The Discovery Blueprint

Ask Questions That Build Trust, And Reveal Truth

Scott Sylvan Bell MBA

Join The Email Publication - Jointheparty.email

Copyright Notice

©2025 Aries 711LLC. All rights reserved.

Aries 711LLC

Legal Disclaimer

The information presented in *The Discovery Blueprint – Ask Questions That Build Trust and Reveal Truth* is intended for educational and informational purposes only. It is not legal, financial, psychological, therapeutic, or professional advice. While every effort has been made to ensure the accuracy, relevance, and usefulness of the material, the authors, publishers, and contributors do not make any guarantees regarding the completeness or applicability of the concepts, strategies, or examples contained in this book.

Discovery conversations, advisory discussions, and client interactions often involve complex interpersonal, ethical, financial, legal, and organizational considerations. These factors can vary widely depending on jurisdiction, industry, and specific circumstances. Readers are strongly encouraged to seek the guidance of qualified professionals—such as licensed legal, financial, or mental health experts—before applying any discovery questions, communication strategies, or decision-based frameworks from this book to real-world situations.

The authors, publishers, and contributors expressly disclaim any liability for actions taken or not taken based on the information provided. By using this book, you acknowledge that no professional, coaching, consulting, therapeutic, or advisory relationship is formed between you and the authors, publishers, or contributors. You agree to hold them harmless from any claims, damages, or consequences that may arise from the use or misuse of the material.

Fiction Disclaimer

Some examples, dialogues, scenarios, and illustrations within this book are fictional or partially fictionalized. While certain situations may be inspired by real-world experiences, they are presented for instructional purposes only. Any resemblance to actual persons, organizations, or events—living or dead—is purely coincidental.

The Dedication From Scott Sylvan Bell

Thank you to the Bell Family Dale, Laurie, Tammy, James & Misty, Brian & Liz, Crystal & Matt, Nancy and all of your kids, Grandma Joan and Grampa Mel, The Bell Uncles and Aunt: Mark, Jerry, Kenny, Steve, Bonnie & Jay. I have to include Ka'e, Rooty, and Tonka

The Hawaii Ohana and Connections: Pat, Ric, Jen, Amy and Peggy Guinther, Mike and Kathryn Quist and their 257 kids.

The Kevin Hogan Group - Dr Kevin Hogan, April Braswell, Bob Beverly, Deborah Cole AKA @Coachdeb, Hing and Team Indonesia, Jason Sisneros, Ken Ownes, Kris McAulay, Mark J Ryan, Rhonda Johnson, Roberto Monaco, Steve Chambers, Tom Vizzini and Kim McFarland, Tonya Reiman, Trisha Chambers,

The Late Night and Early Morning Crew Dr. Fern Kazlow, Jeremy Knauff, Alex Nigh, Bill Hamilton, Bond Halbert, Bryce Beaver, Christine Udasco, Christopher Shaw, Darnell Davis, Dennis Yu, Doug Brown, Doug Wyatt, Earl Flomata, Joel McGuire, Jos Aguiar, Josh Wilkerson, Lacy Horn, Len Wright, Liana Ling, Marty Fahnke, Mitchell Smith, Paul Stoddard, Samuel Duffy and Ed Weeks (The Trio Of Thunder), Sam Wakefield, Scott Plamondon, Troy Assignon & Alicia Repp and Thomas.

The Abraham Group: Jay Abraham, Michelle Abraham, Brian Oney, Brett Anderson, Keith Johnson, Carlos Charre, Desiree Lopez, Laura Sellers, John Howe, Rob Colasanti, Rob Mosqera, Yuki Izoe, Andrea Hedges, Chris Gylseth, Eric Gesinski, Frank Matuk, Gia Cilento, Lyn Kitchen, Matt Smith, Mona Trejo, Nader Fadaee, Robert Anderson and Zenon Isle

The Team from EPIC and Scalable.co: Roland Frasier, DeAnna Rogers, Sam Khorramian, Baily Naab, Michelle Grumbles, Bailey McNamarra, Mattieu Grey, Ryan Frasier, Adam Lyons, Ryan Diess, Richard Linder, Sharon Otoguro, Josh Lannan and Kevin Daly

The EPIC Coaches: Casey Eberhart, Daniel Sweet, Delores Hirsch, Jessie Jackson, Mathew Bergvinson, Matt Bodnar, Nick Thiroes, Richard Reid and Yelitza Mora

The Wealthy Consultant Crew Taylor Welch, Payton Welch, Bijal Patel, Mike Walker and the rest of the team

The CopyPro Team – Jon Benson, Adil Amarsi, Bogdan Bolas, Brennan Hopkins (The Pineapple Pizza King), Craig Dave, Daniella Gattel, Jay White and LeeAnn Price

The Todd Brown crew – Todd Brown, Damian Lanfranchi and Co.

The Copywriters: Alen Sultanic, Carlos Redlich, Dan Ferrari, Danial Doan, David Deutsch, Lori Haller, Paris Lampropoulos, Lori Morgan, Mike Morgan, Paula Longdon & Rae Brent

5

Special Influencers: Anik Singal, Alan Eagle, Aleric Heck, Blair LaCorte, Chet and Amanda Homes, Daymond John, Dr Alan Barnard, Dr. Arun Garg, Geroge Mumford, Jeffrey Gitomer, Joseph McClendon III, Les Brown, Nick Sonnenberg, Perry Marshall, Rich Schefren, Stephan Spencer, Stephen MR Covey, Steve Sims and Tony Robbins.

The Hawaii Reyn Spooner Crew: David, Glen, Hiilei, Curtis, Traci and the rest of the team on the Island!

Join The Email Publication - Jointheparty.email

Table Of Contents

The Elements

CHAPTER 1 — Establishing the Current Landscape

1. Problem-Definition Questions   74

2. Impact-Mapping Questions   78

3. Constraint-Identification Questions   82

4. Misalignment-Detection Questions   86

5. Root-Cause Tracing Questions   90

6. Information-Flow Questions   94

7. Cultural-Readiness Questions   98

8. Order-of-Operation Questions   102

CHAPTER 2 — Diagnosing Past Attempts & Performance

9. Past-Attempt Questions   107

10. Failure-Timeline Questions   111

11. Performance Metric Review Questions   115

12. Escalation-Point Questions   119

13. Bottleneck-Sequence Questions   123

14. Loss-Analysis Questions   127

15. Underutilized-Asset Questions   131

16. Untapped-Upside Questions   135

17. Abandoned-Opportunity Questions   139

CHAPTER 3 — Revealing Hidden Costs & Consequences / Mapping the Decision Environment

18. Stakeholder-Landscape Questions   144

19. Influence-Pattern Questions   148

20. Stakeholder-Motivation Questions   152

Join The Email Publication - Jointheparty.email

CHAPTER 4 — Revealing Operational Realities

CHAPTER 5 — Uncovering Value, Potential, and Strategic Opportunity

CHAPTER 6 — Understanding Collaborative Dynamics and Team Alignment

CHAPTER 7 — Understanding Organizational Dynamics and Cultural Alignment

CHAPTER 8 — Understanding External Pressures, Market Forces

BONUS CHAPTER 1 - Advanced Human Dynamics, Emotion, and Personal-Level Discovery

BONUS CHAPTER 2 – Future-State, Innovation, and Strategic Foresight Discovery

BONUS CHAPTER 3 — Hidden Drivers, Ethical Pressures & Deep-Structure Discovery

The Reason I Wrote This Book And Why It's Important

For most of my Sales and Consulting career, I have watched one pattern repeat itself across every industry, every sales team, every consulting engagement, and every advisory environment: The discovery process is completely misunderstood, underdeveloped, and poorly executed. People treat discovery as a preliminary step instead of a transformational moment. They believe it is a list of questions rather than a structured pathway into clarity, truth, and emotional safety. And because of this, most professionals never see the full picture of what their buyers are facing.

When I was a corporate sales trainer, the weakness in discovery was unmistakable. Salespeople could walk through their presentation, they could defend their pricing, and they could handle predictable objections — but when it came to uncovering what truly mattered, they fell short. Later, as a consultant and coach working with business owners, executives, operators, and entrepreneurs, the pattern didn't change. Whether someone was running a $500K business or a $50M operation, they struggled with the exact same issue: discovery was shallow when it needed to be deep, rushed when it needed to be slow, and scripted when it needed to be human.

That's when I knew the marketplace needed something far stronger — a complete system for discovery, not just a list of questions.

My goal was simple: create the world's most comprehensive, most structured, and most practical repository of discovery questions ever assembled. A book so exhaustive that you could open it to any section, in any situation, and find clarity, direction, and a better way to guide the conversation.

I didn't intend to write another 550 page book. Once the framework took shape, the size of the opportunity became impossible to ignore. Each category opened a doorway to another category. Each question revealed the need for more questions. What began as a structured resource expanded into a full decision-making system.

And once the first major version of the book was complete, something became obvious: two additional chapters and twenty-one additional sections were required to ensure the book addressed 99% of discovery scenarios you will ever face. Without those final sections, the book was strong; with them, the book became a complete reference guide.

Everything in this book was placed in a very specific order for a reason. Discovery has a rhythm. It has a sequence. It has a psychological arc. This book mirrors the discovery process. From understanding the problem, to mapping impact, to identifying constraints, to uncovering internal tension, to exploring consequence, to revealing decision dynamics, to testing commitment — every chapter builds upon the previous one to create a complete advisory system.

How To Use This Book

Think of this book the same way top copywriters think of a "swipe file". A Copywriter creates ads that sell on the page or the website they are on. Copywriters don't start with a blank screen; they start with inspiration, frameworks, angles, and proven structures. They study what has worked before so they can apply it to the present situation with speed and confidence.

This book gives you that same advantage for your discovery process.

Each section includes at least twenty-five examples — not as scripts, but as structural variations. They show you how a question can soften, sharpen, expand, narrow, warm, cool, or deepen depending on your tone, your intention, and the prospect's emotional state. Before any meeting, flip to the relevant section and compare your planned question to the options in this book. Sometimes your version will be strong. Other times you'll find a phrasing that opens a doorway you didn't realize was there… or… another way to ask a question that is boring in your industry.

And those 2 extra chapters and 21 sections added after the first draft? They exist because there were psychological angles, decision dynamics, and consequence-based patterns that needed to be addressed to truly cover the full terrain. Those sections make this book a complete system — not just a resource.

You now have more tools, more range, and more precision than 99% of the people you compete against. Use this book as your secret weapon and your ultimate advantage.

The Fortune Is In the Follow-Up

Almost no sales training material discusses follow-up questions in any meaningful way — yet follow-up is where real discovery begins. You can find it but is isn't the norm, most "sales trainers" want to talk about mindset or closing. It's a shame they miss the point. Anyone can ask an industry standard initial question. Only a skilled advisor can take a second bite at the apple, revisit a point, slow a moment down, or deepen the clarity.

Every section of this book includes ten follow-up questions created to help you see what most people miss: the hidden emotion, the real fear, the unspoken consequence, the political tension, the risk beneath the surface. These follow-ups turn a simple question into a breakthrough moment. Follow-up questions are where you stop collecting information and start revealing truth.

How AI Supported the Creation of This Book

This book was conceptualized, structured, architected, and authored by me — Scott Sylvan Bell.

The thinking is mine.
The frameworks are mine.
The sequence is mine.
The psychology is mine.

AI served as a tool — nothing more, nothing less. It accelerated production. It helped maintain consistency across hundreds of pages. It generated phrasing variations that I could evaluate, refine, restate and improve. It allowed me to explore angles that might have taken months to uncover manually. It gave me speed, breadth, and leverage — but not direction. The structure, strategy, and intellectual ownership remain fully mine. This book is based upon my experience as a salesperson, Corporate Sales Trainer and finally a trusted Consultant.

AI made it possible to create a more complete library, faster. But the mapping, the categorization, the emotional nuance, the consequence-based logic, and the depth of the questions all come directly from real-world experience: decades of training, thousands of conversations, and years of high-level consulting where discovery was the differentiator.

This book was not written by a machine.
This book was written by a practitioner — with a machine assisting the workflow.

Final Thoughts

This book is the result of thousands of hours spent observing human behavior, mapping decision patterns, solving difficult problems, guiding leadership teams, and helping people reach clarity they could not reach alone. It is not simply a collection of questions; it is a philosophy, a structure, a diagnostic tool, and a complete system for building trust and uncovering truth.

If used correctly, this book will do more than help you ask better questions — it will help you think more clearly, operate more strategically, and lead conversations with confidence and depth. It is meant to become a lifelong reference tool, a companion to your advisory skillset, and a swipe file you return to before every meaningful conversation.

Discovery doesn't begin with asking questions.
Discovery begins with seeing.
And this book will help you uncover client's needs by seeing more than you ever have before.

You may have asked good questions before, now its time to make them great.

Understanding the Elements of the Discovery Blueprint

This book is intentionally structured in two parts. You begin with **Elements** before you reach the chapters. These Elements exist to establish the underlying thinking, principles, and strategic frameworks that govern effective discovery. They are not tactics and they are not scripts. They are the conceptual foundation required to understand *why* certain questions work, *when* they should be used, and *how* discovery functions as a system rather than a sequence of steps.

The Elements are designed to shape perception before instruction. Discovery fails most often not because people lack questions, but because they misunderstand the role discovery plays in decision-making, influence, qualification, and risk. The Elements address that problem directly. They explain the ideas, mental models, and strategic dynamics that make discovery effective in the real world. By working through these Elements first, you develop the ability to recognize patterns, read situations accurately, and choose the right approach before moving into application.

Each Element represents a distinct structural function within discovery, much like an architectural element serves a specific role within a blueprint. Some Elements establish stability and safety. Others expose pressure points, hidden constraints, decision friction, or unseen consequences. None exist in isolation, and none are decorative. Each Element is designed to do work—work that prepares you to engage more skillfully, ethically, and confidently when the conversation matters most.

Only after this foundation is established do the chapters move into applied question sets and execution. The Elements give context to the questions that follow. They ensure you are not asking questions mechanically, but with intention and understanding. When the Elements are understood first, the rest of the book becomes more than a collection of examples—it becomes a cohesive system for clarity, influence, and trust. This is why the Elements come first. They are the architecture that supports everything that follows.

Element 1 — Introduction: What Discovery Really Is

Most people believe discovery is simply a list of questions to rattle off. They see it as an early fact-finding step, something to "get through" before moving into the real conversation. That belief is wrong and is a mistake. Discovery is not about collecting data. It is about understanding the human being behind the data and their needs. It is about learning how they think, how they interpret pressure, how they decide, and how they respond when uncertainty shows up. Discovery is the moment when someone tells you, often without realizing it, who they are.

Before the first question is asked, discovery is already happening. The way a prospect greets you, the speed of their voice, the level of detail they offer, the hesitation in their tone, or the confidence in their pacing all give you signals long before you enter the "discovery phase." Discovery begins the moment the conversation begins. Every movement, every pause, every emotional shift is part of the story. Most people miss these cues because they are "asking questions". Elite business advisors and salespeople see the possibilities on the horizon.

Discovery is also a moment where the prospect evaluates you. Even if they booked the meeting, they may still be testing your steadiness. They might challenge you early to see how you handle pressure. They might give short answers to see whether you chase them or stay calm. They want to know if you are the kind of person who listens, or the kind of person who reacts. They want to know if they can trust you to guide them through a problem they haven't been able to solve on their own.

This is why discovery often becomes a **resell of the meeting itself**. The prospect is deciding whether you are worth opening up to. Whether your presence feels safe. Whether your questions feel intentional. Whether your tone communicates confidence or neediness. Whether your questions and follow up are good enough. Most salespeople try to prove themselves. Elite advisors and salespeople do something different: they model steadiness. They anchor the room. They create emotional clarity by staying neutral, curious, and patient. Their authority comes from calm, not pressure. The key is to remain relaxed even under pressure.

One of the biggest misconceptions about discovery is that "if the prospect agreed to the meeting, they agreed to depth of conversation." That is not true. People grant you surface-level access by default. Depth of conversation must be earned. More time it is earned through emotional safety, not through technique. When someone feels safe, they reveal the real issues, the real frustrations, the real conflicts, and the real fears that drive their decisions. When safety is low, they protect themselves with short answers, vague statements, and polite half-truths.

This book views discovery as a **clarity-building experience**, not a quick technical exercise. Your responsibility is not to interrogate. Your responsibility is to help the prospect understand their own situation more clearly than they ever have before. Great discovery is transformative. It shifts how a person thinks about their problem. It reveals the cost of inaction. It brings hidden consequences to the surface. It reframes the challenge in a way that finally makes sense. When this happens, objections disappear because the prospect now sees the full picture.

In this book, you will learn the deeper purpose of discovery and how elite advisors use it to create trust, authority, and momentum. You will learn how to read tone and emotional shifts, how to sequence questions ethically, and how to interpret answers with precision. And most importantly, you will learn how to ask questions in a way that gives the prospect clarity — not pressure. This book is not about memorizing phrases. It is about learning how to guide a human conversation with skill, stability, and intention. You must learn how to ask great questions.

When you understand what discovery really is, the discovery system and ideas in this book becomes far more than a set of prompts. It becomes a tool for insight, pattern recognition, emotional awareness, and strategic alignment. The real goal is not to ask a lot of questions — it is to ask the right questions, in the right order, with the right presence at the right time. This section introduces that philosophy. Everything that follows brings it to life.

Element 2 — Why Most Salespeople and Consultants Fail at Discovery

Most salespeople and consultants fail at discovery for one simple reason: they think the goal is to get quick answers. They rush through questions like they're checking boxes, waiting for the moment they can talk about themselves, their offer, or their solution. But prospects can feel this. They know when the person asking questions isn't genuinely curious. And people do not open up when they feel like they're being interviewed instead of truly understood.

Failure often begins before the first question is even asked. Many advisors enter the call with the wrong internal story running in their head. They're anxious about closing the deal. They're attached to the profitability of the outcome. They're focused on sounding smart or proving their value. These internal pressures always leak through. You may not hear them, but the prospect feels them immediately. When **you** are tense, the prospect becomes guarded. When **you** are insecure, they become vague. When **you** try too hard to impress, they pull away. This is the formula that quietly sabotages thousands of discovery conversations every day.

Another reason discovery fails is because most advisors never learned that **you must sell the discovery process before you perform it**.

Prospects won't automatically give you honesty, depth, or vulnerability. They only do that when they feel you've earned the right to hear it. Discovery collapses when the advisor tries to skip emotional steps. You jump into deep questions before the prospect feels safe. You escalate too fast. You probe too early. You ignore the follow-up questions that actually matter. You chase clarity before you've created trust — and the prospect shuts down or quits.

Prospects also test your emotional stability. This matters more than most advisors ever realize. They challenge your frame to see how strong it is. They push against your question structure to see whether you stay steady. They shorten answers to see if you retreat or lean in. They interrupt the flow to see if you get flustered. They toss out "micro objections" — "We only have a few minutes," "I'm not sure this will help," "We're just exploring." These are not real objections. They're **probing behaviors** designed to see if you can remain calm, clear, and in control. Most advisors fail this test because they react instead of regulate. They push, defend, speed up, or abandon their structure completely. You must stay in control of your emotions in discovery.

Another common failure: discovery becomes a **lecture** instead of a conversation. The advisor explains, clarifies, justifies, and educates far too early. They answer questions that weren't asked. They get uncomfortable with silence and start filling space. They confuse clarity with talking. But talking is the enemy of discovery. When **you** talk, the prospect stops thinking. When **you** talk, the prospect hides their truth. When **you** talk, discovery dies.

A deeper challenge is the lack of emotional neutrality. Many advisors react when the prospect resists. They tighten up when the conversation gets difficult. They avoid asking certain questions because they fear they'll sound pushy. They soften too much in some moments and push too hard in others. Emotional neutrality is rare — and without it, you will never reach deeper insight. Great discovery requires a calm center, even when the prospect is chaotic, uncertain, or defensive.

Another failure pattern appears often: the advisor prioritizes being liked over being effective. They focus on comfort and or rapport instead of clarity. They choose politeness over progress. They try to build rapport instead of revealing the problem. But prospects don't need a friend — they need someone who can guide them. They need someone willing to ask the questions that will move them toward victory instead of allowing them to remain stuck in mediocrity. Great discovery is respectful, but not timid. Gentle, but never fragile. Open, but never passive. You must apply the right amount of pressure — not force, but a steady nudge toward truth.

Finally, discovery fails because advisors misread the moment. A short answer doesn't always mean disinterest — it often means the prospect doesn't feel safe yet. A quick "yes" doesn't mean agreement — it often means avoidance. A prospect who talks a lot isn't necessarily being transparent — they might be hiding behind noise. Discovery requires reading people in layers, not taking everything at face value. You should plan for some level of conflict in your discovery process, as this is normal. You cant agree with everything, you will have some disagreements. These interactions are also a test of your skills both communication and emotions.

This book exists because most discovery training is shallow, scripted, or built to memorize instead of master. It teaches what to ask, but not how to think. It teaches steps, but not psychology. It teaches technique, but not presence. This section marks your turning point — the moment where you stop approaching discovery like a common practitioner and start approaching it like an elite advisor.

Element 3 - Real-Time Discovery Awareness: How Elite Advisors Operate in the Moment

Elite advisors and salespeople don't just prepare well before the call — they stay aware during it. Real-time awareness is what separates advisors who simply ask questions from advisors who guide the conversation with clarity and control. When you understand what's happening in the moment, you begin to hear more than the words. You notice the important shifts. You interpret tone. You sense tension. You detect avoidance. You recognize when the prospect is protecting something or hiding behind something. This is the skill that turns generic conversations into breakthroughs.

The average advisor is focused on the next question. Elite advisors are focused on the **state** of the conversation. They ask themselves:

- "What is this answer really telling me?"

- "What emotional tone did that come from?"

- "Did the pace change?"

- "Is this person opening up or closing down?"

- "Is there something they're afraid to say?"

You can only guide a conversation when you're paying attention to what is happening underneath the surface.

Real-time awareness also means controlling the pace. Prospects often talk fast when they're anxious or trying to stay in control. They talk slow when they're unsure. They go silent when something sensitive comes up. Elite advisors adjust without reacting. If the prospect speeds up, you slow down. If the prospect becomes vague, you become more specific. If the prospect avoids a topic, you gently return to it later. The person who controls the pace controls the clarity.

Another key skill is noticing contradictions. Most prospects will say one thing and later say something that doesn't match. They may talk about wanting growth but describe behaviors built around safety. They may claim a decision is "simple" while revealing a complex political environment. Elite advisors catch these contradictions quietly. When this happens you simply re-enter the topic with curiosity:
"Earlier you mentioned X. Now I'm hearing Y. Help me understand the difference."
This brings truth to the surface without creating conflict.

Elite advisors and salespeople also recognize when the prospect is answering from **logic** versus **emotion**. Logical answers tend to be clean, structured, and distant. Emotional answers tend to be messy, detailed, and revealing. When you sense emotion beneath a logical response, you don't ignore it. You slow down. You investigate gently. You allow space for the truth to surface. Most advisors rush past emotional signals because they're focused on their agenda. You can't do that if you want real clarity. You want and need the emotional answers and raw feelings.

Real-time discovery awareness also includes reading **defensive patterns**. When a prospect becomes short, dismissive, overly detailed, overly confident, or overly agreeable, they're protecting something. They may be avoiding blame. They may be hiding fear. They may be uncertain how honest they can be with you. Elite advisors never punish defensiveness — they soften their tone, reduce pressure, and create more safety. You must earn your way through defenses, not force your way past them.

You also need to recognize when a prospect is trying to control the conversation. They may redirect questions. They may answer with unrelated stories. They may try to move ahead when they feel uncomfortable. Elite advisors and salespeople don't fight this. They simply guide the conversation back:
"Before we move on, I want to understand something you said a moment ago."
This maintains your frame without confrontation.

Finally, real-time awareness means knowing when to go deeper and when to pause. Some moments require a follow-up question. Some moments require silence. Some moments require a gentle challenge. And some moments require you to back off and return later. When you trust yourself enough to slow down and follow the emotional signals of the conversation, discovery becomes smoother, safer, and far more effective.

You must learn how to read the room — not through guesswork, but through patterns. Once you can recognize these patterns in real time, every question you ask becomes more meaningful, more precise, and more likely to reveal the truth.

It's ok to not have the answer or the question immediately, you can pause a moment to gather your thoughts and or ideas. You can use taking notes to your advantage in discovery to slow the process down. When you take notes, you can control the clock. In society it's not considered polite to interrupt someone when they are writing down thoughts or ideas. This time can be extended a few moments to gather thoughts and direct attention.

Next, we move into the concept that ties every great discovery conversation together: **Aftermath** — and why it changes everything.

Element 4 — Why Aftermath-Based Discovery Changes Everything

Your clients may not change because things are going well. People change when the cost of staying the same becomes too heavy to carry. They move when the consequences become real. Discovery becomes powerful when you stop focusing only on the problem and start helping the prospect understand the **impact** of that problem over time. This is the foundation of consequence-based discovery, and it is one of the most important skills you will ever develop.

Most advisors talk about benefits, features, logic, and solutions. Elite advisors and salespeople talk about **aftermath**—not in a forceful way, but in a truthful way. They understand that people often minimize their problems because minimizing feels safer than confronting what's actually happening. When you help someone see the hidden cost of their situation clearly, they naturally begin to move toward change. This is not pressure. This is insight.

Aftermath-based discovery works because people rarely see their situation accurately. They're too close to it. They've adapted to the pain. They've normalized the stress. They've accepted delays, breakdowns, and limitations as "just how things are." You help them step back far enough to see the bigger picture. You ask the questions that link their present decisions to their future outcomes. You help them trace the chain of events they've been ignoring.

The shift from problem to aftermath, is what transforms a simple conversation from casual to meaningful.

Why People Avoid Aftermath

People avoid aftermath because it creates discomfort.
You've seen this pattern:

- They laugh it off.
- They downplay the issue.
- They blame timing, circumstances, or other people.
- They give vague explanations.
- They say "It's not ideal, but we're getting by."

When you hear this, understand something important:
they aren't lying to you — they're protecting themselves and their image.

It feels safer to stay in vagueness than to admit the truth. Most people know something is wrong, but they don't want to think about what it actually means. This is why you play such an important role. You create the safety that allows them to explore the truth without feeling judged or pressured.

Switch From Pressure And Create Clarity

Pressure creates resistance - Clarity creates movement - Movement creates activity

When you explore aftermath, you're not trying to "push" someone. You're guiding them through a process that lets them understand what's really happening in their world. You help them articulate the cost of inaction *in their own words*. That is what makes this approach ethical, honest, and effective.

With proper pause, tone and cadence you might ask:

- "What happens if you leave this unresolved for another six months?"
- "How has this been affecting you day to day?"
- "When this pops up, who else pays the price?"
- "If this continues, what does it mean for the rest of the year?"

These are not aggressive questions, These are respectful reality checks.

The Four Layers of Aftermath

It's a huge mistake stop at the superficial layer of consequence. You will want to explore the deeper layers most people miss. There are four main layers you must pay attention to:

1. Surface Aftermath

These are the obvious costs for the people you serve.

- Lost time and or momentum
- Wasted money and or investments
- Inefficiency
- Repeated mistakes

Most advisors stop here. You won't:

2. Emotional Aftermath

This is what people feel but rarely say out of fear, worry or shame:

- Frustration
- Anxiety
- Stress
- Disappointment
- Embarrassment
- The fear of making a mistake
- The feeling of being "behind"

This is where conversations become real, because emotion drives action.

3. Strategic Aftermath

These are the long-term impacts that shape the future:

- Missed opportunities
- Stalled growth
- Damaged momentum
- Weaker competitive position
- Higher downstream risk

These consequences matter more than most prospects initially realize.

4. Identity Aftermath

This is the deepest level you may be trusted enough to hear:

- "I feel like I should be further ahead."
- "I'm letting people down."
- "I'm not operating at the level I know I can."

When a prospect voices identity-level consequences, the conversation shifts permanently. You've reached the truth behind the facts.

How Aftermath Creates Clean, Ethical Urgency

People don't move because of pressure. They move because:

- They finally understand what's at stake
- They connect their current decisions to their future outcomes
- They see the real cost of waiting
- They recognize the downside of inaction
- They understand what happens if nothing changes

When you help someone see Aftermath clearly, urgency becomes natural. You don't need to push. You don't need to close aggressively. You don't need to convince. The clarity you help create becomes its own motivator.

Why Most Advisors Fail at Using Aftermath

Most advisors make the common mistakes of:

- Going too early and or pushing too hard
- Skipping the emotional foundation
- Not listening deeply enough
- Not following the moment

- Afraid to ask the question that matters or the question that needs to be asked

Aftermath answers must be earned.
You escalate when the prospect feels understood.
You explore impact when the prospect feels safe.
You guide them into the future when they trust your presence in the present.

How to Know When It's Time to Explore Aftermath

Here are some important cluse when the conversation is ready for aftermath when:

- The prospect has shared the facts
- They've explained their frustrations
- They've loosened up emotionally
- The trust level is high enough for depth
- Their tone softens and their guard lowers

That's when you ask,
"Can I ask something that may help us understand this a little more clearly?"

Permission creates safety.
Safety creates honesty.
Honesty creates insight.
Insight creates movement.

Aftermath Creates the Turning Point

Once a prospect sees the true cost of staying the same, they experience a shift:

- Their answers become more honest
- Their urgency becomes internal
- Their clarity becomes sharper
- Their avoidance disappears
- Their willingness to explore increases

The right questions open the door to the next question and you can get to the consequence.

Discovery becomes more than a "check the box conversation", it becomes and exploration. Your discovery process becomes a moment where someone sees themselves differently — and begins to choose a better path. The next section shows you how to use this book across different roles and industries so you can apply aftermath-based thinking in every call you lead.

Element 5 — How to Use This Book Across Roles and Industries

Discovery is not a sales skill, It is a decision-making skill. It is the process of helping another person reach clarity about their situation, their priorities, and their best path forward. Because of this, discovery applies across every advisory role: sales, consulting, coaching, M&A, leadership, and professional services. The questions you learn in this book work everywhere because they are based on psychology, not tactics. The questions are simple and to the point.

The biggest mistake people make is assuming discovery is different depending on the industry. The language may shift. The examples may change. But the core principles do not. Every industry has uncertainty. Every industry has hidden problems. Every industry has decision-makers, influencers, bottlenecks, politics, consequences, and unspoken fears. When you learn how to uncover these patterns, you can walk into any environment and lead the conversation with confidence.

Your role in discovery changes slightly depending on what seat you're sitting in. If you're in sales, your job is to help the buyer understand what is blocking their progress. If you are a consultant, your job is to help the client see the difference between symptoms and root causes. If you're an M&A advisor, your job is to surface risk and opportunity that both sides may be ignoring. If you are a coach, your job is to help the person see their own limiting patterns. The mechanics shift, but the psychology is identical.

This book is structured so you can adapt the questions to any environment without losing integrity. The goal is not to memorize the questions. The goal is to understand the thinking behind them. When you understand the intention, you can adjust the phrasing to fit the context. The questions become tools, not scripts. You can pick the right question at the right time because you understand what you're trying to reveal.

You may find that certain sections are more relevant to your role than others. That is normal. A consultant may be drawn to the sections on bottlenecks and hidden assets. A coach may use the identity questions more frequently. A salesperson may lean heavily on aftermath and decision-making. An M&A advisor will pay close attention to leadership dynamics and approval risk. The book is designed to give you a full toolbox, not a single method.

The most important thing to understand is that discovery does not change just because the environment changes. People still resist when they feel judged. They still avoid the truth when it creates discomfort. They still test your stability before they trust your guidance. They still downplay problems until they understand the consequences of actions or inactions. They still give vague answers when they feel uncertain. Your ability to work with these patterns remains the most valuable skill you can build.

When you use this book, treat each section as a reference point, not a rigid instruction manual. You may read a section and think, "I won't use those exact words," and that is correct. You are not meant to. You are meant to understand the purpose of the questions. You are meant to understand the psychological moment when a question should be asked and the emotional tone required to deliver it. This is what makes discovery truly dynamic.

As you move deeper into the book, you will notice that some questions are softer and more rapport-driven, while others are sharper and more direct. Use them as needed. If the person feels guarded, start with softer questions that build safety. If the person feels open, use intermediate questions to explore the problem. If the person is avoiding responsibility, use direct questions to surface consequence. Mastery is knowing which level to use in the moment.

Another way to use this book is as a tool for diagnosing your own discovery conversations. After each call, you can revisit sections and ask yourself where you lost momentum, where you rushed, where you backed off too early, or where you missed an opening. This book becomes a mirror. It allows you to see your own patterns clearly, so you can adjust your approach on the next call.

Leaders and managers can use this material to train their teams. Instead of teaching scripts, you can teach thinking. Instead of forcing memorization, you can teach how to interpret signals. Instead of pressuring people to close, you can teach them how to create clarity. This approach builds confidence, reduces fear, and improves performance naturally because it gives people the ability to understand what is happening, not just respond to it.

Finally, this book can be used as a swipe file. If you ever feel stuck, skim the questions in the 80-section framework. You don't need to read them in order. You can scan until one fits the moment. Because the questions are organized by intention, you can quickly find the category that matches the situation you're facing. This system allows you to stay present, calm, and prepared, even in difficult conversations.

This book is designed to grow with you. The more you use it, the more you will see. The more conversations you lead, the more naturally these insights will appear. Over time, you will stop thinking about discovery as something you do and start thinking of it as a way of seeing the world. The next section will introduce you to the deeper philosophies that make discovery such a powerful form of influence and guidance, no matter what role you play.

Element 6 — How to Build Discovery Strength Over Time

Discovery is not something you master after a weekend of training. It is a skill that strengthens with repetition, reflection, and intentional practice over your career. Most advisors struggle because they expect discovery to feel natural immediately. They expect the right questions to appear in the moment, even though they've never trained their mind to notice the cues that make a question necessary. Discovery becomes powerful when you treat it as a craft that sharpens gradually through experience.

Questions skills grow exponentially when you study your own conversations and discovery sessions. Every call or appointment gives you a chance to notice what worked, what didn't, and where the turning points were. After a conversation, take a moment to ask yourself a few simple questions. Where did the prospect open up? Where did they shut down? Where did you speed up too early? Where did you soften too much? These small reflections build awareness, and awareness becomes instinct. Over time, you stop repeating the same mistakes and ask better questions.

You also build discovery strength by slowing your internal pace. Most advisors move too quickly because they fear losing the prospect's interest or objections. Interest is gained when you demonstrate control, curiosity, and stability. When you slow down, you begin to hear details you would have missed. You start noticing emotional shifts in the conversation, contradictions, vague language, hesitations, and small signals that point to the real story. Speed hides truth. Calm reveals it the need of the client.

Another way to build strength is by practicing emotional neutrality. Neutrality does not mean being cold or detached. It means you remain steady even when the prospect is stressed, frustrated, or defensive. You do not rise or fall with their emotions. You create a stable space where honesty becomes easier. When neutrality becomes your baseline, you stop reacting and start leading. You ask better questions because you're not trying to rescue, push, or prove anything.

It is also helpful to practice the skill of holding silence. Silence is one of the most underused tools in a discovery process. When you pause after a prospect speaks, you allow their thoughts to settle. You give them space to reveal something deeper. Most advisors interrupt silence because it feels uncomfortable. But silence is where the prospect thinks, and thinking is what creates insight. When you get comfortable with silence, your conversations gain depth naturally.

Building discovery conversations strength requires learning how to hear what is not said. People reveal truth indirectly. They give hints. They drop signals. They use certain phrases to avoid admitting a problem directly. When you train yourself to listen for patterns instead of words, your ability to guide the conversation increases instantly. Discovery becomes more intuitive because you're not reacting to sentences—you're responding to meaning.

Finally, you build discovery strength by practicing patience and then layered curiosity. When the prospect gives an answer, your next question should come from genuine interest. Not scripted curiosity. Not mechanical follow-up. You become a better advisor when you let the conversation unfold naturally and allow your curiosity to guide the sequence. You stop trying to impress the prospect and start trying to understand them. This shift elevates the entire dynamic. The key to this process is you must be strategic and intentional.

The more you practice these question skills, the more discovery becomes part of your identity. You stop thinking about what to ask next and start noticing what the moment requires. You stop chasing answers and start creating clarity. You stop operating from pressure and start operating from presence. Discovery becomes less about technique and more about awareness. The next section introduces the philosophy that supports every question you will learn in this book—why discovery is not just information gathering but a form of strategic influence that shapes the entire outcome of the relationship.

Element 7 — Discovery as Leverage

Discovery creates leverage for you long before you ever discuss a solution. Leverage is not pressure. Leverage is not persuasion. Leverage is the natural shift that occurs when someone begins to see their situation with clarity and cannot return to the old way of thinking or action. When you ask the right questions, the prospect starts to feel the weight of what is happening in their world. They see the trend, the cost, the direction, and the aftermath of action or inaction. That clarity becomes the leverage that moves the conversation forward.

Leverage begins the moment the prospect recognizes that their current path is not sustainable. Most people live in cycles. They repeat the same patterns, make the same decisions, and tolerate the same problems because those problems have become familiar. Discovery when performed correctly disrupts that familiarity. It wakes people up from what they don't see. It helps them realize that their situation is not random; it is the result of choices, habits, systems, or avoidance. When someone sees this clearly, you gain natural leverage because they start to lean toward change on their own.

Another form of leverage emerges when you help the prospect connect scattered problems into a single story or narrative. People often describe issues in pieces: a slow month here, a breakdown there, a challenge with a team member, an inconsistent system, a stalled goal. They see the events, but they don't see the pattern. When you guide the conversation and help them connect these events into a clear narrative, the story becomes undeniable. The truth becomes visible. Patterns create leverage because patterns carry meaning.

Discovery also creates leverage by revealing contradictions. Prospects often say one thing but describe something that contradicts it. They may say they're satisfied, but later admit they're frustrated. They may claim things are stable, but list problems that show instability. They may say timing is fine, but reveal deadlines that prove the opposite. You don't confront the contradiction aggressively. You bring the contradiction to the forefront. When you do, the prospect feels the weight of the inconsistency. They feel the need to reconcile it. That internal tension becomes its own form of leverage.

Leverage also comes from consequence. Once someone sees the true cost of staying the same, they may begin to move naturally. You're not forcing anything. You're revealing what they've been avoiding. This type of leverage is clean, honest, and ethical because it's grounded in reality. When they feel the aftermath of delay, they start to explore options. When they feel the long-term impact, they begin to prioritize differently. When they understand the deeper risk, they commit more fully. These actions bring you closer to the sale or the deal.

Another source of leverage is clarity around responsibility. Prospects often describe problems that sound like external issues, but when you ask deeper questions, they begin to recognize their own role in the outcome. This recognition is powerful. When someone sees where they've allowed something to continue, they feel a natural urgency to correct it. This is not blame. This is ownership. Ownership creates leverage because people take action on what they feel responsible for.

Discovery also creates leverage by showing the prospect the gap between where they are and where they actually want to be. People often live with a diluted vision of what they're capable of. They compromise too quickly. They accept too little. When you explore their goals, frustrations, and missed opportunities, the gap becomes visible. Once the gap is visible, they feel compelled to close it. A person will climb a hill they can see. They will not climb a hill they are blind to.

Another powerful source of leverage is the emotional relief that discovery provides. When someone feels understood at a deep level—more deeply than they've been understood anywhere else—they become open. People move toward the person who understands them. They move away from the person who pressures them. When someone feels heard, they naturally want more clarity. They lean into the conversation. They trust the process. Emotional relief creates leverage that no amount of selling can match. Let prospects open up to you about their professional problems.

The final form of leverage is stability. When the advisor remains calm, steady, and unbothered—even when the prospect is stressed, uncertain, or avoidant—the prospect recognizes that you are the point of certainty in the conversation. Certainty attracts attention. Certainty builds trust. Certainty reduces resistance. When the prospect sees that you are not reactive, they naturally follow your lead. Your stability becomes leverage.

Discovery becomes leverage when you help people see what they couldn't see before, connect what didn't connect before, feel what they had been avoiding, and understand what they had misunderstood. Leverage is the outcome of clarity. Clarity is the outcome of discovery. When you master this, the conversation begins to shift in your direction without force.

The next section will explore how discovery becomes a source of influence—not manipulation, not pressure, but the kind of influence that comes from insight, honesty, and the ability to help someone make a better decision for themselves.

Element 8 — Discovery as Influence

Influence is often misunderstood. Many people treat influence as persuasion or pressure. True influence isn't about getting someone to agree with you. It isn't about controlling the conversation. It isn't about convincing someone to accept your viewpoint. Influence occurs when the other person begins to think more clearly because of the questions you ask and the presence you hold. When your discovery is strong, influence becomes the natural byproduct of helping someone see their situation with honesty and depth. True influence comes from empathy.

Influence begins when the prospect realizes you understand them better than they understand themselves. People rarely encounter someone who listens with intention and asks questions that reveal deeper truth. When you demonstrate that level of understanding, the prospect begins to trust your guidance. They start to see you as someone who can help them make better decisions. That shift in perception is one of the strongest forms of influence you can create.

Another aspect of influence is helping someone slow down long enough to examine their thinking. Most people make decisions from a state of urgency or emotional pressure. They move fast because slowing down forces them to confront uncomfortable realities. When you maintain steady pacing, the prospect matches your rhythm. They begin to reflect instead of react. Reflection creates better decisions. Influence happens when you help someone think with clarity instead of speed.

Influence is also created through the way you frame questions. Surface-level questions lead to surface-level thinking. But when you ask deeper questions—questions about impact, consequence, conflict, responsibility, and future outcomes—the prospect shifts into a different mental space. They begin processing the conversation differently. They start seeing connections they've ignored. They begin understanding the real cause of their challenges. This deeper thinking is what allows influence to take root.

Another source of influence comes from the way you interpret what the prospect says. Most advisors repeat what they hear. You reflect what it means to you and them. When the prospect describes a frustration, you help them explore the root cause. When they describe a delay, you help them trace the long-term impact. When they describe a goal, you help them understand what is blocking it. Interpretation is influence because it helps the prospect see the truth beneath the explanation.

Influence also requires you to hold your emotional center. People follow stability. When the prospect becomes uncertain, avoidant, defensive, or chaotic, your ability to stay grounded becomes a form of leadership. They may not say it out loud, but they feel it. When your tone stays calm, their guard lowers. When your pacing stays steady, their anxiety eases. When your questions stay clear, their thinking becomes sharper. Influence is built through presence as much as through skill.

Another form of influence comes from the way you handle inconsistency. When the prospect contradicts themselves, avoids an answer, or offers something vague, you don't challenge them with intensity. You surface the moment with curiosity. You might say, "Can I ask something about what you just said?" or "The previous question had a similar answer"—can we explore that connection?" You're not correcting them. You're helping them see the gap in their own logic. This creates influence because you help them reach clarity they couldn't reach alone.

Influence deepens when the prospect begins to feel the consequences of their situation. When someone understands the cost of staying the same, they become more open to guidance. They shift from avoiding the problem to exploring solutions. You are not pushing them. You are revealing what is already true. This is why influence through aftermath is ethical. It helps the prospect understand their reality accurately so they can make informed decisions.

Another powerful aspect of influence is helping the prospect articulate what they actually want. Many people describe goals that are vague or half-formed. They talk about solutions without understanding the deeper desire behind them. When you explore their goals, frustrations, hopes, and fears, they begin to understand what they want with more maturity. Clarity about desire creates forward movement. Influence occurs when you help someone see a clearer version of their future.

Ultimately, discovery becomes influence when the prospect realizes the conversation is helping them think better. Influence is not something you apply. It's something the prospect grants you based on how you show up. When you ask the right questions, maintain the right tone, and guide the conversation with confidence, the prospect begins to follow your lead naturally.

Discovery is influence because discovery reveals truth. Truth leads to clarity. Clarity leads to better decisions. When you operate this way, you become someone the prospect trusts—not because you pushed them, but because you helped them understand themselves.

You must be willing to ask the difficult questions with the prospects you meet with as part of your influence strategy.

In the next section, we'll explore another important function of discovery: qualification, and how insight-based qualification protects your time, your energy, and your reputation.

Element 9 — Discovery as Qualification

Conversational qualification is not about filtering people out. It is about understanding whether the conversation is worth continuing, whether the prospect is capable of change, and whether you can actually help them. Most advisors think of qualification as a checklist—budget, authority, timing, need. Elite advisors see qualification as a deeper process. It is the ability to understand how someone thinks, how they make decisions, and whether they are willing to move when clarity appears.

Discovery becomes qualification the moment you begin to understand the prospect's internal world. You learn how they process information. You learn what they avoid. You learn what they value. You learn how they respond to tension, uncertainty, and responsibility. These internal patterns matter far more than surface-level qualification metrics. You're not looking for people with need and money. You're looking for people who will act on clarity.

One of the strongest qualification indicators is how the prospect talks about their problem. Some describe problems with ownership. Others describe them with excuses. Some take responsibility for the outcome. Others blame external factors. People who consistently point outward are far less likely to move forward. People who recognize their own role in the situation are far more qualified—not because they are perfect, but because they are willing to change. Your discovery can be used for qualification of activity or inactivity.

Another important qualification signal is how the prospect participates in the discovery process. A qualified prospect leans into the conversation, even if slowly. They answer questions with honesty, not hesitation. They engage with the process, not resist it. They think when asked to reflect. They stay open when the conversation gets uncomfortable. Their behavior shows interest before their words do. Qualification is often visible long before it is verbal.

You also qualify someone through the clarity of their goals. A prospect with a vague goal is harder to help. A prospect with a shifting goal is harder to guide. A prospect with a fragmented or unrealistic goal may need more foundational clarity before they can move forward. But a prospect who can clearly articulate what they want—even if imperfectly—is far easier to serve. Clarity of desire is one of the strongest indicators of qualification.

Another aspect of qualification is timing, but not in the traditional sense. You're not asking whether the timing is "right." You're listening to whether the timing is real. Some prospects use timing as a shield. They say, "Now isn't ideal," but they have stable patterns of delay. Others say the same words, but they feel the consequences of inaction. You are qualifying the truth behind the timing, not the statement of it.

A deeper layer of qualification comes from understanding how the prospect handles emotional pressure. When you ask a difficult question, a qualified prospect does not shut down. They may slow down, but they don't withdraw. They may feel discomfort, but they don't collapse. They stay in the conversation because they recognize the value of clarity. Someone who cannot tolerate the slightest emotional tension is unlikely to make a meaningful decision later.

You also qualify someone by examining their consistency. Throughout the conversation, people reveal patterns—how they think, how they adapt, how they deflect, how they rationalize, how they handle contradiction. When someone's narrative shifts too frequently, or their explanations lack alignment, they may not be ready for the kind of work you do. When someone speaks with steady alignment, even if they are struggling, they are far more qualified because they are stable enough for change.

Another form of qualification is understanding the prospect's internal priority structure. Some people care deeply about solving the problem, but not enough to act. Some care intellectually, but not emotionally. Some care emotionally, but not strategically. You qualify by listening for whether the problem actually matters to them. If the problem does not matter enough, they are not qualified. If the problem touches their identity, their future, or their sense of responsibility, they are. You may need to have your prospect map out what their future plans are to reveal information from them.

Qualification is also tied to trust. When the prospect trusts you, they tell the truth. When they don't, they stay on the surface. Trust is a qualification indicator because it shows whether the conversation has the depth required to make a real decision. You cannot qualify someone who will not be honest with you. Honesty is the gateway to qualification, not the outcome of it. Depending upon you

Ultimately, discovery becomes qualification when you understand the prospect's readiness. Readiness is not about budget or timing or authority. Readiness is about clarity, emotional openness, alignment, and willingness to explore the truth. You qualify not by asking, "Can they buy?" You qualify by asking, "Can they change?" If the answer is yes, the conversation moves forward with momentum. If the answer is no, you have saved both sides time, energy, and frustration.

The monumental key is you must be willing to put in the work by asking the right question, the proper follow up and saying what needs to be said.

In the next section, you'll learn how discovery protects you from risk—political risk, emotional risk, decision risk, and reputation risk—and why uncovering these risks early prevents deals from dying later.

Element 10 — Discovery as Risk Protection & Trust

Discovery is not just about insight. It is also your primary form of risk protection. Every deal carries risk— inactivity risk, financial risk, emotional risk, political risk, reputational risk, and execution risk. Most advisors underestimate how much risk sits beneath the surface of a conversation. They hear interest, assume alignment, and move forward too quickly. Elite advisors use discovery to expose the risks early, not late. When you uncover risk up front, you protect yourself, the prospect, and the future of the project.

Every prospect carries emotional risk. Some resist accountability. Some shut down under pressure. Some avoid difficult topics. Some hide frustration behind polite answers. Some say they want clarity but become defensive when clarity appears. These behaviors aren't random. They reveal the prospect's readiness. Discovery allows you to see whether someone can handle the emotional truth of their situation. If they can't tolerate honest reflection, the risk of failure increases.

Discovery also protects you from political risk. Many deals fail not because of the problem or the solution, but because of hidden politics in the office. There may be someone behind the scenes who will block the decision. There may be a department that wants something different. There may be a leader who is quietly opposed. There may be internal conflicts the prospect didn't mention. Discovery uncovers these dynamics before you invest time in building a solution that someone else will quietly veto. You may "sell the prospect" but miss the gatekeeper.

Another risk comes from inconsistency. Prospects often give you two different stories without realizing it. They say they want stability, then describe behaviors that create instability. They claim urgency, then describe timelines that contradict urgency. They say the decision is simple, then reveal layers of complexity. These inconsistencies signal risk. When you surface these gaps with curiosity instead of confrontation, you help the prospect reconcile their own thinking. This protects you from surprises later.

Discovery also reveals execution risk. Some prospects want the result but not the work. Some want change without discomfort. Some want improvement without responsibility. Some want clarity without truth. When someone speaks passionately about their goals but resists the reality of what improvement requires, you're looking at execution risk. If someone cannot follow through, the deal becomes dangerous. Discovery allows you to identify this risk before you commit your time and reputation to a client who won't do their part.

Another critical area of risk is expectation risk. Expectations shape satisfaction. If the prospect's expectations are vague, unrealistic, or unstructured, they will become frustrated later. When you explore expectations early—how they see success, how they define progress, what they hope to avoid—you protect the relationship. You cannot meet expectations that were never discussed.

Clear expectations prevent future conflict. Discovery is where those expectations are revealed and aligned.

Trust is another form of protection. Without trust, the prospect stays guarded. They hide the truth. They avoid meaningful answers. They protect their image instead of revealing their reality. When trust is low, qualification is impossible because the person will not share the information you actually need. Discovery creates trust by showing the prospect you understand them, you hear them, and you care about clarity more than closing. Trust is not created through rapport. Trust is created through depth.

A major risk in any deal is hidden fear. Prospects rarely say, "I'm afraid of making the wrong decision." Instead, they mask fear as hesitation, uncertainty, or delay. They talk about timing when the real issue is self-doubt. They talk about budget when the real issue is fear of committing. They talk about options when the real issue is fear of failure. When you use discovery to surface these unspoken fears, you protect the deal from collapsing due to emotions the prospect couldn't articulate.

Discovery also protects your reputation. Advisors damage their reputation when they accept deals they should have declined. When you don't explore readiness, politics, expectations, or responsibility, you take on clients who are not in a position to succeed. When the engagement goes poorly, the blame often returns to you. Discovery protects you from working with clients who will create problems you cannot solve and then hold you responsible for the outcome.

Another layer of protection comes from alignment. When the prospect's goals, behaviors, expectations, and circumstances are aligned, the risk of failure decreases. When they are misaligned, the risk increases. Discovery reveals alignment or misalignment early. If misalignment appears, you can correct it, slow the process, or decide not to move forward. This saves time, energy, and frustration for both sides.

Ultimately, discovery protects you because it reveals truth. Truth eliminates surprise. Truth reduces risk. Truth clarifies expectations. Truth exposes readiness. Truth uncovers politics. Truth reveals fear. The more truth you uncover early, the more stable the entire engagement becomes. You protect yourself by refusing to move forward in the dark.

Discovery is not just a diagnostic tool. It is your personal defense system. It prevents you from stepping into situations that will fail. It protects the prospect from making decisions they aren't ready for. And it protects the relationship by ensuring that both sides understand what is at stake before any commitments are made.

In the next section, you'll learn how to craft world-class discovery questions using rules that keep you clear, effective, and in control of the conversation without ever sounding forceful or interrogative.

Element 11 — Rules for Crafting World-Class Discovery Questions

Some discovery questions may be born from scripts. Great discoveries are built from intention, clarity, and psychology. A world-class question is well thought out but simple, direct, calm, and purposeful. It guides the prospect toward deeper truth without creating pressure, confusion, or defensiveness. Most advisors ask questions that are too vague, too soft, too complicated, or too self-serving. Elite advisors follow specific rules that make their questions more effective and easier for the prospect to respond to.

The first rule is no "why" questions. "Why" has the power to put people on the defensive. It implies judgment. It forces justification from the prospect. It triggers the part of the brain that protects image. When you ask someone, "Why did you do that?" they will defend their behavior instead of exploring it. Replace "why" with softer language such as, "What led you to that?" or "How did that come about?" These versions create the same insight without triggering resistance.

The second rule is no compound questions. When you ask two or three questions at once, the prospect answers the easiest one and ignores the rest. Compound questions create confusion. They overwhelm the mind. They interrupt the natural flow of the conversation. You should ask one question at a time, then wait. A clean question leads to a clean answer. When you speak in single directions, you guide the prospect more effectively.

Another rule is no leading questions. Leading questions steer the prospect toward the answer you want instead of the truth they need to explore. When you ask, "So would you say the team is the real problem?" you're not exploring. You're influencing through suggestion. Elite advisors ask questions that are neutral. You hold space for the prospect to arrive at their own insight. Anything that sounds like a statement hidden inside a question breaks the integrity of discovery.

The next rule is the one-intent-per-question rule. Every question should accomplish exactly one thing. If your question tries to reveal emotions, clarify timelines, and uncover consequences all at once, it fails at all three. A powerful discovery question has a single purpose: clarify, explore, surface, redirect, or deepen. When you collapse intentions, the prospect becomes confused. When you stay focused, the prospect stays clear.

Softening statements are another essential part of world-class discovery. A softening statement creates psychological permission. It reduces resistance. It helps the prospect feel comfortable stepping into a deeper question. Examples include, "Can I ask you something about that?" or "Would it be alright if we explored that a little more?" These statements prepare the mind for reflection. They make difficult questions feel safer.

Another rule is to avoid sounding like you are in an Interrogation. You are not interrogating the prospect. You are guiding them. Tone matters as much as content. A calm tone lowers defenses. A slow pace encourages reflection. A neutral expression of curiosity invites honesty. When your tone is rushed, sharp, or aggressive, the prospect retreats. When your tone is steady and open, they share more than they planned to.

You must also control conversational pace. If you move too quickly, the prospect feels pressured. If you move too slowly, the prospect feels lost. The right pace matches the emotional moment. After a significant insight, you pause. After a vague answer, you clarify. After a contradiction, you explore. Pace is not about speed. Pace is about timing. It is one of the most important tools in discovery. There is a good rhythm to a discovery process.

The Sequencing Rule is another pillar of great questioning. You cannot escalate too quickly. Before exploring consequence, you must create clarity. Before exploring clarity, you must create safety. Before challenging, you must build rapport. Before going wide, you must go narrow. This sequence is not rigid, but it is essential. When you jump ahead emotionally, the prospect shuts down. When you move in the right order, the conversation feels natural.

The Redirection Rule helps you keep the conversation on track without overpowering the prospect. If they drift into irrelevant details or avoid the core issue, you redirect gently. You might say, "Can I bring us back to something you mentioned earlier?" or "Let me ask about the part that seemed most important a moment ago." Redirection is not control. It is clarity. You keep the conversation aligned with what matters.

The Clarification Loop is another rule that prevents misunderstandings. When the prospect gives an unclear answer, you don't assume you know what they meant. You loop back with a gentle prompt such as, "When you say it's been challenging, what does that mean for you specifically?" or "Help me understand the part that has been most frustrating." Clarification ensures accuracy. Accuracy ensures insight.

Another rule of a world-class discovery process is to avoid interpreting too soon. If you interpret before the prospect has finished explaining, you disrupt their thought process. You distort the insight. You take ownership of the moment instead of letting them reach the realization on their own. Wait until the prospect fully articulates their thought before offering reflection or observation. Discovery is not a race to the answer. It is a process of unveiling.

You can use recapping or a repeat and approve method to your discovery process. You will want to ensure that you cycle between statements to signal you are aware of the conversation. This clarity counts as a semi-follow up statement. It's ok if you are corrected in the conversation as it allows to the potential client to expand upon their conversation. In some conversations it works to your advantage to be corrected as it also brings stated clarity to the potential client.

Here are 25 ways to repeat what you think you hear to get clarity on the conversation:

- "Here's what I'm hearing from you…"
- "Here's what it sounds like you mean…"

- "If I'm understanding you correctly, you're saying…"
- "It seems like the core of what you're saying is…"
- "It sounds like the concern underneath this is…"
- "It sounds to me like you're saying…"
- "Let me check my understanding — you're saying…"
- "Let me make sure I'm hearing you right — you're saying…"
- "Let me make sure I'm tracking — you're saying…"
- "Let me reflect this back — you're saying…"
- "So from your perspective, it feels like…"
- "So the impression I'm getting is…"
- "So the sense I'm getting from you is…"
- "So the takeaway I'm hearing from you is…"
- "So the way this is landing for you is…"
- "So what you're expressing is…"
- "So what you're telling me is…"
- "So what's coming across to me is…"
- "So your main point is…"
- "Sounds like what you're saying is…"
- "The message I'm hearing from you is…"
- "The way I'm understanding you is…"
- "What I'm gathering from what you're saying is…"
- "What I'm picking up from you is…"
- "What you seem to be conveying is…"

Finally, your questions must maintain emotional neutrality. If your question carries frustration, intensity, eagerness, or tension, it shifts the emotional balance of the conversation. Prospects follow your energy. If you stay calm, they stay calm. If you become anxious, they retreat. Emotional neutrality allows you to guide without pressure. It signals confidence, stability, and safety—qualities prospects instinctively follow.

When you follow these rules, your discovery questions become cleaner, sharper, and easier for the prospect to answer. You create clarity without force. You guide without pushing. You uncover truth without triggering defensiveness. The next section will show you the most common discovery mistakes advisors make—and how to avoid them—so your questioning remains effective even under pressure.

Element 12 — The 10 Most Deadly Discovery Mistakes

Most advisors fail at discovery not because they lack skill, but because they make avoidable mistakes that weaken the entire conversation. These mistakes break trust, disrupt clarity, and prevent the prospect from sharing the truth. When you understand the most common pitfalls, you can avoid them with confidence and maintain control of the moment even when the conversation becomes difficult. These ten mistakes are the ones that quietly destroy discovery without most advisors realizing it.

The first deadly mistake is guessing before asking. Many advisors make assumptions about the problem, the cause, or the motivation behind the prospect's situation. They jump ahead mentally, and their assumptions leak into their tone and phrasing. When you guess before you ask, you create resistance. The prospect feels misunderstood and pulls back and can lose trust. Curiosity is your protection. The moment you assume, you lose clarity. If you have been in an industry or service for a long period of time you must be aware of this mistake.

The second mistake is asking shallow questions. Shallow questions produce shallow answers. Advisors who stay at the surface do so because they fear going deeper. They hesitate to ask questions about impact, consequence, responsibility, or emotion. But without depth, the prospect stays vague, and the truth stays hidden. Shallow questions make the conversation feel transactional. Depth creates honesty. When you are up against a time constraint this is a common action. If your "frame" is being questioned you may also reduce the quality of your questions.

The third mistake is premature questioning. This happens when you escalate the conversation too quickly. You ask about aftermath before you've created safety. You challenge before you've built rapport. You explore conflict before you've established clarity. Premature questioning creates emotional whiplash. The prospect shuts down because the moment wasn't ready for the question. Timing is as important as the question itself. Salespeople and Consultants create this mistake when the assume the solution early on in the conversation.

The fourth deadly mistake is talking too much. Talking feels safe for the advisor, but it destroys discovery. When you talk, the prospect stops thinking. When you explain, the prospect retreats. When you dominate the conversation, you lose access to the truth. Your job is not to convince. Your job is to create space. Silence reveals more than speech. Reflection reveals more than explanation. In a sales slump or under pressure to close the deal it is common to talk too much.

The fifth mistake is the pressure-based response. Some advisors respond to vagueness, hesitation, or resistance with more intensity. They push for faster answers. They increase their volume. They force the pace. Pressure does not create clarity. Pressure creates defensiveness. When the prospect feels pushed, they protect themselves. When they feel safe, they speak honestly. Pressure destroys safety. If you are using pressure it could be that you are uncomfortable with the stature of the person you are with, a sales slump or loss of focus on the deal.

The sixth mistake is the rescue response. Many advisors rush to solve the problem too early. They interpret the situation, offer solutions, or give advice before the prospect has fully explored their own reality. This creates dependency, not clarity. It interrupts the prospect's thought process. When you rescue too early, you rob the person of their own insight. Discovery dies when the advisor tries to be the hero. You can use silence as a tool in the discovery process when you let it work. Sometimes rush to rescue mistake is made when a targeted commission is the thought instead of how to work with the client.

The seventh deadly mistake is missing contradictions. Prospects often reveal inconsistencies without noticing them. They say the problem is small but describe consequences that are large. They claim stability but describe a pattern of instability. They talk about clarity but reveal confusion. When you miss these contradictions, the conversation loses direction. Surfacing contradictions gently helps the prospect align their thinking. If you have personal struggles and self worth issues, this part of the process is skipped as it can create fear of loss.

The eighth mistake is making assumptions about emotion. Advisors sometimes assume the prospect feels stressed, frustrated, overwhelmed, or uncertain based on tone or content. But unless the prospect says it, you do not know it. When you project emotion onto someone, they may feel judged or misunderstood. Instead of assuming, explore. Ask, "How has this been affecting you personally?" Let them talk. If you have the need to talk you may make the mistake of not waiting after the question is asked. You must get great at silence after you ask a question.

The ninth deadly mistake is failing to ask a follow up question. When the prospect gives an answer that deserves exploration, many advisors move on too quickly. They skip opportunities for depth. They miss moments of insight. The follow-up question is often the one that reveals the truth. Without follow-up, discovery becomes a checklist instead of a conversation. Depth appears only when you stay in the moment long enough to see it. Each question you ask should have a follow up question tied to it. These follow up questions reveal more than a quick hit of content.

The tenth mistake is the lack-of-aftermath error. Many advisors identify the problem but never explore its impact of the idea or concept. They understand the surface issue but never uncover the deeper cost. When the prospect doesn't feel the aftermath of staying the same, they have no reason to move. Discovery without aftermath is information without insight. It is clarity without urgency. Without consequence, decisions stall. The fear of "no answer" is what causes salespeople and consultants to not look for the consequences of actions or inactions.

When you eliminate these ten mistakes, your discovery becomes steadier, more effective, and more influential. You stop losing the prospect's trust. You stop rushing the emotional process. You stop missing the moments that matter. You begin to see the patterns inside the conversation instead of reacting to the words on the surface.

Element 13 — The Discovery Order of Operations

Discovery collapses when the conversation moves out of order. You cannot escalate before establishing clarity. You cannot ask about aftermath before creating safety. You cannot explore conflict before understanding the facts. You cannot discuss authority before understanding criteria. When you violate sequence, the prospect feels pressured, confused, or exposed. The order of operations protects the conversation. It keeps the emotional tempo balanced and ensures that the prospect remains open instead of guarded.

Discovery is not rigid, but it is structured. The steps flow into each other naturally when you hold the right presence and follow the emotional logic of the conversation. When you move in the correct order, each question prepares the prospect for the next one. When the order breaks, the prospect protects themselves. This chapter gives you a clear model for sequencing so your discovery conversations become smoother, deeper, and more effective.

The first stage is Establish: Before you can diagnose anything, you must create the conditions for honesty. This means setting expectations, establishing authority through tone rather than force, and giving the prospect permission to speak with transparency. Establishment is not small talk. It is not rapport. It is clarity about what this conversation is and how it will work. When the prospect understands the structure, they relax. When they relax, they open up.

The second stage is Diagnose: This is where you identify what is happening in the prospect's world. You explore symptoms without assuming causes. You ask calm, open questions. You look for patterns. You let the prospect speak long enough to reveal their thinking. This is where most advisors rush. They hear one problem and jump to solutions. Elite advisors diagnose with patience. You collect data without judgment. Diagnosis is understanding, not problem solving.

The third stage is Aftermath: Once the prospect has shared the facts, you help them understand the impact. This stage requires emotional neutrality and precision. You ask questions that guide the prospect toward recognizing the cost of staying the same. You move slowly and patiently. You explore without pushing. You help them connect symptoms to outcomes. When aftermath is handled correctly, the prospect feels clarity, not pressure. They begin to lean in instead of retreat.

The fourth stage is Conflict: Conflict does not mean argument. Conflict is the internal tension the prospect feels between where they are and where they want to be. You surface this tension by exploring contradictions, misalignments, competing priorities, and blocked paths. You help them see the gap between their current reality and their desired outcome. When conflict becomes visible, the prospect starts to recognize that change is necessary. This stage creates movement because it reveals the friction that has been hiding in the background.

The fifth stage is Criteria: Once conflict and aftermath is clear, the prospect is ready to define what a good solution actually looks like. Most advisors skip this and jump into presenting their offer. Elite advisors and salespeople explore criteria first. You ask, "What would you need to see to feel confident moving forward?" or "What matters most in making this decision?" or "What would need to be true in order for us to work together". Your potential clients criteria reveals the decision-making framework the prospect will use. When you understand criteria, you understand how to lead the rest of the conversation. You can map out the decision process with this information.

The sixth stage is Authority: Now that the prospect is clear on the problem, the consequence, the conflict, and the criteria, you explore who else is involved in the decision. You do not ask aggressively. You ask in a grounded way: "Who else needs to be comfortable with this?" Authority is not just about titles. It is about influence, politics, and emotional power inside the organization or household. When you map authority after criteria, the prospect feels safe discussing it because they now understand the importance of the decision.

The seventh stage is Budget: Budget is not about numbers. It is about feasibility, readiness, and alignment. Budget is sensitive because it touches identity and safety. When you ask too early, the prospect shuts down. When you ask after they've explored consequence, conflict, criteria, and authority, the conversation feels natural. You ask questions that help them clarify what they have allocated, what they have planned, and what the cost of not solving the problem might be. Budget becomes a logical step, not a confrontation. In order to get to the closing of a deal you must get to the budget. If you do not talk about the budget, at some point it will come back to haunt you.

The eighth stage is Timeline: Once budget is understood, you explore when change needs to happen. Timeline is not just about when they want something done. It is about how the problem evolves if nothing changes. You compare their ideal timeline with the aftermath timeline. You reveal any gaps, risks, or conflicts. When the timeline is explored late in the process, the prospect has the clarity needed to be honest about urgency and next steps.

The ninth stage is Commitment: Commitment is not a closing technique. It is the natural outcome of layered clarity. Commitment means the prospect understands the problem, the impact, the tension, the criteria for a solution, the people involved, the required investment, and the timeline for action. When all these pieces are aligned, commitment becomes easy. You don't push for it. You guide the prospect into confirming what they already understand.

The discovery order of operations is not a script. It is a psychological sequence. Every stage prepares the mind for the next. When you follow this order, the conversation feels safe, logical, and guided. When you violate the order, the conversation becomes chaotic, pressured, or unclear. Mastering this sequence allows you to lead the prospect with confidence—even when the conversation becomes complicated or emotional.

The next section will teach you how to follow up on answers in a way that deepens trust, sharpens clarity, and opens the door for more meaningful insight. This is where discovery becomes dynamic and where many advisors struggle to maintain control without force.

Element 14 — How To Follow Up On An Answer

Following up on an answer is one of the most important skills in discovery. It is also one of the most neglected. Most advisors ask a question, get a surface-level response, and immediately move on. They treat the answer as the destination instead of the doorway. Elite advisors understand that the first answer is rarely the real answer. The truth sits underneath the explanation, and follow-up questions are the only way to reach it. You must know how you will follow up for any question asked in discovery.

The power of follow-up lies in what it signals. It tells the prospect that you're listening, not waiting to speak. It tells them that their thoughts matter. It tells them the conversation is safe enough to go deeper. Follow-up questions show presence, understanding, and curiosity. Without follow-ups, discovery remains shallow. With follow-ups, discovery becomes a layered exploration that reveals patterns, meaning, and insight. Without follow ups you run the potential of losing the deal.

The first part of follow-up is pausing. When the prospect finishes speaking, most advisors rush to the next question. They fear silence, so they fill the space. But silence is where reflection happens. When you pause after an answer, you give the prospect room to think—often revealing more than they planned to. A well-timed pause is a form of leadership. It shows the prospect that you're not in a hurry, and it encourages them to continue without prompting. A common strategy is to ask a question and then stay quiet for a 10 count.

Verbal mirroring is another essential follow-up tool. Verbal mirroring is simply repeating the last few words of what the prospect said in a calm, curious tone. This draws them deeper into their own thought process. For example, if they say, "It's been overwhelming," you might respond with, "Overwhelming?" This small reflection invites expansion. It helps the prospect clarify what overwhelming means to them instead of assuming you already understand. This strategy has been talked about in sales training for decades, but is often overlooked as a powerful tool.

Looping is the technique of bringing the conversation back to something important the prospect said earlier. People often reveal meaningful details without realizing it. They mention frustration, tension, or a pattern, but then move past it quickly. When you loop back—"Something that stood out to me from your answer earlier…"—you show that you're tracking the conversation in a precise way. Looping deepens trust and turns scattered thoughts into structured insight.

Digging is the process of moving from general statements to specific examples. Prospects often speak in broad terms because broad language feels safer. They say things like, "It's been challenging," or "Things have been inconsistent." These statements lack detail. Digging helps you get to the real story. You might ask, "What does challenging look like for you specifically?" or "Can you walk me through an example of that?" Specifics reveal truth. Without them, discovery stays foggy. You must be aware that you can ask for these insights but it cant become a pattern. You only have so many "at bats" with digging into questions.

Escalating the aftermath is another form of follow-up. Once the prospect gives you clarity, you help them understand what that clarity means for their future. You move gently from the present into the consequences of inaction. You might ask, "I am curious, what happens if this continues for another three months?" or "Help me understand, how does this affect things long-term?" This is not pressure. It is exploration. Escalating consequences helps the prospect feel the weight of their situation without feeling forced.

Redirecting keeps the conversation aligned with what matters. Prospects often drift into stories, tangents, or explanations that are unrelated to the core issue. Redirection allows you to regain the thread while still honoring their contribution. You might say, "That makes sense. Can I bring us back to something you said earlier?" or "Let me ask about the part that seemed most important a moment ago." Effective redirection prevents discovery from becoming scattered.

Clarifying vague responses is another essential follow-up skill. Many prospects speak in unclear terms because clarity exposes the truth. When you hear vague language—"We're doing okay," "It's been a bit rough," "We're figuring it out"—you ask, "What does that mean for you?" or "Help me understand the part that's been most difficult." Clarification transforms emotional fog into usable insight. You cannot diagnose or explore aftermath without clear definitions.

Surfacing contradictions gently is another form of follow-up that separates elite advisors from average ones. When a prospect says two things that don't align, you don't confront them. You explore the contradiction with calm curiosity. You might say, "Can I ask about something that doesn't quite line up?" or "Earlier you mentioned X, but now you're saying Y—can we explore that?" This technique helps the prospect reconcile their own thinking. Contradictions are not problems; they are invitations for deeper conversation.

Challenging without breaking rapport is one of the highest forms of follow-up. Challenge is not aggression. Challenge is the ability to ask the question the prospect has been avoiding. You do it slowly, respectfully, and with permission. "Can I ask you something that might help us see this more clearly?" Challenge reveals truth, and truth creates movement. When you challenge properly, trust increases. When you challenge poorly, trust collapses. The difference is tone and timing.

The final part of follow-up is connecting the dots. Prospects rarely see how their answers relate to one another. They describe isolated issues, not patterns. When you connect their answers—"It sounds like the challenges with your team and the delays you described earlier are linked"—you reveal the structure behind their experience. This insight is often the moment where everything clicks for the prospect. Dot-connecting is where discovery elevates from conversation to transformation.

Following up on answers turns ordinary discovery into powerful exploration. It prevents you from rushing. It prevents premature assumptions. It prevents surface-level conversations. Follow-up is how you uncover the emotional truth, not just the stated facts. It is how you maintain control of the conversation without force. It is how you build trust through depth, not rapport. When you master follow-up, the prospect feels seen, understood, and guided—three conditions that create movement without pressure.

The next section will show you how to put all of this together in a complete, structured discovery conversation. You'll see how each stage, question type, and follow-up technique fits into a real conversation from start to end.

Element 15 — The Complete Discovery Conversation (Scripted Examples)

A complete discovery conversation is not a script. It is a sequence of moments that follow psychological logic. Each moment prepares the prospect for the next. When executed correctly, the conversation feels natural, steady, and honest. There is no pressure. There is no interrogation. There is only clarity. This section demonstrates what a full discovery conversation can look like—from the opening statement to the close.

This example is not meant to be memorized. It is meant to show you the rhythm, pacing, tone, transitions, and emotional flow of a strong discovery conversation. As you read it, pay attention to how the advisor moves slowly, listens deeply, and escalates tension without creating pressure. Notice where pauses appear. Notice how follow-ups reveal truth. Notice how the advisor never jumps ahead or abandons structure. This is discovery done well. Below is a complete example with annotations embedded in the flow. You can adjust to level from mild to aggressive in this script. This is about as generic as it gets.

Opening Authority Statement (modify as needed)

Advisor:
"Before we dive in, let me set us up for success. My role today is simple. I'm here to understand your situation clearly enough to see what's working, what's not, and what it might take to move things forward. I'll ask you a few questions, you can be as open as you're comfortable being, and if I need to slow us down or circle back, I'll do that.
If at any point something doesn't make sense, just let me know.

I am going to answer with 100% honesty and ask that you do the same ok?
Ready?"

This opening creates structure, permission, and authority without pressure.

Prospect:
"Yes, that works."

Warm Discovery

Advisor:
"Let's start here—what led you to take this call today?"

The initial question is broad on purpose. It reveals direction without forcing depth too early.

Prospect:
"We've been dealing with some inconsistencies in performance."

Advisor:

"Can you tell me more about what inconsistencies means for you?"

This early clarification prevents vague language from taking over the conversation.

Prospect:

"Some weeks our numbers look solid, and other weeks they fall off a cliff."

Advisor:

"That sounds frustrating. How long has that pattern been happening?"

Notice the emotional acknowledgment paired with a clarity question.

Prospect:

"About eight months."

Core Discovery (Diagnose)

Advisor:

"Walk me through one of those weeks when things dropped. What was happening at that time?"

Digging through examples reveals patterns.

Prospect:

"We had issues with staff coverage and internal miscommunication."

Advisor:

"Is that something that happens occasionally, or is it showing up more often?"

A narrowing question moves from event to pattern.

Prospect:

"It's been happening more often."

Advisor:

"Based on what you're seeing, what do you think is driving the inconsistency?"

Inviting the prospect's interpretation uncovers self-awareness and responsibility.

Prospect:

"I think leadership hasn't been on the same page."

Aftermath Exploration

Advisor:

"Let me ask something about that. When leadership isn't aligned, what tends to happen downstream?"

The advisor moves gently into aftermath without pressure.

Prospect:

"Everyone ends up confused. Projects stall, people point fingers, and our clients feel the effects."

Advisor (pause):

"That's a heavy ripple. What has that been costing you so far?"

The pause signals depth; the question makes aftermath visible.

Prospect:

"Lost revenue. Stress. Delays. We constantly feel behind."

Advisor:

"And if nothing changes, where does this lead a few months from now?"

Escalating aftermath reveals urgency without aggression.

Prospect:

"Honestly, we could lose key people."

Conflict (Gap Awareness)

Advisor:

"That's serious. Let me ask something that might help us see the bigger picture. Where do you want things to be instead?"

This shifts from aftermath to desired outcomes.

Prospect:

"I want a stable, consistent operation where people know their responsibilities."

Advisor:

"So the gap between where you are and where you want to be—is it getting wider or staying the same?"

This surfaces internal conflict.

Prospect:

"It's definitely getting wider."

The Recap

Advisor: "So what I'm picking up from you is this: you're dealing with performance swings that have been happening for about eight months, the miscommunication and coverage issues are showing up more often, leadership isn't aligned, and that disconnect is creating confusion, stalled

projects, and client impact. It's costing you revenue, momentum, and stability—and if nothing changes, you're worried you could lose key people. At the same time, the operation you want is steady, predictable, and clear… and it feels like the gap between the two is widening.
Did I capture that correctly?"

Prospect: You nailed it

Criteria Exploration

Advisor:
"Given the gap you're seeing, what needs to be true for you to feel confident moving forward with any solution?"

Criteria reveals the prospect's decision-making framework.

Prospect:
"I need a clear plan, accountability systems, and someone who can guide us through implementation."

Advisor:
"And what else?"

Prospects almost always stop short. Gentle expansion reveals the full list.

Prospect:
"Consistency. We need a consistent process we can stick to."

Authority Mapping

Advisor:
"When you think about making a change like this, who else needs to feel comfortable with the direction?"

The advisor explores the authority chain only after clarity and criteria exist.

Prospect:
"My operations director and our CFO."

Advisor:
"What's their perspective right now?"

This uncovers political alignment or friction.

Prospect:
"They know things need to improve, but they're overwhelmed."

Budget & Feasibility

Advisor:

"Based on what you've described—the revenue loss, the risk of turnover, the widening gap—how are you thinking about the investment required to fix this?"

Notice the budget question is grounded in aftermath and readiness, not cost.

Prospect:

"If the plan is solid and the execution is real, we're prepared to invest."

Timeline

Advisor:

"When do these issues need to be addressed for the year not to slip further?"

Timeline is anchored to consequence, not preference.

Prospect:

"Within the next 60 days."

The Recap 2

Advisor: "So the impression I'm getting is this: you need a solution that gives you a clear plan, real accountability systems, and guidance through implementation — not theory, but hands-on execution. You also want a consistent process your team can rely on. On the decision side, your operations director and CFO both need to feel aligned, even though they're already overwhelmed by the current instability. From a feasibility standpoint, as long as the plan is strong and the execution is real, you're ready to invest in fixing this. And based on everything you've shared, the timeline isn't flexible — these issues need to be addressed within the next 60 days for the year not to slip any further.
Did I get that right?"**

Prospect: Yes, you are spot on

Commitment

Advisor:

"Based on everything you've shared—the inconsistency, the downstream effects, the leadership alignment, the risk of losing people—what feels like the right next step for you?"

The advisor doesn't close. They guide the prospect into self-clarity.

Prospect:

"We need help implementing a solution. I want to explore what working together could look like."

Advisor:

"Good. Let's take the next step together."

Conclusion

This example demonstrates how a complete discovery conversation unfolds when the advisor stays calm, clear, and steady. There is no rush. There is no force. There is no selling. Each step naturally leads to the next because the advisor follows the order of operations with discipline. The prospect opens up because the advisor creates safety. Clarity becomes momentum. Momentum becomes commitment.

The next section will take these principles even further by showing how discovery shifts depending on the industry you're speaking to—and how to adapt your questions without losing integrity, depth, or control.

Element 16 — Industry-Specific Discovery Frameworks

Discovery does not change from industry to industry. The human psychology behind it stays the same. What changes is the context—how the problem shows up, how the prospect experiences it, and what consequences matter most in their environment. Elite advisors know how to adjust their questions without losing structure, tone, or intention. This section gives you industry-specific angles so you can adapt your discovery approach to different fields while maintaining the same level of depth and clarity.

These are not scripts. They are frameworks. They show you how to think, not what to memorize. Each industry carries its own form of risk, consequence, and emotional pressure. Your job is to understand the environment well enough to ask questions that uncover the truth the prospect is not yet saying. When you adjust your angle but maintain your structure, you remain in control of the conversation no matter who you're speaking to.

HVAC & Home Services

In home services, the prospect often minimizes problems because they've learned to tolerate discomfort. They delay decisions until something breaks. The key is helping them understand the long-term consequences of avoidance.

Focus on:

• safety and comfort
• rising costs
• system longevity
• homeowner stress
• emergency risk

You might explore:

• "How long have you been noticing these signs?"
• "What happens if this system fails during peak season?"
• "What's been the impact of these issues on comfort or routine?"
• "If nothing changes, what does this mean for the rest of the year?"

Home service discovery revolves around helping the prospect understand the escalating costs of inaction.

Pest Control

Pest issues carry emotional weight. People feel embarrassment, frustration, and fear. Discovery must be gentle but direct.

Focus on:

- severity of infestation
- spread and recurrence
- sanitation or health concerns
- emotional discomfort
- financial impact of delay

You might ask:

- "Where have you been noticing activity?"
- "Has this been getting better, worse, or staying the same?"
- "How is this affecting your ability to use the space?"
- "What happens if this continues another month?"

Pest control discovery explores impact, not just identification.

Roofing & Exterior Construction

Roofing prospects often avoid replacement because of cost anxiety. You must explore risk without pressure.

Focus on:

- structural integrity
- water intrusion
- escalating repair costs
- resale value
- timeline sensitivity

You might ask:

- "What first made you think it was time to get this checked?"
- "What concerns you most about waiting?"
- "How long has the roofing issue been on your mind?"
- "If the situation worsens, what areas of the home are most vulnerable?"

Roofing discovery centers on future risk and financial exposure.

Plumbing

Plumbing problems create urgency, but people often underestimate their severity until a major failure occurs.

Focus on:

- hidden damage
- water contamination

- mold or structural risk
- operational disruption
- repair vs. replacement clarity

You might explore:

- "What symptoms have you noticed and for how long?"
- "Has the issue changed or spread?"
- "How is this affecting your daily routine?"
- "What's the risk if this worsens?"

Plumbing discovery helps the prospect connect small signs to bigger consequences.

Construction & Remodeling

Construction prospects often lack clarity about what they actually want. You must explore vision, constraints, and readiness.

Focus on:

- project scope
- timeline expectations
- material or design preferences
- budget alignment
- long-term goals

You might ask:

- "What's motivating you to consider this project now?"
- "How do you want the space to feel or function when it's done?"
- "What concerns you most about starting this project?"
- "What's your ideal timeline for completion?"

In construction, discovery uncovers clarity of vision and decision readiness.

Coaching & Consulting

In advisory roles, the prospect's thinking patterns matter as much as their problem. You must understand the emotional and strategic layers.

Focus on:

- limiting beliefs
- internal conflict
- accountability readiness

- leadership behavior
- long-term goals

You might ask:

- "What patterns have you noticed repeating for you?"
- "Where do you feel most stuck?"
- "What's the part of this situation you've been avoiding?"
- "How would fixing this change your life or business?"

Coaching discovery uncovers the deeper truth behind surface-level frustrations.

M&A and Exit Advisory

These prospects deal with high-stakes decisions. Discovery is about alignment, risk, valuation clarity, and emotional readiness.

Focus on:

- why the prospect wants to sell
- exit timeline
- business health
- internal political risk
- deal-breakers

You might explore:

- "What prompted you to consider an exit?"
- "How prepared do you feel the business is for due diligence?"
- "What risks concern you most in a potential transaction?"
- "What would a successful exit allow you to do next?"

In M&A, discovery exposes decision risk and internal alignment.

SaaS & Technology

In software sales, the primary challenges revolve around inefficiency, productivity loss, and operational breakdowns. Discovery must surface friction, cost, and workflow disruption.

Focus on:

- manual processes
- team adoption challenges
- workflow inefficiencies
- cost of delays
- integration complexity

You might ask:

- "Where are things slowing down right now?"
- "What's the impact of those delays on your output?"
- "Who is most affected when the system breaks down?"
- "What happens to productivity if nothing changes?"

SaaS discovery reveals operational drag and hidden costs.

Professional Services

These prospects seek expertise but often lack clarity about what they actually need. Discovery must uncover expectations, risks, and misalignment.

Focus on:

- service expectations
- readiness for guidance
- internal constraints
- previous failures
- desired outcomes

You might ask:

- "What has made this a priority now?"
- "Where have you seen results fall short in the past?"
- "What would a successful engagement look like for you?"
- "What risks are you hoping to avoid this time?"

Professional service discovery builds alignment and expectation clarity.

Health & Wellness

These prospects experience emotional pressure, self-judgment, and fear of failure. Discovery must balance empathy with direction.

Focus on:

- emotional triggers
- previous attempts
- physical limitations
- lifestyle constraints
- identity-level motivation

You might ask:

• "What made you decide it's time to make a change now?"
• "Where have things been breaking down for you?"
• "How has this been affecting your daily life?"
• "What becomes possible for you if this improves?"

Health and wellness discovery uncovers readiness, motivation, and identity.

Industry-specific frameworks allow you to apply elite discovery principles anywhere. You adjust your angle, not your philosophy. You adapt your language, not your depth. You maintain structure, presence, and neutrality while exploring the parts of the prospect's world that matter most in their environment. This adaptability is what makes you effective across diverse industries without losing control or clarity.

The next section will shift into advanced qualification and scoring—how to determine which prospects are worth investing in and which conversations should end early.

Element 17 — The Qualification Blueprint

Below is a **tightened version that is ~80 words shorter**, with **no loss of meaning, structure, or authority**.

I removed redundancy, compressed phrasing, and simplified a few explanations while preserving your voice.

Qualification determines where you invest your time, energy, and attention. It protects you from entering engagements that drain resources or damage your reputation. Most advisors qualify at the surface—budget, authority, need, timing. Elite advisors qualify at depth. They understand that internal readiness, emotional stability, and commitment to change matter far more than technical details.

The qualification blueprint is not a checklist. It is a diagnostic tool that helps you interpret the person across from you. It reveals whether they can make clear decisions, take responsibility, and follow through once clarity appears. When qualification is done well, you avoid bad fits, wasted time, and fragile deals that collapse under pressure.

The first pillar of qualification is Fit. Fit is not about whether the prospect needs what you offer. It is about alignment—between their problem and your expertise, their expectations and your process, and their personality and your communication style. Poor-fit prospects resist guidance or demand unrealistic outcomes. Strong-fit prospects respect structure and process.

The second pillar is Budget, though not in the traditional sense. Budget reflects willingness, priority, and allocation. You are listening for whether the problem matters enough to invest in. Some prospects have funds without commitment. Others lack funds today but will find a way because the issue is meaningful. Budget qualification reveals seriousness, not affordability.

Authority is the third pillar. Authority is not about titles. It is about influence, decision power, and veto risk. You must understand who can approve, block, or quietly influence the outcome. Many deals fail because hidden decision-makers were never uncovered.

Decision Certainty is the fourth pillar. Certainty is the ability to decide once clarity exists. Some people gather information without acting. Others hesitate under pressure. You are listening for clarity-driven decisiveness. Low-certainty prospects stall or retreat as commitment approaches.

The fifth pillar is Constraints. Every prospect has limits—time, bandwidth, competing priorities, emotional resistance, or structural barriers. These must be surfaced early. When constraints dominate, deals become unstable and execution fails.

The sixth pillar is Appetite for Change. This is one of the strongest indicators of qualification. Some prospects are uncomfortable yet complacent. Others are frustrated and ready. Appetite reflects urgency, ownership, and willingness to act. Without it, no solution works.

Alignment is the seventh pillar. Alignment means goals, expectations, and behaviors match. When they conflict, risk increases. Alignment creates momentum.

The eighth pillar is Long-Term Potential. You are qualifying both the immediate opportunity and the relationship's future value. Long-term potential influences whether the investment of time is worth it.

The ninth pillar is the Scoring System. Each pillar is rated on a simple scale:
1 = Risk
3 = Neutral
5 = Strong

Consistent scores above three signal a qualified prospect. Scoring keeps you objective and prevents emotional decision-making.

The tenth pillar is Pattern Recognition. Beyond scores, you watch behavior. How prospects speak, respond to tension, and handle difficulty reveals the truth. Single statements can mislead. Patterns do not.

Qualification is not about excluding people. It protects the integrity of your work and ensures readiness. When done well, decisions become easier and outcomes more predictable. When rushed, everything becomes unstable.

The next section introduces the Red Team / Blue Team Discovery Test—a method for stress-testing deals, revealing hidden risk, and exposing weak points before they become problems.

Element 18 — Preliminary And Softening Statements

The way a question begins often determines how it is received. Even the most thoughtful "what" or "how" question can feel interrogative if it arrives without context, intention, or emotional awareness. Preliminary statements exist to regulate the moment before the question is asked. They signal care, precision, and purpose. They help the other person understand why you are asking and create enough safety for reflection instead of reaction. When used correctly, these statements lower resistance, slow the conversation, and invite collaboration. They are not filler. They are subtle tools that shape how your questions land and how deeply the other person is willing to engage

1.Accuracy & Respect

- "Before I connect any dots…"
- "I want to be precise here…"
- "I want to make sure I'm understanding this correctly…"
- "I want to understand this clearly…"
- "Let me check that I'm tracking with you…"

2. Permission & Soft Entry

- "Can I ask you something to understand this better?"
- "I want to approach this thoughtfully…"
- "If you're open to it, I'd like to ask…"
- "This may help us get clearer—may I ask…"
- "Would it be okay if I explored this a bit?"

3. Normalizing & Safety

- "Many people find this challenging to articulate…"
- "People often reflect on this when they slow down…"
- "There's value in exploring this…"
- "This comes up frequently…"
- "This is something I hear often…"

4. Context Setting

- "The reason I'm asking is to understand the full picture…"
- "This gives me better context…"
- "This helps clarify the situation…"
- "This helps me see how this shows up for you…"
- "This will help us focus on what matters most…"

5. Slowing the Conversation

- "Before we move on, let's stay here briefly…"
- "I want to explore this more fully…"
- "I'd like to spend a moment here…"
- "Let's pause on this…"
- "Let's slow this down for a moment…"

6. Curiosity Without Pressure

- "I want to understand this more deeply…"
- "I'd like to explore something with you…"
- "I'd like to learn more about your perspective…"
- "I'm curious…"
- "I'm interested in how you see this…"

7. Emotional Sensitivity

- "I want to approach this with care…"
- "Take your time with this…"
- "This can carry some weight…"
- "This may take a moment to think through…"
- "This often requires reflection…"

8. Shared Problem-Solving

- "I want to align as we look at this…"
- "I'd like to work through this with you…"
- "Let's think through this together…"
- "Let's unpack this…"
- "So we can get clear together…"

9. Neutral Framing

- "This brings alignment…"
- "This gives us a clearer picture…"
- "This helps create clarity…"
- "This is about understanding…"
- "This supports better decisions…"

10. Ownership & Reflection

- "As you reflect on this…"

- "From your perspective…"
- "In your experience…"
- "The way you see it…"
- "When you think about this…"

Preliminary statements are not about softening your authority; they are about strengthening your influence. They allow you to ask direct questions without triggering defensiveness and to explore meaningful topics without creating pressure. When used with restraint and intention, they make your questions feel human, thoughtful, and customized to the moment. Over time, they also change how you listen. You become more deliberate, more present, and more precise. The result is discovery that feels less like an interview and more like a guided conversation—one where clarity emerges naturally and trust builds quietly through how you ask, not just what you ask.

Element 19 — The Power Of A Conversational Recap

The most important moment in discovery does not happen when you ask the first question. It happens at the end of the conversation, when you reflect everything back to the potential client and give them space to agree, disagree, or correct you. This moment determines whether clarity actually exists or whether the conversation only felt productive. Most salespeople and consultants rush past it because they believe discovery is about gathering information. In reality, discovery is about confirming understanding. The recap is where that confirmation happens.

The purpose of the recap is not to convince the prospect that they have problems. It is not to dramatize the situation or amplify urgency. It is to demonstrate—clearly and unmistakably—that you heard them. When a prospect hears their own words reflected back accurately, something important happens internally. They stop evaluating you and start evaluating their situation. Agreement follows naturally, not because you pushed, but because the truth feels familiar.

A discovery recap is not a summary. A summary lists facts. A recap organizes meaning. It connects what the prospect said about their current situation, how it affects them, why it matters, and where they want to go instead. When you do this well, you turn a scattered conversation into a coherent narrative the prospect can see themselves inside of. This allows them to decide whether that narrative is accurate. That decision is far more powerful than anything you could persuade them to accept.

When you deliver the recap, tone matters more than language. You must be calm, neutral, and precise. This is not the moment for enthusiasm or performance. Speak slowly. Leave space between thoughts. Use the prospect's own phrasing as closely as possible. Do not improve their story. Do not add insight. Do not connect dots they did not connect themselves. Accuracy is the goal. Accuracy is what builds trust.

The structure of the recap should feel natural, not scripted. You remind them why they took the call in the first place, reflect what is happening now, state why it matters based on the consequences they described, and acknowledge what they want instead. You also reflect where they stand emotionally and mentally—whether they feel clear, uncertain, frustrated, or hesitant. Everything you say should already belong to them. Nothing should feel new.

Once the recap is complete, the most important part begins. You invite response—not validation, but correction. Instead of asking questions that pressure agreement, you ask questions that invite accuracy. You create room for them to say you missed something, misunderstood something, or need to adjust a detail. This is where many advisors get uncomfortable, but this is exactly where alignment is built. When a prospect corrects you, they are not resisting. They are engaging. They are taking ownership of the truth.

Disagreement during the recap is not a problem. It is proof that the person is thinking. It means they are listening carefully. It means they care about getting it right. Passive agreement, on the other hand, often signals avoidance or disengagement. When someone says, "That part is right, but let me explain this piece more clearly," the conversation deepens. The prospect is now participating in defining the reality of the situation instead of reacting to it.

This moment also gives you critical diagnostic information. When prospects expand on the recap, readiness is high. When they thoughtfully clarify, engagement is strong. When they minimize, deflect, or soften what they previously said, something important is unresolved. The recap shows you whether the problem is real enough, clear enough, and meaningful enough to move forward. It protects you from false momentum and fragile commitments.

When the recap is done correctly, the dynamic of the conversation changes. The prospect no longer feels guided or influenced. They feel understood. You are no longer perceived as someone trying to move the conversation forward. You become someone who can reflect reality without distortion. This is where authority is earned—not through control, but through presence.

The recap proves that you were listening at a level most people never experience. It allows the prospect to agree with their own truth, correct inaccuracies, and feel seen without being pressured. This is why great advisors do not close conversations. They confirm clarity. And once clarity exists, the next step takes care of itself.

Here are 10 ways to introduce the Recap or the Summary process:

1. Before we go any further, I want to make sure I'm understanding this correctly.
2. Before we talk about next steps, I want to confirm I didn't miss anything important.
3. Before we wrap up, I want to reflect the full picture back to you so we're aligned.
4. Can I walk through how I'm currently seeing this, and you can adjust anything that doesn't fit?
5. Here's how I currently understand the situation—what would you change or add?
6. I want to reflect this back in your words, not mine—tell me where I need to refine it.
7. I'd like to pause for a moment and summarize what you've shared so far.
8. I'm going to recap what I've heard—not to move things forward yet, just to make sure it's accurate.
9. Let me make sure I'm tracking with you so far.
10. Let me reflect back what I'm hearing so you can tell me where I'm right and where I'm off.

If you are not closing sales, one of the first places to look is your discovery process. Are you asking set discovery questions. Once you ask the questions are you following up with another question. Lastly are you recapping the conversation to confirm the need, want and or desire? Having a recap or summary can help you close more deals almost immediately.

Element 20 — Turning Practice Into Discovery Mastery

Discovery mastery is not built by knowing the right questions. It is built by repeatedly placing yourself inside real conversational tension and learning how to remain steady while navigating it. Reading frameworks creates awareness. Practicing discovery creates competence. Analyzing that practice is what creates mastery. Without analysis and refinement, even the best questions flatten into habit instead of skill.

This chapter exists to close the gap between understanding discovery and *becoming* a strong discovery practitioner. The goal is not familiarity. The goal is instinct.

Why Practice Must Be Treated as an Asset

Every role play, rehearsal, or solo practice session is raw material. These sessions are not disposable exercises; they are intellectual assets. When captured and reviewed, they become a growing library of insight, patterns, and language that compounds over time. This is the difference between casual practice and deliberate training.

Most professionals practice without extracting value. They repeat conversations but never slow down to see what actually happened. Mastery requires you to turn experience into data.

Action Items

- Decide that every practice session will be recorded in some form.

- Treat practice as training, not warm-up.

- Create a single folder or system where all recordings and notes will live.

Role Play: Where Discovery Becomes Instinct

Role play is where discovery moves from theory into behavior. Discovery is not a cognitive exercise—it is a live interaction that requires emotional regulation, patience, and precision under uncertainty. Role play conditions your nervous system to stay calm when answers are vague, when resistance appears, or when the conversation does not go as planned.

Your role-play partner should challenge you. Some sessions should include clipped answers that test your follow-up discipline. Others should introduce confusion, guardedness, or subtle pushback. These moments expose where you rush, soften, over-explain, or abandon structure.

You must also practice with cooperative prospects. The market contains both extremes. Versatility comes from handling both without changing your presence.

Action Items

- Role play at least once per week with another person.

- Rotate scenarios: guarded, rushed, resistant, open, and cooperative.

- Practice the *entire* discovery arc from opening to recap.

Recording Practice: Turning Repetition Into Acceleration

Recording is what separates improvement from repetition. Video recordings reveal posture, facial expressions, pacing errors, and emotional leakage you cannot see in real time. They show whether your presence communicates steadiness or urgency.

Audio recordings sharpen awareness of tone, rhythm, cadence, and silence. Without visual cues, you hear rushed phrasing, filler language, and moments where your voice tightens. Audio is also practical—it can be reviewed during daily routines, making improvement continuous instead of occasional.

Action Items

- Record video for role play when possible.

- Record audio for solo practice and quick review.

- Review at least one recording within 24 hours of practice.

Using Transcripts to Identify Patterns

Transcripts convert conversation into structured learning. Once sessions are transcribed, patterns become visible. You can see where you stop following up, where you accept vague answers, and which phrases reliably unlock clarity.

Transcripts remove emotion and memory bias. They show you what actually happened—not what you *think* happened.

Action Items

- Transcribe key practice sessions.

- Highlight strong questions, weak follow-ups, and missed moments.

- Track repeated behaviors across multiple sessions.

Using AI as a Discovery Accelerator

AI adds leverage when used with intention. Modern tools can summarize sessions, identify objection patterns, surface emotional shifts, and suggest alternative phrasing. AI becomes an objective second set of eyes and ears.

AI does not replace judgment. It sharpens it. It helps you turn raw practice into refined language and repeatable frameworks.

Action Items

- Run transcripts through AI for pattern analysis.

- Ask AI to identify missed follow-ups and alternative phrasing.

- Capture insights and add them to your personal library.

Building a Personal Discovery Library

Over time, your recordings and insights become a private intellectual property archive. This archive contains your strongest questions, best phrasing, signature follow-ups, and breakthrough moments. Organized intentionally, it becomes a personalized training system that compounds year after year.

Action Items

- Create categories: questions, follow-ups, objections, breakthroughs.

- Store your best language in a searchable format.

- Review your library monthly to reinforce learning.

Solo Training: Mastery Built in Private

Solo training allows you to slow down, remove pressure, and study your own patterns honestly. Many breakthroughs happen alone, where experimentation is safe and uninterrupted.

One of the most effective solo practices is recording yourself asking discovery questions out loud. Speak as if you were in a live meeting. Then review from three perspectives: what you said, how you said it, and how the moment felt.

Action Items

- Record yourself asking questions weekly.

- Analyze tone, pace, and emotional steadiness.

- Refine delivery until presence matches intention.

Refining Questions Through Variation

Comparing your questions to the variations in this book builds flexibility. You learn how to adjust question weight based on safety, resistance, and readiness. This conditioning allows you to adapt naturally without sounding scripted.

Action Items

- Take one question per week and test multiple variations.

- Practice softer and stronger versions intentionally.

- Notice which versions create the deepest reflection.

Learning by Studying Other Advisors

Observing other professionals accelerates awareness. Watch interviews, podcasts, coaching sessions, or sales calls. Pay attention to pacing, silence, hesitation, and timing. Notice where clarity was missed or tension escalated.

Reverse-engineer strong moments. Identify why a question worked and how it was delivered.

Action Items

- Study one external conversation per week.

- Pause and analyze strong and weak moments.

- Integrate one insight into your next practice session.

From Practice to Mastery

Training builds discipline. Discipline builds awareness. Awareness builds mastery. Over time, discovery stops being something you perform and becomes something you embody. Your presence steadies. Your listening deepens. Your questions land with precision.

Discovery is an art.
Practice is where the art becomes instinct.
Recording, analysis, and refinement are where instinct becomes mastery.

Elements Conclusion:

Discovery is not a technique, a script, or a preliminary step. It is the operating system behind every meaningful advisory relationship—the discipline that reveals truth, clarifies thinking, exposes consequence, and allows people to see themselves with uncommon honesty. When done correctly, discovery transforms uncertainty into insight, confusion into clarity, and resistance into momentum. It becomes the moment where people recognize their own patterns and where change becomes possible.

This book was created to give you a complete system for discovery at the highest level—not a list of clever questions, but a methodology rooted in psychology, emotional safety, sequencing, and strategic clarity. You learned how elite advisors slow the moment down, listen for what isn't said, follow emotional cues, create safety before depth, and guide conversations without force. You learned why aftermath, follow-up questions, silence, and presence—not pressure—shape the direction of the conversation.

More importantly, you now understand the architecture behind discovery: its rhythm, order of operations, psychological layers, and the way each stage prepares the prospect for the next. You've seen how discovery becomes leverage, influence, qualification, and risk protection. You've learned how it uncovers contradictions, reveals identity-level friction, exposes political dynamics, and clarifies readiness. You now know how to shape conversations ethically so people move because the truth is clear.

If you practice these frameworks, discovery will stop being something you "do" and will become the way you see the world. You will notice patterns earlier, hear inconsistencies faster, read people more accurately, and ask sharper questions. Prospects will trust you more quickly and make decisions with greater confidence. Clarity becomes the natural outcome—not because you forced it, but because you guided it.

When you master discovery at this level, you become the advisor people follow. Not because of charisma, but because of clarity and presence. You become the person who helps others think better, decide better, and operate at a higher level.

Let this book be your reference guide and your advantage. Revisit it often. Let it sharpen your instincts until discovery becomes second nature.

Great advisors don't ask more questions—they ask better ones.

This book has given you everything you need to become one of them.

CHAPTER 1 — Establishing the Current Landscape

Every effective discovery conversation begins with a clear understanding of the buyer's current landscape. Before exploring causes, consequences, politics, or decision dynamics, an advisor must first understand what the buyer is actually experiencing. Chapter 1 establishes that foundation. It begins with the simple act of listening — not for surface-level complaints, but for the deeper signals that reveal how the buyer's world functions. These early insights create the stability needed for every later stage of discovery.

Most buyers arrive with some idea of their problem, but their view is rarely complete. Thought patterns blur details, familiarity hides patterns, and internal pressure encourages people to minimize what's really happening. This chapter guides the advisor through a structured process that moves from defining the problem to understanding how it spreads, what restricts progress, where perspectives diverge, and how work truly unfolds inside the organization. Each section adds a layer of clarity to the one before it.

The sequence begins with **Problem-Definition Questions**, which help the buyer articulate their challenge in plain terms. This step alone often reveals gaps, uncertainty, or hidden emotional weight. From there, **Impact-Mapping Questions** uncover how the problem affects people, processes, outcomes, and confidence. Buyers often realize their situation is larger and more interconnected than they initially believed.

Next, **Constraint-Identification Questions** explore what blocks progress. These constraints often include limited resources, unclear responsibility, or environmental conditions the buyer has unconsciously accepted. **Misalignment-Detection Questions** then expose where perspectives differ across the team — a frequent source of confusion and friction. These insights help the advisor understand not only the problem, but the social reality surrounding it.

The chapter continues by tracing patterns through **Root-Cause Tracing Questions**, which reveal why the problem keeps appearing. **Information-Flow Questions** show how communication helps or harms progress, exposing gaps that shape execution. Finally, **Order-of-Operation Questions** reveal how the workflow actually functions step-by-step — the true operational rhythm that determines outcomes.

By the time these eight sections are complete, the advisor has a well-defined picture of the buyer's environment: what they face, how it affects them, what blocks progress, how their people think, and how their workflows break down. This understanding is not about collecting data — it is about uncovering the truth beneath symptoms and assumptions. Chapter 1 creates a foundation strong enough to support the deeper discovery work ahead.

CHPATER 1 - SECTION 1 - Problem-Definition Questions

Introduction

Every discovery conversation begins with one simple truth: you cannot help someone change what they cannot clearly describe. Problem-definition questions serve as the stabilizing force that brings a scattered situation into focus. Many buyers arrive with a mix of assumptions, guesses, and partial narratives. They often feel the symptoms of the problem long before they understand its shape. This section helps the advisor slow the moment down, frame what is known, and begin uncovering what is still hidden.

The strategic purpose of problem-definition questions is to build the first anchor in the buyer's mind. When the buyer hears themselves describe the issue out loud, their internal viewpoint begins to shift. People think more clearly when guided by an outside voice that helps them organize their reality without judgment. These questions take the buyer from a vague sense of frustration to a clear, shared understanding of what is actually happening. That clarity creates permission for deeper work later in the conversation.

The psychological purpose is just as important. Buyers often carry emotional weight tied to uncertainty — frustration, embarrassment, worry, or even fear of being judged for letting a problem grow. Calm, steady problem-definition questions help relieve that pressure. When you help someone define the problem without rushing them, you become a source of stability. A buyer who feels understood becomes more open, more honest, and more willing to explore the truth.

Interpretation Tip: Listen for how concrete or vague their explanations are. Vague answers usually signal that the buyer hasn't fully examined the issue. Concrete answers reveal that they have been thinking about the problem for some time, which often indicates urgency or impact. Pay attention to emotional tone — frustration, confusion, or resignation can reveal how long the problem has been active.

Coaching Note: If a buyer gives a short or general answer, resist the urge to fill the silence or explain what you think they mean. Instead, gently ask for clarity. When buyers explain something in more detail, they deepen their own awareness. Your role is to help them verbalize the parts of the problem they've never fully articulated.

Here is a sample phrasing you might use in real conversation:

- *"Before we explore anything else, could you walk me through what you're noticing on your side?"*

- *"Let's start simple — what feels off, incomplete, or not working the way it should?"*

With this foundation in place, the following questions will help you guide the buyer to define the problem with greater accuracy, depth, and confidence.

Standard Problem-Definition Questions (8)

Tone: calm, open, rapport-building.

1. "Can you describe what first made you feel something needed attention?"

2. "What part of the situation stands out as the main issue to you right now?"

3. "When you think about the problem, what's the simplest way you would explain it?"

4. "What were you hoping would be happening that isn't happening yet?"

5. "What feels unclear or confusing about the current situation?"

6. "What has changed recently that made this worth discussing now?"

7. "What do you see happening that tells you something isn't lining up?"

8. "If you had to sum up the challenge in one sentence, how would you put it?"

Intermediate Problem-Definition Questions (9)

Tone: probing, curious, professional.

1. "What parts of the issue do you feel confident you understand, and what parts feel blurry?"

2. "When did you first notice early signs that something wasn't working as expected?"

3. "What patterns or recurring moments make the problem more obvious?"

4. "How would you explain the difference between what you expected and what actually happened?"

5. "Which people or processes seem most affected by the problem so far?"

6. "If you had to break the issue into smaller pieces, what would the top three be?"

7. "What has your team observed that adds to your understanding of the problem?"

8. "What do you believe is driving the issue beneath the surface?"

9. "What information do you wish you had that would help you see the situation more clearly?"

Aggressive Problem-Definition Questions (8)

Tone: direct, respectful, truth-seeking — NOT abrasive.

1. "What part of this problem has been ignored the longest?"

2. "What signs told you this was serious, even if no one said it out loud?"

3. "What have you been tolerating that you know shouldn't continue?"

4. "If nothing changed, what's the most likely outcome you're quietly expecting?"

5. "Where do you feel the problem may be bigger than you've admitted so far?"

6. "Which assumption about this issue do you think might be wrong?"

7. "Who is most frustrated by this problem but hasn't voiced it directly?"

8. "What truth about this situation have you been avoiding because it's inconvenient?"

Follow-Up Problem-Definition Questions (10)

Tone: empathetic, reflective, clarifying.

1. "Can you give an example of when that showed up most recently?"

2. "What did you notice in that moment that confirmed this was a real issue?"

3. "When you say it's been building for a while, what do you mean by that?"

4. "How did that impact your team or workflow the day it happened?"

5. "What surprised you most when you realized the problem wasn't temporary?"

6. "What makes that specific detail important to you?"

7. "How long has that part of the issue been occurring in the same way?"

8. "What changed after you noticed that pattern more clearly?"

9. "What were you hoping would happen instead?"

10. "How would you know for certain that this part of the problem has been solved?"

Conclusion

Defining a problem with clarity is the first act of leadership in any advisory conversation. Many buyers arrive with ideas shaped by incomplete information or emotional fatigue. Helping them express the issue in a grounded, coherent way creates an internal shift: they begin to see the problem as something that can be understood, measured, and ultimately resolved. That shift establishes you as the person who brings order to what feels chaotic.

Strategically, problem-definition questions create alignment between you and the buyer. Without a shared definition, every later step — diagnosing causes, exploring consequences, mapping decisions — becomes harder. With a clear definition, the path ahead becomes simpler, calmer, and more predictable.

Psychologically, these questions allow the buyer to lower their guard. When someone feels heard and unjudged while describing a difficult situation, they experience relief. That relief leads to openness. Openness leads to honesty. Honesty leads to deeper discovery.

As you move into later sections of this chapter, remember that every advanced discovery question depends on the strength of the foundation you build here. Clarity enables insight. Insight enables momentum. And momentum makes change possible.

Reflection Prompt:
Think about a recent conversation where a buyer struggled to explain their problem. What question could you have asked that would have helped them define it more clearly? What made that moment difficult, and how would you approach it differently now?

CHPATER 1 - SECTION 2 - Impact-Mapping Questions

Introduction

Once a buyer can describe the problem, the next step is understanding what the problem is doing to their world. Many prospects underestimate the true weight of an issue because they are so used to living with it. Impact-mapping questions help uncover the practical, emotional, operational, and strategic consequences that the buyer has normalized. When asked calmly and clearly, these questions reveal how the problem affects people, workflows, timelines, and results.

Strategically, impact mapping helps the advisor shift the conversation from *"What's happening?"* to *"What is this costing you?"* Buyers often come in with a surface-level description but lack a structured view of the ripple effects. These questions help them articulate pressures, delays, inefficiencies, and unintended outcomes that sit beneath the surface. Once a buyer hears themselves describe specific impacts, they begin to feel urgency in a grounded, self-generated way — not through persuasion, but through clarity.

Psychologically, impact mapping gives the buyer permission to express concerns they may have been holding inside. People often protect themselves by minimizing the consequences of a problem. When you give them space to describe what the issue disrupts, slows down, or complicates, they begin to confront the reality they've been carrying alone. This creates emotional relief and often deepens trust because the buyer feels safe acknowledging the full picture.

Interpretation Tip: Listen for signs that the buyer is discovering new impacts as they speak. Phrases like "now that I think about it…" or "I hadn't realized until saying this out loud…" indicate that your questions are expanding their awareness. These moments signal readiness for deeper exploration in later sections.

Coaching Note: Do not rush when the buyer describes impact. Allow them to pause, collect their thoughts, and continue. When a buyer slows down, they often reveal the most valuable insights. After they finish, reflect back a short summary to confirm accuracy before moving forward. This strengthens alignment and prevents misunderstanding.

Here are a couple of phrasing examples used in real conversations:

- *"Help me understand how this shows up day to day. What happens when the issue hits your workflow?"*

- *"When this problem is active, who feels it first — and how do they feel it?"*

The following questions will help you guide the buyer in mapping the real effects of the problem across their environment.

Standard Impact-Mapping Questions (8)

Tone: steady, open, rapport-based.

1. "How does this issue affect your day-to-day work?"

2. "Who else feels the impact when this problem shows up?"

3. "What tasks or responsibilities does this make harder than they should be?"

4. "How does this problem change the way your team has to operate?"

5. "What part of your week gets disrupted the most because of this?"

6. "What usually gets delayed when this challenge comes up?"

7. "How does this affect the confidence your team has in their work?"

8. "What results do you notice slipping when the problem becomes active?"

Intermediate Impact-Mapping Questions (9)

Tone: curious, probing, professional.

1. "What are the biggest ripple effects you've seen across your team or process?"

2. "When this problem occurs, what secondary issues appear because of it?"

3. "How does this influence your ability to hit deadlines or stay on schedule?"

4. "Which metrics or outcomes take the biggest hit when this shows up?"

5. "How does the problem change the way people communicate or coordinate?"

6. "What additional work gets created because of the issue?"

7. "Which part of the operation absorbs the most pressure when the impact grows?"

8. "How does this problem affect the experience of your customers or stakeholders?"

9. "If you had to estimate the weekly or monthly strain this creates, how would you describe it?"

Aggressive Impact-Mapping Questions (8)

Tone: direct, respectful, consequence-focused.

1. "Which part of the business is getting damaged more than you've been willing to admit?"

2. "What's the impact that no one talks about but everyone feels?"

3. "Where do you see the most avoidable waste or loss because of this issue?"

4. "If this continues for another six months, what do you expect to break first?"

5. "What's the hardest part of dealing with a problem no one has fully addressed?"

6. "Who is absorbing consequences they shouldn't be absorbing?"

7. "What numbers or results are being quietly dragged down by this?"

8. "Where is this problem holding you back even if you haven't said it aloud yet?"

Follow-Up Impact-Mapping Questions (10)

Tone: empathetic, reflective, clarifying.

1. "You mentioned this slows things down — can you tell me where the slowdown is most noticeable?"

2. "How did that specific impact show up the last time this problem occurred?"

3. "What stands out to you about the way people respond when the issue happens?"

4. "Can you walk me through what a typical bad day looks like when this problem hits?"

5. "What makes that particular impact frustrating or stressful for your team?"

6. "How long has the impact been getting worse in this way?"

7. "What changed after the problem began affecting this part of your operation?"

8. "What do you think the team expects will happen if the impact keeps expanding?"

9. "When you say it affects results, which result matters most to you?"

10. "How would you know that the impact has been fully resolved or neutralized?"

Conclusion

Impact-mapping questions create a turning point in the discovery conversation. By this stage, the buyer is no longer speaking about the problem in abstract terms. They are describing the real-world friction, delays, and losses that shape their experience. This shift deepens their understanding and brings urgency into the open without any pressure from you.

Strategically, mapping impact gives structure to the buyer's situation. It transforms a vague challenge into a measurable one. When the buyer recognizes specific areas being affected — people, processes, outcomes, confidence, communication — the conversation becomes grounded in evidence rather than assumptions. This prepares you for later sections where you will trace causes, estimate costs, and explore consequences with far greater accuracy.

Psychologically, impact mapping helps the buyer feel validated. Many decision-makers have been carrying burdens alone, trying to compensate for the problem without acknowledging how much it drains them. When they articulate these impacts out loud, they experience relief and often a sense of partnership — someone finally understands what they've been dealing with.

As you move forward, remember that impact mapping is not about exaggerating the situation; it's about helping the buyer see the truth clearly. Clarity reduces doubt. Reduced doubt increases readiness for change. This makes future conversations more honest, more focused, and more productive.

Reflection Prompt:
Think back to a discovery call where the buyer minimized the problem. What impact question could you have asked that might have helped them recognize how wide the ripples actually were?

CHPATER 1 - SECTION 3 - Constraint-Identification Questions

Introduction

After defining the problem and exploring its impact, the next step is identifying what stands in the way of improvement. Constraints are the hidden forces that limit progress: missing resources, unclear responsibilities, outdated systems, bottlenecks, or even mental models that no longer fit the situation. Constraint-identification questions help the buyer recognize the specific factors that prevent them from fixing the problem themselves. Most buyers feel the constraints long before they understand them.

Strategically, identifying constraints gives you a realistic map of the buyer's operational environment. Before any solution can be considered, you need to understand what is blocking progress and why those obstacles exist. Many deals stall not because the problem is unclear, but because the advisor never identifies what restricts the buyer's ability to move forward. These questions reveal capacity limits, decision barriers, resource shortages, and environmental pressures that define the buyer's reality.

Psychologically, constraint identification often brings relief to the buyer. When people struggle to fix an issue, they sometimes blame themselves or their team. Helping them see the structural or contextual constraints behind the struggle reduces guilt and increases clarity. When the buyer realizes, "This isn't just us — there are real barriers here," they feel less pressure and more motivation to explore solutions.

Interpretation Tip: Listen for constraints described as "just the way things are." These phrases signal resignation rather than analysis, which means the buyer may have accepted a barrier as permanent. That is often where the most powerful discovery work happens.

Coaching Note: Avoid immediately suggesting solutions when a constraint appears. Your goal is understanding, not fixing. Solutions become far more effective — and welcomed — after the buyer fully explores what restricts them. Hold space, ask calmly, and keep the focus on their internal landscape.

Here are two example prompts you might use:

- *"What makes this problem harder to address than it should be?"*

- *"Walk me through what gets in the way when you try to make progress."*

The following questions help uncover hidden restrictions, barriers, and environmental factors shaping the buyer's situation.

Standard Constraint-Identification Questions (8)

Tone: open, calm, rapport-oriented.

1. "What tends to get in the way when you try to address this?"

2. "What makes this issue harder to manage than you expected?"

3. "Which parts of your process feel the most restrictive right now?"

4. "What slows things down when you try to make changes?"

5. "Who or what needs more support to move this forward?"

6. "What resources do you feel are stretched thin because of this?"

7. "What would you say is the biggest barrier to making progress?"

8. "When you think about solving this, what feels out of your control?"

Intermediate Constraint-Identification Questions (9)

Tone: curious, probing, professional.

1. "What are the predictable moments when the constraints become most visible?"

2. "Which dependencies or handoffs tend to create friction?"

3. "What part of the workflow becomes fragile when pressure increases?"

4. "How do current roles or responsibilities contribute to the limitation?"

5. "What decision-making delays make progress difficult?"

6. "What missing information or unclear expectations contribute to the constraint?"

7. "Which part of the operation is most vulnerable when this barrier appears?"

8. "What would need to change internally for this constraint to ease?"

9. "When you've tried to improve this before, what stopped the effort?"

Aggressive Constraint-Identification Questions (8)

Tone: direct, respectful, truth-seeking.

1. "Where do you see an obvious bottleneck that no one has addressed?"

2. "What restriction has been accepted as normal even though it's holding everything back?"

3. "Who is blocking progress — intentionally or unintentionally?"

4. "What internal rule or habit creates more problems than it solves?"

5. "What part of the system breaks first under pressure?"

6. "Which constraint keeps you from fixing the issue even if you want to?"

7. "What barrier has been ignored because addressing it feels uncomfortable?"

8. "What truth about your limitations do you think the team avoids acknowledging?"

Follow-Up Constraint-Identification Questions (10)

Tone: empathetic, reflective, clarifying.

1. "Can you walk me through a recent moment when that constraint showed up?"

2. "What did you notice happening right before the limitation became a problem?"

3. "How did the team respond when the barrier appeared?"

4. "What part of that experience was most frustrating or draining?"

5. "How long has that constraint been influencing the situation?"

6. "What changed after the constraint became more obvious?"

7. "Which detail about that restriction worries you most?"

8. "How have you tried working around this barrier in the past?"

9. "What makes that particular constraint difficult to address?"

10. "How would you know the barrier has been removed or reduced?"

Conclusion

Constraint-identification questions reveal the hidden architecture of the buyer's challenge. Without understanding what blocks progress, even the clearest problem definition and strongest impact map will fall short. These questions uncover the invisible limitations that shape the buyer's capacity to act. Once constraints are visible, the rest of the discovery process becomes more grounded, practical, and credible.

Strategically, knowing the constraints allows you to design solutions that fit the buyer's reality. Buyers trust advisors who understand their limits — time, budget, people, processes, and political factors. When you identify these early, you prevent unrealistic expectations and build a foundation for alignment.

Psychologically, acknowledging constraints creates relief. Buyers often believe they "should" be able to solve the problem on their own. When you help them see the environmental and structural limitations working against them, it shifts the conversation from self-blame to strategy. This leads to more open dialogue and clearer decision-making.

As you move forward to the next section, remember this principle: **progress is determined not only by the size of the problem, but by the strength of the constraints surrounding it.** The better you understand those constraints, the more precisely you can guide the buyer toward clarity and momentum.

Reflection Prompt:
What constraints do prospects most commonly overlook in your conversations, and how could identifying them earlier change the direction of your discovery work?

CHPATER 1 - SECTION 4 - Misalignment-Detection Questions

Introduction

Misalignment is one of the most common sources of hidden friction inside any organization, yet it is also one of the least discussed. Buyers often assume that their team, leadership, or partners share the same understanding of the problem, the same priorities, and the same expected outcomes. In reality, misalignment quietly weakens progress, slows decisions, and causes people to work against one another without realizing it. This section helps you uncover where perspectives, expectations, and responsibilities are out of sync.

Strategically, misalignment-detection questions act as an early-warning system. Even the best solution will fail if the people involved do not agree on what the problem is or how it should be addressed. These questions reveal discrepancies between departments, roles, and stakeholders — gaps that often go unnoticed until they cause major setbacks. When you detect misalignment early, you help the buyer avoid wasted time, unnecessary conflict, and stalled initiatives.

Psychologically, misalignment often creates frustration, confusion, and quiet tension within teams. People hesitate to speak openly about conflicting viewpoints because they fear escalation. By asking structured, non-confrontational questions, you give the buyer a safe way to acknowledge differences that may have been building beneath the surface. This lowers emotional pressure and helps them see where communication has broken down.

Interpretation Tip: Listen for clues that different people describe the issue in different ways. When the buyer says, "Well, it depends who you ask," or "Some people see it differently," you've entered the misalignment zone. These moments reveal that the organization lacks a unified narrative — a key driver of inefficiency and stalled progress.

Coaching Note: When the buyer reveals misalignment, resist the urge to assign fault. Your role is not to diagnose who is right, but to understand the range of perspectives. Once the differences are visible, the buyer can begin the work of establishing clarity, alignment, and ownership.

Here are two example prompts:

- *"How consistent are the perspectives across your team?"*

- *"If I asked two different people about this issue, what would they each say?"*

The questions below help uncover where viewpoints, expectations, goals, and interpretations diverge.

Standard Misalignment-Detection Questions (8)

Tone: open, calm, rapport-focused.

1. "How aligned do you feel your team is on what the main issue actually is?"

2. "What differences in perspective have you noticed among the people involved?"

3. "When the problem comes up in conversation, how do others describe it?"

4. "Which parts of the situation do people seem to agree on most?"

5. "Which parts are interpreted differently depending on who you talk to?"

6. "How often do discussions about this issue lead to confusion or mixed messages?"

7. "Who tends to see the situation in a completely different way?"

8. "What expectations vary the most from person to person?"

Intermediate Misalignment-Detection Questions (9)

Tone: probing, thoughtful, professional.

1. "What are the biggest gaps between how different stakeholders view the issue?"

2. "How do priorities differ between departments or teams when this comes up?"

3. "Which responsibilities are unclear or interpreted inconsistently?"

4. "What assumptions do you think people are making without checking for accuracy?"

5. "Where do you see communication breaking down around the problem?"

6. "Which voices or perspectives tend to get overlooked in discussions?"

7. "How does misalignment affect the speed or quality of decisions?"

8. "What examples come to mind where two people acted based on different understandings?"

9. "How often do goals or expectations shift depending on who is leading the conversation?"

Aggressive Misalignment-Detection Questions (8)

Tone: direct but respectful, truth-exposing.

1. "Who is working from a completely different playbook than everyone else?"

2. "Which assumptions are driving conflict even if no one has said it out loud?"

3. "Where is misalignment costing you the most time or credibility?"

4. "Who disagrees with the current direction but hasn't voiced it openly?"

5. "What expectation is most unrealistic or out of sync with reality?"

6. "Which person or group is pulling the project sideways without realizing it?"

7. "Where are commitments being made that others cannot actually support?"

8. "What truth about internal disagreement would surprise leadership if they heard it?"

Follow-Up Misalignment-Detection Questions (10)

Tone: empathetic, clarifying, reflective.

1. "Can you describe the moment you first noticed people weren't aligned?"

2. "What happened in that conversation that made the differences obvious?"

3. "How did people react when the conflicting viewpoints came up?"

4. "What part of the misalignment created the most confusion?"

5. "How long has this difference in perspective been affecting progress?"

6. "Which recent decision shows the impact of these misaligned viewpoints?"

7. "What has the team been doing to work around the disagreement?"

8. "What makes this misalignment tough to bring up openly?"

9. "How would things change if everyone saw the situation the same way?"

10. "What would a fully aligned version of this team look like on this issue?"

Conclusion

Misalignment-detection questions illuminate the silent forces that cause confusion, tension, and stalled progress. By helping the buyer uncover these differences early, you protect them from avoidable conflict and costly missteps. Many organizations operate with the illusion of alignment

— until a key initiative fails. Your questions bring reality to the surface in a calm, constructive way.

Strategically, identifying misalignment gives you insight into how decisions are made, how communication flows, and where disconnects originate. When you understand whose perspectives differ and why, you can guide the buyer toward clarity and cohesion. This insight becomes invaluable as the conversation deepens into causes, consequences, and decision dynamics.

Psychologically, surfacing misalignment offers the buyer relief and validation. Many leaders feel stuck because they can sense disagreement but lack a neutral way to uncover it. Your questions provide that pathway. As differences become clear, the buyer gains confidence in addressing the issue and in establishing clearer expectations.

As you move forward, remember that misalignment is one of the most significant sources of hidden risk in any organization. The better you uncover these differences early, the smoother and more productive the rest of your discovery process will become.

Reflection Prompt:
Think of a recent situation where a buyer assumed everyone was aligned but later discovered they weren't. What question from this section could have revealed that truth earlier?

CHPATER 1 - SECTION 5 - Root-Cause Tracing Questions

Introduction

After defining the problem, mapping its impact, identifying constraints, and revealing misalignment, the next step is tracing the root causes beneath the surface. Buyers often describe symptoms as if they *are* the problem. Root-cause tracing questions shift the conversation from "what is happening" to "why this is happening." This is where discovery becomes diagnostic rather than descriptive.

Strategically, understanding root causes prevents you from solving the wrong issue. Many organizations treat visible symptoms — delays, errors, communication breakdowns — without examining the underlying drivers. When you guide the buyer to uncover the deeper forces shaping the problem, you help them avoid another cycle of temporary fixes. Root-cause questions create leverage because they allow you to address the structural conditions instead of the surface-level noise.

Psychologically, these questions help the buyer slow down long enough to examine patterns they may have overlooked. People naturally react to symptoms because they are immediate and disruptive. But the root causes usually involve older decisions, outdated assumptions, or internal dynamics the buyer has normalized. When you help them notice these patterns, they often experience a mix of clarity and relief — clarity because things finally make sense, and relief because they see a path forward.

Interpretation Tip: Listen for moments where the buyer describes a pattern that repeats regardless of who is involved. Recurring issues often point to deeper mechanical or structural causes. Pay attention to anything they say that begins with "It always happens when…" or "It started around the time that…" — these are natural entry points into the real drivers of the problem.

Coaching Note: Avoid jumping to conclusions. Your questions are not meant to prove your theory; they are meant to help the buyer explore theirs. When the buyer discovers the root cause themselves, the insight is more powerful and the motivation to address it is stronger.

Sample phrasing you might use:

- *"What do you think is driving this beneath the surface?"*

- *"Has anything upstream changed that could be influencing this?"*

The questions below help you guide the buyer into deeper analysis and pattern recognition.

Standard Root-Cause Tracing Questions (8)

Tone: open, calm, exploratory.

1. "What do you believe is sitting underneath the problem you're seeing?"

2. "When this issue occurs, what usually leads up to it?"

3. "What patterns have you noticed over time?"

4. "When did the problem first start showing signs of developing?"

5. "What changed around that time that might be relevant?"

6. "Who or what is closest to the point where the issue begins?"

7. "What part of the process feels like the starting point of the problem?"

8. "What early signals do you notice before things start to go wrong?"

Intermediate Root-Cause Tracing Questions (9)

Tone: curious, probing, pattern-focused.

1. "Which moments in the workflow seem to trigger the issue most reliably?"

2. "What deeper factors do you think are influencing the situation?"

3. "How do previous decisions contribute to the current problem?"

4. "Which assumptions might be shaping the behavior that leads to the issue?"

5. "Where does the breakdown first become visible before it spreads?"

6. "What upstream steps seem most connected to the downstream symptoms?"

7. "What root causes have you ruled out, and why?"

8. "How do recurring mistakes or delays point back to a deeper source?"

9. "If you had to name the most likely underlying driver, what would it be?"

Aggressive Root-Cause Tracing Questions (8)

Tone: direct, respectful, truth-oriented.

1. "What decision from the past is still creating problems today?"

2. "Where do you see the real origin of the issue, even if it's uncomfortable to admit?"

3. "Who is closest to the root cause but least aware of it?"

4. "What long-standing habit or assumption is keeping this problem alive?"

5. "Which part of the system is outdated and dragging everything down?"

6. "If you stripped away all excuses, where does the problem actually begin?"

7. "What root cause has been ignored because addressing it feels politically risky?"

8. "What truth about how this started do people avoid acknowledging?"

Follow-Up Root-Cause Tracing Questions (10)

Tone: empathetic, reflective, clarifying.

1. "Can you walk me through what happened right before the problem appeared?"

2. "What did you notice during the first instance that now seems relevant?"

3. "When you say it 'always happens this way,' what do you mean by that?"

4. "What part of the pattern stands out the most to you?"

5. "How long has this deeper cause been influencing the situation?"

6. "What detail makes you think this is the real source of the issue?"

7. "How does this root cause show up in different parts of the team or process?"

8. "What changed after you realized the issue had a deeper origin?"

9. "What would confirm that this is, in fact, the true cause?"

10. "If this root cause disappeared tomorrow, what would be different immediately?"

Conclusion

Root-cause tracing is where discovery shifts from identifying what's visible to understanding what's responsible. Many organizations spend years fixing symptoms without ever addressing the deeper forces driving them. By guiding the buyer through the process of uncovering these causes, you help them break cycles that have been repeating for far too long.

Strategically, root-cause clarity changes everything. Solutions become more precise, risks become easier to anticipate, and decisions become more confident. When you understand the source of the problem, your recommendations carry more weight because they speak directly to what needs to change.

Psychologically, tracing root causes helps the buyer untangle confusion and frustration. Many leaders feel stuck because they know something is wrong but can't articulate why. When they discover the deeper pattern, they often feel a sense of empowerment — the fog lifts, and the path forward becomes visible.

As you move to the next section, remember that strong discovery is not about collecting information — it's about revealing truth. Root-cause tracing brings truth to the surface in a structured, thoughtful, and emotionally safe way.

Reflection Prompt:
Think of a recurring issue you've seen across multiple prospects. What deeper pattern do they usually overlook, and which root-cause question could help them see it faster?

CHAPTER 1 - SECTION 6 - Information-Flow Questions

Introduction

Even when a problem is well-defined, its impact is clear, constraints are visible, and root causes are emerging, there is still one foundational element that shapes everything inside an organization: **how information moves**. Information flow is the bloodstream of any operational system. When communication is slow, incomplete, fragmented, or distorted, every other part of the workflow suffers. Information-flow questions help uncover how knowledge, updates, tasks, expectations, and decisions travel between people — and where those flows break down.

Strategically, understanding information flow reveals whether the organization operates with clarity or confusion. Many problems are not the result of poor intentions or lack of skill, but simply poorly structured communication pathways. These questions expose delays, missed handoffs, outdated reporting methods, unclear channels, and hidden communication bottlenecks. Once you understand how information actually moves — not how it *should* move — you gain powerful insight into the real engine of the buyer's operations.

Psychologically, information flow reflects trust, transparency, and confidence within a team. When people hesitate to share updates, simplify details, or delay communication, it often signals fear of conflict, fear of judgment, or uncertainty about expectations. Information-flow questions help the buyer surface these subtle emotional dynamics without placing blame. This creates an honest view of how people are thinking, feeling, and responding to the environment around them.

Interpretation Tip: Pay close attention to inconsistencies between what is "supposed" to happen and what "actually" happens. Most organizations have formal communication processes on paper that look nothing like what is used in real life. When the buyer describes workarounds, shortcuts, or informal channels, you are getting closer to the real truth.

Coaching Note: Keep the tone neutral and curious. People sometimes feel defensive when discussing communication issues because it touches their habits, speed, and reliability. Your goal is to explore the system, not to critique individuals. Use soft phrasing and allow pauses — buyers often reveal valuable details when they feel safe.

Example prompts you might use:

- *"Walk me through how information travels from one person to the next."*

- *"How does your team keep each other updated when things change?"*

The questions below will help you uncover where information flow supports progress — and where it breaks it.

Standard Information-Flow Questions (8)

Tone: open, calm, easy to answer.

1. "How does information usually get shared across your team?"

2. "When something important happens, how does that update reach the right people?"

3. "Which communication channels do you rely on most?"

4. "How consistent are your team's methods for sharing updates?"

5. "What usually works well about the way information moves?"

6. "Where do updates tend to get delayed or overlooked?"

7. "How clear are expectations when information gets passed along?"

8. "What tools or systems do you use to keep everyone informed?"

Intermediate Information-Flow Questions (9)

Tone: curious, probing, situational.

1. "What part of the workflow relies most heavily on accurate information flow?"

2. "Where do you see the biggest gaps between what is shared and what is needed?"

3. "How do you handle information that requires quick attention or rapid response?"

4. "What happens when someone misses a key update?"

5. "Which teams or individuals communicate most effectively, and why?"

6. "Where does information tend to get distorted or simplified?"

7. "How does the current communication flow affect accuracy or execution?"

8. "What steps, if any, are taken to confirm that updates were understood correctly?"

9. "How does information move differently during stressful or busy periods?"

Aggressive Information-Flow Questions (8)

Tone: direct, respectful, truth-seeking.

1. "Where is communication breaking down the most?"

2. "Who is out of the loop far more often than they should be?"

3. "Which updates get lost because the process is outdated or inefficient?"

4. "What information is being withheld — intentionally or unintentionally?"

5. "Who tends to share updates late, inconsistently, or incompletely?"

6. "Where does miscommunication quietly damage results?"

7. "What critical information is not being documented or tracked properly?"

8. "What would leadership be surprised to learn about how communication actually happens?"

Follow-Up Information-Flow Questions (10)

Tone: empathetic, reflective, clarifying.

1. "Can you walk me through the last time an important update didn't reach everyone?"

2. "What happened in that moment that revealed a communication gap?"

3. "How did the team respond once they realized the information was missing?"

4. "What consequences came from that breakdown?"

5. "How long has that communication issue been showing up in similar ways?"

6. "Which part of the process created the most confusion?"

7. "What did people assume would happen that didn't happen?"

8. "What makes this part of the information flow difficult or unreliable?"

9. "What would a smoother or more predictable process look like?"

10. "How would you know that communication is flowing the way it should?"

Conclusion

Information-flow questions reveal the communication architecture that shapes the buyer's entire environment. When information moves well, decisions are faster, people feel aligned, and the organization operates with clarity. When information moves poorly, even small issues can become major obstacles. This section helps you understand not just how communication is intended to work, but how it truly functions in everyday reality.

Strategically, uncovering information flow issues gives you a deeper understanding of operational risk. Many problems originate not in poor strategy but in poor communication. When you see where updates get stuck, distorted, or delayed, you gain insight into the most vulnerable parts of the buyer's system.

Psychologically, exploring information flow helps buyers feel seen and understood. Communication issues often create stress, frustration, and mistrust — but people rarely talk about them openly. By asking structured, neutral questions, you bring hidden communication dynamics to the surface without blame or judgment. This creates clarity and reduces tension.

As you continue to the next section, remember this principle: **information is only power when it is shared clearly and consistently.** The smoother the flow of information, the stronger the organization's ability to execute, adjust, and grow.

Reflection Prompt:
Think about the last time a deal stalled because the buyer was working with incomplete or inconsistent information. Which question from this section might have uncovered that breakdown earlier?

CHPATER 1 - SECTION 7 - Cultural-Readiness Questions

Introduction

Even when a problem is clear, its impact is mapped, constraints are understood, misalignment is exposed, and communication patterns are visible, there is still one question left: **Is the organization ready for change?** Cultural readiness determines whether a team can accept new ideas, adapt to new expectations, and follow through on necessary adjustments. Many deals fail not because the solution is wrong but because the culture isn't prepared to support it. This section helps you determine whether the environment can handle progress — or whether deeper cultural issues must be addressed first.

Strategically, cultural-readiness questions reveal the emotional and behavioral landscape that surrounds the problem. Culture shapes how people communicate, how they respond to conflict, how they handle accountability, and how open they are to change. Understanding this allows you to design recommendations that fit the organization's actual capacity. If the team is resistant, fatigued, or divided, pushing forward prematurely can create friction or even failure. These questions help you avoid missteps and help the buyer see their unseen barriers.

Psychologically, cultural readiness touches the group's identity and shared beliefs. People often hold unspoken norms — "This is just how we do things," "Change never sticks here," or "Leadership doesn't follow through." When you surface these mindsets, the buyer gains insight into the invisible forces that shape behavior. Many leaders have a sense that something is "off culturally," but they struggle to articulate it. These questions help them put language around what they feel.

Interpretation Tip: Listen for emotional cues — frustration, fatigue, resignation, or defensiveness. These signals reveal whether the culture is stretched thin or capable of adapting. Also notice whether the buyer speaks in terms of possibility ("We could…") or limitation ("We can't because…"). These patterns reveal openness or resistance.

Coaching Note: Avoid labeling a culture as "good" or "bad." Culture is complex and shaped by history, leadership style, communication patterns, and shared experiences. Your role is to help the buyer explore what is true, not to judge it. Focus on clarity, not criticism.

Example phrasing you might use:

- *"How ready do you feel your team is for change right now?"*

- *"What norms or habits might make improvement difficult?"*

The questions below help uncover how prepared the organization is — emotionally, behaviorally, and structurally — for meaningful progress.

Standard Cultural-Readiness Questions (8)

Tone: open, steady, rapport-focused.

1. "How would you describe your team's overall openness to change?"

2. "What is the general attitude when new ideas or processes are introduced?"

3. "How consistent is follow-through when the team commits to improvements?"

4. "What behaviors or habits support change?"

5. "Which habits make change more difficult?"

6. "How would you rate the team's trust in leadership during transition periods?"

7. "How do people typically respond when expectations shift?"

8. "What recent changes went well, and why?"

Intermediate Cultural-Readiness Questions (9)

Tone: probing, curious, diagnostic.

1. "What cultural patterns stand out as supportive or resistant to improvement?"

2. "How does the team handle accountability when things get difficult?"

3. "What beliefs or assumptions shape how people react to new initiatives?"

4. "Where do you see the strongest momentum for change?"

5. "Where do you see the strongest resistance?"

6. "How does conflict influence people's willingness to try something new?"

7. "What communication behaviors help or hurt the team during transition?"

8. "Which groups or individuals tend to adapt quickest, and why?"

9. "How would you describe the team's current emotional bandwidth for change?"

Aggressive Cultural-Readiness Questions (8)

Tone: direct, respectful, truth-revealing.

1. "Who resists change the most, even if they don't say it directly?"

2. "What cultural habit is holding the team back more than anyone admits?"

3. "What part of the culture feels outdated or misaligned with new expectations?"

4. "Which leaders say they support change but behave inconsistently?"

5. "What unspoken rule keeps people from trying new approaches?"

6. "Where does fear — of conflict, failure, or judgment — shape behavior?"

7. "What part of the culture creates the most drag on progress?"

8. "What truth about your culture have people been avoiding because it feels uncomfortable?"

Follow-Up Cultural-Readiness Questions (10)

Tone: empathetic, clarifying, reflective.

1. "Can you walk me through a recent change and how the team reacted?"

2. "What did people do or say that revealed their readiness level?"

3. "Which part of that experience stood out to you most?"

4. "How long has this cultural pattern been influencing the team?"

5. "What has reinforced the team's current attitudes toward change?"

6. "What specific moment showed the clearest sign of resistance or openness?"

7. "How did leadership respond when the cultural pressure increased?"

8. "What emotions did you observe — stress, frustration, optimism, hesitation?"

9. "What would need to shift internally for the culture to support improvement more strongly?"

10. "How would you know the culture is ready for meaningful change?"

Conclusion

Cultural-readiness questions reveal the emotional and behavioral foundation that determines whether progress is possible. No solution, no matter how strong, can thrive in a culture that is unprepared or unwilling to support change. By exploring how people think, respond, and communicate during transition, you help the buyer see the true landscape beneath their operational surface.

Strategically, understanding cultural readiness helps you design recommendations that fit the buyer's real world. It prevents unrealistic plans, reduces risk, and increases the likelihood of successful implementation. A culture that is not aligned with improvement will resist it — silently or openly — until the internal dynamics are addressed.

Psychologically, these questions allow the buyer to acknowledge truths they may have sensed but could not articulate. This creates clarity, reduces frustration, and opens the door to conversations that are honest rather than hopeful. When the buyer sees the cultural patterns clearly, they gain the awareness needed to lead change effectively.

As you move toward the final section of Chapter 1, remember that culture is not just a backdrop — it is an active force. It accelerates progress or restricts it. It shapes behavior and performance. And it determines how any solution will land.

Reflection Prompt:
Think of an organization where cultural resistance undermined a great solution. Which cultural-readiness question from this section might have revealed the issue early enough to prevent failure?

CHPATER 1 - SECTION 8 - Order-of-Operation Questions

Introduction

Every complex situation has a sequence — a chain of events, actions, handoffs, and decisions that determine how work actually gets done. Problems often arise not because the tasks are wrong, but because the *order* of those tasks is flawed, outdated, unclear, or inconsistent. Order-of-operation questions help uncover how the buyer's workflow unfolds step by step, revealing where the sequence breaks, overlaps, or creates unnecessary friction.

Strategically, understanding the true order of operations allows you to map the internal mechanics of the organization. Many buyers describe their workflow in broad strokes, but the real insight comes from exploring the precise sequence: what happens first, what depends on what, where timing matters, and where delays originate. These questions expose missed handoffs, poorly timed actions, unnecessary loops, and steps that no longer serve a purpose.

Psychologically, walking through sequence step-by-step helps the buyer slow their thinking, making invisible issues visible. People often skip over parts of a workflow because the routine feels automatic or familiar. When you ask them to break it down, they begin to notice inconsistencies, assumptions, and gaps they have overlooked. This can create sudden clarity — moments where the buyer says, "Now that I'm explaining it, this doesn't make sense."

Interpretation Tip: Listen for moments when the buyer hesitates while explaining the sequence. Hesitation often signals uncertainty or gaps in the process. Also pay attention to where they jump ahead or skip steps; these are strong indicators that the actual workflow is unclear or not consistently followed.

Coaching Note: Keep the pace slow. Sequencing questions work best when the buyer has room to think. If they rush, you will get a superficial outline. Encourage them to pause, recall specifics, and walk through the process as if they were training a new team member.

Example phrasing you might use:

- *"Can you walk me through the exact steps from start to finish?"*

- *"What happens immediately after that step?"*

The following questions help uncover how the order of operations shapes — or disrupts — performance.

Standard Order-of-Operation Questions (8)

Tone: calm, structured, clear.

1. "Can you walk me through the main steps of the process from start to finish?"

2. "What usually happens first when this situation begins?"

3. "What step tends to take the most time?"

4. "Where does the workflow slow down the most?"

5. "Which steps depend on others being completed first?"

6. "How consistent is the sequence from one person to another?"

7. "What happens immediately before the problem shows up?"

8. "What step gets skipped most often, and why?"

Intermediate Order-of-Operation Questions (9)

Tone: probing, analytical, detail-focused.

1. "What is the ideal sequence supposed to look like, and how does reality differ?"

2. "Which steps create bottlenecks because of timing or dependencies?"

3. "What transitions between steps tend to create confusion or errors?"

4. "Which roles are responsible at each stage of the workflow?"

5. "Where does the process rely on manual actions or judgment calls?"

6. "Which steps feel outdated or unnecessary based on current needs?"

7. "What upstream decisions influence the next stages most heavily?"

8. "Where do handoffs break down or get delayed?"

9. "If you had to simplify the sequence, which parts would you adjust first?"

Aggressive Order-of-Operation Questions (8)

Tone: direct, respectful, truth-exposing.

1. "Which step in the process causes the most avoidable damage?"

2. "Where is the sequence fundamentally out of order?"

3. "What part of the workflow has not been updated despite repeated issues?"

4. "Who is performing steps out of sequence, and how is that affecting results?"

5. "What actions create unnecessary loops that waste time or resources?"

6. "Where does the current order make no operational sense?"

7. "What step exists only because 'it's always been done this way'?"

8. "If you could reset the sequence from scratch, what would you remove or reorder?"

Follow-Up Order-of-Operation Questions (10)

Tone: reflective, clarifying, empathetic.

1. "Can you describe a recent moment when the sequence broke down?"

2. "What happened right before things fell out of order?"

3. "How did the team handle that disruption?"

4. "Which part of the sequence created the most confusion?"

5. "How often does that specific breakdown occur?"

6. "What detail makes you think the order needs to be changed?"

7. "How has the sequence evolved over time, and why?"

8. "What part of the order feels most fragile when pressure increases?"

9. "What would a cleaner, more logical sequence look like?"

10. "How would you know the new order of operations is working better?"

Conclusion

Order-of-operation questions uncover the structural backbone of the buyer's workflow. Every process has a natural rhythm, and when that rhythm is disrupted, performance declines. By exploring the sequence step-by-step, you help the buyer understand where timing, handoffs, dependencies, and outdated practices are creating friction. This clarity becomes essential as you move into more advanced discovery later in the book.

Strategically, understanding operational sequence gives you insight into how decisions are made, how work progresses, and where interventions will have the greatest effect. When you see where the order is broken, you can help the buyer anticipate problems before they occur and design improvements that fit their real-world environment.

Psychologically, sequence mapping helps buyers feel grounded. Many leaders sense chaos or inefficiency but can't pinpoint why. When they walk through the process with you, they often realize the issue is not effort but structure. This realization creates relief and a renewed sense of direction.

As we complete this final section of Chapter 1, remember that sequence reveals truth. It shows how things actually work — not how people assume they work. And that truth becomes the foundation for every deeper insight you will uncover in later chapters.

Reflection Prompt:
Think of a workflow you've seen that looked functional on the surface but broke under pressure. Which order-of-operation question from this section would have revealed the flaw earlier?

Chapter 1 Conclusion

Establishing the current landscape is the essential first act of any advisory engagement. Without it, later insights lose accuracy and recommendations lack credibility. Chapter 1 equips the advisor with a framework for seeing the buyer's world as it truly is — not idealized, polished, or filtered, but real. Each layer of questioning builds clarity, helping both the advisor and the buyer recognize the forces shaping the present situation.

This chapter reinforces a critical principle: meaningful discovery does not begin with solutions. It begins with understanding. Before a buyer can see what needs to change, they must see where they stand. The questions in Chapter 1 help organize confusion, expose hidden patterns, and create shared language around the buyer's reality. This shared understanding becomes the foundation for trust, alignment, and forward momentum.

As the book moves into Chapter 2, the focus shifts from the present to the past — from what is happening now to what has already been attempted. The insights from this first chapter make that transition smoother and more insightful. With the current landscape fully mapped, the advisor can now explore the history behind the problem and identify the lessons, mistakes, and overlooked clues that led to this moment.

CHAPTER 2 - Diagnosing Past Attempts & Performance

Chapter Introduction

Before an organization can move forward, it must understand the history that brought it to its current situation. Most buyers know they've tried things before, but they rarely examine those efforts with depth or structure. Chapter 2 turns past attempts into meaningful insight. Instead of treating failure as a simple result, this chapter explores the pattern behind the result — the sequence of decisions, reactions, breakdowns, and overlooked opportunities that shaped what actually happened. Every past effort contains a story, and this chapter reveals that story in a way that transforms hindsight into clarity.

Understanding past attempts is not about blame; it is about pattern recognition. Buyers often repeat the same mistakes because they never had a clear way to review previous actions. By guiding them through what they tried, when things shifted, what the metrics revealed, where bottlenecks formed, and what potential went unused, you help them see their history as a map rather than a mystery. This perspective gives them the confidence to act more intentionally moving forward.

The chapter begins with **Past-Attempt Questions**, which uncover what the buyer actually did — not their recollection filtered through frustration or disappointment, but the real steps taken. This is followed by **Failure-Timeline Questions**, which reveal the sequence behind the collapse. Buyers often discover that failure didn't happen all at once; it unfolded through a series of turning points.

Next, **Performance-Metric Review Questions** ground the conversation in data, showing measurable effects rather than assumptions. **Escalation-Point Questions** expose the moments when pressure intensified and the system began to strain. These questions help buyers replay their experience with clarity, noticing elements they previously overlooked.

From there, **Bottleneck-Sequence Questions** reveal how slowdowns formed and spread. **Loss-Analysis Questions** illuminate the true cost of the attempt — not just financially, but emotionally and operationally. **Underutilized-Asset Questions** uncover strengths that were available but unused, and **Untapped-Upside Questions** highlight promising signals that never had the chance to grow. Finally, **Abandoned-Opportunity Questions** explore the ideas and pathways that were left behind entirely.

By the end of Chapter 2, the advisor and buyer share a complete understanding of the past: what was attempted, what was missed, what was misjudged, and what was possible. This creates a foundation of truth — one not built on memory or emotion, but on pattern, sequence, evidence, and insight. With this grounding, future decisions become clearer, more intentional, and more aligned with the organization's real capabilities.

CHPATER 2 - SECTION 1 - Past-Attempt Questions

Introduction

Once the current landscape is understood, the next step in discovery is exploring what the buyer has already tried. Every organization leaves behind a trail of past attempts — some thoughtful, some rushed, some half-finished, and some never properly evaluated. These attempts contain valuable clues. They reveal the buyer's assumptions, decision patterns, frustrations, resource limitations, and tolerance for experimentation. Past-attempt questions help uncover the history behind the problem so the advisor can understand not only what was done, but why it didn't work.

Strategically, examining past attempts prevents you from repeating the same failures. Many buyers revisit the same strategies expecting different results, simply because no one has guided them through a structured review. These questions reveal missteps, shortcuts, impatience, miscommunication, or poor sequencing that contributed to previous breakdowns. They also show what the buyer already believes is possible, what they fear will happen again, and where hidden lessons are waiting to be surfaced.

Psychologically, discussing past attempts brings out emotions that often shape decision-making: frustration from wasted effort, embarrassment over failed initiatives, disappointment in past leadership, or hesitation to try again. Buyers may minimize or overstate their previous actions to protect themselves. Your goal is to create a space where they can recount the past without fear of judgment. When handled with calm curiosity, these questions help the buyer shift from blame to insight.

Interpretation Tip: Listen for phrases that signal emotional residue — "We thought it would…" or "That should have worked…" or "We didn't realize until too late…" These statements reveal expectations, blind spots, and pressures that influenced past decisions. Also pay attention to who the buyer references repeatedly; their comments often reveal political or relational dynamics tied to past failures.

Coaching Note: When the buyer describes what they tried, avoid giving immediate feedback. Your job is not to critique the past but to understand it. Let the buyer finish their explanation before asking clarifying follow-ups. Revisit key moments gently — especially where attempts were abandoned early or evaluated poorly — as these areas often contain the most valuable insight.

Example phrasing you might use:

- *"Walk me through what you've tried so far."*

- *"What approaches seemed promising at the time?"*

The questions below help guide the buyer through a clear, honest look at their previous efforts.

Standard Past-Attempt Questions (8)

Tone: open, calm, non-judgmental.

1. "What have you tried so far to address this?"

2. "Which approaches felt like they had potential in the beginning?"

3. "What steps did you take first when the issue became noticeable?"

4. "How did you decide which strategies to try?"

5. "What seemed to work for a while before losing momentum?"

6. "Which past actions helped at least a little?"

7. "What did your team expect those attempts would accomplish?"

8. "What made you realize your earlier efforts weren't enough?"

Intermediate Past-Attempt Questions (9)

Tone: curious, probing, pattern-focused.

1. "Which past attempts came closest to helping, and why do you think they didn't last?"

2. "Where do you think the earlier strategies began to break down?"

3. "What assumptions guided the decisions behind those attempts?"

4. "How consistently were the previous efforts followed across the team?"

5. "What role did timing or workload play in the outcome?"

6. "Which attempt required the most effort but produced the least return?"

7. "How was success measured — and was that measurement clear to everyone?"

8. "What feedback did you receive from others about those earlier efforts?"

9. "What lessons did you take away, even if the attempt wasn't successful?"

Aggressive Past-Attempt Questions (8)

Tone: direct, respectful, truth-revealing.

1. "Which attempt failed fastest — and why?"

2. "What approach looked good on paper but collapsed in practice?"

3. "Where did leadership overestimate what the team could manage?"

4. "Which past move created more problems than it solved?"

5. "Who pushed for an approach that wasn't realistic at the time?"

6. "What warning signs did everyone miss during earlier attempts?"

7. "What part of the past strategy was flawed from the start?"

8. "What effort was continued far longer than it should have been?"

Follow-Up Past-Attempt Questions (10)

Tone: empathetic, clarifying, reflective.

1. "Can you walk me through what happened during that attempt?"

2. "What moment made you realize the plan wasn't working?"

3. "How did people respond when the results weren't improving?"

4. "What specific challenge slowed the effort down?"

5. "How long did the attempt continue before being changed or stopped?"

6. "Which detail stands out most to you looking back?"

7. "How did communication shape the success or failure of that attempt?"

8. "What would you have done differently with what you know now?"

9. "What part of the attempt still feels unresolved or unfinished?"

10. "How would you know if a new approach avoids the same mistakes?"

Conclusion

Past-attempt questions turn history into insight. Every effort, whether successful or not, contains valuable information about the buyer's mindset, capacity, assumptions, and environment. By helping the buyer explore what they have already tried, you prevent them from repeating the same cycles and encourage them to see patterns they may have missed. This transforms failure into understanding and uncertainty into clarity.

Strategically, reviewing past attempts allows you to identify what the buyer has already ruled out, what they are still open to, and what has quietly shaped their expectations. Psychologically, it helps the buyer process any emotional weight tied to previous failures, reducing hesitation and increasing readiness for something new.

As you continue through Chapter 2, the focus will build on this foundation — moving from the history of actions taken to the timing, sequence, and deeper lessons behind each effort. A clear understanding of past attempts is the gateway to analyzing performance more completely.

Reflection Prompt:
Think of a buyer who seemed hesitant to try again after a failure. What past-attempt question from this section could have helped them unpack the experience more clearly?

CHPATER 2 - SECTION 2 - Failure-Timeline Questions

Introduction

Once past attempts have been explored, the next step is understanding *when* things went wrong. Every failed attempt leaves behind a timeline — a sequence of moments that reveal how the problem developed, how expectations shifted, and where the effort began to unravel. Failure-timeline questions help the buyer break the history into clear stages so that you can see patterns, pressure points, and early warning signs. This transforms the failure from a vague memory into a structured source of insight.

Strategically, understanding the timeline allows you to distinguish between isolated issues and recurring cycles. Some failures happen suddenly; others erode slowly through repeated missteps. When the buyer traces the sequence, you can identify which turning points matter most — the moment misalignment emerged, when motivation dipped, when results plateaued, or when constraints became overwhelming. These insights help you anticipate future barriers and design solutions that fit the buyer's real-world rhythm.

Psychologically, revisiting the timeline helps the buyer process the experience with clarity rather than emotion. Many people remember failures as a single moment, but failures rarely happen all at once. They build gradually. Breaking the experience into stages helps the buyer understand what was truly within their control, what conditions shaped the outcome, and what lessons were overlooked. This reduces self-blame and increases readiness for a more intentional next step.

Interpretation Tip: Listen for the moment the buyer's tone changes — frustration, hesitation, relief, or realization. These emotional shifts often signal the true breaking point in the timeline. Pay attention to when communication slowed, expectations changed, or responsibilities became unclear; these moments reveal deeper systemic issues.

Coaching Note: Move gently through the timeline. Some buyers feel vulnerable discussing the details of a failure. Encourage them to describe events factually, stage by stage, without judgment. Once the timeline is laid out, ask clarifying follow-ups to help them see the patterns more clearly.

Sample phrases you might use:

- *"Walk me through the timeline from the start of the attempt to when it stopped working."*

- *"What were the key moments that shaped the outcome?"*

The questions below help reconstruct the sequence of events so the buyer can understand how the failure unfolded.

Standard Failure-Timeline Questions (8)

Tone: calm, clear, step-by-step.

1. "When did this attempt first begin?"

2. "What happened during the first few weeks?"

3. "When did you start noticing early signs that something wasn't working?"

4. "What happened next after those early signs appeared?"

5. "When did the momentum begin to slow down?"

6. "What changed in the middle of the effort?"

7. "When did it become clear the approach needed to be adjusted or stopped?"

8. "How long did the overall attempt last before ending?"

Intermediate Failure-Timeline Questions (9)

Tone: probing, sequential, pattern-focused.

1. "Which moment in the timeline stands out as the first real turning point?"

2. "When did the team's confidence start to shift, and why?"

3. "What events or conditions accelerated the decline in results?"

4. "Which decisions in the middle of the timeline shaped the final outcome?"

5. "What external factors influenced the timeline — deadlines, seasons, workload?"

6. "When did communication begin to change, and how did that affect things?"

7. "What indicators suggested the effort was losing alignment or focus?"

8. "Which stage of the timeline created the most pressure?"

9. "Looking back, where would you have paused or reset the plan?"

Aggressive Failure-Timeline Questions (8)

Tone: direct, honest, precision-focused.

1. "What was the exact moment you knew the attempt was failing?"

2. "Which decision in the timeline did the most damage?"

3. "Who hesitated at a critical moment when follow-through was needed?"

4. "What early warning sign did the team ignore?"

5. "When did leadership lose visibility into what was happening?"

6. "Which turning point was handled poorly and accelerated the failure?"

7. "What part of the timeline showed the clearest breakdown in accountability?"

8. "If you had to name the failure's true starting point, when was it?"

Follow-Up Failure-Timeline Questions (10)

Tone: reflective, clarifying, grounded.

1. "Can you describe what happened right before that key moment?"

2. "What detail from that stage sticks with you most now?"

3. "How did the team react during that part of the timeline?"

4. "What conversations took place around that turning point?"

5. "How did expectations shift during that stage of the process?"

6. "What could have been done differently at that moment?"

7. "What surprised you about how quickly things changed?"

8. "How did the pressure of that moment affect decision-making?"

9. "What part of the timeline revealed the biggest gap in preparation?"

10. "What would confirm that a future attempt doesn't repeat this timeline?"

Conclusion

Failure-timeline questions turn a difficult experience into a blueprint for better decisions. By guiding the buyer through the sequence of events, you reveal where expectations shifted, where communication faltered, and where the underlying weaknesses first appeared. This transforms failure from something foggy and frustrating into something structured and understandable.

Strategically, mapping the timeline clarifies the conditions under which the previous effort broke down. These insights help you anticipate future risks and design solutions that avoid repeating the same pattern. Psychologically, the timeline gives the buyer a sense of control — it helps them see the past with clearer eyes and less emotional weight, which increases readiness for new action.

As you move deeper into Chapter 2, you will build on this timeline by exploring escalation points, bottleneck sequences, and deeper process failures. Each layer brings more precision, helping both you and the buyer understand not just what failed, but how the failure unfolded step-by-step.

Reflection Prompt:
Think of a past conversation where the buyer focused only on the final failure. Which timeline question from this section could have helped them understand the deeper sequence behind it?

CHPATER 2 - SECTION 3 - Performance-Metric Review Questions

Introduction

When an attempt to solve a problem fails or underdelivers, one of the most important clues lies in the numbers, outcomes, or measurable results. Performance-metric review questions encourage a buyer to look at what changed — or what didn't — after prior efforts. Rather than relying on impressions or anecdotes, these questions help surface objective data points, patterns, and gaps that often tell the truth more clearly than memories or explanations.

Strategically, reviewing performance metrics helps both the buyer and the advisor move from vague impressions to concrete evidence. It reveals where the promise fell short, which expectations were unmet, and how measurable outcomes shifted. This clarity prevents wishful thinking or misremembered results from shaping future decisions. Instead, you ground the conversation in reality — in outcomes that can be tracked, compared, and evaluated.

Psychologically, asking about metrics can feel uncomfortable — especially if prior efforts failed. People may fear numbers reflect poorly on their team or their decisions. But when you frame these questions calmly and neutrally, you help the buyer detach emotionally from the outcome and see results with fresh eyes. That detachment often reveals overlooked losses, hidden costs, and subtle shifts that were never acknowledged.

Interpretation Tip: Watch for hesitations, generalizations, or vague language when the buyer speaks of prior results. Phrases like "It seemed better," or "We thought we did okay" often mask weak or inconsistent data. When a buyer struggles to recall numbers, frequency, or timing, it likely means performance was neither tracked nor measured — which itself is a critical insight.

Coaching Note: Encourage specificity. If the buyer can't remember exact numbers, guide them gently toward approximate ranges or qualitative comparisons. The goal isn't perfection — it's clarity. Even approximate or partial data can reveal patterns worth noting. Avoid judgment; treat the answers as data, not as human failure.

Standard Performance-Metric Review Questions (8)

Tone: calm, factual, open.

1. "What key results or metrics did you expect to improve when you tried this before?"

2. "Which performance indicators did you track during and after the attempt?"

3. "Which metrics showed the clearest change — positive or negative?"

4. "What moved in the right direction, even if only slightly?"

5. "What stayed the same despite your efforts?"

6. "Which numbers or outcomes disappointed you the most?"

7. "How did actual results compare to your initial expectations?"

8. "What data or feedback did you collect to evaluate the attempt's success?"

Intermediate Performance-Metric Review Questions (9)

Tone: probing, analytical.

1. "Over what time period did you track the metrics for that attempt?"

2. "How consistent was your measurement or reporting process during that time?"

3. "Which metrics drifted first — and which ones lagged behind?"

4. "When results changed, what other factors were happening simultaneously?"

5. "Were there periods where results improved briefly then reversed — why might that be?"

6. "Which metrics mattered most to stakeholders at the time?"

7. "Were there metrics you wished you had tracked but didn't?"

8. "Did any qualitative feedback — not just numbers — hint at deeper issues alongside the metrics?"

9. "How did the metrics influence the decision to continue or stop the effort?"

Aggressive Performance-Metric Review Questions (8)

Tone: direct, honest, truth-seeking.

1. "Which metric failed the hardest, regardless of the initial optimism?"

2. "What number proved the approach was flawed from the start?"

3. "If you look back, which outcome should have alerted you that this wasn't working?"

4. "What result disappointed stakeholders but was ignored or downplayed?"

5. "Which metric's stagnation caused the most unseen damage?"

6. "Which indicator was rising — yet you failed to notice its significance until too late?"

7. "What missed metric is creating the issues you still face today?"

8. "What data point, if re-examined, reveals the true scale of the failure?"

Follow-Up Performance-Metric Review Questions (10)

Tone: empathetic, clarifying, supportive.

1. "Can you walk me through the last report or result you reviewed after that attempt?"

2. "What did you notice first when you compared before and after metrics?"

3. "How did people react when results didn't meet expectations?"

4. "What specific number or result raised concerns for you?"

5. "Did any metric trends make you pause and reconsider the approach?"

6. "What assumptions did you have about metrics that turned out to be wrong?"

7. "What was more surprising — what improved, or what stayed broken?"

8. "If you could track only three metrics next time, which would you pick and why?"

9. "What extra information would help you understand the numbers more clearly?"

10. "How would you define success now, based on what you learned from those metrics?"

Conclusion

Performance-metric review questions move discovery from assumptions to measurable reality. They help you and the buyer see what success truly looked like — or what failure concealed — in previous attempts. By reviewing real data, you create a clearer picture of what worked, what didn't, and why.

This clarity prevents repeating mistakes and highlights which measures reflected real value, which outcomes were superficial, and where expectations drifted. These insights ensure future strategies are built on evidence, not optimism.

Psychologically, honest engagement with metrics helps the buyer process disappointment or uncertainty without blame. It allows them to view past performance as information, not failure, and creates the space needed to approach new strategies with intention.

Reflection Prompt:

Think of a time when an initiative felt successful but the metrics disagreed. Which question from this section would have uncovered that mismatch earlier?

CHPATER 2 - SECTION 4 - Escalation-Point Questions

Introduction

Every failed or underperforming initiative contains moments when the situation intensified — points where problems accelerated, pressure increased, or unexpected complications forced the team into reactive mode. These escalation points often reveal more about the true dynamics of the situation than the final outcome itself. Escalation-point questions help the buyer trace those critical moments so you can understand how small issues grew into larger ones, and how the team responded under strain.

Strategically, identifying escalation points shows where the organization's resilience breaks down. Early symptoms become major problems not because of the initial trigger, but because the environment is unprepared to absorb the pressure. These questions highlight where communication weakened, responsibilities blurred, emotions spiked, or structural weaknesses became visible. Understanding escalation points helps you design solutions that prevent repeat crises by reinforcing the right parts of the system.

Psychologically, escalation brings out stress responses — avoidance, overreaction, blame, silence, or frantic attempts to regain control. When buyers recount these moments, they often reveal deeper fears, unspoken tensions, or mismatches between expectations and capability. Your role is to help them explore these moments calmly so the history becomes a source of insight rather than embarrassment or frustration.

Interpretation Tip: Listen for sudden changes in tone, pace, or emotional charge when the buyer describes a moment. These signals often indicate a true escalation point. Also pay attention to who became central during the escalation — the individuals involved can reveal political realities, competency gaps, or organizational vulnerabilities.

Coaching Note: Guide the buyer through escalation moments slowly. Many leaders try to skip over these points because they feel uncomfortable revisiting stress or conflict. Encourage them to pause and describe the context, triggers, reactions, and aftermath. The more detail they share, the clearer the underlying pattern becomes.

Example prompts you might use:

- *"When did the situation shift from manageable to urgent?"*

- *"What moment felt like the turning point where everything intensified?"*

Standard Escalation-Point Questions (8)

Tone: calm, structured, exploratory.

1. "When did the issue first begin to escalate?"

2. "What happened right before the situation intensified?"

3. "Who noticed the escalation first?"

4. "What signs told you things were getting worse?"

5. "How did the team respond when pressure started increasing?"

6. "How quickly did the situation change once escalation began?"

7. "What part of the attempt became most difficult during that period?"

8. "What conversations took place as the situation escalated?"

Intermediate Escalation-Point Questions (9)

Tone: probing, diagnostic, pattern-focused.

1. "What specific trigger caused the escalation to begin?"

2. "Which part of the process became unstable or overwhelmed first?"

3. "Who absorbed the most pressure during the escalation?"

4. "How did communication shift once urgency increased?"

5. "What options did the team consider at that point?"

6. "Which earlier warning signs suddenly became more serious during escalation?"

7. "What external factors added intensity to the situation?"

8. "How did leadership involvement change once the issue escalated?"

9. "Which actions taken during escalation helped, and which made things worse?"

Aggressive Escalation-Point Questions (8)

Tone: direct, honest, respectful.

1. "What decision directly triggered the escalation?"

2. "Who panicked first — and what effect did that have?"

3. "Which person or team failed to act at the critical moment?"

4. "What mistake accelerated the escalation instead of slowing it down?"

5. "Where did accountability break down during the crisis?"

6. "What uncomfortable truth became obvious only when things escalated?"

7. "Which reaction — or lack of reaction — did the most damage?"

8. "What blind spot turned a small problem into a major issue?"

Follow-Up Escalation-Point Questions (10)

Tone: empathetic, clarifying, reflective.

1. "Can you describe the moment you realized the situation had escalated?"

2. "What did you notice about the team's energy during that period?"

3. "Which specific detail stands out most from that moment?"

4. "How did the escalation affect morale or communication?"

5. "What part of the response felt rushed or unplanned?"

6. "What conversations happened after the escalation to process what occurred?"

7. "How long did the effects of the escalation linger?"

8. "What would have helped stabilize the situation earlier?"

9. "What did you learn about your team during that moment of intensity?"

10. "How would you know if another escalation was beginning sooner next time?"

Conclusion

Escalation-point questions help the buyer trace the exact moments when pressure, complexity, or confusion overwhelmed the system. These insights reveal structural weaknesses, emotional responses, and hidden dynamics that would otherwise remain unnoticed. Understanding escalation points is essential to preventing history from repeating itself — both for the buyer and for any future solution you design.

Strategically, these moments expose the system's weak links. They show where processes collapse, where communication fails, and where expectations collide with reality. Psychologically, the buyer gains a deeper understanding of how their team behaves under stress, which helps them approach future challenges with greater clarity and leadership.

This section lays the groundwork for the next part of the chapter, where we explore bottleneck sequences, deeper breakdowns, and the internal patterns that shape performance. Escalation-point insight becomes the map that leads directly to those deeper discoveries.

Reflection Prompt:
Think of a time when a project spiraled quickly. Which escalation-point question from this section could have identified the turning point before the break happened?

CHPATER 2 - SECTION 5 - Bottleneck-Sequence Questions

Introduction

Every organization has pressure points — stages in a process where work slows down, decisions stall, or resources become overwhelmed. These are bottlenecks, and they usually follow a recognizable sequence. Bottleneck-sequence questions help uncover *how* bottlenecks form, *where* they appear first, *how* they progress, and *why* they continue to create recurring obstacles. Identifying these sequences transforms random frustration into a predictable pattern the advisor can analyze.

Strategically, bottleneck-sequence questions reveal systemic inefficiencies. When multiple attempts have failed or underperformed, bottlenecks often played a silent role. By understanding the sequence, you uncover which steps are overloaded, which dependencies are unstable, and which handoffs consistently break down. These insights help prevent future failures by redesigning or reinforcing the process where it weakens most.

Psychologically, bottlenecks are emotionally charged. People often feel responsible for slowdowns or fear blame when delays occur. Asking about bottlenecks requires a calm, neutral tone so the buyer feels safe describing what really happens. When handled well, these questions help the buyer see that bottlenecks aren't personal failures — they are structural realities that can be addressed once understood.

Interpretation Tip: Pay attention to repeated mention of the same role, department, or step in the process. Repetition often signals the anchor point of the bottleneck sequence. Also notice whether the buyer describes stress building gradually or appearing suddenly; these patterns indicate whether the bottleneck sequence is triggered by volume, complexity, communication, or time pressure.

Coaching Note: Encourage the buyer to think chronologically. Bottleneck sequences are easiest to see when walked through step-by-step. Guide them to recall specific examples rather than broad statements. Ask follow-ups to uncover what was happening upstream or downstream from each bottleneck moment.

Example prompts you might use:

- *"Walk me through where things tend to slow down first."*

- *"What happens next after the first slowdown begins?"*

Standard Bottleneck-Sequence Questions (8)

Tone: calm, observational, easy to answer.

1. "Where do things typically slow down first in your process?"

2. "What step tends to create the earliest delay?"

3. "When the workload increases, which part of the workflow gets overwhelmed first?"

4. "Which stage usually becomes the second slowdown once the first appears?"

5. "Who or what absorbs the most pressure when things start backing up?"

6. "How does the bottleneck spread to the next part of the process?"

7. "What happens downstream when the first bottleneck forms?"

8. "Which tasks pile up most quickly during busy periods?"

Intermediate Bottleneck-Sequence Questions (9)

Tone: probing, structured, pattern-focused.

1. "What specific conditions trigger the first bottleneck to appear?"

2. "When the first slowdown happens, what issue typically emerges next?"

3. "Which role or function becomes the central point of congestion?"

4. "How do decision delays contribute to the bottleneck sequence?"

5. "Which dependencies fail when pressure increases?"

6. "What communication gaps worsen the bottleneck as it progresses?"

7. "At what stage does the bottleneck begin impacting customer or stakeholder experience?"

8. "Which attempts to address bottlenecks have worked temporarily — and why did they fade?"

9. "What part of the sequence seems most consistent across different situations?"

Aggressive Bottleneck-Sequence Questions (8)

Tone: direct, precise, truth-seeking.

1. "Which step in the sequence is the true choke point everyone avoids acknowledging?"

2. "Who becomes the organizational bottleneck when pressure increases?"

3. "What part of the workflow collapses fastest under strain?"

4. "Which decision-maker consistently slows down the entire process?"

5. "What outdated step in the sequence creates unnecessary congestion?"

6. "Where does the bottleneck expose weak accountability or unclear ownership?"

7. "What unresolved issue keeps triggering the same bottleneck sequence repeatedly?"

8. "What part of the process is structurally incapable of handling current volume or complexity?"

Follow-Up Bottleneck-Sequence Questions (10)

Tone: empathetic, clarifying, detail-oriented.

1. "Can you walk me through a recent example where the bottleneck formed?"

2. "What happened immediately before the slowdown began?"

3. "Which part of the workflow felt the pressure first?"

4. "How did the issue spread from one step to the next?"

5. "What reaction from the team made the bottleneck more noticeable?"

6. "How long did the bottleneck last during that instance?"

7. "Which factors made the bottleneck more intense than usual?"

8. "What temporary fixes were used to get things moving again?"

9. "What detail from that example stands out most now?"

10. "How would you know the sequence was improving or stabilizing?"

Conclusion

Bottleneck-sequence questions reveal how and why processes collapse under pressure. Understanding these sequences allows the advisor to identify recurring structural weaknesses that previous attempts failed to address. Instead of treating bottlenecks as isolated frustrations, this approach frames them as predictable patterns that can be redesigned, reinforced, or strategically bypassed.

Strategically, these insights highlight where improvements will have the greatest effect. Once you know where the sequence begins and how it spreads, you can prevent delays, improve workflow stability, and design solutions grounded in reality rather than assumptions.

Psychologically, bottleneck awareness helps the buyer release self-blame and see the issue clearly. Many teams internalize delays as personal shortcomings when they are truly the result of structural overload or unclear roles. By reframing bottlenecks as solvable design flaws, you empower the buyer to lead change with confidence.

Reflection Prompt:
Think of a recurring workflow slowdown you've observed. Which bottleneck-sequence question from this section would have revealed the underlying pattern sooner?

CHPATER 2 - SECTION 6 - Loss-Analysis Questions

Introduction

Every failed or abandoned attempt carries a set of losses — lost time, lost money, lost opportunities, lost trust, or lost momentum. These losses are rarely examined in detail, yet they shape the buyer's mindset more than anything else. Loss-analysis questions help uncover what the failed attempt truly cost the organization, both tangibly and emotionally. By identifying these losses clearly, you help the buyer understand the full weight of the past so they can make better choices moving forward.

Strategically, loss analysis brings precision to the cost of inaction and the consequences of flawed execution. Buyers often underestimate the ripple effects of failure, focusing only on visible costs. These questions reveal hidden losses: delayed progress, increased workload, strained relationships, missed deadlines, damaged morale, and reduced confidence in future initiatives. Understanding these losses helps you design solutions that not only fix the problem but also repair the damage left behind.

Psychologically, discussing losses can surface frustration, disappointment, embarrassment, or fatigue. Some buyers downplay losses to protect themselves; others inflate them out of frustration. Your goal is to help them articulate the truth — calmly, without blame. Loss-analysis provides emotional clarity, making the buyer more open to change because they finally understand what staying stuck is truly costing them.

Interpretation Tip: Listen for patterns in the buyer's language:

- Loss of trust ("People stopped believing in the plan…")

- Loss of time ("We wasted months on this…")

- Loss of confidence ("After that, people hesitated…")

- Loss of opportunity ("We missed the window…")
  These signals reveal deeper organizational dynamics that will affect future decisions.

Coaching Note: Ask these questions gently but firmly. You're helping the buyer confront reality, not relive past frustration. Use follow-ups to help them quantify or qualify the loss so the impact becomes clear and actionable.

Example prompts you might use:

- *"What did the failed attempt end up costing you?"*

- *"What losses stand out most when you look back?"*

Standard Loss-Analysis Questions (8)

Tone: calm, factual, exploratory.

1. "What did the failed attempt cost in terms of time or effort?"

2. "What results were delayed because the plan didn't work?"

3. "Which resources were used up without producing the return you expected?"

4. "How did the failed effort affect your team's workload?"

5. "What opportunities did you have to set aside while focusing on this attempt?"

6. "What momentum was lost once the effort stopped working?"

7. "How did the past failure affect your timeline for future goals?"

8. "What stands out as the biggest loss from that experience?"

Intermediate Loss-Analysis Questions (9)

Tone: deeper, probing, structured.

1. "Which losses were most visible — and which were hidden at first?"

2. "How did the failure affect morale, confidence, or team energy?"

3. "What delays or setbacks created new problems downstream?"

4. "Which relationships weakened because the effort didn't deliver?"

5. "What long-term opportunities slipped away during the failed attempt?"

6. "How did the failure influence leadership's trust in the process?"

7. "Which departments absorbed the biggest impact?"

8. "What losses have continued to affect performance even after the attempt ended?"

9. "If you had to list the top three losses, what would they be and why?"

Aggressive Loss-Analysis Questions (8)

Tone: direct, respectful, truth-focused.

1. "What loss hurt the organization more than anyone acknowledged at the time?"

2. "Which part of the failure cost you the most credibility?"

3. "What opportunity disappeared permanently because the attempt failed?"

4. "Who paid the highest personal price for that failure?"

5. "What financial or strategic loss was quietly swept aside?"

6. "Which loss shaped how people think about new initiatives today?"

7. "What long-term consequence did the team underestimate?"

8. "If you're honest, what was the most damaging outcome of the entire attempt?"

Follow-Up Loss-Analysis Questions (10)

Tone: empathetic, clarifying, emotionally aware.

1. "Can you give an example of how that loss showed up day-to-day?"

2. "What moment made you realize the loss was bigger than expected?"

3. "How did the team react when the full impact became clear?"

4. "What part of the loss took the longest to recover from?"

5. "How did the loss change the way people approached future decisions?"

6. "What emotion comes up when you think about that particular loss?"

7. "Which part of the loss still affects your workflow or results now?"

8. "What did people hope would happen that never materialized?"

9. "What would have needed to be different to avoid that loss?"

10. "How would you know that future efforts have recovered what was lost?"

Conclusion

Loss-analysis questions illuminate the full impact of past failures — not just the visible costs, but the deeper, often hidden consequences that shape how an organization moves forward.

Understanding these losses provides the buyer with a clearer picture of how the past still influences their present decisions, expectations, and readiness for change.

Strategically, identifying losses allows you to design solutions that repair what was damaged while also preventing similar losses in the future. This helps create more resilient systems, stronger follow-through, and better alignment across the organization.

Psychologically, naming the losses helps the buyer process their experience instead of carrying it silently. It turns frustration into insight and disappointment into information. Once the full weight of the past is understood, the buyer becomes more open to exploring stronger and more effective approaches.

Reflection Prompt:
Think of an initiative that failed quietly but left long-lasting effects. Which loss-analysis question from this section would have uncovered the true impact sooner?

CHPATER 2 - SECTION 7 - Underutilized-Asset Questions

Introduction

Not every failure is caused by what the organization lacked; many failures occur because the organization **already had what it needed but didn't use it well**. Underutilized assets are the hidden strengths — people, skills, tools, relationships, data, time, or opportunities — that were available but never fully leveraged. This section helps the buyer uncover what resources were overlooked, misallocated, or left on the sidelines during past attempts.

Strategically, identifying underutilized assets reveals where the organization had untapped potential that could have changed the outcome. These questions highlight strengths hidden in plain sight: employees who weren't consulted, tools that were deployed too late, insights that were ignored, or partnerships that could have eased the burden. Understanding these assets allows you to shape future solutions around existing strengths rather than starting from scratch.

Psychologically, underutilized assets often come with quiet frustration. Team members may feel unheard, leaders may feel regret, or the buyer may realize they underestimated what they already had. Your role is to help them see these assets without blame. When handled thoughtfully, this exploration can shift the buyer from discouragement to empowerment — because it reveals that the gap between failure and success might be smaller than they believed.

Interpretation Tip: Listen for statements like "We never thought to involve them," "We had the tool, but…," or "We didn't realize what we had at the time." These phrases reveal overlooked strengths or forgotten capabilities. Also pay attention to assets mentioned casually; sometimes the buyer doesn't see their value until you ask deeper questions.

Coaching Note: Guide the conversation with curiosity rather than critique. You are helping the buyer discover potential, not highlighting mistakes. When the buyer recognizes underutilized assets, they often gain renewed confidence because they see possibilities that were always within reach.

Example prompts you might use:

- *"What strengths or resources were available but not fully used?"*

- *"Who had insights you didn't tap into during the attempt?"*

Standard Underutilized-Asset Questions (8)

Tone: open, encouraging, optimistic.

1. "What resources were available that you didn't fully use?"

2. "Who on the team had experience that wasn't leveraged enough?"

3. "What tools or systems could have supported the effort more effectively?"

4. "Which processes or workflows had untapped potential?"

5. "What internal knowledge or data wasn't brought into the decision-making?"

6. "Who could have provided insight if they had been involved earlier?"

7. "What strengths within the team went unnoticed during the attempt?"

8. "What part of your existing capacity was underused at the time?"

Intermediate Underutilized-Asset Questions (9)

Tone: probing, thoughtful, uncovering.

1. "Which skills or talents were available but not assigned to the right tasks?"

2. "What internal relationships or partnerships could have reduced friction?"

3. "Which tools were implemented too late to make a difference?"

4. "Where did communication patterns prevent certain people from contributing?"

5. "What insights emerged only after the attempt ended — and why weren't they discovered earlier?"

6. "Which overlooked strengths could have changed the trajectory of the effort?"

7. "What routines or habits kept valuable resources from being utilized?"

8. "Which person or group had a clearer perspective than others realized?"

9. "What internal assets were undervalued because they weren't measured or recognized?"

Aggressive Underutilized-Asset Questions (8)

Tone: direct, revealing, respectful.

1. "Who had the ability to improve the situation but was never consulted?"

2. "What tool or system was ignored even though it could have prevented the failure?"

3. "Which talented team member was sidelined or overlooked?"

4. "What internal advantage was wasted during the attempt?"

5. "Who held critical information that leadership never accessed?"

6. "Which part of the organization had capacity that went unused?"

7. "What competency was underestimated or dismissed until after the failure?"

8. "Which missed opportunity still frustrates you because the asset was right there?"

Follow-Up Underutilized-Asset Questions (10)

Tone: reflective, supportive, clarifying.

1. "Can you give an example of an asset that wasn't used when it should have been?"

2. "What would have happened if that person or tool had been involved earlier?"

3. "What prevented that asset from being used more effectively?"

4. "How did the team react when they realized the asset was underutilized?"

5. "What made that resource valuable in hindsight?"

6. "How long had that asset been available without being leveraged?"

7. "What would you change to integrate that asset next time?"

8. "What part of the situation would that asset have impacted most?"

9. "Which overlooked asset could still be useful moving forward?"

10. "How would you know that an asset is being fully utilized next time?"

Conclusion

Underutilized-asset questions shine a light on hidden strengths the organization already possessed but failed to bring into play. These insights reveal that many failures are not due to lack of ability, but lack of awareness, coordination, or strategic allocation. By understanding which resources were left untapped, you help the buyer see possibilities they may never have considered.

Strategically, identifying underutilized assets helps you design solutions that maximize what the organization already has, reducing cost, increasing efficiency, and improving confidence. Many organizations underestimate their own capabilities; this section helps correct that perception.

Psychologically, this exploration boosts morale. Buyers often feel discouraged by past attempts, but when they recognize they already had valuable assets, they see a path forward that feels more achievable. It also encourages better collaboration and utilization of talent in future initiatives.

Reflection Prompt:
Think of a buyer who believed they lacked resources but actually had untapped strength within their team. Which underutilized-asset question from this section could have helped them realize that sooner?

CHPATER 2 - SECTION 8 - Untapped-Upside Questions

Introduction

While many diagnostic conversations focus on failure, loss, or breakdown, one of the most overlooked parts of discovery is understanding **what could have gone right but didn't.** Every past attempt contains untapped upside — gains the organization *could* have achieved, opportunities they were close to capturing, and improvements that were within reach but never realized. Untapped-upside questions shift the conversation from regret to potential, showing the buyer that their situation contains more opportunity than they may have noticed.

Strategically, examining untapped upside changes the energy of the discovery conversation. Instead of focusing solely on what went wrong, these questions highlight the value that was almost unlocked. This perspective helps you identify which strategies had promise, which strengths were emerging, and where early signals of improvement appeared before the momentum faded. Recognizing these moments allows you to design future solutions that amplify what *did* work — even if only briefly.

Psychologically, exploring untapped upside provides hope. Buyers often walk away from failed attempts feeling discouraged or cynical. But when they look back and see the progress they were close to achieving, their mindset shifts. They feel energized, more open to new ideas, and more confident that success is still possible. These questions help lighten the emotional weight of failure by reframing it through possibility rather than defeat.

Interpretation Tip: Listen closely when the buyer says things like "We almost…," "If we had just…," "It was starting to work until…," or "We saw early signs that…" These statements often reveal powerful, unused leverage points. You can build future strategies around these latent advantages.

Coaching Note: Encourage optimism grounded in evidence — not hope without structure. When discussing upside, keep the tone forward-looking: "What does this tell us?" "How can this be amplified?" "What would this look like if it had been fully developed?" You are guiding the buyer into a productive mindset that balances realism with possibility.

Example prompts:

- *"What positive results were starting to appear before things stalled?"*

- *"What upside was available that you weren't able to capture?"*

Standard Untapped-Upside Questions (8)

Tone: open, optimistic, opportunity-focused.

1. "What part of the attempt showed the earliest signs of success?"

2. "Which positive trend appeared before the effort slowed down?"

3. "What opportunities were close but not fully realized?"

4. "Which early wins gave you confidence at the time?"

5. "What improvements were beginning to appear before things shifted?"

6. "What strengths emerged during the attempt that weren't fully developed?"

7. "Which ideas seemed promising but didn't get a chance to mature?"

8. "What potential did you see that made the effort worth trying in the first place?"

Intermediate Untapped-Upside Questions (9)

Tone: probing, curious, constructive.

1. "Which parts of the attempt improved faster than expected?"

2. "What metrics or feedback hinted that success was possible?"

3. "Which team members showed surprising capability or initiative?"

4. "Where did the process feel smoother or more aligned than before?"

5. "Which aspects of the strategy felt like they were on the right track?"

6. "What positive momentum did you notice before the slowdown?"

7. "Which ideas or methods could have produced strong results with just a bit more support?"

8. "What advantages became visible that you didn't see beforehand?"

9. "What potential do you believe still exists if the right approach were used?"

Aggressive Untapped-Upside Questions (8)

Tone: direct, energizing, truth-focused (not accusatory).

1. "What opportunity did you clearly see but didn't capitalize on?"

2. "Which promising result was ignored or abandoned too early?"

3. "What upside was obvious in hindsight but wasn't pursued?"

4. "Which early win should have been doubled down on?"

5. "What breakthrough was within reach but slipped away?"

6. "Who showed potential that leadership overlooked?"

7. "Which strategy could have succeeded with just one critical adjustment?"

8. "What promising sign was misinterpreted or undervalued at the time?"

Follow-Up Untapped-Upside Questions (10)

Tone: reflective, clarifying, encouraging.

1. "Can you describe the moment you realized the attempt had real potential?"

2. "What specific result or feedback made you feel things were improving?"

3. "What made that upside possible in the first place?"

4. "How did the team respond to those early signs of progress?"

5. "Why do you think the upside wasn't fully captured?"

6. "Which part of the opportunity still feels relevant today?"

7. "What would it take to unlock that upside now?"

8. "What detail from that promising moment stands out most?"

9. "How would you build on that potential if you could redo the attempt?"

10. "What would success have looked like if the upside had been fully achieved?"

Conclusion

Untapped-upside questions bring balance to the story of past attempts. They remind the buyer that even within failure, there were signs of progress, moments of alignment, and opportunities that could still be pursued. This perspective helps them recognize that success wasn't as far away as it seemed — and that the future may hold more potential than the past revealed.

Strategically, identifying upside helps you design solutions that amplify what worked rather than simply avoiding what didn't. These insights form the foundation for strengths-based strategy, enabling the buyer to move forward with a mix of realism and optimism.

Psychologically, discussing untapped upside rebuilds motivation. It reframes the narrative from "we failed" to "we were close," shifting the buyer from discouragement to possibility. That mental shift plays a major role in their willingness to embrace a more effective next step.

Reflection Prompt:
Think of a buyer who gave up too early on a promising approach. Which untapped-upside question from this section could have helped them see the opportunity they missed?

CHPATER 2 - SECTION 9 - Abandoned-Opportunity Questions

Introduction

Every failed or incomplete initiative leaves behind a set of opportunities that were never explored, never implemented, or never fully developed. These abandoned opportunities are often more valuable than the attempt itself. They represent paths the organization could have taken but didn't — ideas that were dismissed too quickly, improvements that were postponed, experiments that never reached scale, or potential advantages that slipped through the cracks. Abandoned-opportunity questions help uncover these overlooked possibilities so the buyer can recognize what was left on the table.

Strategically, examining abandoned opportunities exposes the gap between *what was possible* and *what was chosen.* This reveals the organization's decision patterns, risk tolerance, prioritization logic, and blind spots. It also helps the advisor understand which options were ignored due to time pressure, resource limitations, internal conflict, or simple lack of awareness. Identifying these missed pathways helps shape future recommendations that avoid the same limitations and capture the potential that remains.

Psychologically, abandoned opportunities often carry emotional residue — regret, frustration, disbelief, or even indifference. Some buyers feel they missed a window; others feel they lacked the confidence to pursue a bold idea. Your role is to help them revisit these opportunities without judgment. When approached thoughtfully, this reflection gives the buyer renewed clarity and a sense of unfinished potential that can be harnessed moving forward.

Interpretation Tip: Listen for "we almost," "we planned to," "we never got around to," "we talked about but didn't," or "we backed off because…" These phrases point directly to abandoned opportunities. Also notice opportunities tied to unassigned ideas — buyers often casually mention a strong idea that no one took ownership of.

Coaching Note: Stay curious, not corrective. Your goal is not to criticize past choices but to illuminate options that could still hold value. When handled with care, this conversation shifts the buyer from focusing on past limits to imagining future possibilities.

Example prompts you might use:

- *"What opportunities were identified but never acted on?"*

- *"What promising ideas were abandoned before they had a chance to develop?"*

Standard Abandoned-Opportunity Questions (8)

Tone: open, reflective, encouraging.

1. "What opportunities were discussed but never fully pursued?"

2. "Which ideas were set aside due to time or resource constraints?"

3. "What improvements did you plan but never implement?"

4. "Which partnerships or collaborations were considered but not explored?"

5. "What potential changes were delayed and then forgotten?"

6. "Which opportunities seemed promising but lost momentum early?"

7. "What part of the strategy was abandoned before you knew if it would work?"

8. "What ideas resurfaced later that you wish you had acted on earlier?"

Intermediate Abandoned-Opportunity Questions (9)

Tone: probing, curious, depth-oriented.

1. "Which opportunity could have created significant improvement if pursued?"

2. "What made the team hesitate when the opportunity first appeared?"

3. "Which internal factors caused the opportunity to be deprioritized?"

4. "What conditions would have allowed you to move forward with that idea?"

5. "Which abandoned idea still feels relevant today?"

6. "What prevented promising concepts from becoming actionable plans?"

7. "Which missed opportunity do you think about most in hindsight?"

8. "What early signals suggested the opportunity had real potential?"

9. "Which abandoned direction aligns well with your current needs?"

Aggressive Abandoned-Opportunity Questions (8)

Tone: direct, honest, truth-seeking.

1. "What opportunity did you walk away from that you now regret?"

2. "Which idea had the highest upside but was dismissed too quickly?"

3. "What opportunity vanished because no one took ownership?"

4. "Which strategic path was abandoned out of fear or uncertainty?"

5. "Who argued against an idea that could have changed the outcome?"

6. "What opportunity slipped through the cracks during internal conflict?"

7. "Which promising direction was ignored because it required uncomfortable change?"

8. "What window of opportunity closed because action wasn't taken in time?"

Follow-Up Abandoned-Opportunity Questions (10)

Tone: empathetic, clarifying, gently challenging.

1. "Can you describe the moment when the opportunity was set aside?"

2. "What caused the conversation around that idea to stop?"

3. "What did people hope the opportunity would accomplish?"

4. "How did the team react when it resurfaced later, if at all?"

5. "What makes you think that opportunity could still matter today?"

6. "What constraints made pursuing it difficult at the time?"

7. "How would things look now if that opportunity had been explored?"

8. "What detail about that abandoned idea stands out most?"

9. "What would need to change to revisit that opportunity now?"

10. "How would you know that the opportunity is worth pursuing today?"

Conclusion

Abandoned-opportunity questions expose the untapped potential hidden in past decisions. They help the buyer recognize that the past contains not only failures, but also paths never traveled — paths that may still hold value today. By exploring these missed opportunities, you help the buyer understand the difference between strategic choices and circumstantial limitations.

Strategically, these insights reveal which opportunities deserve renewed attention and which ones can inform future planning. They also highlight the internal dynamics — hesitation, confusion, competing priorities — that caused promising ideas to be abandoned prematurely. Understanding these patterns helps prevent the same mistakes in future initiatives.

Psychologically, examining abandoned opportunities restores hope. It helps the buyer see that the door to progress was never fully closed — it was simply left unopened. This shift in mindset encourages renewed motivation and a more proactive approach to upcoming decisions.

Reflection Prompt:
Think of a buyer who mentioned an idea they "never got around to." Which abandoned-opportunity question could have given them clarity and created new momentum?

Chapter Conclusion

Chapter 2 transforms hindsight into intelligence. By breaking down past attempts into their components, you help the buyer understand not only what failed, but *why* it failed. This reduces uncertainty and prevents repeated mistakes. It also reveals the organization's strengths — strengths that may have gone unnoticed because they were overshadowed by frustration or time pressure. With a clearer view of their own history, the buyer becomes more willing to consider change, because they finally understand what held them back and what they can build on moving forward.

Strategically, this chapter equips you with historical context, performance evidence, behavioral patterns, and unused potential — all of which strengthen your recommendations. Psychologically, the process helps the buyer release disappointment and replace it with insight. They see that failure was not a dead end, but a source of important lessons. This positions them to enter the next stage of discovery with clarity and confidence.

As the book moves into Chapter 3, the focus shifts from examining the past to understanding the internal forces that influence decision-making today. Having clarified what has already happened, the advisor is now ready to uncover how decisions will be made, who influences them, and which pressures shape the buyer's choices. Chapter 2 sets the stage for that deeper exploration by ensuring the past is understood, respected, and transformed into guidance for the future.

CHAPTER 3 - Mapping the Decision Environment

Chapter Introduction

Every decision unfolds inside an environment shaped by people, pressures, and patterns. Buyers often focus on the problem they want to solve but overlook the human ecosystem that determines whether progress is possible. Chapter 3 brings that ecosystem into focus. Rather than treating the buyer as a single decision-maker, this chapter reveals the full network of stakeholders, influences, motivations, barriers, and timing forces that shape the outcome of any meaningful initiative. Understanding this environment is the key to guiding conversations with clarity and confidence.

The chapter begins with **Stakeholder-Landscape Questions**, which identify every person who plays a role in shaping the decision. From there, **Influence-Pattern Questions** reveal how opinions move inside the group — who shapes conversations quietly, who anchors decisions, and who shifts momentum. Once the environment is visible, **Stakeholder-Motivation Questions** explore each individual's priorities, fears, incentives, and personal pressures, exposing the human forces behind the decision.

The middle of the chapter examines friction: **Objection-Anticipation Questions** help predict resistance, while **Risk-Tolerance Questions** uncover each stakeholder's comfort with uncertainty. Together, these insights explain why decisions may stall. Decision-making isn't just about logic it's shaped by emotional boundaires and learned caution.

Next, the chapter explores **Decision-Sequence Questions**, which expose the real steps behind how approvals unfold. Following that, **Approval-Criteria Questions** clarify the conditions that must be met before leadership commits. These structured insights help the advisor anticipate timing, prepare stronger proposals, and navigate internal processes without confusion or missteps.

The final two sections explore alignment and readiness. **Alignment-Barrier Questions** reveal where stakeholders fall out of sync — the hidden conflicts or missing information that block agreement. **Timing-Pressure Questions** uncover the cycles and workloads that influence when decisions can be made. Finally, **Commitment-Signal Questions** show how to read the shift from interest to true intent, revealing when a buyer is emotionally and strategically ready to move forward.

By the end of Chapter 3, the advisor has a deep, structured understanding of the decision environment: who the players are, how they influence each other, what motivates them, what slows them down, and what signals readiness for action. This perspective transforms discovery from guesswork into clear, navigable insight. With this clarity, the advisor can guide the buyer through complex conversations with confidence and empathy — the foundation for meaningful progress in later chapters.

CHAPTER 3 - SECTION 1 - Stakeholder-Landscape Questions

Introduction

As discovery moves deeper, the focus shifts from understanding the problem and its history to understanding the environment in which decisions are made. No meaningful change happens in isolation. Behind every initiative is a network of people — leaders, influencers, skeptics, supporters, decision-makers, hidden stakeholders, and informal power holders. Stakeholder-landscape questions reveal who these people are, how they think, and how their roles shape the buyer's reality.

Strategically, mapping the stakeholder landscape helps you understand the social architecture surrounding the problem. Organizations rarely make decisions based on pure logic; decisions are shaped by priorities, personalities, politics, relationships, and historical experiences. These questions help uncover the structure behind influence: who holds authority, who holds information, who holds trust, and who holds resistance. Without this clarity, even the best solution can fail simply because the environment wasn't aligned.

Psychologically, people often underestimate the complexity of their own internal dynamics. They may focus on a single decision-maker while ignoring others who quietly affect outcomes. Some stakeholders may have unofficial influence that outweighs formal titles. Others may support change privately but resist publicly due to fear or uncertainty. These questions help the buyer articulate dynamics they sense but have never examined directly.

Interpretation Tip: Pay attention to how the buyer speaks about people — tone, hesitation, pronouns, or repeated mentions. These patterns reveal emotional undercurrents: trust, frustration, respect, or avoidance. Often, the buyer reveals more in *how* they talk about a person than *what* they say.

Coaching Note: Encourage neutrality. Buyers sometimes feel protective or critical of certain stakeholders. Keeping the tone fact-focused helps them explore the landscape without defensiveness. Guide them gently toward clarity, not judgment.

Example prompts you might use:

- *"Who is involved in shaping the outcome of this issue?"*

- *"Whose perspective matters most at each stage of the process?"*

The questions below help illuminate the full map of people influencing the decision environment.

Standard Stakeholder-Landscape Questions (8)

Tone: open, calm, factual.

1. "Who are the key people involved in this situation?"

2. "Whose input is needed for things to move forward?"

3. "Who feels the impact of this issue most directly?"

4. "Who has formal authority over decisions in this area?"

5. "Who tends to be consulted informally before decisions are made?"

6. "Which departments or teams interact with this issue most?"

7. "Who typically champions improvements or new ideas?"

8. "Who usually provides the most resistance when change is discussed?"

Intermediate Stakeholder-Landscape Questions (9)

Tone: probing, curious, structured.

1. "Which stakeholders have the strongest influence over the outcome?"

2. "Who is responsible for gathering information before decisions are made?"

3. "Which roles depend on the success of this initiative?"

4. "Who will feel pressure if the problem continues?"

5. "What relationships matter most to the success of this effort?"

6. "Who communicates most often with leadership about this issue?"

7. "Which stakeholders tend to shape the narrative behind the scenes?"

8. "Who has a perspective that others often overlook?"

9. "Which individuals carry historical context that could affect decisions now?"

Aggressive Stakeholder-Landscape Questions (8)

Tone: direct, truth-focused, respectful.

1. "Who holds the real power in this situation, regardless of titles?"

2. "Which stakeholder could stop progress if they disagreed?"

3. "Who has the strongest personal stake in the outcome?"

4. "What person consistently influences decisions more than people realize?"

5. "Who is likely to resist quietly even if they appear supportive?"

6. "Whose approval is essential even if they're not officially in charge?"

7. "Which stakeholder tends to derail conversations when pressure increases?"

8. "Who shapes opinions informally but avoids taking responsibility publicly?"

Follow-Up Stakeholder-Landscape Questions (10)

Tone: reflective, clarifying, relational.

1. "Can you describe how each stakeholder views this issue?"

2. "What have you noticed about their reactions during past discussions?"

3. "Which stakeholder's opinion seems to shift the group the most?"

4. "What past experiences shape how these individuals think about new initiatives?"

5. "What concerns or motivations drive each stakeholder?"

6. "How do relationships between stakeholders affect collaboration?"

7. "What dynamics would become more visible if tension increased?"

8. "Which stakeholder is the most unpredictable in decision-making?"

9. "How does each person respond when expectations change?"

10. "What would help these stakeholders align more easily?"

Conclusion

Stakeholder-landscape questions reveal the human structure behind every decision. They expose the network of influence that determines how ideas are received, how resistance forms, and how and when decisions take shape. Without this understanding, advisors risk presenting solutions that fail not because of merit, but because they collide with unseen dynamics.

Strategically, a clear stakeholder landscape allows you to anticipate blockers, mobilize supporters, and tailor recommendations to the internal realities of the organization. Psychologically, these questions help the buyer articulate interpersonal dynamics they've sensed but never verbalized. This clarity reduces uncertainty and increases their confidence in navigating internal conversations.

As the chapter continues, the focus will shift from identifying stakeholders to understanding each stakeholder's motivations, objections, influence patterns, and decision criteria. This first section lays the foundation by revealing who is part of the landscape — the next sections uncover how they behave within it.

Reflection Prompt:
Think of a deal that slowed down because of an unseen stakeholder. Which stakeholder-landscape question would have surfaced that person earlier?

CHAPTER 3 - SECTION 2 - Influence-Pattern Questions

Introduction

Once the stakeholder landscape is mapped, the next step is understanding **how influence actually moves** within the group. Influence seldom follows organizational charts. It follows trust, history, confidence, reputation, emotional ties, and sometimes fear. Influence-pattern questions help uncover how stakeholders shape one another's opinions, how decisions form over time, and how conversations evolve from initial thoughts to final outcomes. These patterns determine whether an initiative gains traction or quietly loses momentum.

Strategically, understanding influence patterns allows you to predict how a recommendation will be received and how quickly it can advance. Some stakeholders influence through formal authority; others influence through relationships or the respect they've earned. Some sway decisions subtly through perspective shifts, while others shape outcomes by setting the emotional tone of the conversation. Influence-pattern questions reveal these movement channels so you can guide the buyer effectively through their own decision environment.

Psychologically, people often underestimate the degree to which influence shapes their decisions. They may believe decisions are based on logic alone when, in reality, stakeholders are responding to signals from others — confidence cues, hesitation, enthusiasm, or quiet resistance. These questions help the buyer see these invisible currents. Once understood, influence becomes easier to navigate, manage, and align.

Interpretation Tip: Pay attention to the order in which the buyer describes people. Those mentioned early often hold more influence. Also notice where the buyer hesitates or softens language — these moments often signal a stakeholder whose influence feels sensitive or politically complex.

Coaching Note: Keep the tone neutral, not analytical. Buyers may feel defensive when discussing influence because it exposes internal dynamics. Encourage reflection without pressure: "Let's explore what you've observed," or "Help me understand how opinions shift." This maintains psychological safety while revealing valuable insight.

Example prompts you might use:

- *"How do opinions within the group tend to form?"*
- *"Who influences conversations without needing to lead them?"*

Standard Influence-Pattern Questions (8)

Tone: calm, observational, open.

1. "Whose opinions tend to shape the direction of discussions?"

2. "Who does the team look to for reassurance during uncertainty?"

3. "Whose reactions influence how others speak about the issue?"

4. "Which stakeholders usually speak first — and how does that impact the group?"

5. "Who tends to clarify or reframe ideas during conversations?"

6. "Which individuals help bring the group back on track during debates?"

7. "Who usually helps build consensus when opinions differ?"

8. "How do informal conversations shape the group's thinking?"

Intermediate Influence-Pattern Questions (9)

Tone: probing, curious, insight-seeking.

1. "Which stakeholder has the strongest impact on how others interpret new information?"

2. "Who influences decisions even when they aren't in the room?"

3. "Which relationships seem to drive alignment or division?"

4. "How does the group respond when a particular person voices concern or approval?"

5. "Which individuals help move ideas forward quietly behind the scenes?"

6. "Where do you see influence shifting depending on the topic or timing?"

7. "Which stakeholder's confidence — or lack of it — changes the group dynamic?"

8. "How do disagreements typically get resolved, and who plays a role in that?"

9. "Whose perspective is often adopted by the group, even if others disagree privately?"

Aggressive Influence-Pattern Questions (8)

Tone: direct, respectful, truth-exposing.

1. "Who controls the real momentum of decision-making?"

2. "Which stakeholder sways decisions the most without claiming responsibility?"

3. "Who causes the group to hesitate when they express doubt?"

4. "Which person consistently influences outcomes more than their title suggests?"

5. "Who shifts the room with a single comment — positive or negative?"

6. "Whose approval determines whether an idea even gets considered?"

7. "Which individual disrupts alignment by steering conversations off-track?"

8. "Who quietly influences leadership in ways others don't see?"

Follow-Up Influence-Pattern Questions (10)

Tone: reflective, clarifying, gently revealing.

1. "Can you describe a moment when someone's reaction changed the direction of the discussion?"

2. "What specific behavior signaled that influence at play?"

3. "How did the rest of the group respond to that influence?"

4. "Which recent decision shows influence clearly?"

5. "What pattern have you observed across several meetings or conversations?"

6. "Which stakeholder's influence surprised you once you noticed it?"

7. "How does influence shift when pressure increases or deadlines approach?"

8. "Who tends to mediate conflict, and what influence does that give them?"

9. "What part of the influence pattern creates misalignment or confusion?"

10. "How would you know if influence became more balanced or transparent?"

Conclusion

Influence-pattern questions uncover the hidden mechanics of decision-making. They reveal how opinions form, how pressure builds, and how commitments take shape. Influence is often subtle, emotional, and relational — and understanding it is essential for navigating complex decision environments.

Strategically, these insights help you anticipate resistance, build momentum, and frame recommendations in ways that resonate with the people who truly matter. Psychologically, they help the buyer see their internal environment clearly, often for the first time. This clarity reduces tension and increases confidence as the buyer prepares for deeper discussions involving power, risk, and commitment.

As we move forward in Chapter 3, the next sections will explore stakeholder motivations, risk tolerance, objection patterns, and decision sequencing. Influence patterns form the backbone of this work, revealing how the human environment will respond to change.

Reflection Prompt:
Think of a situation where one person's reaction shifted an entire meeting. Which influence-pattern question would have uncovered that dynamic earlier?

CHAPTER 3 - SECTION 3 - Stakeholder-Motivation Questions

Introduction

Once you understand who the stakeholders are and how influence moves among them, the next step is uncovering **why** they behave the way they do. Stakeholders don't react to ideas randomly — their decisions are anchored in motivations shaped by goals, fears, pressures, incentives, personal history, and emotional investment. Stakeholder-motivation questions help reveal the underlying drivers that determine each person's stance, commitment, and behavior. Without understanding these motivations, even the most logical plan can collapse under unseen resistance.

Strategically, exploring stakeholder motivations helps the advisor see the forces shaping the decision environment. Some stakeholders are driven by performance metrics; others are focused on reputation, stability, efficiency, or control. Some want clarity. Some want autonomy. Some want safety. Others want progress. Understanding these drivers allows you to tailor your message in a way that aligns with each person's priorities. When you meet motivations directly, friction drops and alignment becomes easier.

Psychologically, motivation is rarely expressed outright. People often speak in practical terms, but their actions stem from deeper emotional or experiential realities. A stakeholder may resist change not because they dislike the idea, but because a past attempt hurt their team. Another may support an initiative because it finally gives them the influence or visibility they've been seeking. These questions guide the buyer into examining the human side of decision-making — not just the operational side.

Interpretation Tip: Listen for emotional clues hidden in rational explanations. When the buyer says, "They just want things to be stable," or "They're cautious," or "They push for progress," they're revealing motivational patterns. Pay attention to the words *trust, pressure, safety, ownership, credit,* and *risk* — these often point directly to stakeholder motivations.

Coaching Note: Approach these questions without judgment. People's motivations are shaped by their experiences and responsibilities. When you help the buyer explore them neutrally, they gain a clearer picture of the internal environment, making it easier to communicate effectively with each stakeholder.

Example prompts:

- *"What does each stakeholder hope will happen if this succeeds?"*

- *"What concerns might be motivating their hesitation?"*

Standard Stakeholder-Motivation Questions (8)

Tone: calm, curious, non-judgmental.

1. "What does each stakeholder hope to gain from solving this issue?"

2. "What responsibilities shape their priorities around this decision?"

3. "What part of the outcome matters most to them personally?"

4. "Which goals or targets influence their thinking the most?"

5. "What do they care about protecting or preserving?"

6. "What motivates them to support or challenge new ideas?"

7. "Which pressures are they trying to reduce by solving this problem?"

8. "What would success look like from their point of view?"

Intermediate Stakeholder-Motivation Questions (9)

Tone: probing, insightful, psychologically aware.

1. "Which stakeholder is most driven by performance or measurable results?"

2. "Who is motivated by stability and risk reduction?"

3. "Who values recognition, visibility, or influence the most?"

4. "Which individuals are motivated by protecting their team or workload?"

5. "Who responds most strongly to efficiency or process improvement?"

6. "Which stakeholders are motivated by removing frustration or uncertainty?"

7. "What past experiences shape how each stakeholder views this situation?"

8. "Which long-term goals influence their stance on this issue?"

9. "What motivates them to change their mind once new information appears?"

Aggressive Stakeholder-Motivation Questions (8)

Tone: direct, respectful, revealing deeper truth.

1. "Who is motivated more by avoiding blame than pursuing progress?"

2. "Which stakeholder's reluctance comes from fear rather than logic?"

3. "Who wants this solution because it strengthens their influence or position?"

4. "Who might resist because success would shift control away from them?"

5. "Which stakeholder has the most to lose if things go wrong?"

6. "Who is driven by past failures that still shape their decisions?"

7. "What personal agenda is influencing the conversation more than people admit?"

8. "Who is motivated by proving something — to themselves or to others?"

Follow-Up Stakeholder-Motivation Questions (10)

Tone: empathetic, clarifying, reflective.

1. "Can you describe a moment that revealed what motivates this stakeholder most?"

2. "What did they say or do that signaled their underlying concerns?"

3. "How do they behave when they feel confident versus uncertain?"

4. "What motivates them during times of stress or change?"

5. "What reaction showed you what they value most?"

6. "How does their past experience shape their current stance?"

7. "What detail about their motivation became clearer once you looked back?"

8. "What fears or hopes seem to be driving their involvement?"

9. "How would their motivation change if the situation became more urgent?"

10. "What would increase their confidence in moving forward?"

Conclusion

Stakeholder-motivation questions reveal the inner forces shaping the decision environment. Without this understanding, the advisor is left guessing — and guessing leads to misalignment, missed signals, and stalled progress. By uncovering what each stakeholder values, fears, or hopes for, you gain clarity on how to communicate effectively, where resistance will appear, and what will inspire commitment.

Strategically, knowing motivations allows you to tailor recommendations so they resonate with the people who matter most. Psychologically, it gives the buyer a deeper understanding of their own environment, reducing tension and helping them lead conversations with empathy and precision. When motivations are visible, decision-making becomes clearer and collaboration becomes easier.

As Chapter 3 continues, the next sections will build on these insights by exploring stakeholder objections, risk tolerance, decision sequencing, and internal alignment. Understanding motivation is the key that makes all of those conversations more meaningful and more predictable.

Reflection Prompt:
Think of a stakeholder whose behavior didn't make sense at first. Which motivation question would have revealed the reason sooner?

CHAPTER 3 - SECTION 4 - Objection-Anticipation Questions

Introduction

Once the stakeholder landscape and motivations are clear, the next step is understanding **where objections will come from and why.** Objections are not random; they are signals. They reflect concerns about risk, workload, timing, clarity, trust, budget, capability, past experiences, and internal pressure. Objection-anticipation questions help the buyer forecast resistance before it appears, making future conversations smoother, more predictable, and far less stressful.

Strategically, anticipating objections gives you the ability to prepare the buyer for internal conversations, build stronger proposals, and create messaging that addresses friction points upfront. When objections are identified early, they lose their power to derail progress. Instead, they become manageable elements that can be addressed, clarified, and resolved through thoughtful dialogue.

Psychologically, objections often stem from fear — fear of failure, fear of judgment, fear of increased workload, fear of change, or fear of conflict. These fears rarely appear directly; they are expressed through questions, hesitations, or "practical concerns." By helping the buyer explore these concerns early, you reduce emotional pressure and create space for more honest, productive communication.

Interpretation Tip: Listen for phrases like "They're going to ask…" or "They'll probably worry about…" These statements reveal anticipated objections. Pay close attention to the emotional intensity behind the buyer's predictions — stronger reactions often indicate deeper unresolved tension between stakeholders or past attempts.

Coaching Note: Avoid framing objections as problems or conflicts. Instead, treat them as insights. Reassure the buyer that objections are normal and predictable. The more neutral you remain, the more willing the buyer will be to explore sensitive concerns openly.

Example prompts:

- *"What concerns do you expect from your team when this comes up?"*

- *"Who is most likely to push back, and for what reason?"*

Standard Objection-Anticipation Questions (8)

Tone: calm, neutral, predictive.

1. "What concerns do you expect to hear first when this idea is introduced?"

2. "Who is most likely to ask tough questions early in the conversation?"

3. "Which stakeholders tend to be cautious or skeptical?"

4. "What objections have come up in similar situations before?"

5. "What do you think people will worry about most?"

6. "Which parts of the plan might feel unclear or risky to others?"

7. "Who might need extra information to feel comfortable?"

8. "What common misunderstandings could arise when you share this idea?"

Intermediate Objection-Anticipation Questions (9)

Tone: probing, predictive, thoughtful.

1. "Which stakeholders will be most concerned about workload or capacity?"

2. "Who may hesitate because of past failures or disappointments?"

3. "Which part of the plan is likely to trigger questions about risk or timing?"

4. "Who will push back if they feel excluded from the decision process?"

5. "What internal expectations could conflict with this initiative?"

6. "What concerns might arise around budget, resources, or ROI?"

7. "How might communication gaps create unnecessary objections?"

8. "Which stakeholders will need reassurance about stability or control?"

9. "What objections might appear only after people discuss this privately?"

Aggressive Objection-Anticipation Questions (8)

Tone: direct, respectful, truth-revealing.

1. "Who is most likely to resist this even if they don't say it publicly?"

2. "What objection could undermine the effort if not addressed early?"

3. "Who might shut down the idea due to fear of accountability or visibility?"

4. "Which stakeholder is likely to challenge the plan to maintain influence?"

5. "What concern will people hide rather than express openly?"

6. "Which objection will feel personal rather than logical?"

7. "Who will oppose this because it disrupts their preferred way of working?"

8. "What internal politics could turn a small concern into a major objection?"

Follow-Up Objection-Anticipation Questions (10)

Tone: clarifying, empathetic, reflective.

1. "Can you describe a moment when this stakeholder objected in the past?"

2. "What patterns have you noticed in how they express concerns?"

3. "What past experience might shape their reaction now?"

4. "What specific detail do you think they'll focus on?"

5. "What would help soften their concern before it becomes resistance?"

6. "How would they react if the timeline or workload changed?"

7. "What reassurance would matter most to this stakeholder?"

8. "What makes you believe this objection will resurface?"

9. "How does this person typically respond after their objections are addressed?"

10. "What would make this stakeholder feel confident instead of wary?"

Conclusion

Objection-anticipation questions bring hidden resistance into the open long before it disrupts progress. They help the buyer see where tension is likely to appear, how stakeholders will react, and what concerns will shape the decision process. Anticipating objections doesn't eliminate them — it transforms them into manageable, predictable elements of the conversation.

Strategically, this clarity enables the advisor and buyer to prepare stronger communication, address friction early, and guide decision-makers with confidence. Psychologically, it reduces anxiety on all sides. When objections are discussed before they surface, the environment becomes calmer and more cooperative.

As Chapter 3 continues, later sections will explore risk tolerance, decision timing, approval pathways, and internal alignment. Objection awareness lays the groundwork for these deeper layers, allowing the advisor to navigate the decision environment with both precision and empathy.

Reflection Prompt:

Think of a situation where an unexpected objection derailed a promising initiative. Which question from this section would have predicted it ahead of time?

CHAPTER 3 - SECTION 5 - Risk-Tolerance Questions

Introduction

After understanding objections, the next critical layer in the decision environment is **risk tolerance** — the degree to which stakeholders are willing or unwilling to move forward under uncertainty. Risk tolerance influences every conversation, every objection, and every approval path. Some stakeholders embrace risk as a necessary step toward progress, while others avoid it because past failures, personal pressure, or organizational culture have shaped them to be extremely cautious. Risk-tolerance questions help you uncover these differences so you can predict how decisions will unfold.

Strategically, analyzing risk tolerance helps you determine the pace, structure, and framing required for your solution. If the environment is risk-averse, the advisor must emphasize stability, clarity, and safety. If the environment is more risk-tolerant, the advisor can highlight innovation, opportunity, and growth. Without this understanding, even a well-designed solution can feel misaligned with the organization's comfort level.

Psychologically, risk tolerance is deeply personal. It is shaped by past experiences, workload pressures, fear of judgment, trust in leadership, confidence in the team, and individual emotional thresholds. These factors often operate beneath the surface. People rarely say "I'm afraid of risk," but they demonstrate it through hesitation, softened language, or constant requests for more information. These questions help the buyer articulate feelings they may not have named before.

Interpretation Tip: Listen for emotional keywords ("safe," "stable," "uncertain," "pressure," "exposed"). They reveal risk comfort without the buyer consciously realizing it. Also pay attention to how the buyer talks about past attempts — risk-averse environments often overcorrect after a failure, while risk-tolerant environments tend to minimize caution until pressure rises.

Coaching Note: Approach these questions with sensitivity. Risk touches on vulnerability. Your role is not to judge whether the environment should be more bold or more cautious; your job is to understand it so your guidance aligns with reality.

Example prompts:

- *"How comfortable is your team making decisions when not everything is known?"*

- *"Who leans toward caution, and who prefers to move quickly?"*

Standard Risk-Tolerance Questions (8)

Tone: calm, supportive, exploratory.

1. "How comfortable is your group with making decisions under uncertainty?"

2. "Who tends to prefer cautious, step-by-step approaches?"

3. "Who is more willing to take bold action when needed?"

4. "What level of risk feels acceptable to most stakeholders?"

5. "How do people respond when a situation becomes unpredictable?"

6. "What past experiences influence your team's comfort with risk?"

7. "What helps stakeholders feel safe when considering new ideas?"

8. "Which decisions in the past required more confidence than clarity?"

Intermediate Risk-Tolerance Questions (9)

Tone: probing, contextual, psychologically aware.

1. "Which stakeholders feel pressure to avoid mistakes at all costs?"

2. "Who is motivated by potential upside even when risk is present?"

3. "How does leadership typically react when results are uncertain?"

4. "Which individuals require detailed proof before moving forward?"

5. "Who encourages forward movement even when information is incomplete?"

6. "How does your organization balance speed versus certainty?"

7. "Which recent decisions revealed high or low risk tolerance?"

8. "What part of the process becomes tense when risk increases?"

9. "How do people justify their level of comfort or discomfort with risk?"

Aggressive Risk-Tolerance Questions (8)

Tone: direct, respectful, truth-exposing.

1. "Who is most afraid of making the wrong decision?"

2. "Which stakeholder slows progress out of fear rather than logic?"

3. "Who pushes for action even when it compromises stability?"

4. "Which past failure still makes the team overly cautious today?"

5. "Who resists bold ideas because it threatens their sense of control?"

6. "Which individual embraces risk because it increases their influence?"

7. "What risk is everyone avoiding discussing openly?"

8. "Who feels exposed if this decision goes wrong — and why?"

Follow-Up Risk-Tolerance Questions (10)

Tone: reflective, clarifying, steady.

1. "Can you describe a moment when the team showed clear discomfort with risk?"

2. "What behavior signaled that hesitation most clearly?"

3. "Which stakeholder's reaction changed the group's comfort level?"

4. "What detail from a past risky decision still affects people today?"

5. "How did the team respond once uncertainty became unavoidable?"

6. "What helped restore confidence during that situation?"

7. "Which aspects of risk feel manageable — and which feel overwhelming?"

8. "What does the team need to feel more secure moving forward?"

9. "How would this decision look if everyone were slightly more risk-tolerant?"

10. "How would it look if everyone were slightly more risk-averse?"

Conclusion

Risk-tolerance questions uncover the emotional and practical thresholds that shape how an organization makes decisions. They reveal which stakeholders fear uncertainty, who embraces it, and how past experiences influence the present. Without this insight, advisors risk pushing too hard or too gently — misaligning their approach with the buyer's true comfort zone.

Strategically, risk-tolerance awareness helps tailor the pace, framing, and structure of recommendations. Psychologically, it gives the buyer a deeper understanding of their team's fears, hopes, and limits, enabling them to navigate internal conversations with empathy and foresight.

The next sections in Chapter 3 will dive into decision sequencing, approval paths, and alignment barriers — all of which depend heavily on how risk is perceived and managed. Understanding risk tolerance lays the groundwork for predicting how decisions will actually unfold.

Reflection Prompt:
Think of a buyer who stalled because the environment felt "too uncertain." Which risk-tolerance question would have uncovered the source of that hesitation sooner?

CHAPTER 3 - SECTION 6 - Decision-Sequence Questions

Introduction

Even when the right people are involved and their motivations are understood, decisions rarely happen in a single moment. They unfold through a **sequence** — a series of steps that includes conversations, approvals, reviews, hesitations, clarifications, and internal checkpoints. Many advisors assume decisions move linearly, but in most organizations, decisions move in loops, cycles, and layered stages. Decision-sequence questions help you uncover the real pathway a decision follows, from spark to signature.

Strategically, understanding the decision sequence helps you anticipate timing, momentum, bottlenecks, and hidden dependencies. When the buyer knows which steps must occur and in what order, they can guide the initiative more confidently. This also prevents frustration — instead of expecting immediate movement, the buyer gains a realistic understanding of how their organization makes commitments and what triggers each step in the chain.

Psychologically, decision sequences are shaped by culture, power dynamics, and comfort with uncertainty. Some teams move quickly once a leader shows interest; others require consensus, documentation, and repeated review. Some environments delay decisions until emotional readiness aligns with operational clarity. These patterns are often intuitive to the buyer but unspoken, making them difficult to navigate without careful questioning.

Interpretation Tip: Pay attention to phrases like "usually," "typically," "first we need to…," "after that…," or "before anything else…" These indicate established patterns. Also look for hesitations when the buyer tries to recall steps — uncertainty often signals informal or politically sensitive stages.

Coaching Note: Encourage the buyer to describe the process without idealizing it. Many want to explain how decisions "should" be made rather than how they *actually* unfold. Remind them that clarity is power — knowing the real sequence helps prevent missteps and misunderstandings.

Example prompts:

- *"Walk me through the steps a decision goes through before it becomes final."*

- *"Who gets involved at each stage, and when?"*

Standard Decision-Sequence Questions (8)

Tone: calm, chronological, grounded.

1. "What is the first step your team takes when considering a new idea?"

2. "Who gets involved early in the decision process?"

3. "What typically happens after the initial discussion?"

4. "Which checkpoints or reviews are part of the normal sequence?"

5. "Who needs to give input before anything moves forward?"

6. "What happens between initial agreement and final approval?"

7. "How does the team confirm readiness before making a commitment?"

8. "What steps usually finalize the decision?"

Intermediate Decision-Sequence Questions (9)

Tone: probing, structure-focused, detailed.

1. "Which steps tend to take the longest in the decision process?"

2. "Who must be consulted informally before the official process begins?"

3. "What part of the sequence tends to create the most delays?"

4. "Which approvals depend on earlier conversations going well?"

5. "How does the team handle questions or concerns that arise mid-sequence?"

6. "When decisions stall, where in the sequence does it usually happen?"

7. "What triggers movement from one stage of the process to the next?"

8. "Which documents, reports, or insights are required at specific steps?"

9. "How does the team know when they've gathered enough information to proceed?"

Aggressive Decision-Sequence Questions (8)

Tone: direct, truth-focused, pattern-revealing.

1. "What step in the sequence slows everything down every time?"

2. "Who becomes the bottleneck during the approval process?"

3. "Which part of the process exists only because people are afraid to move too quickly?"

4. "What unofficial step shapes decisions more than any formal requirement?"

5. "Who has the power to pause or derail the sequence without saying 'no' directly?"

6. "Which stage exposes the most confusion or misalignment?"

7. "What step gets skipped when people feel pressured or overwhelmed?"

8. "Which part of the process adds little value but still delays progress?"

Follow-Up Decision-Sequence Questions (10)

Tone: reflective, clarifying, precision-oriented.

1. "Can you describe a recent decision and walk me through each stage?"

2. "What happened at the moment when momentum slowed?"

3. "How did the team respond during the more difficult steps?"

4. "What detail from the sequence became clearer in hindsight?"

5. "Which step required more alignment than expected?"

6. "What conversations occurred between stakeholders during key moments?"

7. "How did tension or pressure affect the sequence?"

8. "Which step required the most explanation or reassurance?"

9. "What would the ideal sequence look like if redesigned?"

10. "How would you know the sequence was becoming faster or smoother?"

Conclusion

Decision-sequence questions reveal the real mechanics behind how commitments form. They uncover the timing, dependencies, conversations, and checkpoints that shape whether an initiative moves forward or stalls. Many advisors focus solely on the "final yes," but the path to that yes is far more important — and far more complex.

Strategically, understanding the decision sequence prevents surprises. It helps you anticipate friction, prepare the right information at the right time, and support the buyer in guiding their internal process with confidence. Psychologically, these questions reduce frustration by transforming vague pathways into clear, navigable steps.

In the next sections, we will explore approval criteria, alignment barriers, timing pressures, and commitment signals — all of which build on the foundation created here. When an advisor understands the decision sequence, they gain the ability to navigate the organization's environment with precision and influence.

Reflection Prompt:
Think of a deal that moved slowly for reasons no one could explain at the time. Which decision-sequence question would have exposed the true cause earlier?

CHAPTER 3 - SECTION 7 - Approval-Criteria Questions

Introduction

Understanding the decision sequence reveals *how* decisions move through the organization, but approval-criteria questions reveal **what must be true** for a final "yes" to occur. Every organization has explicit requirements and implicit expectations that shape which initiatives get approved. These criteria may involve budget justification, strategic alignment, leadership confidence, risk assessment, timing, or emotional readiness. Without clarity on these conditions, even strong proposals struggle to gain approval.

Strategically, identifying approval criteria helps you design a recommendation that matches the organization's real standards. It prevents the advisor from presenting ideas that feel promising but fail to meet essential conditions. Clear criteria also help the buyer advocate internally — when they know what decision-makers require, they can position the initiative more effectively and anticipate what information needs to be prepared in advance.

Psychologically, approval criteria are often shaped by past disappointments, leadership preferences, or internal culture. Stakeholders may avoid stating these criteria directly because they feel political, sensitive, or overly strict. Some decision-makers rely on instinct more than process. Others rely on process more than instinct. Exploring these realities helps the buyer navigate approval conversations with confidence rather than guesswork.

Interpretation Tip: Listen closely when the buyer references phrases like "They'll need to see…," "Leadership usually wants…," "Finance always checks…," or "They won't move forward unless…" These statements reveal approval expectations that may not appear in any document or official process.

Coaching Note: Focus on clarity without pressure. The goal is not to force the buyer into rigid criteria but to help them articulate what matters most in their environment. Encourage them to separate essential requirements from preferences — this distinction often clarifies why some initiatives succeed and others stall.

Example prompts:

- *"What has leadership required before saying yes to similar initiatives?"*

- *"What elements must be in place for this to earn approval?"*

Standard Approval-Criteria Questions (8)

Tone: clear, structured, grounded.

1. "What factors matter most when leaders decide whether to approve an initiative?"

2. "What information does the team usually need before giving a final yes?"

3. "Which criteria are considered essential in your approval process?"

4. "What level of detail is expected in proposals or recommendations?"

5. "How does leadership determine whether something aligns with strategic goals?"

6. "What evidence or examples help strengthen approval conversations?"

7. "What conditions need to be met before funding or resources are allocated?"

8. "What makes leadership feel confident that an initiative is worth pursuing?"

Intermediate Approval-Criteria Questions (9)

Tone: probing, clarifying, insight-focused.

1. "Which stakeholders emphasize financial justification the most?"

2. "Who cares more about long-term alignment than short-term results?"

3. "What qualitative factors influence the final decision?"

4. "Which risks must be addressed before approval is possible?"

5. "What part of the plan typically requires the most justification?"

6. "What criteria have blocked past initiatives from moving forward?"

7. "Which aspects of an initiative receive the closest scrutiny?"

8. "How does leadership evaluate timing when considering approval?"

9. "What proof or validation has helped past initiatives gain approval quickly?"

Aggressive Approval-Criteria Questions (8)

Tone: direct, truth-seeking, respectful.

1. "What is the real reason leadership says no — even when the idea seems strong?"

2. "Which criterion is treated as non-negotiable, regardless of circumstances?"

3. "What part of your proposal would leadership reject immediately if not addressed?"

4. "Who demands the strictest justification before approving anything?"

5. "Which approval conditions are driven more by fear than by strategy?"

6. "What hidden criteria influence decisions behind closed doors?"

7. "Which requirement has nothing to do with logic yet shapes approval every time?"

8. "What would cause leadership to pull support even after showing initial interest?"

Follow-Up Approval-Criteria Questions (10)

Tone: reflective, clarifying, detail-oriented.

1. "Can you describe a recent initiative that met the criteria successfully?"

2. "What made leadership confident in that situation?"

3. "What part of the criteria created challenges during the approval process?"

4. "Which stakeholder insisted on specific details or proof?"

5. "How did the team respond when a requirement wasn't met?"

6. "What did you learn about approval expectations from that experience?"

7. "Which criteria felt more flexible, and which felt rigid?"

8. "What would help the next proposal meet these criteria more easily?"

9. "What detail did leadership focus on most when reviewing the idea?"

10. "How would you know that this initiative is fully prepared for approval?"

Conclusion

Approval-criteria questions bring clarity to the conditions that determine whether an initiative earns a final yes. Without understanding these criteria, advisors and buyers make assumptions that lead to frustration, misalignment, and stalled progress. With clarity, however, the decision environment becomes predictable — and the pathway to approval becomes much easier to navigate.

Strategically, approval criteria help you shape recommendations that resonate with leadership expectations. Psychologically, they give the buyer confidence that they understand what truly matters in internal conversations. Approval becomes less mysterious and more manageable.

As Chapter 3 continues, upcoming sections will explore alignment challenges, decision timing, political dynamics, and commitment signals. Understanding approval criteria sets the stage for all of these — because it defines the standards against which every idea will be measured.

Reflection Prompt:

Think of a project that failed not because it was weak, but because it didn't meet hidden expectations. Which approval-criteria question would have revealed that earlier?

CHAPTER 3 - SECTION 8 - Alignment-Barrier Questions

Introduction

Even when the right stakeholders are identified, their motivations are understood, objections are anticipated, and approval criteria are clear, initiatives can still stall due to **alignment barriers**. These are the hidden points of friction that prevent stakeholders from moving together in a unified direction. Alignment barriers may arise from communication gaps, historical tension, conflicting priorities, workload pressures, or simple misunderstandings. Alignment-barrier questions help the buyer uncover what stands in the way of collective agreement, even when everyone seems to want progress.

Strategically, alignment barriers are often the true cause of sluggish decision-making. They reveal why meetings feel productive but nothing changes afterward, why one stakeholder always hesitates, or why teams nod in agreement but act inconsistently. By identifying the specific blockers, you make it possible to address them proactively — clearing the path for faster, coordinated action.

Psychologically, alignment barriers often carry emotional weight. Some stakeholders may fear conflict and avoid voicing concerns. Others may feel unheard, leading to silent resistance. Some may prioritize their own team's workload over organizational goals. These dynamics rarely appear in surface-level conversations. Alignment-barrier questions help the buyer see the interpersonal realities beneath the formal structures.

Interpretation Tip: Listen for signs of tension or avoidance when the buyer describes certain individuals or departments. Hesitation, softened language, or references to "mixed feelings," "different priorities," or "not on the same page" point directly to alignment barriers. Pay attention to whether the buyer describes resistance as passive ("nothing happened") or active ("they pushed back") — each reveals a different type of barrier.

Coaching Note: Approach these questions gently. Alignment issues often touch on sensitive relationships. Encourage the buyer to describe patterns rather than assign blame. The goal is clarity, not criticism. When handled with care, these conversations help the buyer understand where alignment must be strengthened for progress to occur.

Example prompts:

- *"Where do stakeholders tend to fall out of sync?"*

- *"What makes it hard for people to agree or move forward together?"*

Standard Alignment-Barrier Questions (8)

Tone: calm, clear, exploratory.

1. "Which stakeholders tend to see this issue differently?"

2. "Where do perspectives begin to diverge during discussions?"

3. "What parts of the conversation usually create tension or confusion?"

4. "Who tends to move faster than others feel comfortable with?"

5. "What priorities compete with this initiative?"

6. "Which teams or departments have different expectations?"

7. "What makes alignment difficult even when everyone agrees on the goal?"

8. "What information is missing that keeps people from aligning?"

Intermediate Alignment-Barrier Questions (9)

Tone: probing, clarifying, pattern-finding.

1. "Which stakeholders struggle to agree on the problem itself?"

2. "What assumptions differ across the group?"

3. "Which responsibilities or workloads create friction?"

4. "What part of the plan raises concerns that others dismiss too quickly?"

5. "Which alignment issues come from past experiences, not the current situation?"

6. "Who needs more clarity before they feel comfortable aligning?"

7. "What communication gaps create unnecessary disagreement?"

8. "Which priorities conflict with this initiative's timing or requirements?"

9. "What pattern of misalignment has repeated across past efforts?"

Aggressive Alignment-Barrier Questions (8)

Tone: direct, honest, truth-focused.

1. "Who consistently slows alignment due to hidden resistance?"

2. "Which stakeholder says they support the initiative but acts differently?"

3. "Who holds a conflicting agenda that prevents full alignment?"

4. "Which interpersonal tension undermines group unity?"

5. "What unspoken disagreement is shaping stakeholder behavior?"

6. "Who wants influence over the outcome but avoids taking responsibility?"

7. "Which department's priorities block alignment most often?"

8. "What internal tension no one is willing to name but everyone feels?"

Follow-Up Alignment-Barrier Questions (10)

Tone: reflective, stabilizing, clarifying.

1. "Can you describe a recent moment when alignment suddenly weakened?"

2. "What triggered the change in stakeholder energy or agreement?"

3. "Which detail revealed the misalignment most clearly?"

4. "How did different stakeholders react when tension appeared?"

5. "What conversations happened afterward to restore alignment?"

6. "What part of the plan felt the most sensitive or divisive?"

7. "What information would have prevented the alignment issue?"

8. "What insight did you gain about the group from that moment?"

9. "How has misalignment affected timing or momentum in the past?"

10. "What signs would show that alignment is strengthening now?"

Conclusion

Alignment-barrier questions expose the friction that prevents stakeholders from acting in unison. They reveal where priorities diverge, where communication breaks down, and where hidden concerns block progress. Without identifying these barriers, even the most well-designed solution will struggle to move forward — because alignment is the engine that drives organizational commitment.

Strategically, these insights help the advisor and buyer create messaging, sequencing, and support structures that unify stakeholders. Psychologically, they help the buyer navigate sensitive interpersonal dynamics with greater awareness and empathy. When alignment barriers are visible, they become fixable.

As Chapter 3 continues, the next sections will explore decision timing, internal pressure cycles, political dynamics, and signals of true commitment. Alignment is the bridge between understanding stakeholders and guiding them toward decisive action.

Reflection Prompt:
Think of a deal where everyone "agreed" in the meeting but nothing happened afterward. Which alignment-barrier question would have revealed the real issue?

CHAPTER 3 - SECTION 9 - Timing-Pressure Questions

Introduction

Even when stakeholders are aligned and approval criteria are clear, the **timing** of a decision can dramatically influence whether an initiative moves forward. Organizations operate within cycles — planning seasons, budget windows, performance reviews, peak workload periods, and leadership transitions. These cycles create timing pressures that shape when decisions are welcomed, delayed, or avoided entirely. Timing-pressure questions help uncover the rhythms, constraints, and external forces that influence when stakeholders feel ready — or unready — to take action.

Strategically, understanding timing pressure allows you to position recommendations in a way that matches the organization's natural flow. You avoid pushing when the environment is overwhelmed and instead guide the buyer toward windows where decision-making is easier, faster, and more productive. Advisors who ignore timing often misinterpret hesitation as lack of interest, when in reality, the organization simply isn't in a position to act yet.

Psychologically, timing pressure creates invisible emotional strain. When workload rises or uncertainty increases, people become more cautious, less open to change, and more sensitive to perceived risk. During stable or energetic periods, stakeholders feel more confident and willing to explore new approaches. Timing-pressure questions help the buyer see these emotional cycles clearly, allowing them to navigate decisions without frustration or unrealistic expectations.

Interpretation Tip: Listen for references to deadlines, quarters, seasons, staffing cycles, major events, or "busy periods." These indicate timing constraints. Also notice when the buyer says "not right now," "after this," or "once we get through…" — these phrases reveal patterns of cyclical pressure.

Coaching Note: Encourage a balanced perspective. Timing is neither an excuse nor an obstacle — it is a variable to understand. Help the buyer see where timing creates opportunity and where it creates limitation. When they understand the rhythm, they can plan conversations more strategically.

Example prompts:

- *"What timing factors influence how quickly decisions move?"*

- *"When does your organization feel most open to new initiatives?"*

Standard Timing-Pressure Questions (8)

Tone: calm, chronological, practical.

1. "Which periods of the year make decision-making easier or harder?"

2. "What busy cycles tend to slow momentum?"

3. "When does your team typically review new initiatives?"

4. "What deadlines or seasons shape the timing of decisions?"

5. "Which times of year bring more pressure or uncertainty?"

6. "How does workload affect your team's ability to focus on new ideas?"

7. "When do people feel most able to consider change?"

8. "What timing constraints should be considered for this effort?"

Intermediate Timing-Pressure Questions (9)

Tone: probing, pattern-focused, context-aware.

1. "Which stakeholders experience the highest pressure at certain times?"

2. "What internal events influence when decisions are made?"

3. "Which external factors affect decision timing?"

4. "How do budget cycles shape when approvals are likely?"

5. "Which recurring deadlines impact the team's openness to new ideas?"

6. "What timing-related patterns have delayed past initiatives?"

7. "How do seasonal or quarterly targets affect decision energy?"

8. "What timing pressures create the most hesitation?"

9. "Which time-related factors could accelerate a decision?"

Aggressive Timing-Pressure Questions (8)

Tone: direct, truth-seeking, clear.

1. "What timing issue will kill this initiative if not addressed now?"

2. "Which stakeholder hides behind timing pressure to avoid making a decision?"

3. "What time window is far smaller than people realize?"

4. "Who is pushing this decision too fast for their own benefit?"

5. "Which upcoming event will make action significantly harder?"

6. "What timing excuse is used repeatedly to avoid commitment?"

7. "Who loses influence if this decision is delayed?"

8. "What timing risk no one wants to acknowledge?"

Follow-Up Timing-Pressure Questions (10)

Tone: reflective, clarifying, steady.

1. "Can you describe a recent decision that was delayed due to timing?"

2. "What sign made it clear the timing wasn't right?"

3. "How did stakeholders respond once the delay became unavoidable?"

4. "What detail from that situation still shapes timing decisions now?"

5. "What timing factors created the most stress for the team?"

6. "What helped the group regain momentum afterward?"

7. "Which timing pressures were predictable — and which were unexpected?"

8. "What would need to change to make timing less restrictive?"

9. "What timing patterns do you expect to repeat this year?"

10. "How would you know the timing is now more favorable for action?"

Conclusion

Timing-pressure questions uncover the rhythms that shape decision-making within an organization. They reveal when stakeholders feel overloaded, when energy is high or low, and when the environment supports — or resists — new initiatives. Without understanding timing, advisors risk misreading hesitation and misaligning efforts with the organization's natural flow.

Strategically, these insights help position recommendations during windows of openness and avoid periods of strain. Psychologically, they give the buyer clarity about why movement slows and how to plan conversations without feeling discouraged. Timing isn't just a variable — it's a force that shapes momentum.

As Chapter 3 moves forward, the next sections will explore internal politics, commitment signals, and how decisions solidify once timing aligns. Understanding timing pressure creates a foundation for navigating these deeper dynamics with confidence and foresight.

Reflection Prompt:
Think of a deal that would have closed if timing had been better. Which timing-pressure question would have revealed the issue earlier?

CHAPTER 3 - SECTION 10 - Commitment-Signal Questions

Introduction

After exploring stakeholders, motivations, influence patterns, objections, risk tolerance, decision sequencing, approval criteria, alignment barriers, and timing pressure, the final element of the decision environment is understanding **commitment signals** — the behaviors, statements, actions, and decisions that reveal when a stakeholder is truly ready to move forward. Commitment is rarely expressed directly. Instead, it appears gradually through subtle shifts in energy, behavior, clarity, and engagement. Commitment-signal questions help the buyer identify these signs and distinguish between curiosity, consideration, and genuine readiness.

Strategically, recognizing commitment signals allows the advisor to guide the process with precision. When commitment increases, next steps become easier, objections soften, and conversations become more forward-looking. When commitment is missing, pushing too aggressively creates resistance or erodes trust. Understanding these signals helps prevent false positives — situations where a buyer seems supportive but is actually unprepared to take action.

Psychologically, commitment grows when confidence increases and fear decreases. Stakeholders begin asking deeper questions, request clarity, involve additional decision-makers, or explore logistics. These behaviors show that they are mentally and emotionally moving toward a decision. Lack of commitment appears as hesitations, vague language, or delay behaviors. Commitment-signal questions teach the buyer to interpret these cues accurately, reducing confusion and frustration.

Interpretation Tip: Pay close attention to the verbs stakeholders use — "should," "could," "might," versus "need to," "will," or "let's." Word choice often reveals commitment level. Also listen for increased specificity; committed stakeholders move from generalities to details like timing, budget, and implementation.

Coaching Note: Encourage the buyer to view commitment as a spectrum rather than a binary yes/no state. This reduces pressure and allows them to guide stakeholders confidently from early interest into full readiness. Your questions should help them notice patterns and make informed decisions about when to advance the conversation.

Example prompts:

- *"What signals tell you someone is genuinely ready to move forward?"*

- *"How do you know when commitment is increasing or fading?"*

Standard Commitment-Signal Questions (8)

Tone: calm, observational, grounded.

1. "What signs show you that a stakeholder is becoming more engaged?"

2. "How do people usually express interest in moving forward?"

3. "What behaviors indicate they're taking the idea more seriously?"

4. "Which questions signal curiosity versus true commitment?"

5. "How do stakeholders act when they feel confident about next steps?"

6. "What changes in tone or energy show growing commitment?"

7. "What details do people ask about when they're close to deciding?"

8. "How do you know when a stakeholder is still undecided?"

Intermediate Commitment-Signal Questions (9)

Tone: probing, clarifying, insight-driven.

1. "What specific behaviors indicate that someone is ready to take action?"

2. "Which stakeholders start involving others once commitment grows?"

3. "How does the conversation change when people move from interest to intent?"

4. "What signals show that a stakeholder is imagining implementation?"

5. "Which steps do people take when they feel ready for real progress?"

6. "What questions reveal that someone is preparing to make a decision?"

7. "Which stakeholders request timelines or logistics when commitment rises?"

8. "How does reduced hesitation show up in their communication?"

9. "What signals reveal fading commitment before it becomes obvious?"

Aggressive Commitment-Signal Questions (8)

Tone: direct, revealing, truth-focused.

1. "Who talks about action but never follows through — what signal exposes that?"

2. "Which stakeholder gives false commitment signals to avoid saying no?"

3. "Who backs away once next steps require real responsibility?"

4. "What behavior shows the difference between real intent and polite interest?"

5. "Which stakeholder signals commitment only when others are watching?"

6. "What action would prove someone is genuinely ready right now?"

7. "Which signals mean commitment is weak, even if their words sound supportive?"

8. "What behavior clearly shows a stakeholder has moved into true decision mode?"

Follow-Up Commitment-Signal Questions (10)

Tone: reflective, clarifying, perceptive.

1. "Can you describe a moment when a stakeholder's behavior revealed true commitment?"

2. "What detail signaled that shift most clearly?"

3. "How did their communication change once they became serious?"

4. "What did they ask or request that showed readiness?"

5. "What behavior helped you realize they were imagining the outcome?"

6. "Which signal surprised you when you noticed it later?"

7. "What conversation revealed growing certainty or confidence?"

8. "Which action or request showed they needed fewer reassurances?"

9. "What signs would help you catch fading commitment earlier next time?"

10. "How do you personally distinguish between interest and real intent?"

Conclusion

Commitment-signal questions reveal the moment when a conversation transforms from exploration to action. They help the buyer recognize readiness, avoid false assumptions, and guide stakeholders through the final steps of the decision process with accuracy and care.

Strategically, these insights enable better pacing, more precise next steps, and a clearer understanding of when to advance conversations. Psychologically, they help the buyer interpret subtle cues, reducing uncertainty and preventing frustration. Instead of guessing, they gain the ability to read commitment with confidence.

This section completes Chapter 3's exploration of the decision environment. Together, these insights give the advisor a powerful understanding of the human, emotional, political, and practical dynamics that shape whether — and how — decisions are made.

Reflection Prompt:
Think of a time when a stakeholder gave mixed signals. Which commitment-signal question would have clarified their real intent?

Chapter Conclusion

Chapter 3 reveals that decisions are not made in isolation — they are shaped by a web of stakeholders, motivations, tensions, and timing pressures. By mapping this environment, you gain insight into the emotional and structural forces that determine whether progress is possible. Understanding these dynamics prevents surprises and reduces the friction that often derails change.

Strategically, this chapter equips you to predict challenges before they arise. You learn who influences decisions informally, who hesitates under pressure, and what approval criteria shape the final outcome. Psychologically, the chapter helps you interpret behavior more accurately, allowing you to respond with empathy rather than assumption. When you understand how commitment forms and how alignment dissolves, you become a more effective guide for the buyer.

As the book moves forward, later chapters will build on this foundation by exploring needs, value, solution fit, and strategic change. Because you now understand the environment in which decisions are made, you can navigate upcoming conversations with clarity, precision, and confidence. Chapter 3 gives you the map — the chapters ahead show you how to travel it.

CHAPTER 4 - Revealing Operational Realities

Chapter Introduction

Every organization has an operational reality — a day-to-day rhythm filled with routines, expectations, shortcuts, frustrations, and hidden pressures. Yet most buyers describe these realities in vague terms: "We're stretched thin," "Things could run smoother," or "We're doing our best with what we have." These descriptions capture emotion, but they lack the clarity needed to create meaningful change. Chapter 4 brings the operational world into focus by examining it from the inside out, layer by layer, until the true structure of daily work becomes unmistakably clear.

The chapter begins with **Current-State Mapping Questions**, which anchor the conversation in what is happening right now — not assumptions, not hopes, not idealized versions, but the concrete reality of daily operations. Once that foundation is laid, **Constraint-Identification Questions** reveal what limits the team's ability to move forward. These constraints define the boundaries within which performance must operate and the edges that any solution must respect.

Next, the chapter examines the emotional and practical strain created by **Workload Pressure**. Workload affects how people think, communicate, and prioritize. It influences their openness to change and their capacity for improvement. From there, **Resourcing-Gap Questions** expose the missing tools, capabilities, support, or personnel that make current expectations harder than they appear — gaps that often go unnoticed because teams adapt quietly and heroically.

The chapter then explores the friction created by **Prioritization Conflicts**, where competing demands shape decisions more than strategy does. These conflicts reveal how intentions often lose to urgency. **Process-Inefficiency Questions** uncover the structural slowdowns that erode performance one small step at a time. Each inefficiency becomes a signal of how the system has evolved and where it is silently draining energy.

From there, the conversation shifts to **Dependency Chains**, the interconnected steps that determine how work moves from one person or function to another. Dependencies create both structure and fragility. When they fail, the entire workflow absorbs the impact. **Breakdown-Pattern Questions** bring attention to the failures that repeat — the moments when systems collapse in predictable ways. These patterns expose the deeper structural weaknesses that cannot be ignored.

Finally, the chapter closes with **Operational Risk** and **Performance-Threshold Questions**, which reveal vulnerabilities and limits. These insights help leaders understand not only when things break but why they break — and what happens when demand exceeds capacity. By naming these thresholds, the buyer gains a clearer sense of how much pressure the system can realistically handle.

Chapter 4 gives the advisor and buyer a complete, unfiltered picture of how the organization functions today. It surfaces the obstacles, limits, tensions, and vulnerabilities that shape performance. More importantly, it transforms operational challenges from frustrations into data — practical, actionable information that sets the stage for meaningful improvement in the chapters ahead.

CHAPTER 4 - SECTION 1 - Current-State Mapping Questions

Introduction

Before any organization can make meaningful progress, it must understand its current state with clarity rather than assumption. Buyers often describe their situation in broad terms — "it's messy," "we're behind," "we're stretched thin," or "things aren't working." These statements feel true, but they aren't precise enough to build solutions on. Current-state mapping questions bring structure to that uncertainty by helping the buyer articulate what the environment actually looks like today.

Strategically, mapping the current state prevents you from building solutions on incomplete or inaccurate understanding. These questions expose the real conditions inside workflows, communication patterns, resource allocation, and day-to-day operations. They reveal the difference between how the organization thinks it operates and how it actually operates. This clarity allows the advisor to identify gaps, constraints, and opportunities with accuracy instead of assumptions.

Psychologically, current-state conversations can feel vulnerable. When buyers talk about their current struggles, they often worry about judgment, blame, or appearing disorganized. Your role is to create an atmosphere of acceptance. Remind them that clarity is valuable — not something to fear. When the buyer feels safe describing their present reality, they are more willing to explore what needs to change.

Interpretation Tip: Listen for inconsistencies between what the buyer *wants* the current state to be and what it *actually* is. When a buyer says, "We're doing okay, but…" or "We should be fine, except…" pay attention to what follows — these statements often point directly to hidden friction points.

Coaching Note: Guide the buyer toward specificity. Instead of accepting generalities, help them describe concrete examples, numbers, routines, and patterns. The more precise the picture, the more meaningful the future solutions will become.

Example prompts:

- *"Help me understand what a typical day looks like for your team."*

- *"What's happening now that makes improvement feel necessary?"*

Standard Current-State Mapping Questions (8)

Tone: calm, open, descriptive.

1. "How would you describe your current situation in practical terms?"

2. "What does a normal day look like for your team?"

3. "What is working well in your process right now?"

4. "What's creating the most friction or delay today?"

5. "Where does your workflow feel smooth — and where does it feel strained?"

6. "Who is most affected by the current challenges?"

7. "What responsibilities take up the most time or energy?"

8. "What recent changes have shaped your current environment?"

Intermediate Current-State Mapping Questions (9)

Tone: probing, detail-oriented, structural.

1. "Which steps in your current workflow feel essential yet inefficient?"

2. "Where do current processes break down most often?"

3. "How consistent is performance across different team members or functions?"

4. "Which tasks require the most manual effort or workaround?"

5. "What gaps exist between your expectations and current results?"

6. "Where does communication feel unclear or incomplete?"

7. "Which responsibilities lack clear ownership today?"

8. "What situations create predictable slowdowns or bottlenecks?"

9. "How does the current state compare to where you expected to be by now?"

Aggressive Current-State Mapping Questions (8)

Tone: direct, honest, precise.

1. "What part of your current operation is visibly failing?"

2. "Which process is outdated but still being used out of habit?"

3. "Where is the team losing the most time or money today?"

4. "Which responsibilities fall through the cracks because no one owns them?"

5. "What current behavior is hurting performance the most?"

6. "Who is overwhelmed in a way leadership hasn't acknowledged?"

7. "What problem has become so normal that people stopped noticing it?"

8. "Where is the gap between expectation and reality widest right now?"

Follow-Up Current-State Mapping Questions (10)

Tone: clarifying, reflective, supportive.

1. "Can you share an example that illustrates what you just described?"

2. "When did you first notice this part of the process becoming strained?"

3. "What happens on days when the issue feels most noticeable?"

4. "How does the team work around this challenge when it appears?"

5. "What reaction did you observe from stakeholders when this issue surfaced?"

6. "What detail about the current state stands out most to you now?"

7. "Which part of the current process feels most unpredictable?"

8. "How has the current state changed over the past few months?"

9. "What would help you understand the situation more clearly?"

10. "What signal would tell you that the current state is improving?"

Conclusion

Current-state mapping questions transform vague frustration into a structured picture of reality. They help the buyer understand what is happening, where friction lives, and how people experience their daily environment. This clarity becomes the foundation for every future decision — because without understanding the present, it is impossible to design an effective path forward.

Strategically, these questions reveal the gap between expectation and reality, uncover inefficiencies, and identify hidden complexities. Psychologically, they help the buyer replace uncertainty with awareness. When people feel seen and understood in their current struggles, they become more open to exploring the next step.

This section sets the stage for the rest of Chapter 4, where we will examine constraints, resourcing, prioritization, and operational pressure in deeper detail. Understanding the current state is the first layer of operational truth — the layers ahead will uncover why the current state exists and how it can be improved.

Reflection Prompt:
Think of a buyer who described their situation vaguely or inconsistently. Which current-state mapping question would have helped clarify their reality faster?

CHAPTER 4 - SECTION 2 - Constraint-Identification Questions

Introduction

Once the current state is clearly mapped, the next layer of operational insight involves understanding the **constraints** that shape the environment. Constraints are the limits, boundaries, and pressures that restrict what an organization can do today. They might be structural (tools, processes, bandwidth), human (skills, energy, experience), environmental (timing, workload, external demands), or emotional (confidence, fear, hesitation). Constraint-identification questions help the buyer articulate these limitations so you can see what is possible, what isn't, and what will need to change for progress to occur.

Strategically, constraints are not obstacles to avoid — they are design parameters. They define the edges within which any realistic solution must operate. By identifying constraints early, you avoid recommending strategies that cannot be implemented or supported in the real world. Instead, you work with the buyer to build solutions that fit their actual capacity, not their ideal capacity.

Psychologically, talking about constraints can feel uncomfortable for buyers. Some worry it will make their team look weak. Others fear acknowledging limits because it forces them to face the gap between what they want and what they can currently support. Your role is to normalize this conversation. Every organization has constraints. Understanding them is a sign of strength, not failure.

Interpretation Tip: Listen for words like "can't," "don't have," "not enough," "too much," "limited," "stretched," or "overloaded." These words reveal constraints even when the buyer is trying not to emphasize them. Also notice when the buyer pauses or hesitates — constraints often live in the details they avoid mentioning first.

Coaching Note: Help the buyer see constraints as data, not judgment. Encourage honesty and specificity. When the buyer feels safe naming what limits them, they gain the clarity needed to move forward intentionally and confidently.

Example prompts:

- *"What limits your ability to change this today?"*

- *"Where do constraints show up most clearly in your current operations?"*

Standard Constraint-Identification Questions (8)

Tone: calm, neutral, clarifying.

1. "What limits your team's ability to improve this area right now?"

2. "Where does capacity feel stretched the most?"

3. "What resources do you wish you had more of?"

4. "Which responsibilities take priority over this effort?"

5. "What part of your workflow feels restricted or overloaded?"

6. "Which tasks or processes feel constrained by time or bandwidth?"

7. "What current limitations are slowing progress?"

8. "Where do you feel the most pressure in your operations?"

Intermediate Constraint-Identification Questions (9)

Tone: probing, structured, insight-oriented.

1. "Which constraints come from external factors rather than internal ones?"

2. "What parts of the process depend on a person or tool that's already overwhelmed?"

3. "Which responsibilities pull your team away from improvement work?"

4. "What skills or capabilities feel insufficient for your current needs?"

5. "What assumptions about capacity shape what you believe is possible?"

6. "Which steps rely on resources that are inconsistent or unreliable?"

7. "What constraints get overlooked because they've become normal?"

8. "Which limitations create the most tension between teams?"

9. "What constraints would become urgent if demand increased suddenly?"

Aggressive Constraint-Identification Questions (8)

Tone: direct, honest, boundary-exposing.

1. "What part of your operation is completely maxed out?"

2. "Which team or individual simply cannot take on more work?"

3. "What resources are so limited that they are restricting growth?"

4. "Which outdated process is creating the harshest constraint?"

5. "Where do you lack the capability to meet your current expectations?"

6. "What constraint is everyone aware of but no one addresses?"

7. "Which limitation has become a convenient excuse instead of a real barrier?"

8. "What constraint will break first if pressure increases?"

Follow-Up Constraint-Identification Questions (10)

Tone: thoughtful, reflective, clarifying.

1. "Can you describe a specific moment when this constraint became evident?"

2. "How does this limitation affect daily workflow or performance?"

3. "What workarounds does the team use when this constraint appears?"

4. "How does the constraint impact customers or stakeholders?"

5. "What has been tried to reduce this constraint, and what happened?"

6. "How long has this limitation been influencing your operations?"

7. "Which parts of the organization feel the constraint most intensely?"

8. "What would happen if this constraint worsened?"

9. "What small change could ease this limitation temporarily?"

10. "What long-term change could reduce or remove this constraint entirely?"

Conclusion

Constraint-identification questions reveal the boundaries within which the organization must operate. They show where capacity is stretched, where resources are lacking, and where processes are incapable of supporting current demands. These insights create a clearer picture of what is possible and what will require structural change.

Strategically, understanding constraints helps the advisor design realistic solutions that respect operational limits while still moving the organization forward. Psychologically, this section helps the buyer release shame or frustration around their limitations and instead embrace clarity as a strength.

As Chapter 4 continues, the next sections will dive deeper into workload patterns, resourcing gaps, prioritization conflicts, and internal pressure cycles. Constraints are the foundation — once they're understood, the rest of the operational landscape becomes far easier to navigate.

Reflection Prompt:
Think of a time when a buyer wanted progress but simply didn't have the capacity. Which constraint-identification question would have uncovered that truth sooner?

CHAPTER 4 - SECTION 3 - Workload-Pressure Questions

Introduction

Once constraints are identified, the next operational layer involves understanding **workload pressure** — the emotional and practical strain created by the volume, pace, and unpredictability of daily work. Workload pressure doesn't just influence how people feel; it shapes how they think, decide, communicate, and prioritize. When pressure is high, stakeholders become more cautious, less flexible, and more reactive. When pressure is moderate or low, they are more open, creative, and willing to explore change. Workload-pressure questions reveal these invisible forces so you can understand how they shape behavior inside the organization.

Strategically, identifying workload pressure helps you see why certain initiatives stall or why teams struggle to engage with new ideas. It explains why people may agree in meetings but fail to follow through — not because of lack of interest, but because their bandwidth is depleted. These questions help you understand the conditions under which stakeholders can absorb change and when they simply can't.

Psychologically, workload pressure affects energy levels, emotional resilience, and attention span. When people feel overloaded, they avoid complexity, resist change, and gravitate toward familiar routines. When pressure lifts, the same people may suddenly become engaged and forward-thinking. By understanding these cycles, you help the buyer interpret team behavior with empathy instead of frustration.

Interpretation Tip: Listen for signs of exhaustion disguised as practicality — phrases like "we're fine," "we'll manage," or "it's just busy right now" often indicate deeper strain. Notice when the buyer pauses before answering workload questions; this often reveals internal conflict between wanting improvement and fearing overload.

Coaching Note: Normalize the conversation. Many leaders hesitate to discuss workload pressure because they fear it reflects poorly on their management. Reassure them that pressure is a natural part of any operation — and understanding it is the first step toward sustainable improvement.

Example prompts:

- *"How stretched does your team feel right now?"*

- *"Where does workload pressure affect performance the most?"*

Standard Workload-Pressure Questions (8)

Tone: calm, practical, empathetic.

1. "How would you describe your team's current workload?"

2. "Where does the team feel the most pressure day to day?"

3. "Which tasks create the most stress or urgency?"

4. "What part of the workload feels hardest to keep up with?"

5. "Who is carrying more than their fair share right now?"

6. "What recent changes have increased workload strain?"

7. "Where does the team feel rushed or behind?"

8. "What work consistently piles up faster than it can be completed?"

Intermediate Workload-Pressure Questions (9)

Tone: probing, clarifying, pattern-aware.

1. "Which responsibilities increase pressure during peak periods?"

2. "What tasks consistently get postponed because of workload?"

3. "How does high workload affect communication or collaboration?"

4. "Which roles experience the most sudden spikes in pressure?"

5. "What triggers workload stress most predictably?"

6. "What part of the workload requires constant multitasking?"

7. "How does workload pressure influence decision-making speed?"

8. "Which tasks create emotional strain beyond the practical effort involved?"

9. "What patterns of overload have repeated throughout the year?"

Aggressive Workload-Pressure Questions (8)

Tone: direct, truth-seeking, pressure-exposing.

1. "Who is burned out but hiding it?"

2. "Which tasks are overwhelming the team the most?"

3. "What workload problem is leadership underestimating?"

4. "Which responsibilities are unsustainable at current levels?"

5. "Where is workload pressure causing noticeable performance decline?"

6. "What critical task is consistently rushed because there's no time?"

7. "Who is close to disengaging due to workload strain?"

8. "What part of the workload would fail first during a surge in demand?"

Follow-Up Workload-Pressure Questions (10)

Tone: reflective, empathetic, grounding.

1. "Can you describe a recent moment when workload pressure peaked?"

2. "What signs showed that the team was overwhelmed?"

3. "How did people respond emotionally during that time?"

4. "What did the team stop doing because pressure became too high?"

5. "How long does it take for the team to recover after heavy workload periods?"

6. "What changes have helped reduce pressure, even temporarily?"

7. "What issue becomes more visible when workload rises?"

8. "How does workload pressure affect your ability to lead effectively?"

9. "What would make workload more manageable for the team?"

10. "What signal would show you that workload pressure is easing?"

Conclusion

Workload-pressure questions uncover the emotional and operational weight carried by the team. They reveal how strain affects performance, decision-making, communication, and readiness for change. Without understanding workload pressure, advisors risk recommending solutions that add burden rather than relieve it.

Strategically, these questions show where capacity is limited, where pressure spikes occur, and where sustainable improvement must begin. Psychologically, they help the buyer see their team more compassionately, understanding that resistance often reflects fatigue rather than unwillingness.

As Chapter 4 continues, the next sections will explore resourcing gaps, prioritization conflicts, process inefficiencies, and operational risks — all of which connect directly to workload. When workload pressure is understood clearly, the rest of the operational puzzle becomes far easier to interpret.

Reflection Prompt:
Think of a team that struggled to implement a change even though they agreed it was important. Which workload-pressure question would have revealed why?

CHAPTER 4 - SECTION 4 - Resourcing-Gap Questions

Introduction

After examining workload pressure, the next layer of operational truth involves identifying **resourcing gaps** — the missing people, skills, tools, capacity, or support structures that prevent the organization from performing at its full potential. These gaps are often the quiet root cause behind frustration, inefficiency, and stalled progress. Buyers often assume their teams "should" be able to handle everything, even when the resources simply don't exist. Resourcing-gap questions bring these realities into focus.

Strategically, resourcing gaps define the difference between what the organization *wants* to do and what it is *equipped* to do. Without this clarity, leaders tend to overextend teams, create unrealistic expectations, or misinterpret operational breakdowns as performance issues rather than capacity issues. Identifying these gaps early helps shape practical strategies that match real capability, not imagined capability.

Psychologically, resourcing gaps carry emotional weight. Leaders may feel guilty for not providing enough support or embarrassed to admit limitations. Team members may feel hesitant to voice their needs for fear of appearing incapable. Your role is to create a safe space for honest exploration. When resourcing gaps are acknowledged without judgment, organizations gain a clearer path to sustainable improvement.

Interpretation Tip: Listen for statements like "We make do," "We figure it out," "We patch things together," or "We're doing our best with what we have." These are polite disguises for deeper resourcing issues. Also notice when the buyer describes individuals who are "stretched," "holding everything together," or "wearing too many hats" — these are signals of hidden gaps.

Coaching Note: Encourage the buyer to view resourcing gaps as information, not failure. Gaps exist in every organization. Understanding them is an advantage because it illuminates where investment, support, or restructuring can create meaningful change.

Example prompts:

- *"Where do you feel under-resourced compared to your goals?"*

- *"Which capabilities or tools would make the biggest difference today?"*

Standard Resourcing-Gap Questions (8)

Tone: calm, open, factual.

1. "Where do you feel the team is lacking the resources it needs?"

2. "Which responsibilities require more support than you currently have?"

3. "What skills or capabilities feel limited within the team today?"

4. "Where does the team rely too heavily on one or two individuals?"

5. "What tools or systems do you wish were stronger or more reliable?"

6. "Which roles feel understaffed for the workload they carry?"

7. "What tasks take longer because the right resources aren't available?"

8. "Where does the team spend time compensating for missing support?"

Intermediate Resourcing-Gap Questions (9)

Tone: probing, structural, insight-driven.

1. "Which gaps create delays or inconsistencies in performance?"

2. "What expertise is needed but not currently present on the team?"

3. "Which resourcing issues become more obvious during busy periods?"

4. "What responsibilities are being handled by people who aren't trained for them?"

5. "Which outdated tools create unnecessary friction or rework?"

6. "What critical tasks depend on limited or unreliable resources?"

7. "Where do resourcing gaps create risk if someone is absent?"

8. "Which parts of the process would improve immediately with more support?"

9. "What resourcing assumptions no longer reflect your current reality?"

Aggressive Resourcing-Gap Questions (8)

Tone: direct, truth-revealing, respectful.

1. "What role or capability is completely missing from your operation?"

2. "Which team is operating at unsafe or unsustainable resource levels?"

3. "Who is performing tasks they should never have to own?"

4. "What tool or system is so outdated that it creates daily failure points?"

5. "Where is the organization ignoring an obvious resourcing need?"

6. "Which gap is costing you the most time or money right now?"

7. "What capability is essential—but simply not present—in your current structure?"

8. "Which resourcing issue would cause immediate chaos if pressure increased?"

Follow-Up Resourcing-Gap Questions (10)

Tone: reflective, clarifying, supportive.

1. "Can you describe a recent moment when a resourcing gap became painfully clear?"

2. "What workaround did the team use to compensate for the missing resource?"

3. "How did the gap affect performance, morale, or timing?"

4. "What pattern shows that this gap has been present for a long time?"

5. "Which team members feel this gap most intensely?"

6. "What small improvement would help ease the gap right away?"

7. "What long-term change would eliminate this gap entirely?"

8. "How does this gap affect your ability to plan or forecast?"

9. "What does the gap reveal about the organization's priorities or structure?"

10. "What signal would show you that this resourcing issue is finally being addressed?"

Conclusion

Resourcing-gap questions uncover the missing elements that shape operational challenges — the people, tools, skills, and support structures the organization needs but doesn't yet have. Without acknowledging these gaps, leaders often push for unrealistic performance and misinterpret systemic limitations as individual shortcomings.

Strategically, these questions help you design solutions grounded in reality rather than optimism. Psychologically, they help the buyer see their environment more clearly and compassionately, understanding that gaps do not indicate failure but opportunity for improvement.

As Chapter 4 continues, we will explore prioritization conflicts, operational dependencies, inefficiencies, and performance thresholds. Resourcing gaps are the thread that connects all of these — once you understand what the organization is missing, the path forward becomes far more apparent.

Reflection Prompt:
Think of a team that struggled because a key capability or resource was missing. Which resourcing-gap question would have surfaced that truth earlier?

CHAPTER 4 - SECTION 5 - Prioritization-Conflict Questions

Introduction

After uncovering resourcing gaps, the next operational layer involves exploring **prioritization conflicts** — the competing demands, shifting expectations, and misaligned priorities that influence what gets done, what gets delayed, and what gets ignored. Organizations rarely struggle because people don't care; they struggle because they care about many things at once. Prioritization conflicts reveal the tension between what the team *wants* to do, what it *must* do, and what it *does* because of pressure, urgency, or habit.

Strategically, understanding prioritization conflicts helps you see why certain initiatives never gain traction despite strong interest. It explains why teams feel overextended, why tasks pile up, and why workload doesn't reflect organizational goals. These questions illuminate the friction between stated priorities and lived priorities — the difference between the plan and reality.

Psychologically, prioritization conflicts often carry emotional weight. People may feel guilty for neglecting work they value, or frustrated when urgent tasks overshadow meaningful progress. Others fear disappointing leadership or falling behind, so they focus on immediate demands instead of strategic ones. These conversations help the buyer understand that misalignment isn't a personal failure — it's a natural outcome of operating under competing pressures.

Interpretation Tip: Listen for contradictions between what the buyer says is important and what the team actually spends time on. Phrases like "We want to, but…" or "We should, except…" signal conflicting priorities. Also notice when the buyer describes frequent context switching or tasks being "pushed aside" — these patterns reveal deeper misalignment.

Coaching Note: Help the buyer separate *intent* from *capacity*. When they understand the real forces shaping prioritization, they can make cleaner decisions and communicate expectations more effectively. Encourage honesty without blame; prioritization conflicts happen in every environment.

Example prompts:

- *"What important work gets overshadowed by urgent tasks?"*

- *"Where do conflicting priorities slow down progress?"*

Standard Prioritization-Conflict Questions (8)

Tone: calm, clarifying, observational.

1. "What priorities compete for your team's attention right now?"

2. "Which important tasks get delayed because of urgent demands?"

3. "Where does the team struggle to decide what to focus on first?"

4. "Which responsibilities feel mismatched with their assigned priority level?"

5. "What work receives the most attention, and why?"

6. "What tasks consistently get pushed to the side?"

7. "Where does conflict arise around what should come first?"

8. "What priorities feel unclear or inconsistently communicated?"

Intermediate Prioritization-Conflict Questions (9)

Tone: probing, structured, insight-driven.

1. "Which priorities are driven by leadership expectations rather than team needs?"

2. "What tasks consume time but contribute little to long-term goals?"

3. "Which responsibilities create tension between departments?"

4. "What part of the workload is influenced most by unexpected interruptions?"

5. "Which priorities shift the most throughout the week or quarter?"

6. "What assumptions drive how work is prioritized today?"

7. "Which tasks rely on stakeholders who have competing priorities of their own?"

8. "What part of your planning process becomes strained by conflicting expectations?"

9. "How do competing priorities affect communication and collaboration?"

Aggressive Prioritization-Conflict Questions (8)

Tone: direct, truth-focused, revealing.

1. "What priority consistently wins, even when it shouldn't?"

2. "Which important project is being sacrificed for less meaningful work?"

3. "Who is setting priorities that do not match the team's reality?"

4. "What responsibility is no one admitting is no longer important?"

5. "Which priority conflict creates the most inefficiency?"

6. "What urgent tasks distract from strategic goals the most?"

7. "Which team suffers most because priorities are unclear or unrealistic?"

8. "What priority decisions cause resentment or confusion?"

Follow-Up Prioritization-Conflict Questions (10)

Tone: reflective, clarifying, empathetic.

1. "Can you describe a recent moment when priorities clashed?"

2. "What decision did the team make in that moment, and why?"

3. "Which priority felt neglected afterward?"

4. "How did the team feel about the trade-off that was made?"

5. "What pattern of conflict have you noticed over time?"

6. "What made the situation more stressful or confusing?"

7. "What clarity would have helped resolve the conflict sooner?"

8. "Which people or teams experienced the conflict most intensely?"

9. "What adjustments would reduce future prioritization tension?"

10. "What signs would show that priorities are finally aligning?"

Conclusion

Prioritization-conflict questions uncover the silent battles that shape daily work. They reveal where important tasks lose momentum, where urgency overrides strategy, and where misalignment creates inefficiency and frustration. Without understanding these conflicts, solutions remain superficial — treating symptoms rather than causes.

Strategically, these insights help the advisor design approaches that respect both the organization's goals and its operational realities. Psychologically, they help the buyer understand their team's behavior through the lens of competing pressures rather than disappointment or blame. When prioritization becomes visible, the path to clearer alignment emerges.

As Chapter 4 continues, the next sections will explore process inefficiencies, resource dependencies, operational breakdowns, and performance thresholds. Prioritization conflicts are the emotional and structural bridge between intention and execution — understanding them strengthens every step that follows.

Reflection Prompt:
Think of a team that always felt "too busy" for strategic work. Which prioritization-conflict question would have revealed why?

CHAPTER 4 - SECTION 6 - Process-Inefficiency Questions

Introduction

Once prioritization conflicts are clear, the next operational layer involves identifying **process inefficiencies** — the friction points, repetitive tasks, redundant steps, and outdated routines that slow down performance. Inefficiencies are often accepted as "just how things are," even though they drain energy, increase errors, and limit capacity. Process-inefficiency questions help the buyer examine these hidden slowdowns and understand how they shape daily work.

Strategically, uncovering inefficiencies allows you to see where improvement would have the greatest impact. Some inefficiencies create minor annoyances; others quietly cost teams hours each week. When you identify the processes that consistently slow progress, you reveal opportunities to streamline workflows, improve communication, and free up capacity without increasing workload or adding new resources.

Psychologically, inefficiencies create frustration, fatigue, and a sense of stagnation. When people spend excessive time on manual workarounds or correcting preventable errors, they lose momentum and motivation. By bringing inefficiencies into the open, you help the organization understand that these frustrations are not personal failures — they are structural problems that can be improved.

Interpretation Tip: Listen for phrases like "it's just always been like this," "we don't love it, but it works," or "we've adapted to it." These are signals that an inefficient process has become normalized. Also pay attention to moments when the buyer describes unpredictable delays or constant interruptions — these often trace back to broken processes.

Coaching Note: Encourage the buyer to describe processes step by step rather than summarizing them. The inefficiencies usually appear in the details. When you help them narrate how work really flows, blind spots become visible, and improvement opportunities naturally emerge.

Example prompts:

- *"Which steps in your workflow feel heavier than they should?"*

- *"Where do processes break down or require repeated rework?"*

Standard Process-Inefficiency Questions (8)

Tone: calm, observational, descriptive.

1. "Which parts of your process take longer than they should?"

2. "Where do tasks get repeated unnecessarily?"

3. "What step consistently causes delays or confusion?"

4. "Which processes rely on too many manual steps?"

5. "Where do people get stuck waiting for information or approval?"

6. "What tasks require more effort than the value they produce?"

7. "Which workflow feels the most outdated or clunky?"

8. "Where do simple tasks regularly become more complicated?"

Intermediate Process-Inefficiency Questions (9)

Tone: probing, analytical, insight-focused.

1. "Which inefficiencies cause the most frustration for the team?"

2. "What steps create the highest risk of error or rework?"

3. "Where does communication slow down the process?"

4. "What part of the workflow is handled differently by each person?"

5. "Which tasks require constant clarification or correction?"

6. "Where does poor handoff between stakeholders create delays?"

7. "What part of the process becomes unreliable during busy periods?"

8. "Which recurring inefficiencies leadership tends to overlook?"

9. "What bottleneck appears most often across different projects?"

Aggressive Process-Inefficiency Questions (8)

Tone: direct, truth-revealing, precision-focused.

1. "What process is clearly broken but still used daily?"

2. "Which step wastes the most time for the least payoff?"

3. "What outdated system is dragging down performance?"

4. "Where is inefficiency harming results the most?"

5. "Which manual task should have been automated long ago?"

6. "What process requires so much effort it drains morale?"

7. "Where is the organization clinging to a process because 'it used to work'?"

8. "What inefficiency is costing you the most time or money right now?"

Follow-Up Process-Inefficiency Questions (10)

Tone: reflective, clarifying, practical.

1. "Can you describe a recent example of this inefficiency in action?"

2. "What adjustment or workaround did the team use in that moment?"

3. "How often does this inefficiency appear throughout the week?"

4. "What caused the problem the last time the process broke down?"

5. "How does this inefficiency affect other parts of the workflow?"

6. "What detail makes this process feel especially frustrating?"

7. "What has been tried to fix or improve this step?"

8. "What prevented the solution from holding over time?"

9. "What short-term change would ease the inefficiency immediately?"

10. "What long-term change would remove the inefficiency entirely?"

Conclusion

Process-inefficiency questions illuminate the hidden drag inside organizational systems. They reveal where time, energy, and attention are wasted — often without people realizing it. By surfacing these inefficiencies, you help the buyer see opportunities for improvement that offer high impact with relatively low cost.

Strategically, these insights allow you to prioritize operational changes that improve performance and free up capacity. Psychologically, they help the team understand that many frustrations are structural rather than personal — a shift that reduces blame and increases motivation to improve.

As Chapter 4 continues, the following sections will explore resource dependencies, breakdown patterns, operational risks, and performance thresholds. Process inefficiencies form the backbone of operational friction; once exposed, they become stepping stones toward meaningful improvement.

Reflection Prompt:
Think of a team that constantly felt behind despite working hard. Which process-inefficiency question would have exposed the real cause sooner?

CHAPTER 4 - SECTION 7 - Dependency-Chain Questions

Introduction

After exploring inefficiencies, the next operational layer involves revealing the **dependency chains** that shape how work flows — the people, processes, tools, and approvals each task relies on before it can move forward. Most operational breakdowns don't occur because a single step fails; they occur because one dependency slows, breaks, or shifts unexpectedly. Dependency-chain questions help the buyer understand where their operations hinge on the performance, timing, or clarity of others.

Strategically, understanding dependency chains allows you to identify the true sources of delay. A process may seem inefficient on its own, but the real slowdown may come from a step that depends on something upstream — a missing approval, a delayed input, an unavailable tool, or a person stretched too thin. When you uncover dependencies, you reveal the hidden structure that explains where friction forms and why it repeats.

Psychologically, dependency chains influence how teams perceive control. When people rely on others for key steps, they may feel anxious, frustrated, or powerless. These emotions surface quietly in conversations about delays or miscommunication. By mapping dependencies, you help the buyer see the system's complexity and understand why expectations often collide with operational reality.

Interpretation Tip: Listen for moments when the buyer mentions "waiting," "holding," "depending on," "after they do this," or "once we receive that." These phrases highlight key dependencies. Notice also when a dependency is tied to a single person — single points of failure are often the most fragile parts of the operation.

Coaching Note: Encourage the buyer to view dependencies as part of the system rather than weaknesses of individuals. When discussed without blame, dependency mapping becomes a powerful tool for improving collaboration, timing, and resource planning.

Example prompts:

- *"What needs to happen before your team can begin its part of the work?"*

- *"Which tasks depend on others to move forward?"*

Standard Dependency-Chain Questions (8)

Tone: calm, structured, descriptive.

1. "What steps must occur before your team can begin its work?"

2. "Which tasks rely on information from other teams?"

3. "Where do you see the most waiting or holding in your workflow?"

4. "Who needs to provide input before work can continue?"

5. "Which tools or systems your team depends on most?"

6. "What approvals or handoffs are required for the process to move forward?"

7. "Where do dependencies feel the most fragile or inconsistent?"

8. "What happens when one part of the chain slows down?"

Intermediate Dependency-Chain Questions (9)

Tone: probing, pattern-aware, revealing.

1. "Which dependencies create the most frequent delays?"

2. "What part of the chain relies on a single person or limited resource?"

3. "Which handoffs create confusion or miscommunication?"

4. "Where does the team feel most impacted by upstream decisions?"

5. "What steps require coordination across multiple functions?"

6. "Which dependency causes unpredictable timing?"

7. "What part of the process depends on information that's often incomplete?"

8. "Where do you see the widest gap between expectation and reality?"

9. "Which dependencies create additional workload when they break down?"

Aggressive Dependency-Chain Questions (8)

Tone: direct, truth-focused, precise.

1. "What dependency fails most often — and why?"

2. "Which person or step is the biggest single point of failure?"

3. "What part of the chain is chronically unreliable?"

4. "Which dependency causes the most rework or frustration?"

5. "What upstream behavior consistently slows your team down?"

6. "Which tool or system breaks the chain most frequently?"

7. "What dependency is too risky to continue ignoring?"

8. "Where would your entire process collapse if pressure increased?"

Follow-Up Dependency-Chain Questions (10)

Tone: reflective, clarifying, detail-oriented.

1. "Can you describe a recent moment when a dependency broke down?"

2. "What caused that breakdown, and how did the team respond?"

3. "How long did work stall because of the dependency issue?"

4. "What workaround did the team use to keep things moving?"

5. "How did the breakdown affect downstream steps?"

6. "What part of the chain became more visible during that moment?"

7. "What insight did you gain about the system from that incident?"

8. "Which stakeholders felt the impact most strongly?"

9. "What would help strengthen this part of the dependency chain?"

10. "What sign would show that a dependency is becoming more stable?"

Conclusion

Dependency-chain questions uncover the hidden architecture of workflow. They reveal where processes interlock, where timing must align, and where breakdowns occur most frequently. Without understanding dependencies, leaders often misdiagnose problems — addressing symptoms while ignoring the upstream causes.

Strategically, dependency awareness allows you to predict slowdowns, restructure workflows, strengthen handoffs, and eliminate single points of failure. Psychologically, it helps the buyer understand why their team often feels stuck or powerless — not because of lack of effort, but because of structural reliance on others.

As Chapter 4 progresses, the next sections will explore failure patterns, operational risks, and performance thresholds. Dependency chains are the backbone of operational stability; once they are visible, the organization can address the true roots of its challenges.

Reflection Prompt:
Think of a situation where work stalled because one person or step wasn't ready. Which dependency-chain question would have revealed that vulnerability earlier?

CHAPTER 4 - SECTION 8 - Breakdown-Pattern Questions

Introduction

Even when workflows, dependencies, priorities, and resources are understood, every operation still contains **breakdown patterns** — recurring moments where things fail, stall, or fall apart. These breakdowns aren't random; they follow predictable rhythms tied to timing, communication gaps, resource shortages, handoff issues, unclear expectations, or emotional strain. Breakdown-pattern questions help the buyer trace these moments back to their origins, revealing the systemic issues behind repeated failures.

Strategically, understanding breakdown patterns allows you to distinguish between isolated incidents and chronic structural problems. Many organizations try to fix breakdowns with temporary solutions—more meetings, more reminders, more pressure—without addressing the underlying pattern. By identifying where breakdowns repeat, you uncover the deeper operational flaws that must be corrected for sustainable improvement.

Psychologically, breakdowns often create frustration, tension, or even blame. People remember these moments vividly because they interrupt momentum and expose vulnerabilities. When discussing breakdown patterns, your role is to help the buyer explore these experiences without slipping into defensiveness. The goal is understanding, not fault-finding.

Interpretation Tip: Listen for emotional charge—sighs, humor, frustration, or sharp tone—when breakdowns are mentioned. Emotional spikes often indicate recurring issues the buyer feels are out of their control. Also pay attention to language like "again," "every time," "usually," "it always happens when…," or "I knew this was coming." These reveal strong breakdown patterns.

Coaching Note: Anchor the buyer in curiosity rather than judgment. Encourage them to explore the sequence leading up to the breakdown, not just the moment it occurred. This helps separate the event itself from the root cause, making patterns easier to understand and improve.

Example prompts:

- *"Where do things seem to break down most often?"*

- *"What patterns do you notice when work stalls or goes off-track?"*

Standard Breakdown-Pattern Questions (8)

Tone: calm, observational, objective.

1. "Which parts of your process break down most frequently?"

2. "Where do delays tend to occur again and again?"

3. "What tasks often have to be redone due to errors?"

4. "Which handoffs or transitions are most vulnerable to breakdown?"

5. "Where does communication tend to fall apart?"

6. "What steps feel the most unpredictable or unstable?"

7. "Which responsibilities regularly cause stress or confusion?"

8. "What situations lead to things slipping through the cracks?"

Intermediate Breakdown-Pattern Questions (9)

Tone: probing, pattern-oriented, clarifying.

1. "What breakdowns follow a consistent sequence or trigger?"

2. "Which issues resurface during peak workload periods?"

3. "Where do breakdowns occur due to unclear expectations?"

4. "What common factor appears each time the process fails?"

5. "Which stakeholders experience the breakdown most directly?"

6. "What specific conditions make breakdowns more likely?"

7. "Where does misalignment contribute to repeated failures?"

8. "Which dependencies tend to collapse under pressure?"

9. "What breakdowns have become so common they feel normal?"

Aggressive Breakdown-Pattern Questions (8)

Tone: direct, revealing, truth-focused.

1. "What breakdown is everyone aware of but no one addresses?"

2. "Which part of the operation fails reliably under stress?"

3. "What recurring error costs the team the most time or money?"

4. "Where is accountability unclear, causing repeated failure?"

5. "Which breakdown exposes the biggest structural weakness?"

6. "What problem keeps returning no matter how often it's 'fixed'?"

7. "Which part of the system collapses fastest when expectations increase?"

8. "What breakdown is quietly damaging performance the most?"

Follow-Up Breakdown-Pattern Questions (10)

Tone: reflective, clarifying, gently precise.

1. "Can you walk me through a recent breakdown from start to finish?"

2. "What was happening right before the breakdown started?"

3. "Who felt the impact first, and how did they respond?"

4. "What signals showed the breakdown was beginning?"

5. "Which actions—intentional or unintentional—made it worse?"

6. "What workaround did the team use to recover?"

7. "What did the situation reveal about the system as a whole?"

8. "Which part of the breakdown surprised you?"

9. "How did emotions influence the reaction to the failure?"

10. "What would need to change to prevent this breakdown from recurring?"

Conclusion

Breakdown-pattern questions reveal the recurring failures that shape an organization's daily experience. They expose where systems are fragile, where processes are misaligned, and where operational risks accumulate over time. Without this visibility, leaders react to symptoms rather than addressing root causes.

Strategically, identifying breakdown patterns helps the advisor pinpoint systemic weaknesses and propose targeted improvements. Psychologically, it gives the buyer a framework for understanding failure without blaming individuals. When breakdowns are recognized as structural rather than personal, teams become more willing to explore meaningful change.

As Chapter 4 continues, the next sections will explore operational risk, performance thresholds, and systemic bottlenecks. Understanding breakdown patterns prepares the way for these deeper insights, creating a clearer foundation for diagnosing and improving operational health.

Reflection Prompt:
Think of an issue that resurfaced repeatedly despite attempts to fix it. Which breakdown-pattern question would have revealed the underlying cause sooner?

CHAPTER 4 - SECTION 9 - Operational-Risk Questions

Introduction

After mapping breakdown patterns, the next layer of operational truth involves identifying **operational risks** — the conditions, behaviors, or structures that could lead to future failure. Operational risk is not just about what has already gone wrong; it's about what *could* go wrong if pressure increases, resources shrink, or conditions shift. Operational-risk questions help the buyer explore vulnerabilities, assess exposure, and understand how fragile or resilient their system truly is.

Strategically, operational risk determines the limits of growth, the speed of change, and the reliability of performance. Organizations often underestimate risk because things haven't failed *yet*. But risks accumulate quietly — through dependency fragility, resource shortages, communication gaps, process inefficiencies, and unclear ownership. By identifying these risks early, you help the buyer protect performance and prevent avoidable crises.

Psychologically, discussing risk can trigger discomfort. People may fear acknowledging risk because it exposes uncertainty or suggests that leadership hasn't prepared adequately. Your role is to create a tone of grounded curiosity. Operational risk is not a sign of poor leadership — it is a natural result of complexity. When the buyer approaches risk with calm clarity, they gain the power to strengthen their system rather than fear it.

Interpretation Tip: Listen for uncertainty markers: "hopefully," "as long as," "usually," "if everything goes right," "assuming nothing changes," or "when things don't pile up." These indicate instinctive awareness of operational risk. Also observe when the buyer mentions people who "save the day" — systems that depend on heroics are inherently risky.

Coaching Note: Encourage the buyer to think in terms of vulnerability rather than failure. A vulnerability doesn't need to be catastrophic to matter. The goal is to understand exposure so risk can be managed intelligently rather than reactively.

Example prompts:

- *"Where could things break if pressure increased?"*

- *"What risks would emerge if the current system were tested more heavily?"*

Standard Operational-Risk Questions (8)

Tone: calm, steady, awareness-building.

1. "What parts of your operation feel most vulnerable to disruption?"

2. "Where would a sudden increase in workload create risk?"

3. "Which responsibilities depend on a very limited number of people?"

4. "What tasks would fail if a key resource became unavailable?"

5. "Where do small mistakes create outsized consequences?"

6. "What processes lack clear backup or redundancy?"

7. "Where does uncertainty create the most concern?"

8. "Which areas feel stable only when everything goes exactly right?"

Intermediate Operational-Risk Questions (9)

Tone: probing, analytical, systemic.

1. "Which risks grow larger during busy periods?"

2. "What unspoken risks have become normal over time?"

3. "Which tasks rely on outdated or unreliable systems?"

4. "Where does unclear accountability create exposure?"

5. "Which roles or tools create single points of failure?"

6. "What operational risks stem from communication gaps?"

7. "Which recurring issues suggest deeper structural risk?"

8. "Where does the system rely too heavily on individual effort?"

9. "What risks would appear if expectations suddenly increased?"

Aggressive Operational-Risk Questions (8)

Tone: direct, truth-focused, risk-exposing.

1. "What vulnerability would cause the most damage if ignored?"

2. "Which part of your operation is one failure away from a crisis?"

3. "What risk leadership underestimates the most?"

4. "Which area poses a hidden threat to performance or reputation?"

5. "What operational habit has become dangerously outdated?"

6. "Where is the current system most likely to collapse under pressure?"

7. "Which risk is being managed by hope instead of structure?"

8. "What failure scenario is more likely than people want to admit?"

Follow-Up Operational-Risk Questions (10)

Tone: reflective, clarifying, focused.

1. "Can you describe a past moment when risk became unexpectedly visible?"

2. "What early warning signs appeared before the issue surfaced?"

3. "How did the team respond to the risk once it became clear?"

4. "What part of the environment made the situation more severe?"

5. "What insight did the event reveal about your system's vulnerability?"

6. "Which stakeholders were most affected by the risk?"

7. "What has been done since then to reduce the exposure?"

8. "What remaining gaps could still lead to similar risk?"

9. "What would help you identify risks earlier going forward?"

10. "What signal would tell you that operational risk is increasing again?"

Conclusion

Operational-risk questions illuminate the fragilities that threaten performance and stability. They reveal where pressure could create failure, where resources are stretched too thin, and where systems lack the resilience needed to sustain growth. Without understanding operational risk, leaders are forced into reactive mode — responding to problems only after they appear.

Strategically, these insights empower you to guide the buyer toward stronger processes, more reliable support structures, and a more resilient operation. Psychologically, they help the buyer move from fear of failure to clarity about vulnerability. When risk becomes visible, it also becomes manageable.

As Chapter 4 moves toward its final sections, we will explore performance thresholds and structural load — understanding how much the organization can truly handle before performance begins to break down. Operational risk is the bridge between breakdown patterns and capacity; once understood, the rest of the operational picture comes into sharper focus.

Reflection Prompt:
Think of a situation where a hidden risk suddenly became urgent. Which operational-risk question would have revealed that vulnerability earlier?

CHAPTER 4 - SECTION 10 - Performance-Threshold Questions

Introduction

After examining risk, the final layer of operational reality involves identifying **performance thresholds** — the limits at which people, systems, or processes begin to weaken, stall, or break. Every operation has a tipping point: a moment when workload, pressure, volume, or complexity exceeds its ability to function reliably. Performance-threshold questions help the buyer understand exactly where those limits lie, how close they are to being reached, and what happens when the organization crosses them.

Strategically, knowing performance thresholds allows you to guide the buyer with precision. It helps determine the pace of change the organization can support, the workload it can absorb, and the volume at which quality begins to slip. When you understand thresholds, you avoid recommending solutions that overload the system or expecting performance that cannot be sustained. Instead, you work within the organization's true capacity while planning for long-term expansion.

Psychologically, performance thresholds are often misunderstood or ignored. Leaders want to believe their teams can handle more than they realistically can. Teams often hide signs of strain until breakdown becomes unavoidable. These questions help the buyer confront the truth of their operational limits — not to judge or restrict them, but to empower them to make better decisions with clearer expectations.

Interpretation Tip: Listen for comments that reveal stress points: "We were barely holding on," "Things started slipping," "We couldn't keep up," or "Quality dropped." These statements are clues to thresholds already being crossed. Also observe when the buyer describes frantic shortcuts, rising tension, or increased errors — these are signals that the system is approaching or exceeding its limits.

Coaching Note: Encourage the buyer to view thresholds as indicators, not warnings. A system that hits its limit is not failing — it is providing valuable information. When leaders understand where thresholds lie, they can strengthen their operation without pushing their people or processes into unhealthy territory.

Example prompts:

- *"What happens when demand increases faster than capacity?"*

- *"Where do you see performance start to slip under pressure?"*

Standard Performance-Threshold Questions (8)

Tone: calm, descriptive, grounding.

1. "Where do you see performance begin to decline when workload increases?"

2. "What tasks become harder to complete when pressure rises?"

3. "Which roles reach their limit the fastest during busy periods?"

4. "What signs show that the team is approaching capacity?"

5. "Which responsibilities become inconsistent when strain increases?"

6. "Where do errors start to appear as workload grows?"

7. "What parts of the system struggle most when expectations change?"

8. "What does the team stop doing when they reach their limit?"

Intermediate Performance-Threshold Questions (9)

Tone: probing, clarifying, analytical.

1. "Which processes reach their breaking point sooner than expected?"

2. "What tasks require the most recovery time after heavy workload?"

3. "Which responsibilities shift from proactive to reactive under pressure?"

4. "What patterns appear when the team is operating near its limit?"

5. "Where does quality drop first when demand increases?"

6. "Which dependencies weaken most under strain?"

7. "What thresholds have been crossed in the past without noticing at first?"

8. "How do team members' behaviors change as they approach overload?"

9. "What early-warning signs appear before performance begins to slip?"

Aggressive Performance-Threshold Questions (8)

Tone: direct, revealing, honest.

1. "What part of your operation collapses first when stretched?"

2. "Which team is closest to overload right now?"

3. "What threshold has already been crossed and not acknowledged?"

4. "Where is performance being protected by unsustainable effort?"

5. "Which roles operate at their limit even on normal days?"

6. "What responsibility is dangerously close to failing under pressure?"

7. "What limit is leadership unintentionally ignoring?"

8. "Which performance gap becomes obvious only during stress?"

Follow-Up Performance-Threshold Questions (10)

Tone: reflective, clarifying, insight-focused.

1. "Can you describe a moment when performance clearly hit its limit?"

2. "What did people say or do that showed the threshold was reached?"

3. "What broke down first during that situation?"

4. "How quickly did the team recover afterward?"

5. "What long-term impact did crossing the threshold have?"

6. "Which part of the workflow was most exposed during that moment?"

7. "What pattern did you notice once pressure eased?"

8. "What insight did that experience reveal about your true capacity?"

9. "What adjustment would raise the threshold in the future?"

10. "What sign would help you spot an approaching threshold earlier?"

Conclusion

Performance-threshold questions reveal the limits of your operational system — where team capacity peaks, where quality declines, and where pressure becomes unsustainable. They transform invisible limits into usable insight, allowing leaders to understand exactly how far their team can push before performance falters.

Strategically, these insights inform pacing, planning, resource allocation, and expectations. Psychologically, they reduce frustration by helping leaders see that poor performance often results from structural overload, not lack of effort. When thresholds are understood, teams can work more sustainably and confidently.

With this section complete, Chapter 4 has now fully mapped the operational landscape: the current state, constraints, workload pressure, resourcing gaps, prioritization conflicts, inefficiencies, dependencies, breakdown patterns, risks, and performance limits. These insights give the advisor and buyer a clear understanding of the operational truth — the foundation on which all future recommendations must be built.

Reflection Prompt:
Think of a time when a team looked overwhelmed without warning. Which performance-threshold question would have revealed the approaching limit sooner?

Chapter Conclusion

Chapter 4 brings structure to the operational realities that shape daily performance. By examining current state, constraints, workload pressure, resource gaps, prioritization conflicts, inefficiencies, dependencies, breakdown patterns, risks, and thresholds, the buyer gains a level of clarity that most organizations never take the time to develop. With this clarity, problem-solving becomes grounded, practical, and realistic.

Strategically, the insights from this chapter ensure that future recommendations will match the organization's actual capacity and limitations. They help the advisor design solutions that account for hidden friction points and reduce exposure to risk. Psychologically, they give the buyer a deeper understanding of their environment — not as a chaotic collection of problems, but as a coherent system with patterns, limits, and opportunities.

As the book moves into the next chapter, the focus will shift from diagnosing operational truth to uncovering value, potential, and future possibilities. Chapter 4 ensures that this exploration is grounded in reality. With operational truth clearly visible, the advisor and buyer can pursue change with confidence, precision, and alignment.

CHAPTER 5 - Uncovering Value, Potential, and Strategic Opportunity

Chapter Introduction

Every meaningful transformation begins with clarity — not only about what must improve, but about what *could* become possible. Chapter 5 shifts the discovery journey from diagnosing present challenges to exploring the buyer's deeper motivations, future aspirations, and strategic possibilities. This chapter helps the buyer articulate what they want, why they want it, and how far they believe they can go. It bridges operational truth with emotional meaning and long-term vision.

The chapter opens with **Desired-Outcome Questions**, which help the buyer define what "better" looks like in their own terms. These questions translate broad hopes into direction, creating the foundation for every conversation that follows. From there, **Core-Priority Questions** reveal what the buyer refuses to compromise — the commitments and responsibilities that define their choices and shape their leaders' expectations.

The next layer involves identifying **Untapped Potential** within the organization. This exploration shifts the narrative from constraint to capability. Teams often overlook their strengths because they are buried under daily pressures or overshadowed by more urgent challenges. When these strengths come into focus, the buyer begins to see that growth is not only possible — it is already underway in subtle ways.

From there, the chapter reveals **Hidden Opportunities** that the organization has not yet explored. These opportunities reflect unused insights, emerging demands, process advantages, or creative ideas that could meaningfully advance performance. Once the buyer recognizes these openings, the conversation expands from problem-solving into forward-looking possibility.

The middle of the chapter centers on **Value Definition** and **Significance Recognition**. Value clarifies what the buyer considers meaningful and beneficial, while significance uncovers the emotional reasons the effort matters in the first place. These sections introduce the psychological dimension of discovery — the motivations that give change its meaning, urgency, and staying power.

With value and significance established, **Strategic-Ambition Questions** and **Future-Vision Questions** help the buyer articulate the scale and direction of their aspirations. Ambition reveals how far they want to go; vision reveals what they want the future to look and feel like. These sections shift the buyer into a creative mindset, enabling them to imagine possibilities beyond current limitations.

The chapter closes with **Strategic-Lever Questions** and **Long-Term-Potential Questions**, which identify the actions and capabilities that can accelerate progress and shape future growth.

These insights bring structure to the future — showing the buyer not only what is possible, but how it can realistically unfold over time. Together, these sections create a complete map of value, possibility, and strategic direction.

CHAPTER 5 - SECTION 1 - Desired-Outcome Questions

Introduction

Every meaningful change begins with a desired outcome — a clear picture of what the buyer hopes to achieve, improve, or transform. But most buyers describe their desired outcomes in broad, hopeful terms: "We want to grow," "We want things to run smoother," or "We want better results." These statements express intent, but they don't reveal the deeper vision behind the change. Desired-outcome questions help uncover that vision in a way that becomes specific, grounded, and emotionally resonant.

Strategically, understanding desired outcomes allows you to anchor the entire discovery process in direction rather than symptoms. When you know what the buyer is reaching for, you can align every later question to the path that leads there. Without this clarity, conversations drift or become reactive. With it, opportunities become sharper, decisions become easier, and priorities become more aligned across stakeholders.

Psychologically, desired-outcome conversations tap into motivation, hope, aspiration, and the buyer's sense of possibility. People often suppress their real desires because they fear disappointment, feel restricted by constraints, or lack confidence that improvement is reachable. Your role is to create space where the buyer can articulate what they *actually* want — not what they think they're allowed to want. When a buyer reconnects with genuine possibility, they become more open, more engaged, and more willing to explore change.

Interpretation Tip: Listen for the difference between "would be nice" outcomes (soft desires) and "must happen" outcomes (core motivations). Pay attention to emotional cues: excitement, relief, hesitation, or emphasis. These signals reveal how strongly the buyer feels about each desired outcome and what meaning it carries.

Coaching Note: Encourage the buyer to stay future-focused. When they drift back into describing problems, gently redirect them to the outcomes they ultimately want to create. Clarity of direction becomes the compass for the rest of the chapter.

Example prompts:

- *"What would a successful future look like for your team?"*

- *"What outcome would make all the effort feel worthwhile?"*

Standard Desired-Outcome Questions (8)

Tone: calm, open, aspirational yet practical.

1. "What improvements would you most like to see in the near future?"

2. "How would you describe a successful outcome for this effort?"

3. "What changes would make your day-to-day work feel more manageable?"

4. "What results would show you that things are moving in the right direction?"

5. "What would make your team feel more confident or supported?"

6. "What outcome would feel meaningful, not just helpful?"

7. "Which goals matter most to you right now?"

8. "What would a better version of your current situation look like?"

Intermediate Desired-Outcome Questions (9)

Tone: probing, clarifying, outcome-focused.

1. "What specific results would show that the change was successful?"

2. "Which outcomes would make the biggest difference to your team?"

3. "What long-term improvements are most important to sustain?"

4. "What outcome would reduce the most stress or uncertainty?"

5. "Which measurable results matter most to leadership?"

6. "What outcome would restore momentum or confidence?"

7. "How do you want the team or process to feel once improved?"

8. "What outcome would strengthen your ability to plan ahead?"

9. "Which desired result would eliminate the most frustration?"

Aggressive Desired-Outcome Questions (8)

Tone: direct, truth-seeking, clarity-focused.

1. "What outcome are you afraid to ask for — but truly want?"

2. "Which desired result matters more than all the others?"

3. "What outcome would change everything if you achieved it?"

4. "What result must happen, or the effort wasn't worth it?"

5. "Which goal is non-negotiable, even if others fall short?"

6. "What outcome would leadership refuse to compromise on?"

7. "What result would prove this initiative was the right decision?"

8. "Which outcome is the real reason you're exploring this?"

Follow-Up Desired-Outcome Questions (10)

Tone: reflective, clarifying, gently revealing.

1. "Can you describe a moment that made you realize this outcome truly matters?"

2. "What would change for you personally if this outcome were achieved?"

3. "How would your team's daily experience improve?"

4. "What difference would stakeholders notice first?"

5. "Which part of the outcome feels most important emotionally?"

6. "What would success allow you to focus on next?"

7. "What previous attempts fell short of this outcome — and why?"

8. "What made this outcome hard to reach in the past?"

9. "What smaller wins would signal progress toward the bigger outcome?"

10. "What would achieving this outcome unlock for the organization?"

Conclusion

Desired-outcome questions illuminate the future the buyer wants to create. They turn vague hopes into concrete direction and transform aspiration into clarity. Without understanding desired outcomes, discovery lacks purpose; with them, every subsequent conversation gains focus and momentum.

Strategically, these questions help sharpen priorities, define success criteria, and guide the buyer toward choices that align with their deeper goals. Psychologically, they reconnect the buyer with possibility — a powerful motivator that fuels commitment and resilience.

As Chapter 5 continues, we will explore potential, value, opportunity, and the deeper significance of change. Desired outcomes represent the horizon line; the sections ahead reveal what stands between the present and that future.

Reflection Prompt:
Think of a buyer who struggled to articulate what they wanted. Which desired-outcome question would have helped them clarify their vision?

CHAPTER 5 - SECTION 2 - Core-Priority Questions

Introduction

Once desired outcomes are clear, the next step is understanding **core priorities** — the essential goals, responsibilities, and principles that guide the buyer's decisions. Priorities determine what gets attention, what gets delayed, and what gets protected even during times of pressure or constraint. While desired outcomes reveal where the buyer wants to go, core priorities reveal what matters most during the journey. These questions help uncover the commitments that the organization refuses to compromise.

Strategically, core priorities serve as the stabilizing force behind decision-making. They anchor the buyer's choices and act as filters that determine which opportunities align and which do not. When core priorities are unclear, organizations struggle to stay focused, waste energy on conflicting goals, or make decisions that don't support their long-term direction. Core-priority questions reveal the hierarchy that every meaningful change must respect.

Psychologically, understanding priorities requires honesty and sometimes vulnerability. Buyers may feel torn between what they *want* to prioritize and what they *have* been prioritizing out of habit, pressure, or expectation. Your role is to help them separate those forces and identify the priorities that truly matter to them — the ones that feel essential, not optional.

Interpretation Tip: Listen closely for differences between **stated priorities** ("We say this matters") and **lived priorities** ("This is where time and energy actually go"). Discrepancies between these two reveal hidden tension. Also notice when the buyer describes something as "non-negotiable," "critical," or "the foundation." These are clues to their true core priorities.

Coaching Note: Encourage specificity. General priorities ("growth," "efficiency," "team success") hide important nuance. Guide the buyer toward clarity by asking what each priority *means*, *influences*, or *protects*. The clearer the priority, the easier it becomes to align solutions with it.

Example prompts:

- *"What priorities guide your decision-making when things feel uncertain?"*

- *"Which commitments matter more than anything else right now?"*

Standard Core-Priority Questions (8)

Tone: calm, focusing, clarifying.

1. "What priorities guide your team's decisions on a daily basis?"

2. "Which responsibilities matter most, regardless of workload?"

3. "What goals feel essential to pursue right now?"

4. "Which tasks or initiatives take priority when time is limited?"

5. "Where do you believe resources should be focused most?"

6. "What commitments feel non-negotiable to your team?"

7. "Which outcomes outweigh all others in importance?"

8. "What principles guide your approach to decision-making?"

Intermediate Core-Priority Questions (9)

Tone: probing, revealing, structured.

1. "Which priorities shape how you allocate time and resources?"

2. "What responsibilities receive focus even when the team feels overloaded?"

3. "Which goals reflect the organization's deeper mission?"

4. "What priority becomes most visible during stressful periods?"

5. "Which initiatives must succeed to support broader objectives?"

6. "What expectations drive the decisions you make under pressure?"

7. "Which priorities influence cross-department alignment the most?"

8. "What priority becomes your default when everything feels urgent?"

9. "Which long-term priorities rarely get attention despite their importance?"

Aggressive Core-Priority Questions (8)

Tone: direct, truth-revealing, boundary-setting.

1. "What priority is more important than anything else — truly?"

2. "Which stated priority is actually not a priority in practice?"

3. "What priority are you afraid to admit is slipping?"

4. "Which responsibility is taking precedence even though it shouldn't?"

5. "What goal has been neglected but remains critical?"

6. "Which priority is leadership forcing that the team does not support?"

7. "What priority is stealing attention from more important work?"

8. "Which commitment is non-negotiable even if everything else must wait?"

Follow-Up Core-Priority Questions (10)

Tone: reflective, clarifying, nuanced.

1. "Can you describe a moment that revealed your true priority?"

2. "What trade-offs did you have to make to protect this priority?"

3. "How do your priorities shift when pressure increases?"

4. "What tension exists between your top priorities?"

5. "Which priority feels most aligned with your long-term direction?"

6. "What commitment becomes clearer the more you think about it?"

7. "How do your priorities influence team morale or energy?"

8. "Which priority would you strengthen if you had more resources?"

9. "What smaller priorities support your most important one?"

10. "How would your ideal priority structure look if nothing restricted you?"

Conclusion

Core-priority questions reveal the forces that shape decision-making beneath the surface. They help the buyer articulate what truly matters — not just what sounds important, but what guides action, demands protection, and influences long-term direction. Once these priorities are known, every decision becomes easier to evaluate.

Strategically, these questions help align recommendations with the buyer's deepest values and commitments. Psychologically, they help the buyer express priorities they may have struggled to name, giving them a renewed sense of clarity and purpose. When a buyer understands their true priorities, they can move toward their desired outcomes with confidence and consistency.

As Chapter 5 continues, the next sections will explore untapped potential, hidden opportunities, value definition, and strategic ambition. Desired outcomes show the vision; core priorities show the foundation. Together, they anchor the rest of the discovery journey.

Reflection Prompt:
Think of a buyer who seemed torn between multiple directions. Which core-priority question would have helped them clarify what mattered most?

CHAPTER 5 - SECTION 3 - Untapped-Potential Questions

Introduction

Once desired outcomes and core priorities are clear, the next step is uncovering **untapped potential** — the strengths, opportunities, and latent capabilities within the organization that have not yet been fully utilized. Untapped potential is the bridge between what the buyer *dreams* of achieving and what they are *actually capable* of achieving. These questions help the buyer discover internal advantages that may be hidden beneath daily pressures, operational strain, or outdated assumptions.

Strategically, understanding untapped potential allows you to guide the buyer toward possibilities they may not see. Most organizations underestimate themselves in meaningful ways. They overlook strong performers who haven't been fully leveraged, processes that could scale, data that could be used more intelligently, or ideas that were never given proper attention. By uncovering potential, you help the buyer see that improvement isn't only about fixing problems—it's also about elevating strengths.

Psychologically, these conversations create a sense of hope and empowerment. Instead of focusing solely on constraints, risks, and breakdowns, untapped-potential questions shift the narrative toward capability. This shift helps the buyer reconnect with optimism and possibility, making them more open to exploring strategic change. People are more motivated when they feel they already possess seeds of success.

Interpretation Tip: Listen for opportunities hidden in passing comments—praise for a team member, admiration for a recent success, or references to resources that are "underused," "overlooked," or "not consistent yet." These statements often point directly to areas of untapped potential.

Coaching Note: Encourage the buyer to think broadly. Untapped potential can be human, structural, strategic, cultural, technological, or even emotional. Guide the conversation in a way that expands their field of view rather than narrows it.

Example prompts:

- *"What strengths do you have that aren't being fully utilized?"*

- *"Where do you see potential that hasn't been explored yet?"*

Standard Untapped-Potential Questions (8)

Tone: open, positive, exploratory.

1. "Where do you see strengths that aren't fully leveraged today?"

2. "Which team members have skills that could be used more effectively?"

3. "What successful habits or routines could be expanded?"

4. "Which processes show promise but lack consistency?"

5. "What opportunities feel close but not yet realized?"

6. "Where do you see room for growth inside your existing structure?"

7. "What capabilities are present but underused?"

8. "Which resources could make a bigger impact with more focus?"

Intermediate Untapped-Potential Questions (9)

Tone: probing, encouraging, insight-building.

1. "Which strengths could create significant improvement if developed further?"

2. "What team members show potential that hasn't been nurtured yet?"

3. "Where does the team perform better than leadership realizes?"

4. "Which processes or tools could scale with the right support?"

5. "What ideas have been mentioned but never seriously explored?"

6. "Where do small wins show the possibility for larger success?"

7. "Which internal capabilities could replace current limitations?"

8. "What opportunities are emerging that fit your existing strengths?"

9. "Which successes haven't been fully translated into repeatable outcomes?"

Aggressive Untapped-Potential Questions (8)

Tone: direct, challenging, possibility-expanding.

1. "What potential are you ignoring because you're too focused on problems?"

2. "Which skill or capability could transform performance if taken seriously?"

3. "Who has been undervalued despite strong potential?"

4. "What hidden strength would surprise leadership if highlighted?"

5. "Which opportunity is bigger than anyone realizes right now?"

6. "What internal capability could eliminate your biggest constraint?"

7. "Which strength has been overlooked because it feels too new or untested?"

8. "What resource do you undervalue simply because it's familiar?"

Follow-Up Untapped-Potential Questions (10)

Tone: reflective, clarifying, insight-focused.

1. "Can you describe a moment when you noticed untapped potential?"

2. "What made that moment stand out to you?"

3. "How has that potential shown itself in subtle ways over time?"

4. "What prevented this potential from being used more widely?"

5. "Which stakeholders would benefit most from unlocking this potential?"

6. "What support or structure would help develop it further?"

7. "What small investment could amplify this potential right away?"

8. "How would unlocking this potential influence team morale?"

9. "What broader opportunities might become possible afterward?"

10. "What signal would show you that this potential is finally being realized?"

Conclusion

Untapped-potential questions shift the conversation from limitation to possibility. They help the buyer see the strengths that already exist — the people, ideas, habits, tools, and capabilities that could accelerate progress if properly supported. When buyers recognize their own potential, they become more confident, more engaged, and more willing to pursue meaningful change.

Strategically, these insights help design solutions that build on strengths rather than relying solely on corrective action. Psychologically, they reinforce motivation, showing the buyer that progress is achievable not only through fixing problems but also through unlocking existing value.

As Chapter 5 continues, we will explore hidden opportunities, value definition, strategic ambition, and future vision. Untapped potential provides the fertile ground on which all those conversations grow.

Reflection Prompt:
Think of a buyer who underestimated their team's capabilities. Which untapped-potential question would have helped them see what they already had?

CHAPTER 5 - SECTION 4 - Hidden-Opportunity Questions

Introduction

After uncovering untapped potential, the next step is revealing **hidden opportunities** — the openings, advantages, and strategic paths that the organization has not yet explored. These opportunities often sit just beneath the surface, overshadowed by daily demands, legacy processes, or outdated assumptions. Hidden-opportunity questions help the buyer discover what could be gained, expanded, or leveraged if certain conditions were recognized and acted upon.

Strategically, identifying hidden opportunities shifts the conversation from "what is" to "what could be." Many organizations operate in a narrow frame, limiting themselves to familiar routines and reactive problem-solving. When hidden opportunities are revealed, the buyer gains access to a wider field of possibility — new efficiencies, stronger performance, expanded capabilities, or strategic advantages that were always present but never highlighted.

Psychologically, this exploration encourages curiosity. It helps the buyer step out of the mindset of constraint and into a mindset of growth. Hidden-opportunity questions spark imagination, optimism, and a sense of agency. They show the buyer that progress isn't limited by their current state; it can emerge from overlooked strengths, untested ideas, and dormant potential waiting to be activated.

Interpretation Tip: Listen for clues in the buyer's descriptions of "almost successes," "unused data," "ideas that never took off," "customer needs we haven't tapped," or "areas we haven't fully explored." These statements often point directly to hidden opportunities. Also note moments when the buyer expresses frustration with missed chances — frustration is often a signal of opportunity underneath.

Coaching Note: Guide the buyer toward opportunities that align with their priorities and desired outcomes. Not every opportunity deserves focus. Help them distinguish between appealing possibilities and meaningful opportunities that support their strategic direction.

Example prompts:

- *"Where do you see opportunity that hasn't been explored?"*

- *"What strengths or insights could open new doors if used differently?"*

Standard Hidden-Opportunity Questions (8)

Tone: curious, open, lightly exploratory.

1. "Where do you see opportunities that the team hasn't fully explored yet?"

2. "Which parts of the operation show early signs of promise?"

3. "What strengths could be used in new or expanded ways?"

4. "Where do small successes hint at bigger opportunities?"

5. "What customer needs or requests are only partially addressed today?"

6. "What ideas have been mentioned but never tested?"

7. "Where do you see chance for growth within your current structure?"

8. "What opportunities feel close but underdeveloped?"

Intermediate Hidden-Opportunity Questions (9)

Tone: probing, possibility-expanding, insight-driven.

1. "Which missed opportunities still stand out in your mind — and why?"

2. "What emerging patterns or trends suggest new potential?"

3. "Where is there demand that the organization hasn't capitalized on?"

4. "Which team or process shows growth potential with minimal investment?"

5. "What internal insights or data could reveal stronger opportunities?"

6. "Where could small improvements lead to major gains?"

7. "Which existing capabilities could be repurposed for greater impact?"

8. "What opportunities align with your long-term direction but remain unexplored?"

9. "Where might a simple shift create new strategic leverage?"

Aggressive Hidden-Opportunity Questions (8)

Tone: direct, awakening, challenge-oriented.

1. "What opportunity is obvious in hindsight — and still being ignored?"

2. "Which untapped market, need, or capability could transform your results?"

3. "What opportunity is larger than anyone on the team realizes?"

4. "Where is hesitation preventing you from pursuing a clear advantage?"

5. "Which opportunity has been delayed so long it now carries risk?"

6. "What breakthrough is possible if the organization stops playing small?"

7. "Where are you settling for 'good enough' instead of pursuing opportunity?"

8. "Which hidden opportunity demands action rather than more discussion?"

Follow-Up Hidden-Opportunity Questions (10)

Tone: reflective, clarifying, insight-deepening.

1. "Can you describe an example of a hidden opportunity you noticed recently?"

2. "What made that moment stand out as meaningful or promising?"

3. "How long has this opportunity been present without being used?"

4. "What prevented the team from acting on it before?"

5. "What small step could test or validate the opportunity?"

6. "What skills or resources would strengthen your ability to pursue it?"

7. "Which stakeholders would benefit most if this opportunity were realized?"

8. "How would pursuing this opportunity support long-term goals?"

9. "What risks appear if the opportunity continues to be ignored?"

10. "What sign would indicate that the opportunity is ready for advancement?"

Conclusion

Hidden-opportunity questions illuminate the possibilities that have been overlooked, underestimated, or unrecognized. They help the buyer discover paths that align with their strengths, priorities, and desired outcomes — paths that could create meaningful progress with the right focus and investment.

Strategically, these questions reveal areas where small pivots can create large gains. Psychologically, they reframe the organization's mindset from constraint to opportunity, empowering the buyer to explore future potential with confidence and curiosity.

As Chapter 5 continues, the next sections will explore defining value, understanding significance, shaping ambition, and clarifying long-term potential. Hidden opportunities serve as the doorway to strategic possibility — once visible, they expand what the buyer believes is achievable.

Reflection Prompt:

Think of a buyer who had more opportunity than they realized. Which hidden-opportunity question would have revealed it sooner?

CHAPTER 5 - SECTION 5 - Value-Definition Questions

Introduction

Once hidden opportunities are uncovered, the next step is clarifying **value** — what the buyer considers meaningful, beneficial, or worth investing in. Value is not universal; it varies from organization to organization and from stakeholder to stakeholder. Some value efficiency, others value stability. Some value speed, others value certainty. Value-definition questions help the buyer articulate what "better" actually means to them — not in abstract terms, but in practical, measurable, emotionally grounded ways.

Strategically, defining value gives direction to every future recommendation. When the advisor understands what the buyer values most, they can frame insights, solutions, and next steps through that lens. This helps the buyer see relevance more clearly and builds alignment across the decision group. Without defined value, conversations become scattered, and decisions lose coherence.

Psychologically, value defines meaning. People support change when they feel it supports what they care about. Value-definition questions help the buyer connect their goals to deeper motivations such as pride, recognition, relief, confidence, protection, growth, or accomplishment. These emotional anchors create the energy needed to support long-term change.

Interpretation Tip: Listen for shifts in tone, emphasis, or emotion when the buyer describes what matters to them. Value often reveals itself in the phrases they repeat or return to. Also notice when the buyer describes frustrations — frustrations often show where value is being undermined.

Coaching Note: Push the buyer toward specificity. Avoid vague value statements like "we want to improve." Guide them to define *how* improvement will bring value, *why* it matters, and *what* specific elements define that value for them.

Example prompts:

- *"What does meaningful improvement look like to you?"*

- *"What results or experiences would create the most value?"*

Standard Value-Definition Questions (8)

Tone: calm, clarifying, practical.

1. "What does 'value' mean for your team in this context?"

2. "Which improvements would feel most meaningful to you?"

3. "What results create the greatest sense of progress?"

4. "Which outcomes matter most from a value perspective?"

5. "What part of improvement feels most impactful?"

6. "Which benefits would make the biggest difference day to day?"

7. "What would make this effort feel worthwhile for your team?"

8. "Where do you see the clearest potential for added value?"

Intermediate Value-Definition Questions (9)

Tone: probing, insight-oriented, clarifying.

1. "Which specific results would demonstrate clear value to leadership?"

2. "What improvements would produce measurable gains?"

3. "Where do you expect the highest return on effort or investment?"

4. "Which outcomes would reduce the most friction or cost?"

5. "What value would improved performance create for your customers?"

6. "Which benefits matter most in the long term, not just immediately?"

7. "What part of value connects directly to your core priorities?"

8. "Which aspects of success matter even if they're harder to measure?"

9. "What value do you want the team to experience emotionally?"

Aggressive Value-Definition Questions (8)

Tone: direct, truth-provoking, revealing.

1. "What value matters more than all other benefits — truly?"

2. "Which part of value are you afraid leadership might overlook?"

3. "What value-focused result would make this entire effort unquestionable?"

4. "Which value outcome cannot be compromised?"

5. "What benefit would silence most objections?"

6. "Which value matters enough to justify major change?"

7. "What outcome would prove that staying the same is no longer acceptable?"

8. "Which value does your organization talk about but rarely achieves?"

Follow-Up Value-Definition Questions (10)

Tone: reflective, clarifying, depth-oriented.

1. "Can you describe a moment when you felt real value from a past improvement?"

2. "What made that experience feel meaningful?"

3. "How did it affect your team's energy or performance?"

4. "Which lessons from that moment apply today?"

5. "What value stands out after reflecting on recent challenges?"

6. "How would achieving this value change your daily experience?"

7. "Which stakeholders would notice the value first?"

8. "What signs would show you're receiving the value you expect?"

9. "How would you explain the value of this effort to your team?"

10. "What long-term advantage would this value create?"

Conclusion

Value-definition questions transform vague goals into concrete meaning. They help buyers articulate what "better" actually looks like, why it matters, and how they measure progress. When value is clear, decision-making becomes easier, priorities become sharper, and engagement becomes stronger.

Strategically, these insights allow you to align your guidance with what the buyer cares about most. Psychologically, they help the buyer see the emotional and practical significance behind their choices, creating confidence and connection around the journey ahead.

As Chapter 5 continues, the next sections will explore ambition, future vision, strategic levers, and transformation potential. Value is the lens through which all of these elements gain focus.

Reflection Prompt:
Think of a buyer who struggled to explain why change mattered. Which value-definition question would have helped them uncover what they truly cared about?

CHAPTER 5 - SECTION 6 - Significance-Recognition Questions

Introduction

After understanding how the buyer defines value, the next step is uncovering **significance** — the deeper meaning behind why the change matters. Significance goes beyond measurable outcomes and operational improvements. It speaks to identity, pride, confidence, reputation, relationships, and the emotional weight carried by the work. Significance-recognition questions help the buyer articulate why the effort is important on a human, organizational, and personal level.

Strategically, significance reveals the emotional drivers that influence commitment. Buyers rarely act based on logic alone; they act when something *feels* meaningful. When you understand the significance behind the desired change, you gain insight into what will motivate stakeholders, reduce resistance, and maintain momentum through difficulty. Significance is the "why" that fuels perseverance.

Psychologically, exploring significance helps the buyer move from surface-level goals to core motivations. It uncovers what the buyer is trying to protect, restore, strengthen, or achieve emotionally. Many leaders quietly carry pressure to prove themselves, regain control, show improvement, or protect their team. Significance-recognition questions bring these motivations into the open, turning unspoken feelings into powerful guiding forces.

Interpretation Tip: Listen for tone changes when the buyer explains why something matters. Emotion in the voice—relief, pride, frustration, or hope—signals deeper meaning. Also notice when the buyer talks about team morale, customer trust, leadership confidence, or personal responsibility; these are common areas where significance lives.

Coaching Note: Approach significance with care. These questions are more intimate than operational or strategic ones. Create space for reflection. Allow pauses. Your calm, steady presence gives the buyer permission to think and feel honestly without fear of judgment.

Example prompts:

- *"Why does this outcome matter on a deeper level?"*

- *"What meaning does this effort hold for you or your team?"*

Standard Significance-Recognition Questions (8)

Tone: warm, steady, reflective.

1. "Why is this improvement important to you personally?"

2. "What meaning does this outcome hold for your team?"

3. "Which part of this change feels most significant?"

4. "What deeper reason makes this effort worth pursuing?"

5. "How would achieving this benefit your team beyond the numbers?"

6. "What impact would this have on confidence or morale?"

7. "Why does this matter now compared to earlier?"

8. "What difference would this make in how you feel about your work?"

Intermediate Significance-Recognition Questions (9)

Tone: probing, empathetic, introspective.

1. "What underlying purpose is driving your interest in this change?"

2. "Which emotional or relational factors make this important?"

3. "How would this outcome affect your reputation or credibility?"

4. "What significance does this hold for your leadership role?"

5. "Which team members would feel the impact of this most deeply?"

6. "What would achieving this say about your organization's direction?"

7. "Which frustrations or pressures does this address on a deeper level?"

8. "How would this outcome change the way people work together?"

9. "What personal meaning do you attach to making this succeed?"

Aggressive Significance-Recognition Questions (8)

Tone: direct, revealing, respectfully challenging.

1. "What are you unwilling to admit this outcome means to you?"

2. "Which emotional pressure is driving this more than you expected?"

3. "What would failure here represent on a personal or leadership level?"

4. "What significance is so strong that it makes this effort non-negotiable?"

5. "What deeper need is pushing this to the top of your priorities?"

6. "Who are you trying to protect, reassure, or support through this change?"

7. "What part of your identity is tied to achieving this outcome?"

8. "What meaning would success carry that goes beyond the metrics?"

Follow-Up Significance-Recognition Questions (10)

Tone: gentle, clarifying, emotionally aware.

1. "Can you share a moment when you realized this mattered to you personally?"

2. "What emotion did you feel when that moment happened?"

3. "How has that feeling influenced your decisions since then?"

4. "Who else understands the significance of this change?"

5. "How would success affect the way your team sees you?"

6. "What would achieving this restore, protect, or elevate for you?"

7. "What past experience makes this outcome feel important now?"

8. "Which part of this significance has been difficult to express?"

9. "How does acknowledging the significance change your perspective?"

10. "What deeper meaning becomes clear after reflecting on it now?"

Conclusion

Significance-recognition questions illuminate the emotional foundation of the buyer's goals. They reveal why the change matters—not just what it will accomplish. When significance becomes visible, motivation strengthens, commitment deepens, and decisions gain emotional clarity.

Strategically, these insights help you frame future conversations in ways that resonate with the buyer's deeper motivations. Psychologically, they give the buyer permission to connect with the human meaning behind their work, reducing doubt and increasing confidence.

As Chapter 5 continues, the next sections will explore ambition, future trajectory, strategic levers, and long-term possibility. Significance is the bridge between value and vision — the emotional anchor that gives the future direction its weight.

Reflection Prompt:

Think of a buyer who seemed emotionally invested but never said why. Which significance-recognition question would have helped them express the deeper meaning behind their goals?

CHAPTER 5 - SECTION 7 - Strategic-Ambition Questions

Introduction

With value and significance clarified, the next step is understanding the buyer's **strategic ambition** — the scale, depth, and pace of change they are willing to pursue. Every organization has ambition, but not all ambition is articulated. Some teams dream big but struggle to act. Others act boldly but lack a clear long-term direction. Strategic-ambition questions help uncover the buyer's appetite for growth, their capacity for risk, and the vision they hold for what the organization could become.

Strategically, ambition defines the boundaries of possibility. It influences how far the buyer is willing to go, how quickly they want to move, and how much change they're prepared to embrace. High-ambition environments open pathways for transformation; moderate-ambition environments require a steady, staged approach; low-ambition environments focus on stability and manageable wins. By uncovering ambition, you gain clarity about the scale of recommendations that will feel aligned.

Psychologically, ambition is often shaped by past experiences — successes that created confidence, failures that created caution, or leadership changes that shifted expectations. Buyers may also hesitate to express ambition because it feels vulnerable or unrealistic. Your role is to create space where ambition can be expressed honestly and without judgment. When buyers feel safe to articulate their true aspirations, new possibilities emerge.

Interpretation Tip: Pay attention to how buyers talk about the future. Words like "we hope," "we want," and "we'll try" reveal modest ambition. Words like "we need," "we're ready," and "we will" reveal stronger ambition. Also listen for signs of fear, hesitation, or excitement — these emotions highlight the tension between aspiration and perceived limits.

Coaching Note: Encourage the buyer to think beyond short-term pressures. Strategic ambition lives in the long view — what they want to build, become, or influence years from now. Help them explore that direction without forcing them into unrealistic expectations.

Example prompts:

- *"How far do you want this improvement to take you?"*

- *"What level of change feels aligned with your long-term vision?"*

Standard Strategic-Ambition Questions (8)

Tone: open, future-focused, balanced.

1. "How do you see your organization evolving in the next few years?"

2. "What level of change feels appropriate for your current direction?"

3. "What goals reflect your long-term ambition?"

4. "Which improvements would position you strongly for the future?"

5. "What type of progress would make you feel you're moving forward meaningfully?"

6. "What opportunities align with your broader strategic goals?"

7. "What future outcomes feel both important and realistic?"

8. "Where do you want this effort to take you over time?"

Intermediate Strategic-Ambition Questions (9)

Tone: probing, clarifying, directional.

1. "Which strategic goals inspire you the most?"

2. "What ambition do you feel your team is capable of achieving?"

3. "Where do you want to be stronger, bigger, or more effective?"

4. "Which long-term improvements would elevate your competitive position?"

5. "What ambitions require planning beyond your current capacity?"

6. "Which strategic opportunities excite your leadership?"

7. "Where does ambition exceed current structure — and what does that reveal?"

8. "What does meaningful long-term success look like for your team?"

9. "Which ambitions feel challenging but achievable with support?"

Aggressive Strategic-Ambition Questions (8)

Tone: bold, revealing, challenge-oriented.

1. "What ambition are you afraid to say out loud?"

2. "Which long-term goal feels bigger than anything you've tried before?"

3. "What outcome would redefine your organization if achieved?"

4. "Which ambition do you secretly believe is possible?"

5. "What bold move would shift your entire trajectory?"

6. "Which long-term aspiration is leadership overlooking?"

7. "Where are you thinking too small for what you're capable of?"

8. "What ambition would force you to operate at a higher level?"

Follow-Up Strategic-Ambition Questions (10)

Tone: reflective, clarifying, vision-deepening.

1. "Can you describe a moment that shaped your long-term ambition?"

2. "What experience made you realize you could aim higher?"

3. "Which achievements gave you confidence to pursue bigger goals?"

4. "How has your ambition changed over the years?"

5. "What part of your ambition feels most aligned with your identity?"

6. "Which ambition does your team rally around the most?"

7. "What support would help you pursue your ambition more fully?"

8. "Which ambition feels urgent — and why?"

9. "How would you know you're on the right track toward your long-term vision?"

10. "What becomes possible once your ambition is fully activated?"

Conclusion

Strategic-ambition questions reveal how far the buyer wants to go and how boldly they're willing to pursue the future. By uncovering ambition, you gain insight into the scale of transformation that feels achievable and inspiring for the organization. This understanding helps guide recommendations, pace changes, and shape long-term planning.

Strategically, ambition determines direction and momentum. Psychologically, it reflects identity, confidence, and belief in future possibility. When ambition is acknowledged, the buyer becomes more intentional and more energized about the journey ahead.

As Chapter 5 continues, the next sections will explore future vision, opportunity mapping, strategic levers, and long-term potential. Ambition is the emotional fuel that powers the exploration of what the organization can ultimately become.

Reflection Prompt:
Think of a buyer who held back their true aspirations. Which strategic-ambition question would have helped them express their vision more honestly?

CHAPTER 5 - SECTION 8 - Future-Vision Questions

Introduction

Once strategic ambition is understood, the next step is helping the buyer articulate a **future vision** — a vivid, meaningful, and coherent picture of what they want their organization, team, or process to become. While ambition defines scale, vision defines shape. Future-vision questions guide the buyer beyond short-term goals into a clear, emotionally resonant picture of their desired future state.

Strategically, a strong future vision acts as a north star. It helps clarify priorities, align stakeholders, and guide difficult decisions. When the buyer understands their future vision, they can recognize which paths accelerate progress and which distract from it. Without vision, even strong ambition loses direction.

Psychologically, future vision gives hope and meaning. It taps into imagination, identity, and aspiration. Vision-based thinking breaks the gravitational pull of current limitations and allows the buyer to imagine what could exist if constraints were reduced, risks were managed, and potential was activated. These conversations shift mindset from reactive to creative.

Interpretation Tip: Listen for phrases that reveal emotional resonance—what excites them, what feels inspiring, or what brings relief. Notice contradictions between how they talk about today and how they talk about the future; these contrasts highlight the gap they want to close. Pay attention to any hesitation — sometimes the buyer has a clearer vision than they initially feel comfortable expressing.

Coaching Note: Encourage imagery. Help the buyer paint a picture of the future rather than listing bullet points. The more vivid the vision, the more persuasive it becomes as a guiding narrative for their team and stakeholders.

Example prompts:

- *"What does an ideal future look like for your organization?"*

- *"If everything worked exactly as you hoped, what would the future feel like?"*

Standard Future-Vision Questions (8)

Tone: open, imaginative, grounded in possibility.

1. "How would you describe the future you want to create?"

2. "What does a successful future look like for your team?"

3. "Which improvements would shape the future you imagine?"

4. "What would your operations look like at their best?"

5. "How would the future feel different from today?"

6. "What strengths do you want to see expanded over time?"

7. "What role do you want your team to play in the organization's future?"

8. "What long-term changes matter most to your vision?"

Intermediate Future-Vision Questions (9)

Tone: probing, clarifying, direction-focused.

1. "Which elements of your future vision feel most essential?"

2. "How does your ideal future align with your strategic goals?"

3. "What does long-term success look like in practice?"

4. "Which parts of your vision require the biggest shifts from today?"

5. "How would your team work differently in the future you imagine?"

6. "Which customer or stakeholder experiences would change the most?"

7. "What capabilities would need to grow to achieve your vision?"

8. "How would leadership define success in your ideal future?"

9. "Which parts of your vision feel challenging but achievable?"

Aggressive Future-Vision Questions (8)

Tone: direct, bold, boundary-expanding.

1. "What future do you truly want — even if it feels ambitious?"

2. "Which part of your vision scares you because it's so big?"

3. "What future would transform your organization's identity?"

4. "Which vision are you holding back because you fear pushback?"

5. "What future feels impossible only because of current limits?"

6. "Which bold direction would you pursue if nothing held you back?"

7. "What future outcome would change your entire trajectory?"

8. "Which part of your vision demands courage, not caution?"

Follow-Up Future-Vision Questions (10)

Tone: reflective, clarifying, visualization-focused.

1. "Can you describe a moment when you first imagined this future?"

2. "What inspired that vision?"

3. "How has your vision evolved over time?"

4. "Which parts of the vision feel clearest to you now?"

5. "What would achieving this future change for your team emotionally?"

6. "What small details make this future especially meaningful?"

7. "What would daily work look like in your envisioned future?"

8. "How would this future strengthen your organization's identity?"

9. "What signals would show you're moving closer to this future?"

10. "Which part of this future would you want to experience first?"

Conclusion

Future-vision questions help the buyer articulate a meaningful, motivating picture of what they want to create. Vision turns ambition into direction and transforms possibility into a compelling narrative. When the buyer can clearly see their future, the path forward becomes sharper and more intentional.

Strategically, these insights guide priorities, planning, and decision-making. Psychologically, they create hope, energy, and alignment. A strong vision unites stakeholders, strengthens commitment, and anchors long-term progress.

As Chapter 5 continues, the next sections will explore strategic levers, advantage opportunities, long-term potential, and the deeper implications of future-focused thinking. With vision established, the discovery process can now move into shaping the path to reach it.

Reflection Prompt:

Think of a buyer who had ambition but lacked direction. Which future-vision question would have helped them see their desired future more clearly?

CHAPTER 5 - SECTION 9 - Strategic-Lever Questions

Introduction

Once the buyer's future vision is clear, the next step is identifying the **strategic levers** — the specific actions, behaviors, capabilities, or changes that can exert outsized influence on results. Strategic levers are not just tasks or improvements; they are *force multipliers* that accelerate progress, shape outcomes, and move the organization toward its vision efficiently. Strategic-lever questions help the buyer uncover which levers matter most and which ones will deliver the greatest impact with the least wasted effort.

Strategically, this is where direction becomes actionable. Future vision provides the destination, but strategic levers reveal the mechanisms that can make that future possible. These levers vary across organizations: for some, it's leadership alignment; for others, it's process refinement, talent development, tool adoption, customer insight, or improved communication. When the right levers are identified, organizations can make rapid progress without overwhelming resources.

Psychologically, strategic levers create clarity in moments of uncertainty. They show the buyer that meaningful change doesn't require sweeping transformation — it requires choosing and activating the levers that matter most. This reduces overwhelm and strengthens confidence. It narrows the field of action and highlights the handful of moves that truly shift performance and direction.

Interpretation Tip: Listen for clues that a particular change has disproportionate influence: "When this part works, everything else improves," "If we fixed this, a lot of problems would disappear," or "This team sets the tone for the rest." These are signals of strategic levers. Also note moments when the buyer describes early wins or key behaviors that have ripple effects.

Coaching Note: Encourage the buyer to distinguish between *important tasks* and *high-leverage actions*. Not everything that matters has leverage. Strategic levers are the actions that unlock capacity, direction, alignment, or performance across the system.

Example prompts:

- *"Which improvements would create the biggest shift with the least effort?"*

- *"What actions have the strongest ripple effect across the organization?"*

Standard Strategic-Lever Questions (8)

Tone: practical, clarifying, insight-driven.

1. "Which improvements would have the most noticeable impact?"

2. "What actions tend to influence multiple parts of the operation?"

3. "Where do small changes create meaningful gains?"

4. "Which behaviors strengthen performance across the team?"

5. "What part of your process sets the tone for everything else?"

6. "Which tasks or responsibilities shape the final outcome the most?"

7. "Where does improvement seem to produce the biggest ripple effect?"

8. "What capabilities make the rest of the system work better?"

Intermediate Strategic-Lever Questions (9)

Tone: probing, analytical, leverage-focused.

1. "Which actions accelerate progress more than others?"

2. "What skills or habits create disproportionate value?"

3. "Which team or role drives momentum for everyone else?"

4. "What improvement would help remove multiple obstacles at once?"

5. "Which lever would strengthen alignment or communication the fastest?"

6. "Where do you see the strongest connection between effort and impact?"

7. "Which responsibilities influence performance upstream and downstream?"

8. "What change would raise the baseline performance of the entire team?"

9. "Which lever supports your long-term vision most directly?"

Aggressive Strategic-Lever Questions (8)

Tone: direct, pinpointing, high-impact-focused.

1. "What single lever would change the most if activated today?"

2. "Which lever is so powerful it makes other issues seem smaller?"

3. "What lever is being ignored even though it could accelerate results?"

4. "Which action would create a breakthrough if fully committed to?"

5. "What capability gaps are blocking your strongest levers?"

6. "Which part of the operation has the highest leverage — and highest risk?"

7. "What lever requires courage because it affects entrenched habits?"

8. "Which strategic move would shift your entire trajectory if executed well?"

Follow-Up Strategic-Lever Questions (10)

Tone: reflective, clarifying, deeply analytical.

1. "Can you share a moment when a single action created a big improvement?"

2. "What made that action so influential?"

3. "Which lever revealed its impact through a ripple effect?"

4. "Who recognized the leverage first — and why?"

5. "What conditions helped the lever work effectively?"

6. "How did activating that lever change team behavior?"

7. "What prevented that lever from being used consistently before?"

8. "Which long-term lever will support your future vision most strongly?"

9. "What would help strengthen or support your biggest levers?"

10. "What signal would show you that a lever is starting to take effect?"

Conclusion

Strategic-lever questions reveal the actions and capabilities that carry the greatest influence over performance, direction, and momentum. They help the buyer identify not just what needs improvement, but what will *move the system* most quickly and effectively.

Strategically, these insights highlight the highest-impact pathways toward the buyer's future vision. Psychologically, they reduce the feeling of overwhelm and replace it with focus, clarity, and confidence. When the buyer knows which levers matter most, the journey toward meaningful change becomes far more direct and achievable.

As Chapter 5 continues, the next sections will explore long-term potential, transformation possibility, and deeper strategic alignment. Strategic levers are the tools that make the future real.

Reflection Prompt:

Think of a buyer who tried to change everything at once. Which strategic-lever question would have helped them focus on what mattered most?

CHAPTER 5 - SECTION 10 - Long-Term-Potential Questions

Introduction

With strategic levers identified, the final step in this chapter is understanding the organization's **long-term potential** — the future capacity, performance, and opportunity that could be unlocked over time with the right direction, effort, and support. Long-term potential is not about what the organization *is* today; it's about what it can *become*. These questions help the buyer look far beyond near-term challenges and imagine the capabilities, impact, and competitive strength they could achieve through sustained progress.

Strategically, long-term potential represents the highest horizon line. It influences investment decisions, shapes multi-year planning, and guides leadership in choosing which opportunities deserve long-term commitment. When the buyer understands their long-term potential, short-term decisions gain clearer purpose, and future-focused planning becomes more aligned.

Psychologically, exploring long-term potential lifts the buyer out of the constraints of the present. It gives them permission to imagine a stronger, more capable version of their organization without being limited by current pressures or imperfections. This shift helps reinforce confidence, curiosity, and strategic optimism — essential qualities when pursuing lasting transformation.

Interpretation Tip: Listen for excitement, caution, or hesitation when the buyer talks about the long term. These emotional tones reveal whether they see their future as hopeful, uncertain, or constrained. Also note when the buyer references "if we had ____," "once we get ____," or "after we fix ___." These statements often reveal their intuitive understanding of their long-term potential.

Coaching Note: Help the buyer connect long-term potential with their vision, ambition, value, and priorities. Long-term potential is not fantasy; it's the natural extension of what becomes possible when strengths are developed, opportunities are pursued, and strategic levers are activated.

Example prompts:

- *"What could your organization achieve over the long term with the right support?"*

- *"What potential do you see that hasn't yet been fully cultivated?"*

Standard Long-Term-Potential Questions (8)

Tone: calm, open, future-oriented.

1. "What long-term potential do you see in your team or organization?"

2. "Which capabilities could grow significantly over time?"

3. "Where do you see room for long-term development?"

4. "What areas could become strengths with sustained focus?"

5. "What future opportunities do you believe your team could eventually pursue?"

6. "Which skills or processes could scale as you grow?"

7. "What long-term improvement would create lasting advantage?"

8. "Where do you see potential that will take time to realize?"

Intermediate Long-Term-Potential Questions (9)

Tone: probing, clarifying, horizon-expanding.

1. "Which long-term opportunities align most with your future vision?"

2. "What capabilities do you want to see developed over the next few years?"

3. "Which strengths could become defining features of your organization?"

4. "What potential becomes visible once current obstacles are removed?"

5. "Which long-term improvements would elevate your competitive position?"

6. "What future capabilities could transform how your team operates?"

7. "Which investments would pay off the most over time?"

8. "Where do you see potential for multi-year growth or impact?"

9. "What part of your long-term potential feels underestimated today?"

Aggressive Long-Term-Potential Questions (8)

Tone: bold, challenging, boundary-expanding.

1. "What long-term potential are you overlooking because you're too focused on current limits?"

2. "Which future capability could redefine your organization's identity?"

3. "What potential feels bigger than anything you've attempted before?"

4. "Where could your organization be in five years with strong, steady progress?"

5. "What long-term opportunity do you secretly believe is possible?"

6. "Which future strength would surprise your competitors?"

7. "What long-term potential goes untapped because it feels too distant?"

8. "Which big-picture goal could become real with consistent effort?"

Follow-Up Long-Term-Potential Questions (10)

Tone: reflective, clarifying, vision-deepening.

1. "Can you describe a moment when you recognized your team's long-term potential?"

2. "What sparked that realization?"

3. "How has that potential revealed itself over time?"

4. "What long-term capabilities do you want to develop first?"

5. "Which stakeholders would feel the impact of long-term growth most strongly?"

6. "What internal strengths will support your long-term direction?"

7. "What long-term risks must be managed to unlock your potential?"

8. "What small steps today would contribute to your long-term goals?"

9. "What signs would show that your long-term potential is becoming real?"

10. "What future advantage would you gain once your potential is fully realized?"

Conclusion

Long-term-potential questions encourage the buyer to step beyond present challenges and explore what their organization could become with sustained progress and the right strategic support. These questions help reveal hidden strengths, new possibilities, and capabilities that could take years to fully develop — but would significantly shape the organization's future trajectory.

Strategically, long-term potential guides multi-year planning, investment decisions, and capability-building efforts. Psychologically, it creates hope, momentum, and confidence in the journey ahead. When the buyer understands their long-term potential, they gain a sense of direction that is steadier and more meaningful than short-term progress alone.

Chapter Conclusion

Chapter 5 reveals that discovery is not only about uncovering problems — it is equally about revealing potential, meaning, and direction. By exploring desired outcomes, priorities, opportunities, value, significance, ambition, vision, strategic levers, and long-term potential, the buyer gains a deep understanding of both what they want and what they are capable of achieving. This clarity transforms the discovery conversation from a diagnostic exercise into a forward-looking, energizing exploration.

Strategically, this chapter provides the insights needed to shape effective recommendations and guide multi-stage transformations. It ensures that future planning aligns with the buyer's priorities, aspirations, and definition of success. Psychologically, the chapter reconnects the buyer with hope — showing them that change is not just necessary but meaningful, attainable, and aligned with their deeper purpose.

As the book moves forward, the next chapter will shift toward understanding how value amplifies across teams and systems, and how the organization's broader environment influences decision-making. With the emotional and strategic landscape now visible, the buyer is more prepared to pursue meaningful, sustainable change with clarity and confidence.

CHAPTER 6 - Understanding Collaborative Dynamics and Team Alignment

Chapter Introduction

Collaboration is not defined by how people behave when things are easy. It is defined by how teams communicate, coordinate, and respond when expectations shift, pressure rises, or responsibilities overlap. Chapter 6 explores this deeper dimension of teamwork: the patterns, behaviors, and relational forces that determine how effectively people work together in real conditions. Collaboration is not simply a "team activity"; it is a psychological ecosystem shaped by trust, clarity, influence, and emotional safety.

The chapter begins with **Team-Alignment Clarity Questions**, which uncover whether people truly share the same understanding of goals, responsibilities, and expectations. Many teams assume alignment exists until they are forced to act quickly — and then discover how differently each person interprets their role. Alignment clarity sets the stage for the rest of the chapter by revealing the foundation upon which collaboration either thrives or collapses.

Next, the chapter turns to **Communication Flow** and **Role Interaction**, exploring how information moves and how people work together based on their responsibilities. Communication reveals whether meaning travels consistently. Role interaction reveals how responsibilities and authority intersect. Together, these sections provide insight into the daily rhythms of teamwork — the mechanics that shape how smoothly coordination occurs.

From there, the chapter examines **Cross-Functional Dependencies**, **Influence Dynamics**, and **Collaboration Friction**. These sections highlight the areas where collaboration extends beyond the boundaries of a single team. You see where handoffs succeed or fail, where informal power shapes decisions, and where subtle tension disrupts coordination. This middle of the chapter exposes the invisible forces that either strengthen collaboration or quietly degrade it over time.

The next layers explore **Conflict Patterns** and **Decision Friction**, two of the most important indicators of collaborative health. Conflict patterns show how disagreements form and repeat, while decision friction reveals how easily teams commit to action. These sections shine a light on how the organization responds when stakes rise or expectations diverge. They help identify where alignment breaks down and where uncertainty slows momentum.

Finally, the chapter concludes with **Trust Signals** and **Collaborative Readiness**, which reveal the emotional and behavioral readiness of the team to handle complex, high-pressure situations. Trust determines how openly people communicate; readiness determines how effectively they act together when it matters most. These sections integrate all previous insights into a complete picture of collaborative capability.

Together, the ten sections in this chapter offer a comprehensive framework for understanding how teams interact, support each other, and navigate challenges. Collaboration is not a single behavior — it is the interplay of clarity, communication, trust, and influence. Chapter 6 helps the reader diagnose this interplay with precision, empathy, and depth.

CHAPTER 6 - SECTION 1 - Team-Alignment Clarity Questions

Introduction

Before exploring collaboration, communication flow, influence patterns, or cross-functional dynamics, every organization must understand one fundamental element: **team alignment clarity**. Alignment is the degree to which people share the same understanding of goals, responsibilities, expectations, standards, and success measures. Most teams believe they are aligned, but when asked to describe their priorities or outcomes, their answers often diverge. This section helps reveal the reality beneath that assumption.

Strategically, alignment is the foundation of execution. Teams that lack alignment struggle with mixed expectations, duplicated work, unnecessary friction, and inconsistent performance. Alignment—or the lack of it—shapes how fast teams can move, how well they manage change, and how effectively they coordinate with other groups. These questions illuminate hidden gaps in understanding that weaken collaboration long before problems become visible.

Psychologically, alignment affects trust. When people are unclear about expectations, they experience stress, self-protection, and hesitation. When alignment becomes explicit, confidence increases, communication improves, and relationships strengthen. These questions help the buyer surface alignment gaps without creating blame, allowing them to see how clarity impacts morale and teamwork.

Interpretation Tip: Listen for inconsistencies. If the buyer describes multiple goals, mixed expectations, or shifting standards, you are hearing signs of misalignment. Pay attention when they use phrases like "depends on the day," "we're not all on the same page," or "we interpret things differently."

Coaching Note: Encourage the buyer to separate *agreement* from *clarity*. Even when people get along, they may not share a consistent understanding of expectations. Clarity requires explicit shared meaning, not good intentions.

Example prompts:

- *"How consistently does your team describe its top goals?"*

- *"What expectations feel clear — and which do not?"*

Standard Team-Alignment Clarity Questions (8)

Tone: calm, neutral, clarity-seeking.

1. "How clearly does your team understand its top goals?"

2. "Which expectations feel well-defined to everyone?"

3. "Where does the team seem unsure about responsibilities?"

4. "Which tasks or outcomes generate mixed interpretations?"

5. "What areas require repeated clarification?"

6. "Where does communication seem to drift away from the intended message?"

7. "How consistently do team members describe success?"

8. "Which processes rely on assumptions instead of shared clarity?"

Intermediate Team-Alignment Clarity Questions (9)

Tone: probing, pattern-focused, insight-oriented.

1. "Which responsibilities are understood differently across the team?"

2. "Where do priorities compete for attention instead of aligning?"

3. "What expectations vary depending on who you ask?"

4. "Which goals feel understood at the leadership level but unclear at the team level?"

5. "Where do miscommunications create subtle misalignment?"

6. "Which definitions of success differ between individuals or roles?"

7. "What signs show that alignment slips during busy periods?"

8. "Where does clarity get lost as work moves between functions?"

9. "Which topics spark repeated confusion during discussions?"

Aggressive Team-Alignment Clarity Questions (8)

Tone: direct, truth-seeking, respectfully confronting ambiguity.

1. "Where is the team pretending to be aligned when it isn't?"

2. "Which expectation remains unclear no matter how often it's discussed?"

3. "What part of alignment is currently a weak point for leadership?"

4. "Which responsibility lacks ownership because clarity is missing?"

5. "Where does misalignment create the most wasted effort?"

6. "Which team members hold different interpretations but won't speak up?"

7. "What alignment gap is causing the most tension right now?"

8. "Where is misalignment silently hurting performance or trust?"

Follow-Up Team-Alignment Clarity Questions (10)

Tone: reflective, clarifying, emotionally aware.

1. "Can you describe a recent moment when misalignment became visible?"

2. "What caused the misunderstanding?"

3. "How did team members react when clarity was missing?"

4. "What impact did the misalignment have on performance or morale?"

5. "Which part of the situation revealed the real alignment gap?"

6. "What steps were taken to correct the misunderstanding?"

7. "How effective was that correction?"

8. "What deeper issue did the misalignment reveal?"

9. "What would help maintain alignment more consistently?"

10. "What would alignment look like if the team truly shared the same understanding?"

Conclusion

Team alignment clarity questions expose the degree to which people truly understand their goals, responsibilities, expectations, and definitions of success. They reveal whether the team is aligned in concept or aligned in practice — two very different realities. These insights set the stage for deeper exploration of collaboration, communication, and cross-functional coordination.

Strategically, alignment determines speed, accuracy, and cohesion. Psychologically, it influences trust, confidence, and how safe people feel expressing concerns. When alignment becomes visible, the team can address misunderstanding early rather than respond to problems later.

As Chapter 6 continues, we will explore communication flow, role clarity, interpersonal dynamics, cross-team reliance, conflict points, and deeper layers of collaborative behavior. Alignment is the baseline — the foundation upon which all healthy collaboration is built.

Reflection Prompt:

Think of a team that struggled with coordination. Which alignment-clarity question would have revealed the underlying misunderstanding sooner?

CHAPTER 6 - SECTION 2 - Communication-Flow Questions

Introduction

After establishing team alignment clarity, the next step is understanding **communication flow** — how information moves, how decisions are shared, and how meaning is transmitted between people and teams. Communication is the connective tissue of collaboration. If alignment reveals whether everyone understands the same goals, communication flow reveals *how* that understanding spreads or breaks down.

Strategically, communication flow determines speed, accuracy, and cohesion. Strong communication systems keep teams informed, consistent, and coordinated. Weak communication systems create gaps, misunderstandings, misinterpretations, and unnecessary conflict. Many performance issues originate not from poor work ethic but from communication that is fragmented, delayed, incomplete, or filtered through too many layers.

Psychologically, communication affects trust and emotional safety. People feel secure when they know what's happening and why. When communication is unclear, delayed, or inconsistent, teams fill the gaps with assumptions, fears, or defensive behavior. These questions help uncover where communication supports teamwork — and where it quietly erodes it.

Interpretation Tip: Listen for uncertainty markers like "I think," "I assume," "We usually," or "It depends who you ask." These indicate communication flow issues. Also pay attention to mentions of bottlenecks: individuals or teams who control or slow the movement of information.

Coaching Note: Encourage the buyer to focus on patterns, not isolated incidents. Communication flow is defined by the behaviors that repeat — the way messages move most of the time, not just in a single example.

Example prompts:

- *"How easily does information move through the team?"*

- *"Where do messages tend to get delayed or distorted?"*

Standard Communication-Flow Questions (8)

Tone: calm, structured, descriptive.

1. "How would you describe the flow of communication within your team?"

2. "Where does information move smoothly from person to person?"

3. "Which updates tend to reach everyone consistently?"

4. "Where does communication feel slow or fragmented?"

5. "Which topics get communicated clearly most of the time?"

6. "Where do team members often seek clarification?"

7. "Which channels seem most reliable for sharing information?"

8. "What types of messages get overlooked or delayed?"

Intermediate Communication-Flow Questions (9)

Tone: probing, pattern-oriented, clear.

1. "Which responsibilities rely heavily on consistent communication flow?"

2. "Where do breaks in communication cause friction or confusion?"

3. "Which people or teams act as information bottlenecks?"

4. "What messages lose meaning as they move across the organization?"

5. "Where does communication become overly dependent on individuals?"

6. "Which workflows suffer most from delayed or incomplete updates?"

7. "What patterns appear when communication fails?"

8. "Which topics spark misunderstandings due to unclear messaging?"

9. "Where does the team rely on assumptions instead of confirmed information?"

Aggressive Communication-Flow Questions (8)

Tone: direct, precise, truth-seeking.

1. "Where is communication failing the team most right now?"

2. "Who consistently slows or filters information in unhelpful ways?"

3. "What messages rarely reach the people who need them?"

4. "Which communication habit is causing avoidable issues?"

5. "Where does leadership misjudge how well communication is working?"

6. "Which topics cause confusion because communication is inconsistent?"

7. "What system or channel is no longer reliable?"

8. "Where has communication become reactive instead of intentional?"

Follow-Up Communication-Flow Questions (10)

Tone: reflective, clarifying, detail-oriented.

1. "Can you share a recent moment when communication broke down?"

2. "What effect did the breakdown have on workflow or morale?"

3. "Who noticed the issue first?"

4. "What signal showed that communication wasn't moving as expected?"

5. "What did the team do to recover from the breakdown?"

6. "What part of the situation revealed the deeper communication pattern?"

7. "How often does this type of communication issue occur?"

8. "What would have prevented the breakdown in the first place?"

9. "What would a smoother communication flow look like in practice?"

10. "What small change would make communication meaningfully easier?"

Conclusion

Communication-flow questions reveal how information travels — and where it stalls, weakens, or becomes distorted. They expose hidden friction points that hinder alignment, slow decision-making, or erode trust. When communication becomes clear, predictable, and consistent, collaboration strengthens across every level of the organization.

Strategically, these insights help the advisor understand how fast decisions can move and how effectively teams coordinate. Psychologically, they reveal whether people feel informed, supported, and connected. A healthy communication flow makes the organization more resilient and reduces confusion during change.

As Chapter 6 continues, we will explore role alignment, cross-functional dynamics, influence patterns, tension points, and collaborative readiness. Communication flow sets the stage for understanding how people actually work together day after day.

Reflection Prompt:
Think of a moment when communication shaped a team's success or failure. Which communication-flow question would have revealed the underlying issue sooner?

CHAPTER 6 - SECTION 3 - Role-Interaction Questions

Introduction

After understanding the flow of information, the next step is exploring **role interaction** — how individuals and teams work together based on their responsibilities, authority, expectations, and points of overlap. Role interaction shapes the quality of collaboration more directly than job titles or org charts. It reveals how people depend on each other, how they influence one another, and how responsibilities fit together in practice.

Strategically, role interaction determines whether work moves smoothly or becomes tangled in confusion. Even well-designed processes can struggle when responsibilities overlap, authority is ambiguous, or team members aren't sure who owns which decisions. These questions help uncover where roles complement each other, where they collide, and where hidden gaps undermine performance.

Psychologically, unclear or unhealthy role interaction creates tension. People become protective of their tasks, defensive about their territory, or frustrated by unmet expectations. When role interaction is healthy, trust increases and collaboration becomes easier. When it's weak, even small missteps can escalate into conflict. These questions aim to reveal the real dynamics behind cooperation, handoffs, and shared work.

Interpretation Tip: Listen for signs of confusion ("I'm not sure who handles that"), frustration ("We're stepping on each other's toes"), or hesitation ("It depends who's available"). Also note when the buyer praises a cross-functional partnership — positive examples often highlight what healthy role interaction looks like.

Coaching Note: Encourage the buyer to focus on patterns rather than individuals. Role issues are almost always structural, not personal, and exploring them through that lens keeps the conversation balanced and constructive.

Example prompts:

- *"How do your team's roles intersect during daily work?"*

- *"Where do responsibilities overlap or leave gaps?"*

Standard Role-Interaction Questions (8)

Tone: calm, observational, structured.

1. "How do different roles on the team interact during typical workdays?"

2. "Where do responsibilities overlap in useful ways?"

3. "Which handoffs between roles work smoothly?"

4. "Where do roles rely heavily on each other's support?"

5. "Which tasks require coordination between multiple roles?"

6. "Where does role interaction feel unclear or inconsistent?"

7. "Which responsibilities depend on shared understanding?"

8. "Where do interactions between roles shape overall momentum?"

Intermediate Role-Interaction Questions (9)

Tone: probing, pattern-focused, clarity-seeking.

1. "Which roles interact most frequently — and why?"

2. "Where do misunderstandings between roles create delays?"

3. "Which responsibilities lack clear boundaries across roles?"

4. "What role interactions are heavily influenced by personal relationships?"

5. "Where does one role depend on another to complete critical tasks?"

6. "Which interactions break down when workload increases?"

7. "What patterns appear when roles coordinate poorly?"

8. "Where do teams disagree about who owns certain responsibilities?"

9. "What role interactions should be strengthened to improve collaboration?"

Aggressive Role-Interaction Questions (8)

Tone: direct, truth-seeking, revealing friction points.

1. "Which roles consistently conflict with each other?"

2. "Where does unclear role ownership create the most frustration?"

3. "What responsibilities are falling through the cracks due to poor interaction?"

4. "Who is compensating for gaps caused by unclear roles?"

5. "Which role interaction causes the most avoidable tension?"

6. "Where does the team rely on informal behavior to make up for structural issues?"

7. "Which repeated conflict reveals deeper role confusion?"

8. "Where is role interaction weakening performance the most?"

Follow-Up Role-Interaction Questions (10)

Tone: reflective, specific, insight-deepening.

1. "Can you describe a moment when role interaction worked exceptionally well?"

2. "What made that collaboration effective?"

3. "Who contributed to making the interaction smooth?"

4. "What conditions supported that success?"

5. "Can you recall a moment when role interaction broke down?"

6. "What caused the breakdown and how did it unfold?"

7. "How did team members respond to the confusion?"

8. "What deeper issue did the situation reveal about role dynamics?"

9. "What would help strengthen role collaboration going forward?"

10. "What signal would show that role interaction is improving?"

Conclusion

Role interaction questions reveal how responsibilities, authority, and expectations work in practice — not on paper. They uncover where roles complement one another, where they overlap, and where gaps create friction. When role interaction becomes visible, the organization can strengthen collaboration at its structural core.

Strategically, these insights help identify improvements to ownership, workflow, and coordination. Psychologically, they help reduce frustration, clarify expectations, and build trust between individuals and teams. When people understand how their roles intersect, collaboration becomes more natural and predictable.

As Chapter 6 continues, we will explore influence patterns, cross-team dynamics, conflict points, and the subtle forces that shape how people work together. Role interaction is the bridge between communication clarity and effective teamwork.

Reflection Prompt:
Think of a team where roles were unclear or inconsistent. Which role-interaction question would have revealed the underlying dynamic earlier?

CHAPTER 6 - SECTION 4 - Cross-Functional-Dependency Questions

Introduction

Once role interaction is understood within a team, the next layer is examining **cross-functional dependencies** — where different teams rely on one another to complete tasks, make decisions, share information, and support shared outcomes. These dependencies shape the organization's ability to move as a coordinated system rather than a collection of isolated groups. When cross-functional dependencies are strong, progress accelerates. When they are fragile, slow, or unclear, the entire operation feels it.

Strategically, cross-functional dependencies determine how efficiently work flows across the organization. They influence project timelines, customer experience, quality standards, and decision-making speed. Many systemic problems — delays, rework, misalignment, and miscommunication — originate from cross-functional friction rather than internal team issues. These questions help reveal how the organization's pieces fit together and where the biggest collaborative risks sit.

Psychologically, cross-functional relationships affect trust and influence. When teams feel unsupported or unheard, resentment builds quietly. When dependencies are respected and reliable, collaboration becomes easier and morale improves. These questions explore the relational and structural realities behind how teams work together across boundaries.

Interpretation Tip: Listen for frustration tied to other teams: "We're waiting on them," "They don't see the urgency," "We get incomplete information from them," or "They have different priorities." These are markers of cross-functional dependency strain. Also pay attention to positive examples — they reveal the conditions that create strong interteam cooperation.

Coaching Note: Encourage the buyer to distinguish between *functional differences* (each team has different needs) and *friction* (teams block or misunderstand each other). This helps clarify what issues are natural and what issues need attention.

Example prompts:

- *"Which teams rely on each other most heavily to complete their work?"*

- *"Where do cross-functional dependencies support or slow progress?"*

Standard Cross-Functional-Dependency Questions (8)

Tone: calm, structured, descriptive.

1. "Which teams depend on each other most to complete shared work?"

2. "Where do cross-functional handoffs occur most often?"

3. "Which interactions between teams tend to work smoothly?"

4. "Where does cross-functional support feel reliable?"

5. "Which shared responsibilities require coordination between multiple teams?"

6. "Where do teams rely on timely communication from others?"

7. "Which dependencies shape the overall workflow the most?"

8. "Where do teams feel most connected in their efforts?"

Intermediate Cross-Functional-Dependency Questions (9)

Tone: probing, pattern-focused, clarifying.

1. "Where do cross-functional dependencies cause delays or bottlenecks?"

2. "Which teams struggle most to coordinate expectations?"

3. "Where do information gaps between teams create confusion?"

4. "Which cross-functional handoffs are particularly vulnerable during busy periods?"

5. "Where are responsibilities unclear across team boundaries?"

6. "Which patterns appear when cross-functional coordination breaks down?"

7. "What cross-team dependencies influence decision-making speed?"

8. "Which teams interpret shared goals differently?"

9. "Where is trust strained due to inconsistent dependency support?"

Aggressive Cross-Functional-Dependency Questions (8)

Tone: direct, candid, truth-exposing.

1. "Which cross-functional dependency breaks down the most?"

2. "What team consistently slows progress for others?"

3. "Where is cross-functional support unreliable or inconsistent?"

4. "Which shared responsibility lacks clear ownership across teams?"

5. "Where do teams blame each other instead of collaborating?"

6. "Which dependency is so fragile it threatens major initiatives?"

7. "Where does one team's priorities repeatedly override others' needs?"

8. "What cross-functional dysfunction drains the most energy or time?"

Follow-Up Cross-Functional-Dependency Questions (10)

Tone: reflective, detailed, perspective-deepening.

1. "Can you describe a recent moment when cross-functional dependency created a challenge?"

2. "Which team felt the impact first, and how?"

3. "What signals showed the dependency was beginning to fail?"

4. "How did teams respond — separately or collaboratively?"

5. "What made recovery easier or harder?"

6. "Which part of the situation revealed deeper cross-team issues?"

7. "What changes have been made to improve this dependency?"

8. "How effective have those changes been?"

9. "What would help strengthen this cross-functional relationship?"

10. "What would ideal cross-functional dependency support look like?"

Conclusion

Cross-functional-dependency questions reveal the structural connections that determine how teams collaborate across boundaries. They highlight where coordination succeeds, where it falters, and where systemic improvement can unlock significant organizational value.

Strategically, these insights show which areas require alignment, process refinement, or improved communication to ensure smoother cross-team coordination. Psychologically, they expose where trust is strong or strained — an essential factor for effective collaboration.

As Chapter 6 continues, we will explore influence dynamics, conflict patterns, decision friction, interpersonal trust signals, and readiness for deeper collaboration. Cross-functional dependencies form the skeleton of teamwork; the next sections explore the muscles and connective tissue that move it.

Reflection Prompt:
Think of a situation where delays came from another team rather than your own. Which cross-functional-dependency question would have revealed that tension earlier?

CHAPTER 6 - SECTION 5 - Influence-Dynamics Questions

Introduction

Once cross-functional dependencies are visible, the next layer of collaborative understanding involves **influence dynamics** — the informal forces that shape decisions, momentum, alignment, and team behavior. Influence is not the same as authority. Authority is assigned; influence is earned, perceived, or assumed. Influence dynamics determine whose opinions carry weight, who shapes direction behind the scenes, who accelerates progress, and who slows it down without ever saying "no."

Strategically, influence directs the flow of decisions. A team might have the right process, structure, and communication systems, but the real drivers of action often live in informal networks: trusted advisors, persuasive team members, gatekeepers, validators, skeptics, and quiet deciders who sway others without holding formal titles. Understanding these dynamics helps you see how collaboration actually works, not how it is *supposed* to work.

Psychologically, influence reveals the emotional undercurrent of teamwork. People listen to those they trust, admire, fear, or rely on. Influence can empower teams or create imbalance. Positive influence encourages alignment and initiative. Negative influence encourages hesitation, resistance, or misdirection. These questions help uncover where influence helps collaboration — and where it complicates it.

Interpretation Tip: Listen for references to "checking with someone," "getting buy-in," "they'll want to weigh in," or "they tend to push things one way or another." These signals reveal influential voices. Also pay attention to repeated mentions of the same individuals — consistent reference often highlights informal power.

Coaching Note: Approach influence gently. It's a sensitive area because influence is personal, relational, and sometimes political. Your goal is to create enough psychological safety for the buyer to be honest about the team's informal power structure.

Example prompts:

- *"Whose opinion tends to shape decisions the most?"*

- *"Where do informal influencers accelerate or slow progress?"*

Standard Influence-Dynamics Questions (8)

Tone: calm, observational, curiosity-driven.

1. "Who tends to influence decisions within the team?"

2. "Whose input is usually sought before moving forward?"

3. "Which team members shape momentum through their engagement?"

4. "Where does informal guidance help clarify direction?"

5. "Who helps connect different perspectives across the team?"

6. "Which individuals act as stabilizers during uncertainty?"

7. "Where does influence help align people around shared goals?"

8. "Which conversations tend to shift once certain people weigh in?"

Intermediate Influence-Dynamics Questions (9)

Tone: probing, insightful, pattern-seeking.

1. "Which individuals quietly sway decisions behind the scenes?"

2. "Where does influence override formal authority?"

3. "Which voices carry more weight during disagreements?"

4. "Who tends to amplify concerns or urgency within the group?"

5. "Which influencers shape others' understanding of priorities?"

6. "Where do certain personalities dominate collaboration?"

7. "Which individuals act as bridges between teams or functions?"

8. "Where does influence help resolve conflict or tension?"

9. "Which influencers help maintain stability when things shift quickly?"

Aggressive Influence-Dynamics Questions (8)

Tone: direct, revealing, truth-focused.

1. "Who truly drives decisions — regardless of title?"

2. "Which person has influence that others hesitate to challenge?"

3. "Who consistently slows down initiatives because of their influence?"

4. "Which hidden influencer shapes outcomes without being visible?"

5. "Whose approval determines whether something actually moves forward?"

6. "Who holds informal power that leadership underestimates?"

7. "Which person's resistance has the biggest impact on progress?"

8. "Who controls the narrative in key discussions?"

Follow-Up Influence-Dynamics Questions (10)

Tone: reflective, clarifying, role-revealing.

1. "Can you recall a moment when influence shifted the direction of a decision?"

2. "What did that reveal about the influencer's role?"

3. "How did others respond to that influence?"

4. "Which patterns have you noticed across similar situations?"

5. "Who tends to gather support before sharing their perspective?"

6. "Which influencers help build alignment when stakes are high?"

7. "How does influence change during periods of stress or pressure?"

8. "What influence signals do team members pay close attention to?"

9. "Which influential behaviors strengthen collaboration?"

10. "Which influential behaviors create unintended friction or hesitation?"

Conclusion

Influence-dynamics questions reveal the informal power lines running through the organization. They show who shapes decisions, accelerates progress, guides alignment, or triggers hesitation — insight that is essential for understanding how collaboration truly functions.

Strategically, knowing these dynamics helps you navigate decision pathways with accuracy and anticipate how initiatives will move through the organization. Psychologically, these insights explain why certain individuals inspire trust, why others create tension, and why collaboration sometimes succeeds or fails for reasons no org chart can explain.

As Chapter 6 continues, we will explore conflict patterns, behavioral tension points, trust signals, and collaborative resilience. Influence dynamics form the emotional circuitry of teamwork — knowing them helps illuminate everything that comes next.

Reflection Prompt:
Think of a team where one person shaped decisions more than expected. Which influence-dynamics question would have identified their role sooner?

CHAPTER 6 - SECTION 6 - Collaboration-Friction Questions

Introduction

Once influence dynamics are visible, the next layer of collaborative insight involves identifying **collaboration friction** — the subtle or overt points where teamwork becomes strained, inefficient, or emotionally charged. Every organization experiences friction. It shows up in missed expectations, repeated frustrations, strained interactions, hesitations, or communication gaps. Collaboration-friction questions help uncover where these patterns emerge and what underlying forces sustain them.

Strategically, friction reveals the "drag" that slows execution. Even when teams are aligned and communication flows well, unresolved friction can derail progress, erode trust, and make coordination unnecessarily exhausting. When friction goes unexamined, it becomes normal — but it still drains time, energy, and performance. These questions bring that hidden resistance into focus.

Psychologically, friction often forms around unspoken expectations, personal differences, emotional triggers, unresolved conflicts, or unclear boundaries. When people feel friction, they tend to protect themselves by avoiding conversations, working around others, or withholding effort. Understanding these patterns creates the chance for healthier, more honest collaboration.

Interpretation Tip: Listen for repeated complaints, persistent delays, emotional tones of irritation, or comments like "we always struggle with…" These statements often reveal recurring friction. Also note moments of silence, hesitation, or careful phrasing — people sometimes talk around friction rather than naming it directly.

Coaching Note: Approach friction neutrally. Avoid assigning blame or suggesting fault. Frame friction as a *pattern* the team experiences rather than a *problem* caused by individuals. This makes the buyer more willing to explore the topic honestly.

Example prompts:

- *"What parts of collaboration feel harder than they should?"*

- *"Where do interactions become strained or inefficient?"*

Standard Collaboration-Friction Questions (8)

Tone: calm, neutral, gently revealing.

1. "Where does collaboration feel more difficult than expected?"

2. "Which interactions tend to create frustration or tension?"

3. "Where do handoffs or teamwork slow down?"

4. "Which tasks require extra effort because of friction?"

5. "Where do misunderstandings happen most often?"

6. "Which collaborations work well on some days but not others?"

7. "Where does teamwork feel inconsistent or unpredictable?"

8. "Which situations create avoidable friction between people or teams?"

Intermediate Collaboration-Friction Questions (9)

Tone: probing, pattern-seeking, clear.

1. "Which collaboration challenges appear repeatedly?"

2. "Where does friction emerge when pressure increases?"

3. "Which teams or individuals struggle to coordinate consistently?"

4. "What behaviors contribute to recurring tension?"

5. "Which tasks suffer from mismatched expectations?"

6. "Where do timing or priority differences create strain?"

7. "What collaboration habits create small but persistent friction?"

8. "Where does emotional tension follow certain workflows or processes?"

9. "Which situations highlight deeper alignment gaps?"

Aggressive Collaboration-Friction Questions (8)

Tone: direct, candid, truth-focused.

1. "Which collaboration issue is everyone aware of but avoids discussing?"

2. "Where is friction causing the most wasted effort right now?"

3. "Who consistently contributes to tension — intentionally or not?"

4. "Which repeated conflict reveals a deeper unresolved issue?"

5. "Where does collaboration break down under even mild pressure?"

6. "Which team or role resists working with others?"

7. "What friction point has leadership failed to address?"

8. "Where is collaboration dysfunction harming performance the most?"

Follow-Up Collaboration-Friction Questions (10)

Tone: reflective, clarifying, emotionally aware.

1. "Can you describe a recent moment when collaboration friction became obvious?"

2. "What triggered the tension in that situation?"

3. "How did the individuals involved respond emotionally?"

4. "What impact did the friction have on progress?"

5. "Which underlying issue did the moment reveal?"

6. "How often does this type of tension occur?"

7. "What attempts have been made to address it?"

8. "What part of the issue remains unresolved?"

9. "What would healthier collaboration look like in that context?"

10. "What support or clarity would reduce this friction going forward?"

Conclusion

Collaboration-friction questions reveal the tensions that weaken teamwork from beneath the surface. By examining the moments where coordination becomes strained, the organization gains insight into underlying misalignment, emotional triggers, competing expectations, or structural gaps.

Strategically, these insights help identify where processes, expectations, or workflows need adjustment. Psychologically, they illuminate the feelings, habits, and interpersonal patterns that shape how individuals interact. When friction becomes visible, teams can address it with awareness rather than frustration.

As Chapter 6 continues, we will explore conflict dynamics, decision friction, trust signals, and overall collaborative readiness. Collaboration friction sets the stage for identifying deeper interpersonal complexities that influence teamwork every day.

Reflection Prompt:

Think of a situation where teamwork felt harder than it should have. Which collaboration-friction question would have revealed the underlying issue earlier?

CHAPTER 6 - SECTION 7 - Conflict-Pattern Questions

Introduction

After uncovering collaboration friction, the next level of insight involves understanding **conflict patterns** — the predictable ways in which disagreements, tension, or misunderstandings emerge and repeat within the organization. Conflict is not a sign of dysfunction by itself; it is a natural part of collaboration. What matters is *how* conflict forms, how often it appears, and how it is resolved. Conflict-pattern questions help reveal the recurring dynamics that shape emotional climate, team trust, and problem-solving effectiveness.

Strategically, conflict patterns expose where systems, expectations, or communication habits break down. They reveal the pressure points where teams clash, the decisions that cause disagreements, and the interpersonal triggers that escalate tension. When conflict patterns are understood, the organization gains the ability to anticipate and prevent friction rather than constantly reacting to it.

Psychologically, conflict shapes how safe people feel speaking up, raising concerns, or engaging in honest discussion. Some teams avoid conflict to the point of stagnation; others experience conflict so frequently that it drains morale and trust. These questions surface the deeper layers of emotional and relational dynamics that influence long-term collaboration quality.

Interpretation Tip: Listen for emotionally charged words like "frustrated," "tired of," "always," "never," or "again." These often signal recurring patterns. Also note when the buyer describes conflict avoidance — silence and withdrawal are forms of conflict, too, expressed through absence rather than confrontation.

Coaching Note: Treat conflict neutrally. Don't frame it as negative or problematic. Instead, present it as a signal that reveals what is unclear, unresolved, or misaligned. This allows the buyer to explore conflict with curiosity rather than defensiveness.

Example prompts:

- *"Which disagreements tend to repeat themselves?"*

- *"How does conflict usually unfold on your team?"*

Standard Conflict-Pattern Questions (8)

Tone: calm, neutral, pattern-seeking.

1. "What types of disagreement appear most often on your team?"

2. "Where do conflicts tend to begin?"

3. "Which topics commonly lead to tension?"

4. "How does the team typically respond when conflict arises?"

5. "Which situations create misunderstandings that escalate?"

6. "Where does conflict come from unclear expectations?"

7. "Which recurring disagreements feel familiar at this point?"

8. "Where does conflict tend to fade without ever being resolved?"

Intermediate Conflict-Pattern Questions (9)

Tone: probing, clarifying, insight-oriented.

1. "Which conflict patterns resurface across different projects?"

2. "Where do interpersonal differences influence conflict the most?"

3. "Which conflicts escalate quickly instead of resolving naturally?"

4. "What behavior patterns contribute to repeated disagreements?"

5. "Which roles or teams struggle most to resolve conflict together?"

6. "What situations lead to conflict avoidance rather than discussion?"

7. "Where do conflicting priorities trigger tension?"

8. "Which unresolved conflict continues to affect current work?"

9. "What signs show that a conflict is beginning to repeat?"

Aggressive Conflict-Pattern Questions (8)

Tone: direct, revealing, truth-forward.

1. "Which conflict does the team avoid addressing directly?"

2. "What disagreement has become normalized but remains unresolved?"

3. "Who holds tension with another teammate that impacts collaboration?"

4. "Which conflict drains the most energy or time?"

5. "What issue sparks conflict because expectations are unclear?"

6. "Which conflict appears whenever pressure increases?"

7. "What pattern of conflict leadership has not confronted yet?"

8. "Where does conflict reveal deeper trust issues or fears?"

Follow-Up Conflict-Pattern Questions (10)

Tone: reflective, clarifying, emotionally attentive.

1. "Can you describe a moment when conflict revealed a deeper issue?"

2. "What emotion surfaced first during that conflict?"

3. "How did the individuals involved respond to each other?"

4. "What made the conflict escalate — or de-escalate?"

5. "What part of the conflict reflected older, repeated patterns?"

6. "Who felt the impact of the conflict the most?"

7. "How was the conflict resolved, or left unresolved?"

8. "What did the situation teach you about team dynamics?"

9. "What could have prevented that conflict from repeating?"

10. "What would healthier conflict resolution look like for your team?"

Conclusion

Conflict-pattern questions uncover the rhythms and triggers behind repeated tension. They help reveal which disagreements are structural, which are emotional, and which come from unclear expectations or mismatched priorities. When conflict becomes predictable, it becomes solvable — but only when the patterns are made explicit.

Strategically, these insights help identify where communication, alignment, or process improvements are most needed. Psychologically, they show leaders how conflict influences safety, trust, and the emotional climate of the team. When conflict patterns are understood, teams can replace reactive cycles with more intentional, constructive dialogue.

As Chapter 6 continues, we will explore decision friction, trust indicators, emotional safety, and collaborative readiness. Conflict patterns set the stage for understanding how teams respond when pressure rises.

Reflection Prompt:

Think of a conflict you've seen repeat across a team. Which conflict-pattern question would have surfaced that cycle earlier?

CHAPTER 6 - SECTION 8 - Decision-Friction Questions

Introduction

After exploring conflict patterns, the next step is examining **decision friction** — the delays, uncertainties, hesitations, and bottlenecks that slow or complicate decision-making across the organization. Decision friction is one of the most costly forms of collaborative dysfunction. It affects speed, confidence, accountability, and the team's ability to act with clarity. Decision-friction questions help reveal where decisions get stuck, who slows or accelerates them, and what structural or emotional barriers shape the process.

Strategically, decision friction exposes gaps in authority, unclear expectations, competing priorities, or flawed communication flow. Even highly capable teams falter when decision pathways are ambiguous or overly dependent on certain individuals. Identifying these friction points helps build a decision-making environment that is consistent, transparent, and supportive of organizational momentum.

Psychologically, decision friction reveals the fears and hesitations that influence judgment: fear of making the wrong choice, fear of conflict, fear of leadership reactions, or fear of accountability. When decisions are difficult or risky, people often freeze, delay, or seek excessive validation. Understanding these emotional dynamics allows the advisor to address the deeper causes rather than the surface symptoms.

Interpretation Tip: Listen for statements like "We're waiting on…," "It depends…," "We need more clarity," "We're not sure who decides that," or "Different people give different answers." These are reliable signals of decision friction. Also notice when decisions are described as taking longer than expected — time is one of the best indicators of friction.

Coaching Note: Frame friction as a system-level issue, not a personal flaw. This encourages the buyer to explore the patterns honestly rather than defending individual behaviors or past decisions.

Example prompts:

- *"Where do decisions consistently slow down?"*

- *"Who or what creates hesitation during important choices?"*

Standard Decision-Friction Questions (8)

Tone: calm, structured, clarity-focused.

1. "Where do decisions tend to slow down in your team or organization?"

2. "Which decisions require the most back-and-forth discussion?"

3. "Where does the team seek clarification before moving forward?"

4. "Which roles depend on others before decisions can be made?"

5. "Where do priorities or opinions complicate decision-making?"

6. "Which decisions take longer than they should?"

7. "Where does the decision process feel confusing or unclear?"

8. "Which decisions are frequently delayed due to missing information?"

Intermediate Decision-Friction Questions (9)

Tone: probing, analytical, pattern-seeking.

1. "Which decisions consistently require escalations to leadership?"

2. "Where do unclear roles create uncertainty in decision-making?"

3. "Which bottlenecks appear across multiple projects?"

4. "What patterns show up when decisions get delayed?"

5. "Where does a lack of confidence slow down choices?"

6. "Which individuals or teams require excessive validation before deciding?"

7. "What part of the decision process creates the most confusion?"

8. "Which responsibilities get stuck because no one wants to decide?"

9. "Where does misalignment between teams intensify decision friction?"

Aggressive Decision-Friction Questions (8)

Tone: direct, truth-inducing, pressure-revealing.

1. "Which decisions stall because no one wants to take ownership?"

2. "Who consistently slows down decisions — intentionally or not?"

3. "Which decisions are delayed because of fear or hesitation?"

4. "Where does leadership unknowingly contribute to decision friction?"

5. "What decision process is so unclear that it creates unnecessary risk?"

6. "Which repeated delays reveal deeper structural issues?"

7. "Which person or team acts as a gatekeeper without formal authority?"

8. "What decision pattern drains the most time or energy?"

Follow-Up Decision-Friction Questions (10)

Tone: reflective, clarifying, insight-deepening.

1. "Can you describe a recent moment when a decision got stuck?"

2. "What caused the hesitation or delay?"

3. "Who was affected first by the slowdown?"

4. "What signals suggested the decision was beginning to stall?"

5. "How did individuals respond while waiting?"

6. "What part of the situation highlighted the structural issue?"

7. "What was eventually needed to push the decision through?"

8. "What would have accelerated the choice earlier?"

9. "How often does this type of friction occur?"

10. "What would a clear, confident decision process look like for your team?"

Conclusion

Decision-friction questions illuminate the forces that slow down action, weaken momentum, and complicate collaboration. They reveal where uncertainty, unclear authority, conflicting priorities, or emotional hesitation interfere with progress. When decision friction becomes visible, leaders can strengthen pathways, simplify expectations, and create an environment where decisions move with greater clarity and confidence.

Strategically, these insights help refine processes, improve alignment, and clarify ownership. Psychologically, they help reduce fear-driven hesitation and build a culture of empowered, confident decision-making. Removing decision friction accelerates nearly every aspect of collaborative performance.

As Chapter 6 continues, we will explore trust signals, emotional safety, collaborative readiness, and the deeper patterns that influence how people function together in real time.

Reflection Prompt:
Think about a decision that took far longer than it should have. Which decision-friction question would have revealed the root cause sooner?

CHAPTER 6 - SECTION 9 - Trust-Signal Questions

Introduction

After examining decision friction, the next layer of team dynamics lies in understanding **trust signals** — the subtle behaviors, patterns, and communication cues that show whether trust is strong, fragile, or inconsistent across the team. Trust isn't a single emotion; it's a pattern of behaviors people demonstrate when they feel safe, supported, and aligned. Trust signals are often small, but they have an enormous impact on the quality of collaboration.

Strategically, trust signals reveal the hidden drivers of team cohesion. When trust is strong, teams move quickly, communicate honestly, and handle conflict constructively. When trust is weak, alignment suffers, decision-making slows, and team members retreat into self-protection. Trust determines how willingly people share information, ask for help, take risks, and rely on one another.

Psychologically, trust signals come from how people treat each other in everyday moments — how they listen, follow through, respond to mistakes, and interpret one another's intentions. These signals help uncover whether team members feel respected, valued, and supported. When trust is inconsistent, people hesitate to speak up or take initiative. These questions illuminate the emotional climate beneath the surface of the team's work.

Interpretation Tip: Listen for behavioral clues: whether people volunteer information, follow through reliably, give honest feedback, or hesitate to express concerns. Also note references to safety, vulnerability, or avoidance — these are often tied directly to trust levels.

Coaching Note: Trust is sensitive. Encourage the buyer to describe observations rather than judgments. Focus on what people *do* rather than labeling trust as "good" or "bad." This helps keep the conversation objective and constructive.

Example prompts:

- *"What behaviors show that team members trust one another?"*
- *"Where does trust seem fragile or inconsistent?"*

Standard Trust-Signal Questions (8)

Tone: calm, observational, emotionally aware.

1. "What behaviors show that team members trust one another?"
2. "Where do you see people supporting each other willingly?"

3. "Which team members openly share concerns or ideas?"

4. "Where does communication feel honest and direct?"

5. "Which moments show strong follow-through and reliability?"

6. "Where do people feel comfortable asking for help?"

7. "Which interactions show mutual respect and openness?"

8. "Where does trust seem steady even during stressful moments?"

Intermediate Trust-Signal Questions (9)

Tone: probing, insight-focused, relational.

1. "Where do trust levels vary across different roles or teams?"

2. "Which behaviors suggest hesitation or guarded communication?"

3. "Where do people hold back feedback they should share?"

4. "Which interactions feel polite but not fully open?"

5. "Where do team members struggle to rely on one another?"

6. "What patterns emerge when trust weakens under stress?"

7. "Which moments reveal uncertainty about others' intentions?"

8. "Where do unwritten rules replace honest conversation?"

9. "Which relationships feel strong enough to handle conflict well?"

Aggressive Trust-Signal Questions (8)

Tone: direct, revealing, truth-focused.

1. "Who does the team struggle to trust — and why?"

2. "Where is trust breaking down in ways people rarely talk about?"

3. "Which behaviors undermine trust most consistently?"

4. "Who avoids vulnerability because they fear negative reactions?"

5. "Which team members do others hesitate to rely on?"

6. "Where does distrust show up through silence or avoidance?"

7. "What repeated actions make trust difficult to maintain?"

8. "Which trust issue has lingered without being addressed?"

Follow-Up Trust-Signal Questions (10)

Tone: reflective, emotionally aware, clarifying.

1. "Can you describe a moment when trust noticeably increased?"

2. "What behavior made that moment possible?"

3. "How did the team respond to that trust-building action?"

4. "Can you recall a moment when trust decreased unexpectedly?"

5. "What triggered that shift?"

6. "How did people react emotionally to the change in trust?"

7. "What deeper issue did that moment reveal?"

8. "What helped restore trust afterward — if it was restored?"

9. "What would strengthen trust across the team going forward?"

10. "What daily actions would reinforce trust consistently?"

Conclusion

Trust-signal questions illuminate the emotional foundation of collaboration. They reveal the behaviors that strengthen connection, as well as the patterns that weaken it. Trust is not an abstract concept — it is visible in the everyday signals people send through their actions, tone, and willingness to rely on one another.

Strategically, these insights help leaders understand where alignment is vulnerable and where communication needs more openness. Psychologically, trust signals show whether team members feel safe, valued, and respected — essential conditions for high-quality collaboration and resilience.

As Chapter 6 approaches its final section, we will explore collaborative readiness — the organization's overall capacity to work together effectively when the stakes are high. Trust is the emotional bridge that leads directly into that final topic.

Reflection Prompt:

Think of a team where trust shaped momentum either positively or negatively. Which trust-signal question would have revealed that dynamic earlier?

CHAPTER 6 - SECTION 10 - Collaborative-Readiness Questions

Introduction

After exploring alignment, communication, role interaction, influence dynamics, friction, conflict patterns, decision-making, and trust signals, the final step in understanding team collaboration is assessing **collaborative readiness**. Collaborative readiness reflects the team's ability to work together effectively when stakes are high, pressure is intense, or change demands coordinated action. It is the culmination of all previous elements: clarity, trust, communication, adaptability, and emotional stability.

Strategically, collaborative readiness reveals how prepared the team is to handle complex projects, cross-functional efforts, or transformative initiatives. It shows whether the organization can respond quickly, adapt to changing conditions, and sustain cooperation through difficulty. High readiness means the team can execute with confidence; low readiness signals the risk of breakdowns, delays, or conflict under pressure.

Psychologically, collaborative readiness depends on emotional safety, mutual respect, willingness to communicate, and comfort with shared ownership. A team may appear collaborative during normal conditions but struggle when confronted with uncertainty or competing priorities. These questions help uncover the deeper readiness factors that surface only when the environment becomes demanding.

Interpretation Tip: Listen for hesitation about large initiatives, comments about past breakdowns during stressful periods, or expressions of concern about "getting everyone on board." These often reflect weaknesses in readiness. Also note any optimism tied to trust, clarity, or recent progress — these point to emerging readiness.

Coaching Note: Encourage honesty about weaknesses without judgment. Collaborative readiness is not a measure of worth; it's an assessment of capability. Highlight that readiness can be strengthened with intention and clarity.

Example prompts:

- *"How prepared is your team to collaborate during high-stakes situations?"*

- *"What conditions support or undermine readiness?"*

Standard Collaborative-Readiness Questions (8)

Tone: open, balanced, future-oriented.

1. "How prepared does your team feel for high-stakes collaboration?"

2. "Which conditions support effective collaboration during busy periods?"

3. "Where does the team show readiness to coordinate quickly?"

4. "What behaviors indicate strong collaborative habits?"

5. "Which past experiences demonstrate readiness under pressure?"

6. "Where does the team show confidence in working together?"

7. "Which roles or groups feel most prepared for joint efforts?"

8. "What conditions help your team collaborate at its best?"

Intermediate Collaborative-Readiness Questions (9)

Tone: probing, pattern-oriented, clarity-focused.

1. "Where does collaborative readiness weaken when stakes rise?"

2. "Which teams struggle to adjust quickly when plans change?"

3. "What patterns reveal hesitation during collaborative efforts?"

4. "Where does readiness depend too heavily on specific individuals?"

5. "Which tasks expose readiness gaps most clearly?"

6. "What conditions make the team less willing to coordinate?"

7. "Where does readiness break under pressure or tight timelines?"

8. "Which aspects of readiness feel inconsistent across groups?"

9. "What signals show the team is becoming more collaborative over time?"

Aggressive Collaborative-Readiness Questions (8)

Tone: direct, truth-seeking, high-stakes oriented.

1. "Where is your team least prepared to collaborate when it matters most?"

2. "Which readiness gap threatens major initiatives right now?"

3. "Who struggles to collaborate under pressure — and why?"

4. "What part of the team collapses into silos during stressful periods?"

5. "Which behaviors signal low readiness but go unaddressed?"

6. "What situations reveal the team's biggest collaborative weaknesses?"

7. "Which readiness issues leadership underestimates?"

8. "Where is collaboration fragile enough to fail during major changes?"

Follow-Up Collaborative-Readiness Questions (10)

Tone: reflective, clarifying, insight-deepening.

1. "Can you describe a moment when collaboration succeeded under pressure?"

2. "What made that moment possible?"

3. "Who contributed to creating readiness in that situation?"

4. "Can you recall a time when readiness broke down?"

5. "What triggered the breakdown?"

6. "How did team members respond emotionally and behaviorally?"

7. "What deeper issues did the situation reveal?"

8. "What lessons were learned about readiness?"

9. "What conditions would strengthen readiness going forward?"

10. "What small, consistent actions would help the team stay prepared?"

Conclusion

Collaborative-readiness questions complete the exploration of team alignment and relational health. They reveal how well the team can perform under real-world pressure, not just ideal conditions. Readiness reflects the combined influence of clarity, trust, communication, emotional safety, adaptability, and interpersonal dynamics.

Strategically, these insights indicate the organization's capacity for consistent execution during complex initiatives or major transitions. Psychologically, they highlight whether team members feel supported, confident, and connected — the foundation for strong, resilient collaboration.

Chapter Conclusion

Chapter 6 reveals that collaboration depends on far more than good intentions or teamwork slogans. It is built through clarity, supported by trust, strengthened by communication, and shaped by the subtle interpersonal dynamics that influence decisions. When these elements align, teams become cohesive, resilient, and capable of navigating complexity with confidence. When they drift, collaboration becomes inconsistent and emotionally draining.

Strategically, this chapter equips the reader to analyze collaborative systems with precision — identifying the patterns that shape momentum, the bottlenecks that slow progress, and the relational forces that determine how teams respond under pressure. Psychologically, the chapter highlights how emotional safety, trust, and honest communication influence the team's ability to work together consistently.

With these insights established, the reader is prepared to move into the next chapter, where the focus shifts from internal dynamics to understanding how organizational context, leadership signals, and cultural expectations influence discovery. Chapter 6 serves as the collaborative foundation for everything that follows.

CHAPTER 7 - Understanding Organizational Dynamics and Cultural Signals

Chapter Introduction

Organizations often present themselves through mission statements, values posters, and leadership messaging — but the *real* organization is experienced through its atmosphere, habits, and shared behaviors. Chapter 7 explores this deeper reality by examining the emotional, cultural, and structural signals that shape how people interpret their environment. While teams operate within processes and systems, those systems only work as well as the culture supporting them. To understand discovery at a strategic level, the advisor must understand these cultural signals with precision.

The chapter begins with **organizational climate**, which reveals the emotional tone of daily work. Climate shows how people actually feel — engaged, overwhelmed, calm, uncertain, energised, or cautious. This felt reality sets the stage for all collaboration, communication, and performance. Next, the chapter examines **leadership signals**, the behavioral cues leaders send that shape trust, momentum, and the emotional temperature of the organization. Leadership behavior often sets the tone long before formal messaging arrives.

After setting these foundations, the chapter explores **cultural norms** and **decision hierarchy**, two critical forces that determine how behavior forms and how decisions move through the organization. Cultural norms represent the unspoken rules people follow without thinking. Decision hierarchy reveals who truly holds authority and how clear — or unclear — that authority feels. Both shape how smoothly the organization works, and both influence discovery conversations at every level.

The chapter then moves into **organizational expectations**, **accountability behaviors**, and **cultural pressure**. These sections examine how people interpret what is required of them, how they respond to responsibility, and what forces push them to act in certain ways. Expectations guide behavior. Accountability shows how people follow through. Cultural pressure reveals the emotional undercurrents that shape momentum. Together, they create the structure of performance and the emotional conditions that support or strain it.

The latter part of the chapter focuses on **emotional safety**, **organizational identity**, and **behavioral reinforcement**. These sections highlight the deepest cultural drivers: whether people feel safe to be honest, how they see themselves within the organization, and what behaviors the system reinforces over time. Emotional safety determines openness and vulnerability. Identity shapes belonging and pride. Reinforcement determines which behaviors persist and which fade. Together, they reveal the psychological engine behind culture itself.

By exploring these ten layers, Chapter 7 provides a complete understanding of the forces shaping how people experience their work environment. Organizational dynamics are not abstract theories — they are lived realities that determine how receptive, aligned, resilient, and collaborative teams truly are. This chapter prepares the reader to recognize these signals with clarity and to use them as a powerful lens for discovery.

CHAPTER 7 - SECTION 1 - Organizational-Climate Questions

Introduction

Before exploring leadership signals, cultural expectations, decision hierarchies, or systemic habits, it's important to understand the organization's **climate** — the emotional and psychological atmosphere people experience in their daily work. Organizational climate is the felt reality of the workplace. It reflects how safe people feel speaking up, how supported they feel in their roles, and how connected they feel to the organization's direction. Climate is not a policy; it's an experience.

Strategically, organizational climate shapes performance more directly than most structural elements. A strong climate encourages initiative, collaboration, and resilience. A weak or inconsistent climate creates hesitation, frustration, disengagement, and misalignment. Climate influences how receptive the team will be to change, how well they adapt under pressure, and how naturally they share information.

Psychologically, climate is the emotional tone of the organization. It shows up in daily interactions — in the way people respond to mistakes, discuss challenges, celebrate wins, or react to feedback. Climate influences motivation, stress levels, trust, and belonging. Organizational climate questions help reveal whether people operate from a place of confidence or caution, clarity or confusion, connection or disconnection.

Interpretation Tip: Listen for words like "comfortable," "stressed," "supported," "uncertain," or "overwhelmed." These signal emotional conditions. Also pay attention to inconsistencies — a climate may be healthy in one team but fragile in another. Climate is rarely uniform.

Coaching Note: Encourage the buyer to speak from observation rather than assumption. Climate often varies across individuals, roles, and levels, so seek specific examples where possible.

Example prompts:

- *"How would you describe the general atmosphere of your organization?"*

- *"What emotional tone do people feel most often at work?"*

Standard Organizational-Climate Questions (8)

Tone: warm, observational, emotionally aware.

1. "How would you describe the overall atmosphere in your organization?"

2. "Where does the team seem most engaged and energetic?"

3. "Which parts of the organization feel calm and steady?"

4. "Where do people seem stressed or overloaded?"

5. "Which environments feel supportive and encouraging?"

6. "Where does morale seem lower than expected?"

7. "Which teams appear the most comfortable raising concerns?"

8. "Where does the emotional tone shift depending on the day?"

Intermediate Organizational-Climate Questions (9)

Tone: probing, perceptive, pattern-focused.

1. "Where do emotional patterns influence daily performance?"

2. "Which teams experience inconsistent morale?"

3. "What parts of the climate improve or deteriorate during busy periods?"

4. "Where do people hesitate to share honest feedback?"

5. "Which teams respond most strongly to leadership's emotional tone?"

6. "Where do communication habits reflect underlying stress?"

7. "Which situations highlight emotional openness or emotional withdrawal?"

8. "What climate patterns do new employees notice first?"

9. "Where does climate differ between leadership and frontline perspectives?"

Aggressive Organizational-Climate Questions (8)

Tone: direct, candid, truth-exposing (still respectful).

1. "Where is the climate noticeably unhealthy?"

2. "Which teams struggle because emotional safety is low?"

3. "What emotional tone drains energy or motivation the most?"

4. "Who influences the climate negatively — intentionally or unintentionally?"

5. "What climate issue leadership avoids discussing openly?"

6. "Where does persistent stress signal deeper systemic problems?"

7. "Which part of the climate undermines performance consistently?"

8. "Where do people pretend the climate is healthy when it isn't?"

Follow-Up Organizational-Climate Questions (10)

Tone: reflective, emotionally attuned, clarity-deepening.

1. "Can you describe a moment when the climate felt especially positive?"

2. "What behaviors contributed to that feeling?"

3. "How did the team respond to the positive atmosphere?"

4. "Can you recall a moment when the climate felt unusually tense?"

5. "What triggered the shift in emotional tone?"

6. "How did people react during that moment?"

7. "What deeper pattern did the climate change reveal?"

8. "What helped restore emotional balance afterward?"

9. "What climate improvements would have a noticeable impact?"

10. "What daily habits would help strengthen the overall atmosphere?"

Conclusion

Organizational-climate questions reveal the emotional and psychological environment in which teams operate. They illuminate the daily experiences that influence performance, trust, communication, and openness to change. Climate is the context that determines whether collaborative efforts feel natural or challenging.

Strategically, climate insights help the advisor understand how well the organization can absorb new ideas, handle pressure, and maintain alignment. Psychologically, these insights reveal whether people feel supported, valued, and connected — essential elements of long-term engagement.

As Chapter 7 continues, we will explore leadership signals, cultural expectations, decision hierarchy, organizational norms, and the social forces that shape workplace behavior. Climate is the first layer of cultural understanding — the lived experience that precedes formal culture.

Reflection Prompt:
Think of an organization where the emotional tone shaped performance significantly. Which climate question would have revealed that truth earlier?

CHAPTER 7 - SECTION 2 - Leadership-Signal Questions

Introduction

Once the organization's emotional climate is understood, the next layer involves exploring **leadership signals** — the verbal and nonverbal cues that leaders send through their actions, tone, priorities, expectations, and consistency. Leadership signals shape how people interpret direction, how they respond to challenges, and how they behave when uncertainty appears. Leaders signal far more through behavior than through formal communication.

Strategically, leadership signals reveal the real priorities of the organization. While official messages may outline goals or values, people tend to follow what leadership *demonstrates,* not what leadership *announces.* These signals determine whether teams feel encouraged, cautious, pressured, or inspired. Leadership signals also influence morale, trust, alignment, and willingness to take initiative.

Psychologically, leadership signals shape emotional safety. If leaders respond defensively to feedback, people stop sharing concerns. If leaders remain calm during difficulty, people feel grounded. If leaders model consistency, others follow suit. These questions uncover both the helpful signals and the mixed signals that shape the organizational environment.

Interpretation Tip: Listen carefully for phrases like "leadership says they want… but…" or "they communicate well when…" These contrasts reveal misalignment between intent and impact. Pay attention to differences between what leaders emphasize publicly versus how they behave in day-to-day situations.

Coaching Note: Invite the buyer to reflect on observed behaviors rather than personal judgments. The goal is to understand how leadership influence is *felt,* not to criticize individuals.

Example prompts:

- *"What signals do your leaders send through their everyday actions?"*

- *"How do leadership behaviors shape team confidence?"*

Standard Leadership-Signal Questions (8)

Tone: calm, balanced, observation-focused.

1. "What messages do leaders consistently reinforce through their behavior?"

2. "Which leadership actions strengthen confidence across the team?"

3. "Where do leaders demonstrate clear support for their priorities?"

4. "Which leadership habits create stability during change?"

5. "Where does leadership set a positive tone for communication?"

6. "Which signals show that leaders value team insight?"

7. "Where do leaders model the behaviors they expect from others?"

8. "Which leadership actions help build trust across the organization?"

Intermediate Leadership-Signal Questions (9)

Tone: probing, insight-driven, clarity-focused.

1. "Where do leadership signals differ from formal messaging?"

2. "Which leadership behaviors shape how people interpret expectations?"

3. "Where do leaders unintentionally create mixed signals?"

4. "What patterns appear when teams try to understand leadership priorities?"

5. "Which situations reveal leadership's true values or concerns?"

6. "Where do leadership signals shift under pressure?"

7. "What leader behaviors influence morale the most?"

8. "Where do leadership actions inspire initiative?"

9. "Which signals reveal how leaders feel about collaboration or risk?"

Aggressive Leadership-Signal Questions (8)

Tone: direct, truth-seeking, respectfully confronting contradictions.

1. "Where do leadership behaviors contradict stated priorities?"

2. "Which signals create confusion or hesitation across the team?"

3. "Where is leadership unintentionally discouraging honest communication?"

4. "Which leaders send mixed messages that weaken alignment?"

5. "What leadership habit repeatedly undermines momentum?"

6. "Where does leadership avoid addressing issues directly?"

7. "Which signals cause people to adjust behavior out of caution?"

8. "What leadership behavior sends the strongest negative signal right now?"

Follow-Up Leadership-Signal Questions (10)

Tone: reflective, perceptive, behavior-oriented.

1. "Can you describe a moment when a leadership signal strengthened the team's confidence?"

2. "What specific behavior created that experience?"

3. "How did the team respond afterward?"

4. "Can you recall a moment when a leadership signal caused concern or confusion?"

5. "What triggered that perception?"

6. "How did people react emotionally or behaviorally?"

7. "What deeper issue did the signal reveal about leadership alignment?"

8. "What helped clarify the signal afterward — if it was clarified?"

9. "What leadership behaviors would improve clarity and trust?"

10. "What consistent habits would strengthen leadership's positive influence?"

Conclusion

Leadership-signal questions uncover the behaviors that shape how people interpret expectations, change, and priorities. They reveal the difference between what leadership intends and how leadership is actually experienced by the team. These signals influence trust, motivation, clarity, and the overall tone of the organization.

Strategically, understanding leadership signals helps determine how well the organization can align around shared goals and how effectively it can sustain momentum. Psychologically, these insights highlight whether team members feel encouraged, pressured, uncertain, or supported — essential information when guiding discovery.

As Chapter 7 continues, the next sections will explore cultural habits, decision hierarchies, organizational norms, and the unspoken rules that shape daily work. Leadership signals provide the lens through which culture is interpreted.

Reflection Prompt:

Think of an organization where leadership behavior shaped morale or direction significantly. Which leadership-signal question would have revealed that insight earlier?

CHAPTER 7 - SECTION 3 - Cultural-Norm Questions

Introduction

After examining leadership signals, the next layer in understanding organizational dynamics involves exploring **cultural norms** — the unwritten rules, shared habits, and informal expectations that shape how people behave. Cultural norms aren't documented in handbooks or explained during onboarding; they are learned through observation, repetition, and social reinforcement. They determine how people communicate, how decisions are made, how mistakes are handled, and how conflict is navigated.

Strategically, cultural norms reveal what *actually* happens inside the organization, not what leadership says happens. They influence speed, adaptability, collaboration, and accountability. If formal processes say one thing but norms say another, norms always win. Understanding these norms is critical for assessing whether change is feasible, how quickly it can take root, and where resistance will naturally appear.

Psychologically, cultural norms shape identity and belonging. People often conform to norms unconsciously because that is how they maintain social acceptance. Some norms are healthy, supporting openness, initiative, and shared success. Others are restrictive or discouraging, creating silence, hesitation, or blame. These questions help uncover the invisible behaviors that keep teams comfortable, cautious, engaged, or disconnected.

Interpretation Tip: Listen for phrases like "that's just how we do things," "people know better than to…," or "it wouldn't go over well if…" These are direct windows into cultural norms. Also note inconsistencies — norms vary by team, department, or leadership group.

Coaching Note: Encourage the buyer to describe observable behaviors rather than attributing motives. Norms are best understood through what people consistently do, not what people intend.

Example prompts:

- *"What unwritten rules guide how people work here?"*

- *"What behaviors get reinforced — intentionally or unintentionally?"*

Standard Cultural-Norm Questions (8)

Tone: calm, exploratory, pattern-aware.

1. "What unwritten rules shape daily behavior in your organization?"

2. "Which habits reflect the culture more than official policies?"

3. "Where do people follow norms without being asked?"

4. "Which behaviors get repeated because 'that's how things are done'?"

5. "Where do norms support healthy collaboration?"

6. "Which expectations are understood even if not spoken?"

7. "Where do cultural habits guide decision-making?"

8. "Which norms help people feel comfortable and connected?"

Intermediate Cultural-Norm Questions (9)

Tone: probing, insight-focused, clarity-seeking.

1. "Which cultural norms reinforce consistency across teams?"

2. "Where do norms conflict with stated priorities?"

3. "What norms influence how people handle disagreement?"

4. "Which unwritten rules affect communication speed or tone?"

5. "Where do norms discourage risk-taking or creative thinking?"

6. "Which habits shape how people respond to mistakes?"

7. "Where do norms influence who speaks up and who stays quiet?"

8. "What cultural expectations influence how decisions are made?"

9. "Which norms become more visible during busy or stressful periods?"

Aggressive Cultural-Norm Questions (8)

Tone: direct, truth-seeking, revealing deeper patterns.

1. "Which cultural norm limits performance the most?"

2. "Where does the culture encourage silence instead of honesty?"

3. "What behavior gets rewarded even though it isn't healthy?"

4. "Which norm discourages accountability or initiative?"

5. "Where does culture value speed over quality, or vice versa?"

6. "Which cultural expectations people follow out of fear?"

7. "What unspoken rule makes improvement harder than it should be?"

8. "Where do cultural habits undermine leadership's intentions?"

Follow-Up Cultural-Norm Questions (10)

Tone: reflective, detail-seeking, psychologically aware.

1. "Can you share a moment when a cultural norm became obvious to you?"

2. "What happened that revealed the norm clearly?"

3. "How did people respond to the situation?"

4. "What emotion did the norm create — comfort, pressure, hesitation, or something else?"

5. "How long has this norm been in place?"

6. "Who reinforces the norm intentionally or unintentionally?"

7. "What impact does the norm have on performance or morale?"

8. "Has anyone tried to shift the norm? What happened when they did?"

9. "What would improve if this norm changed or evolved?"

10. "What small behavior could begin shifting the norm in a healthier direction?"

Conclusion

Cultural-norm questions reveal the invisible rules that shape the organization's behavior. These norms determine how people communicate, collaborate, and interpret expectations. When understood, norms provide insight into why certain behaviors persist, why resistance emerges, and why some initiatives succeed while others stall.

Strategically, these insights help predict how the organization will react to change and where the strongest cultural enablers or blockers exist. Psychologically, they reveal whether people feel safe, pressured, supported, or limited by their environment.

As Chapter 7 continues, we will explore decision hierarchy, organizational expectations, emotional climate consistency, and the forces that guide group identity. Cultural norms provide the blueprint for understanding how the organization truly operates.

Reflection Prompt:
Think of a workplace where behaviors were guided more by habit than policy. Which cultural-norm question would have revealed those habits earlier?

CHAPTER 7 - SECTION 4 - Decision-Hierarchy Questions

Introduction

After exploring cultural norms, the next critical layer of organizational understanding involves **decision hierarchy** — the formal and informal structure that determines who makes which decisions, how authority flows, and how quickly choices can be acted upon. Decision hierarchy is not simply a chart; it is the lived reality of how decisions actually move through the organization.

Strategically, decision hierarchy determines speed, accountability, and momentum. If the hierarchy is clear and functional, decisions move efficiently and predictably. If the hierarchy is unclear, overly centralized, or inconsistently applied, decisions slow down, confusion spreads, and teams rely on guesswork. Decision hierarchy questions help reveal whether authority is aligned with responsibility or whether misalignment creates friction and bottlenecks.

Psychologically, decision hierarchy influences emotional safety and confidence. People make better decisions when they know their authority, understand expectations, and feel supported. When authority is inconsistent or invisible, people hesitate, defer upward, or avoid taking initiative altogether. These questions surface the underlying beliefs and experiences that shape the organization's relationship to power, autonomy, and responsibility.

Interpretation Tip: Listen for conflicting statements around empowerment, approval, or ownership — such as "we're empowered, but we still have to…" or "it depends who's involved." These contradictions often reveal hidden hierarchies. Also note when decisions bypass certain roles or stall at predictable points.

Coaching Note: Encourage the buyer to separate *formal authority* from *practical authority*. Many decision pathways function differently than the org chart suggests. Conduct the exploration with curiosity, not critique.

Example prompts:

- *"Who truly makes which decisions — formally and informally?"*

- *"Where does authority support or slow progress?"*

Standard Decision-Hierarchy Questions (8)

Tone: calm, structured, fact-finding.

1. "How would you describe the decision-making structure in your organization?"

2. "Which decisions are made at the team level?"

3. "Which decisions require leadership involvement?"

4. "Where is authority clearly defined and understood?"

5. "Which approvals are routine and predictable?"

6. "Where do people feel comfortable making decisions without escalation?"

7. "Which roles carry natural influence on decisions?"

8. "Where does the hierarchy support smooth coordination?"

Intermediate Decision-Hierarchy Questions (9)

Tone: probing, clarifying, pattern-focused.

1. "Which decisions take longer due to unclear decision hierarchy?"

2. "Where do people escalate decisions unnecessarily?"

3. "Which decisions get caught between levels of authority?"

4. "Where does the hierarchy shift depending on who is involved?"

5. "Which roles believe they hold authority that others do not recognize?"

6. "Where do leaders override decisions that should be made lower in the structure?"

7. "Which decisions cause the most confusion around ownership?"

8. "Where do informal influencers shape decisions more than formal roles?"

9. "What decision patterns reveal gaps in the hierarchy?"

Aggressive Decision-Hierarchy Questions (8)

Tone: direct, truth-seeking, power-aware.

1. "Where is decision authority unclear or inconsistent?"

2. "Which leaders make decisions outside their defined role?"

3. "Who holds authority they should not — or lacks authority they need?"

4. "Where does fear of criticism cause people to escalate decisions unnecessarily?"

5. "Which decision bottleneck harms performance the most?"

6. "Where is the hierarchy so rigid that it slows progress?"

7. "Which decisions are made too high in the organization?"

8. "Where does leadership avoid taking responsibility for hard decisions?"

Follow-Up Decision-Hierarchy Questions (10)

Tone: reflective, clarifying, insight-deepening.

1. "Can you describe a time when the hierarchy worked exactly as it should?"

2. "What made that decision smooth and predictable?"

3. "Who played a key role in making the process work well?"

4. "Can you recall a decision that became more complicated than necessary?"

5. "What caused the breakdown in the hierarchy?"

6. "How did people react to the confusion?"

7. "What deeper issue did the situation reveal about authority?"

8. "How has the organization responded to hierarchy issues in the past?"

9. "What would a healthier decision structure look like in practice?"

10. "What small adjustments would improve clarity and speed?"

Conclusion

Decision-hierarchy questions reveal how authority, responsibility, and ownership actually function inside the organization. They expose where decision pathways support momentum and where they create bottlenecks, hesitation, or confusion. These insights help clarify how deeply structure, culture, and leadership habits influence everyday execution.

Strategically, understanding decision hierarchy enables more accurate forecasting of change readiness and execution speed. Psychologically, it provides insight into whether team members feel confident, supported, and empowered to act within their roles.

As Chapter 7 continues, we will examine organizational expectations, accountability patterns, psychological safety, and cultural pressures that shape how teams operate. Decision hierarchy lays the groundwork for understanding how power and responsibility move within the organization.

Reflection Prompt:
Think of a time when a decision stalled unexpectedly. Which decision-hierarchy question would have clarified the true source of the delay?

CHAPTER 7 - SECTION 5 - Organizational-Expectation Questions

Introduction

After understanding decision hierarchy, the next step in exploring organizational dynamics is examining **organizational expectations** — the standards, behaviors, priorities, and performance assumptions that shape how people believe they should operate. Unlike goals, expectations are not always stated clearly. They form through repeated experiences, leadership behavior, peer pressure, and cultural patterns. Expectations determine how people think they "should" act to be accepted, successful, or seen as competent.

Strategically, organizational expectations reveal what truly drives performance. Formal expectations may be documented, but the expectations people *feel* often determine where they focus, how they spend time, and what they avoid. Expectations influence consistency, accountability, collaboration, and adaptability. When expectations are unclear or contradictory, teams struggle to maintain alignment or confidence.

Psychologically, expectations shape emotional safety and personal identity. People internalize expectations about speed, perfection, independence, communication style, or conflict behavior. When expectations feel unrealistic or unspoken, people experience pressure, hesitation, or self-protection. These questions uncover the emotional and structural dynamics that determine how people interpret what the organization wants from them.

Interpretation Tip: Listen for references to "what's expected," "how things are usually done," "what leadership likes," or "what people try to avoid." These statements reveal the underlying expectations. Also note when the buyer describes expectations that vary across teams or leaders — inconsistency is often a major source of confusion.

Coaching Note: Explore expectations through curiosity rather than judgment. Expectations shape behavior subtly; people often follow them without realizing how much influence they have.

Example prompts:

- *"What expectations guide how people behave or make decisions?"*

- *"Where are expectations clear — and where are they assumed?"*

Standard Organizational-Expectation Questions (8)

Tone: calm, expressive, exploratory.

1. "What expectations guide how people approach their work?"

2. "Which expectations feel clear and well understood?"

3. "Where do expectations help maintain consistent performance?"

4. "Which expectations shape how people communicate with one another?"

5. "Where do expectations support collaboration or teamwork?"

6. "Which expectations help people stay focused on priorities?"

7. "Where do people seem confident in what is expected of them?"

8. "Which expectations reinforce accountability across teams?"

Intermediate Organizational-Expectation Questions (9)

Tone: probing, pattern-seeking, clarity-focused.

1. "Where do expectations feel assumed rather than stated?"

2. "Which expectations vary depending on the team or leader?"

3. "Where do expectations conflict with stated goals or values?"

4. "Which expectations create pressure rather than clarity?"

5. "Where do people hesitate because expectations feel unclear?"

6. "Which expectations shift during busy or stressful periods?"

7. "Where do expectations discourage initiative or risk-taking?"

8. "Which expectations lead to misunderstandings between teams?"

9. "What expectations appear outdated or no longer useful?"

Aggressive Organizational-Expectation Questions (8)

Tone: direct, bold, truth-exposing.

1. "Which expectations are unrealistic or unsustainable?"

2. "Where does the organization rely on unwritten expectations that create confusion?"

3. "Which expectations cause unnecessary stress or hesitation?"

4. "What expectations do people follow only out of fear?"

5. "Where does leadership send mixed messages about what they expect?"

6. "Which expectations undermine teamwork or transparency?"

7. "Where are expectations so vague that people guess instead of knowing?"

8. "What expectation most frequently goes unmet — and why?"

Follow-Up Organizational-Expectation Questions (10)

Tone: reflective, clarifying, psychologically aware.

1. "Can you describe a moment when expectations felt especially clear?"

2. "What made that clarity possible?"

3. "How did the team respond when expectations were well understood?"

4. "Can you recall a moment when expectations caused confusion?"

5. "What triggered the uncertainty?"

6. "How did people react emotionally or behaviorally?"

7. "What deeper issue did that moment reveal about expectations?"

8. "What changes helped improve clarity — if any were made?"

9. "What expectations would benefit from being clarified or simplified?"

10. "What daily behaviors would help reinforce clear, consistent expectations?"

Conclusion

Organizational-expectation questions uncover the assumptions and standards that guide behavior across the organization. They reveal which expectations empower people, which create pressure, and which cause confusion or misalignment. Expectations are a major driver of performance and culture, and understanding them provides insight into both the explicit and implicit rules that shape daily work.

Strategically, these insights help highlight where communication, alignment, or leadership behavior needs refinement. Psychologically, they reveal how people make sense of their roles, responsibilities, and place in the organization — information that is crucial for meaningful discovery work.

As Chapter 7 continues, we will examine accountability behavior, cultural pressure points, emotional safety, and identity patterns that shape how teams function. Expectations set the tone; the next sections explore how people respond to those expectations under real-world circumstances.

Reflection Prompt:
Think of a time when unclear expectations created confusion or stress. Which organizational-expectation question would have surfaced that issue sooner?

CHAPTER 7 - SECTION 6 - Accountability-Behavior Questions

Introduction

After clarifying organizational expectations, the next important layer is understanding **accountability behavior** — how people take ownership, follow through, communicate commitments, and respond when responsibilities aren't met. Accountability is one of the most misunderstood organizational concepts. It is often associated with blame or pressure, but in healthy cultures, accountability is a shared commitment to clarity, reliability, and learning.

Strategically, accountability behavior reveals how effectively the organization executes work. When accountability is strong, progress is predictable, communication is clear, and issues are addressed before they escalate. When accountability is weak or inconsistent, delays increase, responsibilities get blurred, and teams rely more on reactive problem-solving than planned coordination.

Psychologically, accountability behaviors demonstrate the emotional health of the organization. People take greater ownership when they feel safe, supported, and respected. In contrast, avoidance, defensiveness, or inconsistency often stem from fear, uncertainty, or unclear expectations. These questions help illuminate not just the quality of follow-through, but the emotional forces shaping it.

Interpretation Tip: Listen for clues such as "we thought someone else had it," "we were waiting for…," or "it slipped through." These reveal accountability gaps. Also pay attention to how people talk about mistakes — accountability thrives when mistakes are treated as learning opportunities rather than threats.

Coaching Note: Encourage the buyer to frame accountability as a behavior and not a character trait. This keeps the conversation focused on actions, systems, and communication instead of personal criticism.

Example prompts:

- *"How do people show ownership of their commitments here?"*
- *"Where does accountability strengthen or weaken teamwork?"*

Standard Accountability-Behavior Questions (8)

Tone: calm, observational, behavior-focused.

1. "How do team members typically demonstrate ownership of their responsibilities?"
2. "Where do people reliably follow through on commitments?"

3. "Which tasks or roles show consistent accountability?"

4. "Where do handoffs reflect strong responsibility habits?"

5. "Which teams communicate early when they need support?"

6. "Where does accountability reinforce trust within the team?"

7. "Which roles model clear, dependable follow-through?"

8. "Where does accountability help keep projects on track?"

Intermediate Accountability-Behavior Questions (9)

Tone: probing, pattern-seeking, practical.

1. "Where does accountability become inconsistent across teams?"

2. "Which behaviors show hesitation around taking ownership?"

3. "Where do deadlines or commitments get missed frequently?"

4. "Which expectations are unclear enough to weaken accountability?"

5. "Where do people rely on reminders instead of self-management?"

6. "Which situations reveal gaps in ownership during transitions or handoffs?"

7. "Where do accountability issues emerge during busy or stressful times?"

8. "Which accountability patterns repeat across projects?"

9. "Where do informal norms influence accountability more than formal processes?"

Aggressive Accountability-Behavior Questions (8)

Tone: direct, truth-seeking, responsibility-focused.

1. "Where does accountability break down most often?"

2. "Who avoids ownership when tasks become difficult?"

3. "Which team tolerates inconsistent follow-through?"

4. "Where does leadership fail to model accountability?"

5. "Which accountability issue causes the most frustration?"

6. "Where do people rely on excuses rather than action?"

7. "Which recurring failures signal deeper accountability gaps?"

8. "What accountability habit has gone unaddressed for too long?"

Follow-Up Accountability-Behavior Questions (10)

Tone: reflective, clarifying, insight-deepening.

1. "Can you describe a moment when strong accountability made a significant difference?"

2. "What behaviors contributed to that success?"

3. "How did the team respond to the ownership shown?"

4. "Can you recall a moment when accountability was lacking?"

5. "What signs revealed the gap?"

6. "How did people react emotionally or behaviorally?"

7. "What deeper issue did the accountability lapse expose?"

8. "What steps were taken to address the issue — if any?"

9. "What would healthier accountability look like across the team?"

10. "What small, consistent habits would strengthen accountability overall?"

Conclusion

Accountability-behavior questions reveal how ownership, follow-through, communication, and responsibility shape the organization's performance and emotional climate. They expose the patterns that support reliability — and the gaps that create avoidable breakdowns. Accountability is not about assigning blame; it is about understanding how people manage their commitments and respond to challenges.

Strategically, these insights help diagnose whether the organization can sustain consistent execution and respond effectively to pressure. Psychologically, they surface the motivations, fears, and assumptions that shape accountability habits. Understanding these behaviors provides a clearer picture of how aligned and self-sufficient the organization truly is.

As Chapter 7 continues, we will explore cultural pressures, emotional safety, group identity, and behavioral reinforcement patterns. Accountability shows how people act; the next sections explore why they act that way.

Reflection Prompt:
Think of a situation where accountability strengthened or weakened a project. Which accountability-behavior question would have revealed the cause earlier?

CHAPTER 7 - SECTION 7 - Cultural-Pressure Questions

Introduction

After exploring accountability behaviors, the next layer in understanding organizational dynamics involves examining **cultural pressure** — the internal forces that push people to behave a certain way, meet certain expectations, or avoid certain risks. Cultural pressure is powerful because it often operates beneath the surface. People rarely talk about it directly, but they feel it every day through tone, pace, urgency, social norms, leadership behavior, and peer influence.

Strategically, cultural pressure reveals what the organization *prioritizes emotionally*. These pressures determine whether people feel the need to move faster, avoid mistakes, please leadership, stay silent, or remain agreeable. Cultural pressure shapes decision-making, risk tolerance, communication style, and creative thinking. These insights help explain why certain outcomes keep happening — even when formal policies say otherwise.

Psychologically, cultural pressure shapes stress, motivation, and identity. Some forms of pressure create positive energy and focus. Others create fear, burnout, or hesitation. Cultural pressure is often absorbed unconsciously, and people adapt to it to avoid negative consequences. These questions bring those invisible forces into focus so the advisor can understand what drives behavior beneath the level of stated goals.

Interpretation Tip: Listen for phrases like "we have to," "everyone knows," "it's expected," "if you don't," or "it wouldn't look good if…" These statements often reveal pressure sources. Also focus on emotional cues: tension, fear, defensiveness, or guilt often indicate pressure zones.

Coaching Note: Explore cultural pressure neutrally. The goal is not to judge the organization, but to understand how its environment shapes behavior. Many pressures are unintentional — byproducts of ambition, speed, or tradition.

Example prompts:

- *"What pressures do people feel — spoken or unspoken?"*

- *"Where does pressure drive behavior more than values or strategy?"*

Standard Cultural-Pressure Questions (8)

Tone: calm, observant, emotionally aware.

1. "What pressures do people feel in their daily work?"

2. "Where does the team feel the strongest expectation to perform?"

3. "Which responsibilities carry noticeable emotional weight?"

4. "Where do people feel pressured to move quickly?"

5. "Which situations create a sense of urgency — even when not required?"

6. "Where does pressure help people stay focused or motivated?"

7. "Which teams feel the pressure of visibility or leadership attention?"

8. "Where does cultural pressure influence communication style?"

Intermediate Cultural-Pressure Questions (9)

Tone: probing, pattern-focused, psychologically aware.

1. "Where does pressure come more from culture than from leadership direction?"

2. "Which expectations create tension rather than clarity?"

3. "Where do people feel the need to appear busy or productive?"

4. "Which pressures discourage people from speaking openly?"

5. "Where does cultural urgency lead to rushed decisions?"

6. "Which teams or roles feel the most pressure to avoid mistakes?"

7. "What pressure patterns appear during busy periods?"

8. "Where does pressure push people to hide problems or delays?"

9. "Which pressures are absorbed by new employees quickly?"

Aggressive Cultural-Pressure Questions (8)

Tone: direct, truth-exposing, courage-focused.

1. "Which cultural pressure creates the most fear or hesitation?"

2. "Where does pressure lead people to overwork or burn out?"

3. "Which expectations feel impossible to meet consistently?"

4. "What pressure causes people to avoid taking risks?"

5. "Which cultural demands leadership rarely acknowledges?"

6. "Where do people adjust behavior to avoid judgment?"

7. "What pressure leads to decisions that harm quality or collaboration?"

8. "Which pressure is so ingrained that people treat it as normal?"

Follow-Up Cultural-Pressure Questions (10)

Tone: reflective, clarifying, emotionally sensitive.

1. "Can you describe a moment when cultural pressure felt especially strong?"

2. "What triggered that pressure?"

3. "How did people respond emotionally?"

4. "What impact did the pressure have on collaboration or decision-making?"

5. "Which underlying beliefs or habits contributed to that moment?"

6. "How often does this type of pressure appear?"

7. "What helped relieve the pressure — if anything?"

8. "What part of the pressure remains unresolved?"

9. "What would healthier pressure or motivation look like?"

10. "What changes could reduce unnecessary cultural pressure?"

Conclusion

Cultural-pressure questions reveal the emotional forces that shape behavior beneath the surface of strategy, goals, and formal structures. These pressures influence decision-making, communication, risk tolerance, and morale. When understood correctly, they provide insight into why people behave the way they do — not just what they do.

Strategically, cultural pressure highlights systemic influences that drive both positive habits and unintended consequences. Psychologically, it reveals how deeply the organization impacts stress, confidence, and emotional safety. Understanding pressure patterns allows leaders and advisors to support healthier, more sustainable performance.

As Chapter 7 continues, we will explore emotional safety, organizational identity, and behavioral reinforcement — all essential components for diagnosing cultural health. Pressure shows how people react; the next sections explore where they feel safe and how they see themselves within the system.

Reflection Prompt:

Think of a team where pressure shaped behavior more than official guidance. Which cultural-pressure question would have revealed that influence earlier?

CHAPTER 7 - SECTION 8 - Emotional-Safety Questions

Introduction

After examining cultural pressure, the next essential layer of organizational insight involves understanding **emotional safety** — the degree to which people feel comfortable being honest, asking questions, sharing concerns, taking risks, and expressing themselves without fear of judgment or negative consequences. Emotional safety is one of the strongest predictors of team performance, but it is rarely discussed openly. Instead, it is felt in the small moments that shape trust and vulnerability.

Strategically, emotional safety determines how well organizations learn, adapt, innovate, and collaborate. Teams with strong emotional safety speak up early, address issues proactively, and handle conflict constructively. Teams with weak emotional safety avoid difficult conversations, hide mistakes, and hold back insights that could accelerate progress. Emotional safety is the hidden engine behind transparency, accountability, and continuous improvement.

Psychologically, emotional safety reflects whether people feel respected, supported, and valued. It shows whether people believe their voice matters. When emotional safety is strong, people take healthy risks and show initiative. When it is fragile, people protect themselves — often by staying silent, withdrawing, or following the safest path rather than the best one. These questions help uncover how the environment shapes confidence, openness, and vulnerability.

Interpretation Tip: Listen for soft signals such as "we try," "it depends who's in the room," or "people are careful." These phrases often indicate emotional caution. Also watch for differences between formal culture ("we encourage feedback") and lived experience ("people usually stay quiet").

Coaching Note: Approach emotional safety with empathy. This topic is sensitive, and buyers may hesitate to speak openly. Normalize the fact that emotional safety varies across teams and does not indicate failure — it simply reveals important opportunities.

Example prompts:

- *"Where do people feel safe speaking openly?"*

- *"Where do they hesitate, hold back, or stay quiet?"*

Standard Emotional-Safety Questions (8)

Tone: warm, observant, trust-focused.

1. "Where do people feel comfortable sharing their honest thoughts?"

2. "Which environments support open conversation?"

3. "Where do team members ask questions freely?"

4. "Which leaders help create a sense of emotional safety?"

5. "Where do people volunteer ideas without hesitation?"

6. "Which interactions feel respectful and supportive?"

7. "Where do people trust that mistakes will be treated fairly?"

8. "Which teams show confidence in speaking up?"

Intermediate Emotional-Safety Questions (9)

Tone: probing, perceptive, emotionally aware.

1. "Where do people hesitate to express disagreement?"

2. "Which situations make team members cautious about speaking up?"

3. "Where does emotional safety vary across teams or roles?"

4. "Which behaviors suggest fear of judgment or criticism?"

5. "Where do people stay quiet even when they have valuable insight?"

6. "What patterns emerge when emotional safety weakens?"

7. "Which leaders unintentionally reduce emotional openness?"

8. "Where do people soften their feedback to avoid discomfort?"

9. "What signals show that people don't feel fully comfortable being themselves?"

Aggressive Emotional-Safety Questions (8)

Tone: direct, truth-focused, pattern-exposing.

1. "Where is emotional safety the weakest right now?"

2. "Who makes others feel hesitant or uncomfortable sharing openly?"

3. "Which behaviors create fear of speaking up?"

4. "Where does leadership unintentionally shut down honest conversation?"

5. "What situations reveal the absence of psychological safety?"

6. "Which emotional-safety gap threatens collaboration the most?"

7. "Where do people modify their communication to avoid backlash?"

8. "What experiences have made people reluctant to be vulnerable?"

Follow-Up Emotional-Safety Questions (10)

Tone: reflective, clarifying, deeply attentive.

1. "Can you describe a moment when emotional safety was clearly present?"

2. "What allowed people to share openly in that situation?"

3. "How did the team respond to vulnerability?"

4. "Can you recall a moment when emotional safety was noticeably lacking?"

5. "What triggered the shift in behavior?"

6. "How did people react emotionally or physically?"

7. "What deeper issue did that moment reveal about the culture?"

8. "What helped rebuild safety — if it was rebuilt at all?"

9. "What would improve emotional safety across the team?"

10. "What daily behaviors would help reinforce a safer environment?"

Conclusion

Emotional-safety questions reveal the environment in which people express themselves, take risks, and participate in honest dialogue. They illuminate whether individuals feel respected, supported, and psychologically protected — or whether they hold back, stay cautious, and prioritize safety over contribution.

Strategically, emotional safety determines the organization's capacity for learning, innovation, and resilience. Psychologically, it shapes trust, motivation, belonging, and the willingness to collaborate. Understanding emotional safety is essential for diagnosing the health of any cultural system.

As Chapter 7 continues, we will explore identity dynamics, group belonging, and behavior reinforcement — the social mechanisms that determine how people see themselves within the organization. Emotional safety lays the groundwork for understanding these deeper patterns.

Reflection Prompt:
Think of a team where people hesitated to speak openly. Which emotional-safety question would have revealed that hesitation earlier?

CHAPTER 7 - SECTION 9 - Organizational-Identity Questions

Introduction

After understanding emotional safety, the next layer of cultural insight involves exploring **organizational identity** — the shared sense of who the organization believes it is, what it stands for, and how its people define themselves within it. Organizational identity is deeper than brand, messaging, or mission statements. It is the collective self-image that shapes how people interpret challenges, respond to change, and behave under pressure.

Strategically, organizational identity determines consistency. It guides decision-making, influences priorities, and anchors the organization during uncertainty. A clear identity helps teams align naturally, while a fragmented identity creates confusion and inconsistent behavior. Understanding identity helps reveal whether the organization acts from conviction or from habit.

Psychologically, identity shapes belonging and meaning. People want to feel part of something that reflects their values and strengths. When identity is strong, individuals experience pride, loyalty, and clarity of purpose. When identity is weak or contradictory, people feel disconnected, uncertain, or skeptical of change. These questions help reveal the emotional and relational foundation that holds the organization together.

Interpretation Tip: Listen for "we're the kind of company that…," "around here, we believe…," or "this is just who we are." These statements offer direct insight into identity. Also notice tensions between what the organization says it stands for and how it behaves in practice — identity gaps matter.

Coaching Note: Approach identity with curiosity and respect. Identity is personal and often deeply ingrained. Encourage the buyer to reflect on patterns rather than judging whether the identity is "good" or "bad."

Example prompts:

- *"How would you describe the organization's personality or character?"*

- *"What beliefs guide how people see themselves here?"*

Standard Organizational-Identity Questions (8)

Tone: reflective, observational, identity-focused.

1. "How would you describe the organization's personality or character?"

2. "Which values feel genuinely lived in daily work?"

3. "Where do people express pride in the organization?"

4. "Which stories get repeated that reflect the organization's identity?"

5. "Where does the team feel aligned around a shared purpose?"

6. "Which behaviors reflect who the organization believes itself to be?"

7. "Where do people feel connected to the broader mission?"

8. "Which symbols, rituals, or traditions express the organization's identity?"

Intermediate Organizational-Identity Questions (9)

Tone: probing, pattern-oriented, insight-driven.

1. "Where does the organization's identity feel inconsistent across teams?"

2. "Which values appear more aspirational than lived?"

3. "Where do actions contradict the identity leadership promotes?"

4. "Which identity themes emerge during stressful or busy seasons?"

5. "Where does the organization rely on past identity rather than current reality?"

6. "Which groups interpret the organization's identity differently?"

7. "Where do internal stories reveal pride — or frustration?"

8. "What identity expectations shape behavior unconsciously?"

9. "Where does identity influence decision-making more than data or strategy?"

Aggressive Organizational-Identity Questions (8)

Tone: direct, truth-seeking, respectfully challenging.

1. "Where is the organization's stated identity misaligned with its behavior?"

2. "Which identity themes feel outdated or no longer accurate?"

3. "Where does identity create limitations or blind spots?"

4. "Which parts of the identity people question privately?"

5. "What identity-related belief slows progress or innovation?"

6. "Where does the organization cling to identity narratives that no longer serve it?"

7. "Which identity disconnect causes frustration or mistrust?"

8. "What belief about 'who we are' should be reexamined?"

Follow-Up Organizational-Identity Questions (10)

Tone: reflective, exploratory, emotionally intelligent.

1. "Can you describe a moment when the organization's identity was clearly visible?"

2. "What behavior expressed that identity?"

3. "How did people feel during that moment?"

4. "Can you recall a time when the identity felt unclear or fragmented?"

5. "What triggered that sense of disconnect?"

6. "How did the team respond to the identity gap?"

7. "What deeper pattern did the moment reveal?"

8. "How has the identity evolved over time?"

9. "What identity shift would strengthen alignment and performance?"

10. "What small behaviors could reinforce a healthier identity going forward?"

Conclusion

Organizational-identity questions reveal the shared beliefs, stories, values, and assumptions that define how people see themselves within the organization. They highlight the emotional bonds that create belonging, as well as the gaps that create confusion or disconnection.

Strategically, identity shapes alignment, decision-making, level of initiative, and adaptability. Psychologically, identity influences pride, commitment, and trust. Understanding identity offers deep insight into the invisible forces guiding behavior across the organization.

As Chapter 7 moves to its final section, we will explore behavioral-reinforcement patterns — the mechanisms that strengthen or weaken identity, culture, and performance. Identity shows who the organization believes it is; reinforcement shows how that belief is maintained.

Reflection Prompt:
Think of an organization that said one thing about itself but behaved differently. Which identity question would have surfaced that truth early?

Chapter Conclusion

Chapter 7 demonstrates that culture is not what organizations *say* — it is what people feel, observe, and internalize through daily experience. The chapter's ten sections reveal the signals that shape these experiences: the emotional climate, leadership cues, cultural norms, expectations, pressures, and reinforcement patterns that influence every interaction. Understanding these dynamics allows the advisor to see beneath surface-level behaviors and uncover the deeper truths that shape organizational health.

Strategically, these insights help predict how the organization will respond to change, handle complexity, communicate expectations, and support accountability. Psychologically, they reveal whether people feel safe, valued, aligned, and emotionally connected to their work. When these cultural signals are visible, the advisor can guide conversations with empathy and accuracy — uncovering not only what is happening, but *why* it is happening.

With these foundations established, the reader is now ready to move into the next chapter, where we shift from internal organizational culture to the external pressures, market realities, customer expectations, and decision environments that shape complex buying processes. Chapter 7 provides the cultural awareness required to navigate those conversations with insight and confidence.

CHAPTER 8 — Understanding External Pressures, Market Forces, and Buyer Context

Chapter Introduction

Organizations often focus their internal conversations on culture, habits, and workflow, but every decision they make is shaped by something bigger than their internal environment. Chapter 8 expands the lens outward, examining the **external pressures and market forces** that influence strategy, timing, urgency, and willingness to change. Discovery becomes far more accurate when you understand not just how a team operates, but *what the world around them is demanding from them.*

This chapter begins by exploring **market conditions**, the shifting realities that define opportunity and risk. Market dynamics influence whether leaders feel optimistic, cautious, or pressured to evolve. From there, the chapter moves into **customer expectations**, the frontline demands that shape service quality, product decisions, communication style, and operational priorities. Customers often act as the loudest voice shaping the organization's behavior.

Next, the chapter examines **competitive pressure**, the force that pushes organizations to differentiate, defend their position, or accelerate innovation. Competition is often an emotional experience as much as a strategic one, influencing pride, urgency, and fear. After this, the chapter explores **economic constraints**, revealing how budget cycles, cost pressures, and financial realities shape what organizations can do now versus what must wait.

Regulatory influence provides another essential piece of context. Laws, standards, and compliance requirements affect planning, process design, and timing more than most internal leaders admit. This chapter then examines **supply-chain and operational-flow pressures**, the real-world constraints that shape execution speed and reliability. These questions highlight the practical factors that often determine feasibility.

The final sections explore **industry standards**, **external triggers**, **environmental pressures**, and **timing forces**. These elements help reveal how the broader ecosystem affects decision-making, internal alignment, and emotional readiness. Whether through sudden disruptions, societal expectations, geographic realities, or seasonal cycles, external forces frame the boundaries within which every organization must operate.

By the end of Chapter 8, the reader gains a full understanding of the environment surrounding the buyer—an environment filled with pressures, uncertainties, opportunities, and constraints. This chapter helps the advisor approach discovery not simply as a conversation about internal needs, but as a holistic exploration of the world in which the buyer must succeed.

CHAPTER 8 - SECTION 1 - Market-Context Questions

Introduction

Every decision a client makes is shaped by the broader market environment in which they operate. Before exploring competitive pressures, customer expectations, economic constraints, or industry shifts, the first step is understanding **market context** — the landscape that influences how your buyer thinks, prioritizes, and evaluates trade-offs. Market context is not just external data; it is the psychological frame through which the organization interprets reality.

Strategically, understanding market context helps uncover the forces shaping urgency, risk tolerance, and long-term planning. Market signals influence how organizations invest, what opportunities they pursue, and which vulnerabilities they try to guard against. When a buyer feels constrained, uncertain, or pressured by the market, their decisions reflect those conditions. Market-context questions illuminate the external pressures that quietly shape internal choices.

Psychologically, market context affects emotion and narrative. Leaders interpret market conditions through their own experiences, fears, optimism, or skepticism. Teams feel market pressure through expectations for speed, efficiency, and adaptation. These questions help reveal how the buyer *perceives* the market, not merely how the market behaves. Perception drives decision-making just as strongly as data.

Interpretation Tip: Listen for tension between optimism and hesitation. Also pay attention to statements like "the market is changing," "customers expect more," "competitors are moving faster," or "we need to keep up." These reveal the internal story the organization tells about its environment.

Coaching Note: Help the buyer separate the market's objective conditions from the organization's subjective interpretation. This allows you to understand both what is happening *and* how they are making meaning from it.

Example prompts:

- *"How would you describe the current state of your market?"*

- *"Which external forces shape your team's decisions most?"*

Standard Market-Context Questions (8)

Tone: open, descriptive, broad-thinking.

1. "How would you describe the current state of your market?"

2. "Which trends are most influencing your industry right now?"

3. "Where do you see opportunities emerging?"

4. "Which areas of the market feel stable or predictable?"

5. "Where does volatility or uncertainty appear?"

6. "What signals suggest the market is shifting?"

7. "Which customer behaviors are changing?"

8. "Where does your team feel most aligned with market direction?"

Intermediate Market-Context Questions (9)

Tone: probing, pattern-aware, model-building.

1. "Which market trends create pressure on your team's priorities?"

2. "Where do you feel the market is moving faster than your organization?"

3. "Which competitors influence your planning the most?"

4. "What market shifts could redefine your strategy?"

5. "Where do customers' expectations outpace current capabilities?"

6. "What signals show the market becoming more complex?"

7. "Where does your team debate how to respond to market changes?"

8. "Which assumptions about the market need rethinking?"

9. "What parts of the market feel unpredictable or hard to read?"

Aggressive Market-Context Questions (8)

Tone: direct, truth-seeking, strategically bold.

1. "What market reality poses the biggest threat to your current approach?"

2. "Where is your organization falling behind market expectations?"

3. "Which competitor advantage creates real concern internally?"

4. "Where are you underestimating market risk?"

5. "What trend could disrupt your business if ignored?"

6. "Where is the team slow to adapt to market pressure?"

7. "What customer shift your organization is least prepared for?"

8. "What external force is you avoiding confronting directly?"

Follow-Up Market-Context Questions (10)

Tone: reflective, detail-seeking, perspective-deepening.

1. "Can you share a recent moment when a market shift influenced your decisions?"

2. "What signal made the shift visible to you?"

3. "How did your team interpret that change?"

4. "What response did the organization take — if any?"

5. "How confident did people feel in that response?"

6. "What earlier signs might you have missed?"

7. "Who noticed the shift first?"

8. "What concerns surfaced during the transition?"

9. "What new opportunities became clearer afterward?"

10. "How does the market context shape your priorities now?"

Conclusion

Market-context questions reveal the external landscape that shapes internal decision-making. They expose the forces influencing urgency, confidence, and long-term planning. Understanding market context gives the advisor a powerful vantage point: you can see not just what the organization wants, but why it feels the need to pursue certain paths.

Strategically, these insights help uncover constraints and opportunities that shape buyer behavior. Psychologically, they reveal the narratives and assumptions guiding leaders' interpretations of their environment. Market context sets the stage for understanding competitive pressure, customer expectations, economic constraints, and the external signals influencing organizational behavior.

As Chapter 8 continues, we will explore competitive landscape, industry trends, economic pressures, regulatory realities, customer evolution, and the external forces shaping your buyer's world. Market context is the foundation upon which all external discovery rests.

Reflection Prompt:
Think of a time when a market shift suddenly changed priorities. Which market-context question would have surfaced that shift earlier?

CHAPTER 8 – SECTION 1 - Market-Condition Questions

Introduction

Discovery is never only about the internal workings of an organization. Every organization operates inside a broader environment shaped by shifting markets, evolving customer expectations, economic cycles, and competitive forces. To understand a buyer's reality, the advisor must understand the **market conditions** influencing pressure, decision urgency, resource allocation, and strategic priorities. Market conditions create the landscape in which the buyer must navigate every choice.

Strategically, market-condition questions help reveal the external forces shaping your buyer's worldview: supply-demand imbalances, pricing tension, customer behavior, regulatory changes, industry trends, and technological shifts. When these forces are clear, you gain insight into what the buyer sees as opportunity, what they see as risk, and where they feel constrained. These questions ensure that your discovery extends beyond internal dynamics into the broader business ecosystem.

Psychologically, external pressures influence confidence, caution, optimism, and readiness for change. Teams under market pressure may behave more cautiously or more urgently depending on how they interpret the landscape. Some organizations respond with innovation; others respond by tightening budgets or delaying decisions. These questions explore not just the objective conditions, but also the team's emotional interpretation of those conditions.

Interpretation Tip: Listen for hints of uncertainty, confidence, fatigue, or urgency. Comments like "we're watching the market closely," "it's been unpredictable," or "we've had to adjust expectations" signal areas ripe for deeper investigation. Also note what the buyer defines as normal — their version of normal often reveals their tolerance for risk and change.

Coaching Note: Guide the buyer toward clarity rather than prediction. Market conditions are often unpredictable, but the way the team interprets them is highly revealing. Use these questions to uncover mindset and strategic posture, not forecasts.

Example prompts:

- *"How are current market trends influencing your priorities?"*

- *"What external forces are shaping your decisions this quarter?"*

Standard Market-Condition Questions (8)

Tone: calm, curious, landscape-focused.

1. "How would you describe the current conditions in your market?"

2. "Which trends are shaping customer expectations right now?"

3. "Where have you seen noticeable shifts in demand?"

4. "Which external factors influence your strategic decisions most?"

5. "Where do you see stability within your market?"

6. "Which market changes have been easiest to adapt to?"

7. "Where do external conditions support your current goals?"

8. "Which opportunities seem to be emerging from these conditions?"

Intermediate Market-Condition Questions (9)

Tone: probing, pattern-seeking, context-deepening.

1. "Which market shifts have created the most pressure recently?"

2. "Where do you see volatility affecting decision-making?"

3. "Which competitors have adapted more quickly — and how?"

4. "Where are customer behaviors changing faster than expected?"

5. "Which market conditions are shaping your investment choices?"

6. "Where do regulatory or industry standards influence your direction?"

7. "Which trends might reshape your priorities this year?"

8. "Where do external pressures challenge your internal processes?"

9. "Which parts of the market feel oversaturated or underserved?"

Aggressive Market-Condition Questions (8)

Tone: direct, precise, truth-revealing.

1. "Which market pressures are creating the most internal strain?"

2. "Where is the organization struggling to keep pace with change?"

3. "Which competitors threaten your position the most right now?"

4. "Where does the market expose weaknesses in your strategy?"

5. "Which external force you're facing is the least manageable?"

6. "What trend, if ignored, would hurt you the fastest?"

7. "Where is the market forcing you to change your plans?"

8. "Which assumptions about the market may no longer be true?"

Follow-Up Market-Condition Questions (10)

Tone: reflective, clarifying, strategic.

1. "Can you share a moment when market conditions shifted unexpectedly?"

2. "What impact did that shift have on your plans?"

3. "Who recognized the change first?"

4. "What signals made the shift clear?"

5. "How did the team respond to the new conditions?"

6. "What deeper issue did the market shift reveal internally?"

7. "Which adjustments were most effective?"

8. "What opportunities became visible after the shift?"

9. "What risks are still present as a result of those conditions?"

10. "What would help your team respond more confidently to future changes?"

Conclusion

Market-condition questions anchor discovery in the external realities influencing the buyer's perspective. They reveal how the organization interprets opportunity, risk, competition, and change. Understanding market conditions allows you to connect your insights to the environment shaping strategy and execution.

Strategically, these questions help identify the pressures driving urgency or hesitation. Psychologically, they reveal the organization's confidence, resilience, and readiness to adapt.

When combined with internal cultural insights from earlier chapters, market awareness gives you a complete picture of the forces shaping buyer behavior.

As Chapter 8 continues, we will explore customer expectations, competitive pressures, economic constraints, regulatory influences, and external triggers that affect decision-making. Market conditions are the starting point for understanding external context.

Reflection Prompt:
Think of a time when market shifts dramatically altered an organization's strategy. Which market-condition question would have surfaced that shift sooner?

CHAPTER 8 - SECTION 2 - Customer-Expectation Questions

Introduction

Understanding market conditions is only the beginning. To uncover the full external picture, you must also understand **customer expectations** — the beliefs, preferences, and requirements your buyer's customers carry into every interaction. Customer expectations shape how organizations prioritize initiatives, allocate resources, design experiences, and evaluate success. When expectations shift, strategy shifts with them.

Strategically, customer expectations reveal where your buyer feels pressured to evolve, where gaps in service or product fit may be emerging, and where new opportunities might arise. They dictate pace, quality standards, communication preferences, and the definition of value. These questions help you understand the forces shaping the buyer's decision-making from the outside in.

Psychologically, customer expectations create emotional pressure. Customers may be more demanding, more informed, or more selective than ever before. When expectations rise faster than the organization can adjust, teams experience stress, urgency, hesitation, or defensive problem-solving. When expectations align well with capability, teams feel confident and supported. These questions help uncover the emotional patterns tied to serving the customer.

Interpretation Tip: Listen for contrasts such as "customers expect more now," "they've become less patient," or "we're trying to keep up with…" These signal shifting expectations. Also note any hesitation — buyers often fear admitting that customer expectations are outpacing their processes.

Coaching Note: Encourage the buyer to separate *customer expectations* from *customer satisfaction.* Expectations are about what customers believe should happen; satisfaction is how they feel about what actually happens. Keep the focus on expectations.

Example prompts:

- *"What do your customers expect from you today that they didn't expect two years ago?"*

- *"Where do customer expectations drive your priorities?"*

Standard Customer-Expectation Questions (8)

Tone: calm, curious, customer-centered.

1. "What do your customers expect most consistently from your organization?"

2. "Which expectations are easiest for your team to meet?"

3. "Where do customer expectations align with your current strengths?"

4. "Which customer behaviors help clarify what they value most?"

5. "Where do customers respond well to your approach?"

6. "Which expectations shape your communication or service standards?"

7. "Where do customer needs reinforce your strategic goals?"

8. "Which expectations remain stable even as the market changes?"

Intermediate Customer-Expectation Questions (9)

Tone: probing, pattern-focused, clarity-seeking.

1. "Where have customer expectations increased noticeably?"

2. "Which expectations have become harder to meet lately?"

3. "Where do customers compare your organization to competitors?"

4. "Which customer segments express new or evolving requirements?"

5. "Where do expectations shift faster than internal processes can adapt?"

6. "Which scenarios reveal disconnects between customer desire and current capability?"

7. "Where do customers demand more transparency or responsiveness?"

8. "Which expectations shape pricing, delivery, or service models?"

9. "Where do rising expectations create internal tension?"

Aggressive Customer-Expectation Questions (8)

Tone: direct, truth-seeking, pressure-aware.

1. "Which customer expectations your team struggles with the most?"

2. "Where are customer demands outpacing your current capacity?"

3. "Which expectations create the most stress or urgency internally?"

4. "Where are customers dissatisfied because expectations shifted?"

5. "Which expectation is the biggest threat if left unmet?"

6. "Where do customer expectations expose weaknesses in your process?"

7. "What expectation caught the organization off guard?"

8. "Where are customers expecting more value than you're able to deliver today?"

Follow-Up Customer-Expectation Questions (10)

Tone: reflective, clarifying, insight-deepening.

1. "Can you share a moment when customer expectations changed suddenly?"

2. "What sign showed the shift was happening?"

3. "How did the team respond emotionally and operationally?"

4. "What adjustments were made to meet the new expectation?"

5. "Which expectations remain difficult to address?"

6. "How do customers communicate their expectations to you?"

7. "What deeper pattern do these expectations reveal about your market?"

8. "What would meeting rising expectations require internally?"

9. "What opportunity exists because expectations have changed?"

10. "What would help your team anticipate expectations more effectively?"

Conclusion

Customer-Expectation questions uncover how external demands shape internal priorities. They reveal the changing expectations of customers, the emotional pressures these expectations create, and the adjustments organizations make in response. By understanding these forces, the advisor gains insight into what drives buyer urgency, where dissatisfaction may build, and where alignment or misalignment exists between customer needs and organizational capability.

Strategically, these insights help forecast challenges, identify opportunities, and understand why certain initiatives rise in importance. Psychologically, they illuminate how teams interpret and internalize customer pressure — a major driver of decision-making behavior.

As Chapter 8 continues, we will explore competitive forces, economic constraints, regulatory influences, and external triggers that shape buying processes. Customer expectations form the emotional and strategic bridge between internal capacity and external demand.

Reflection Prompt:
Think of a time when customer expectations evolved faster than a team could adjust. Which customer-expectation question would have revealed that shift sooner?

CHAPTER 8 - SECTION 3 - Competitive-Pressure Questions

Introduction

Market conditions and customer expectations set the landscape, but true external pressure often becomes most visible through **competition**. Competitive pressure shapes urgency, influences strategy, and exposes areas where organizations feel vulnerable or behind. Understanding how your buyer perceives competition provides insight into their defensive instincts, their offensive opportunities, and the emotional frameworks shaping their decisions.

Strategically, competitive-pressure questions reveal how your buyer interprets their position in the market—where they feel confident, where they feel threatened, and where they believe differentiation matters most. These insights illuminate why certain projects get prioritized, why budgets shift, and why stakeholders push for or resist change. Competition often determines what the organization believes it *must* do rather than what it *wants* to do.

Psychologically, competitive pressure affects morale, confidence, and risk tolerance. Some organizations respond to competition with determination and creativity. Others experience anxiety, overreaction, or avoidance. Competitive pressure rarely exists in isolation—it blends with identity, expectations, and leadership tone. These questions help surface how competition influences emotional and strategic behavior.

Interpretation Tip: Listen for strong emotional cues—frustration, pride, urgency, defensiveness, or doubt. These emotions reveal how deeply competitive dynamics influence the buyer. Also note references to recent competitor moves — these often trigger internal shifts long before leadership communicates them.

Coaching Note: Encourage objective reflection without judgment. Competition can create both healthy drive and unhealthy tension. The goal is to surface the perceived realities driving decisions.

Example prompts:

- *"How do competitor actions influence your priorities?"*

- *"Where do you see competitors gaining ground—or losing it?"*

Standard Competitive-Pressure Questions (8)

Tone: calm, curious, strategically aware.

1. "How would you describe your competitive landscape right now?"

2. "Which competitors influence your decisions most visibly?"

3. "Where do you feel confident relative to your competitors?"

4. "Which advantages set you apart today?"

5. "Where do competitors struggle in ways that benefit you?"

6. "Which competitor behaviors help you understand market direction?"

7. "Where do you see opportunities to outperform others?"

8. "Which trends shape how you compare yourself to competitors?"

Intermediate Competitive-Pressure Questions (9)

Tone: probing, pattern-focused, insight-driven.

1. "Where do competitors create pressure for faster execution?"

2. "Which recent competitor move demanded internal adjustments?"

3. "Where do competitors outperform you—consistently or occasionally?"

4. "Which markets or segments feel more competitive than others?"

5. "Where does competition influence pricing, service, or product decisions?"

6. "Which competitor investments signal coming changes?"

7. "Where do you see competitors improving at a faster pace?"

8. "Which competitive shifts created the most internal debate?"

9. "Where does competitive pressure highlight gaps in your strategy?"

Aggressive Competitive-Pressure Questions (8)

Tone: direct, precise, truth-excavating.

1. "Which competitor threatens you the most right now?"

2. "Where are you losing ground—and why?"

3. "Which competitor weakness you're not taking advantage of?"

4. "What competitive pressure is causing the most internal strain?"

5. "Which competitor out-innovates you consistently?"

6. "Where does competition expose weaknesses you avoid addressing?"

7. "What competitor action caught your organization unprepared?"

8. "Where do you feel forced into reactive rather than strategic decisions?"

Follow-Up Competitive-Pressure Questions (10)

Tone: reflective, clarifying, scenario-aware.

1. "Can you describe a moment when competitive pressure shifted suddenly?"

2. "What event triggered that shift?"

3. "How did the team learn about the competitor's move?"

4. "What internal reactions did it create?"

5. "Which part of your strategy was most affected?"

6. "What deeper issue did the competitive shift highlight?"

7. "How effective was your response?"

8. "What opportunity emerged from the competitive tension?"

9. "What risk remains open because of that shift?"

10. "What would help the organization respond more proactively?"

Conclusion

Competitive-pressure questions reveal how the buyer perceives their competitive environment — not just in terms of strategy, but in terms of emotion, urgency, and confidence. They shed light on internal debates, external threats, and the motivations shaping buying decisions long before a sales conversation begins.

Strategically, these insights allow you to connect your solution to the competitive realities driving change. Psychologically, they reveal how teams cope with pressure, respond to rivals, and interpret their place in the market. Understanding competitive pressure completes the external context needed for meaningful discovery.

As Chapter 8 continues, we will explore economic constraints, regulatory forces, and external triggers that shape decision timelines. Competitive pressure forms the strategic heartbeat behind many of these influences.

Reflection Prompt:
Think of a moment when a competitor forced an organization to change rapidly. Which competitive-pressure question would have revealed that turning point sooner?

CHAPTER 8 - SECTION 4 - Economic-Constraint Questions

Introduction

No matter how strong the strategy or how compelling the opportunity, every organization makes decisions within the boundaries of **economic constraints**. Budgets, margins, cash flow cycles, cost pressures, revenue forecasts, and profitability goals all shape what is possible and what must wait. Economic constraints are not just financial realities—they are emotional realities, influencing confidence, caution, urgency, and willingness to take risks.

Strategically, economic-constraint questions reveal the financial pressures influencing prioritization. They help uncover where the organization feels limited, where trade-offs are happening, and where investments are most tightly evaluated. These insights clarify whether the buyer is operating in a season of expansion, stabilization, or protection. Economic constraints often explain why decisions accelerate, stall, or shift unexpectedly.

Psychologically, economic pressure creates emotional tension. Teams may feel overloaded, cautious, defensive, or hyper-focused depending on how they interpret financial conditions. Some leaders respond with optimism and creativity, while others respond with restriction and caution. These questions help uncover how financial conditions shape mindset—something that directly influences readiness for change.

Interpretation Tip: Listen for signs of financial stress such as "budget is tight," "we're being cautious," or "we're reviewing all expenses." Also pay attention to internal contradictions— teams may claim they are financially constrained but still invest heavily in certain areas. These contradictions reveal priorities.

Coaching Note: Discuss economic constraints with empathy, not interrogation. Finances often carry emotional weight; create space for the buyer to share openly without feeling exposed or judged.

Example prompts:

- *"How are current financial conditions shaping your decisions?"*

- *"Where do budget or cost constraints influence project timing?"*

Standard Economic-Constraint Questions (8)

Tone: calm, respectful, financially aware.

1. "How would you describe your current financial environment?"

2. "Which areas of the business have the most budget flexibility?"

3. "Where do financial conditions feel supportive of your goals?"

4. "Which investments remain a priority despite constraints?"

5. "Where do budget limits shape project timing or scope?"

6. "Which teams feel financial impact most directly?"

7. "Where do cost considerations guide decision-making?"

8. "Which financial trends are influencing your planning?"

Intermediate Economic-Constraint Questions (9)

Tone: probing, precise, context-seeking.

1. "Where have budgets tightened compared to previous cycles?"

2. "Which financial pressures cause the most internal debate?"

3. "Where does financial uncertainty slow decision-making?"

4. "Which areas require more justification for investment lately?"

5. "Where do finance and operations interpret constraints differently?"

6. "Which financial assumptions guide your current planning?"

7. "Where do revenue fluctuations impact priorities?"

8. "Which cost pressures create tension between teams?"

9. "Where do financial constraints reveal gaps in process or efficiency?"

Aggressive Economic-Constraint Questions (8)

Tone: direct, truth-seeking, pressure-aware.

1. "Which financial constraint is limiting progress the most right now?"

2. "Where is lack of budget hiding deeper operational issues?"

3. "Which investments have been delayed too long due to financial pressure?"

4. "Where does cost-cutting create risk or unintended consequences?"

5. "Which financial assumptions may no longer be realistic?"

6. "Where does financial pressure force short-term decisions over long-term strategy?"

7. "Which budget decisions leadership avoids addressing openly?"

8. "What financial risk is no longer acceptable to ignore?"

Follow-Up Economic-Constraint Questions (10)

Tone: reflective, clarifying, financially insightful.

1. "Can you describe a moment when financial conditions shifted unexpectedly?"

2. "What sign made the shift clear?"

3. "How did the team respond emotionally?"

4. "What adjustments became necessary immediately?"

5. "Which projects were most affected by the change?"

6. "What deeper issue did the financial shift expose?"

7. "Which actions helped stabilize the situation?"

8. "What opportunities, if any, emerged despite the constraints?"

9. "What financial insight would improve decision-making going forward?"

10. "What would help your team navigate economic pressure more confidently?"

Conclusion

Economic-constraint questions reveal how financial conditions shape decision-making, planning, and organizational behavior. They clarify whether the buyer is operating from scarcity, stability, or strategic investment—and how those conditions influence readiness for change. By understanding these pressures, the advisor gains insight into budget cycles, stakeholder caution, and investment appetite.

Strategically, these insights help frame your solution in terms that align with financial realities. Psychologically, they uncover the emotional responses that influence pace, confidence, and risk tolerance. Economic context completes another layer of the buyer's external reality.

As Chapter 8 continues, we will explore regulatory forces, industry standards, external triggers, and environmental influences that affect decision urgency. Economic constraints are the practical boundaries in which all of these forces operate.

Reflection Prompt:

Think of an organization whose decisions were shaped heavily by budget cycles. Which economic-constraint question would have revealed that dynamic earlier?

CHAPTER 8 - SECTION 5 - Regulatory-Influence Questions

Introduction

Beyond market conditions, customer expectations, competition, and financial realities, organizations must navigate a crucial external force: **regulation**. Regulations shape what organizations *must* do, *can* do, and *cannot* do. They create boundaries, obligations, timelines, compliance structures, reporting standards, and operational requirements. Even in less regulated industries, policies and external standards influence decisions in powerful ways.

Strategically, regulatory influences often drive investment, urgency, and resource allocation more forcefully than market pressures. New policies can accelerate projects, delay plans, or fundamentally shift priorities. Regulatory influence questions help uncover which rules, standards, or oversight bodies shape the buyer's decisions—and how strongly. Understanding these forces reveals constraints, risks, and must-win requirements that shape decision urgency.

Psychologically, regulatory pressure can create anxiety, caution, or fear of consequences. Teams may feel overwhelmed by compliance demands or uncertain about new requirements. Others may feel confident because they've built strong compliance structures. These questions uncover the emotional weight behind compliance and how it affects readiness for change, risk tolerance, and operational focus.

Interpretation Tip: Listen for statements like "we have to," "the new rules require," "we're preparing for," or "we can't afford to miss…" These indicate regulatory pressure. Also note when buyers hesitate—regulation often carries sensitivity, and they may fear revealing vulnerabilities.

Coaching Note: Approach regulation with professionalism and reassurance. Regulation is not about fault; it is about structure. Encourage clarity, not defensiveness, and help the buyer articulate where uncertainty or opportunity exists.

Example prompts:

- *"What regulatory requirements influence how you operate?"*

- *"Where do changing rules alter your priorities?"*

Standard Regulatory-Influence Questions (8)

Tone: calm, respectful, compliance-aware.

1. "Which regulatory requirements influence your operations most consistently?"

2. "Where do regulations guide your standard processes?"

3. "Which compliance tasks are easiest for your team to manage?"

4. "Where do regulations support stability in your workflow?"

5. "Which policies or standards shape your decision-making?"

6. "Where does your organization feel confident about compliance?"

7. "Which regulations match your current strengths or capabilities?"

8. "Where does compliance help build trust with customers or partners?"

Intermediate Regulatory-Influence Questions (9)

Tone: probing, structured, clarity-focused.

1. "Where have regulatory changes created new responsibilities?"

2. "Which rules are most difficult to interpret or implement?"

3. "Where do compliance requirements slow down decision-making?"

4. "Which teams carry the heaviest regulatory workload?"

5. "Where do audits or reviews create tension or stress?"

6. "Which emerging regulations you're preparing for?"

7. "Where do compliance standards conflict with operational practices?"

8. "Which regulatory deadlines create the most urgency?"

9. "Where does uncertainty about regulations influence planning?"

Aggressive Regulatory-Influence Questions (8)

Tone: direct, truth-exposing, risk-aware.

1. "Which regulatory requirement poses the biggest risk if unmet?"

2. "Where are you currently out of alignment with regulatory expectations?"

3. "Which compliance gap worries you the most?"

4. "Where have regulatory changes forced unplanned decisions?"

5. "Which regulation stretches your resources the most?"

6. "Where does leadership avoid discussing compliance concerns?"

7. "What regulation could cause a major setback if ignored?"

8. "Where do you feel unprepared for upcoming compliance shifts?"

Follow-Up Regulatory-Influence Questions (10)

Tone: reflective, precision-focused, supportive.

1. "Can you describe a moment when regulatory pressure intensified suddenly?"

2. "What event or announcement triggered that pressure?"

3. "How did the team respond internally?"

4. "Which processes were affected most directly?"

5. "What deeper issue did the regulatory shift expose?"

6. "Which corrective actions worked well?"

7. "What challenges remain unresolved?"

8. "Which resources or tools would help improve compliance confidence?"

9. "What opportunities emerged because of the new regulations?"

10. "What ongoing changes do you expect in your regulatory environment?"

Conclusion

Regulatory-influence questions reveal how external rules, policies, and enforcement shape the organization's decisions, priorities, and operational structure. They highlight compliance-related pressures, fears, and opportunities—offering insight into areas that can't be ignored or delayed. Regulation often creates urgency, elevates risks, and drives investment more strongly than internal motivation.

Strategically, these insights show where the buyer must adapt and where timely support can make a major difference. Psychologically, regulatory responses reveal whether teams feel prepared, overwhelmed, confident, or uncertain. Understanding these forces helps the advisor navigate sensitive topics with precision and empathy.

As Chapter 8 continues, we will explore supply-chain realities, industry standards, external triggers, and environmental influences that shape decision timelines. Regulation is the backbone of constraint; next, we examine the external forces that affect flow and timing.

Reflection Prompt:

Think of a moment when regulation forced an unexpected organizational change. Which regulatory-influence question would have captured that shift sooner?

8

73

CHAPTER 8 - SECTION 6 - Supply-Chain and Operational-Dependency Questions

Introduction

Regulatory forces shape compliance, but another major external pressure comes from **supply-chain and operational dependencies** — the network of suppliers, partners, vendors, manufacturers, logistics providers, and technical systems that support daily operations. These dependencies determine stability, speed, cost, reliability, and the organization's ability to respond to changing demand. When external partners falter, the entire operation feels the impact.

Strategically, supply-chain and operational-dependency questions help uncover where the organization feels stable, where it feels vulnerable, and where disruptions create risk. These insights reveal the hidden forces behind delays, cost fluctuations, operational gaps, or sudden reprioritization. Supply chain issues often shape urgency more than internal priorities do.

Psychologically, supply-chain pressures influence frustration, anxiety, and resilience. Unpredictable partners create tension. Reliable partners create confidence. When teams must absorb variability from outside sources, they may feel stressed, reactive, or cautious. These questions help reveal the emotional effect of external dependencies and how those dependencies shape decision-making.

Interpretation Tip: Listen for statements like "we're waiting on," "they're behind," "we're dependent on," or "we had to adjust." These signals indicate reliance on external parties. Also note which problems the buyer describes as "unexpected"—unexpected disruptions often shape behavior more than planned challenges.

Coaching Note: Approach supply-chain topics with patience. Organizations may feel embarrassed or frustrated by dependency issues. Your role is to create clarity, not critique.

Example prompts:

- *"How do external partners influence your operations?"*

- *"Where do supply-chain dependencies create tension or delay?"*

Standard Supply-Chain & Dependency Questions (8)

Tone: calm, operational, insight-seeking.

1. "How would you describe your current supply-chain stability?"

2. "Which partners or vendors are most reliable for you?"

3. "Where do external dependencies support smooth operations?"

4. "Which processes rely heavily on outside providers?"

5. "Where does your supply chain align well with your pace of work?"

6. "Which logistics or vendor relationships help maintain consistency?"

7. "Where do you feel confident about your operational dependencies?"

8. "Which parts of your process run smoothly because of strong partnerships?"

Intermediate Supply-Chain & Dependency Questions (9)

Tone: probing, pattern-seeking, clarity-focused.

1. "Where have external partners struggled to keep up with demand?"

2. "Which supply-chain issues appear most frequently?"

3. "Where do delays from vendors cause internal disruption?"

4. "Which processes are vulnerable to external interruptions?"

5. "Where do dependency failures create unexpected costs?"

6. "Which partners require more oversight than expected?"

7. "Where do supply-chain issues force changes in timelines?"

8. "Which dependencies slow down decision-making or execution?"

9. "Where do external relationships influence your operational strategy?"

Aggressive Supply-Chain & Dependency Questions (8)

Tone: direct, candid, risk-focused.

1. "Which supply-chain dependency poses the highest current risk?"

2. "Where are you overly reliant on a single vendor or partner?"

3. "Which partner consistently underperforms?"

4. "Where do dependency failures damage customer experience?"

5. "Which supply-chain issue leadership avoids confronting?"

6. "Where have external breakdowns hurt your margins or timelines?"

7. "Which dependency gap could cause a major operational failure?"

8. "What supply-chain risk has gone unaddressed for too long?"

Follow-Up Supply-Chain & Dependency Questions (10)

Tone: reflective, clarifying, detail-oriented.

1. "Can you share a moment when a supply-chain shift disrupted your workflow?"

2. "What triggered the disruption?"

3. "How did the team respond internally?"

4. "What adjustments were necessary to stay on track?"

5. "Which partners communicated well during the challenge?"

6. "Which partners made the situation more difficult?"

7. "What deeper issue did the disruption reveal about your dependencies?"

8. "What changes improved reliability afterward?"

9. "What risks still remain within your network?"

10. "What would strengthen your supply-chain resilience going forward?"

Conclusion

Supply-chain and operational-dependency questions reveal the external relationships and systems the organization relies on to function effectively. They expose the vulnerabilities, strengths, and bottlenecks that shape internal stability and decision urgency. Many internal challenges are actually symptoms of external dependencies — understanding these connections is essential for meaningful discovery.

Strategically, these insights help identify hidden risks and opportunities. Psychologically, they uncover how dependency pressures affect morale, stress, and confidence. This understanding allows your discovery work to extend beyond internal structures into the broader operational ecosystem.

As Chapter 8 continues, we will explore industry standards, environmental triggers, and external catalysts that influence strategic direction. Dependencies define stability; next, we examine the external forces that define momentum.

Reflection Prompt:
Think of a time when an external partner's performance forced internal changes. Which supply-chain question would have surfaced that dependency risk earlier?

CHAPTER 8 - SECTION 6 - Supply-Chain and Operational-Flow Questions

Introduction

Beyond regulation, organizations must contend with a set of external and semi-external forces that directly affect how work gets done: **supply chain dependencies** and **operational flow realities**. These forces determine how reliably materials, information, products, and services move through the system. When supply chains run smoothly, operations feel predictable. When they don't, even strong internal teams become reactive, stressed, or hesitant.

Strategically, supply-chain and operational-flow questions reveal delays, bottlenecks, reliance on external partners, inventory risks, vendor constraints, and timing issues that influence both short-term execution and long-term planning. These issues often define project feasibility far more than internal enthusiasm. Understanding operational flow also helps uncover hidden friction points—places where capacity, timing, or availability shape the buyer's readiness for change.

Psychologically, supply-chain challenges create pressure, uncertainty, and frustration. Teams may feel powerless when external partners fail, or overwhelmed when demand spikes unexpectedly. Operational flow issues also contribute to stress patterns that spill into communication, decision-making, and pacing. These questions help surface the emotional weight tied to operational predictability.

Interpretation Tip: Listen for signals like "we're waiting on…," "lead times have increased," "we're dependent on…," or "the delay cost us…" These reveal external constraints. Also note where the buyer expresses tension, fatigue, or resignation—operational friction often creates emotional fatigue long before strategic fatigue appears.

Coaching Note: Treat operational challenges with empathy. These issues are often outside the buyer's control, and your tone should reinforce that this is a collaborative effort to understand—not criticize—their environment.

Example prompts:

- *"What external operational factors influence your ability to move quickly?"*

- *"Where do supply-chain dependencies shape your planning?"*

Standard Supply-Chain & Operational-Flow Questions (8)

Tone: calm, practical, systems-aware.

1. "Which supply-chain partners your team relies on most?"

2. "Where do operational processes feel predictable and steady?"

3. "Which workflows experience the least disruption?"

4. "Where does the team feel confident about lead times and availability?"

5. "Which vendors or partners support your operations reliably?"

6. "Where does operational flow help you stay aligned with customer needs?"

7. "Which logistics patterns have remained stable over time?"

8. "Where do external partners contribute to smooth execution?"

Intermediate Supply-Chain & Operational-Flow Questions (9)

Tone: probing, pattern-focused, detail-oriented.

1. "Where have lead times increased or become less predictable?"

2. "Which supply-chain partners experience frequent disruption?"

3. "Where do operational delays influence customer experience?"

4. "Which workflows break down during periods of high demand?"

5. "Where do dependencies on external vendors create pressure?"

6. "Which materials, tools, or inputs are most difficult to secure consistently?"

7. "Where do operational bottlenecks cause misalignment between teams?"

8. "Which disruptions force you to adjust timelines or scope?"

9. "Where does operational flow shape how fast your organization can adopt new initiatives?"

Aggressive Supply-Chain & Operational-Flow Questions (8)

Tone: direct, truth-exposing, constraint-aware.

1. "Which supply-chain gap hurts your performance the most right now?"

2. "Where are external delays causing internal frustration or rework?"

3. "Which operational weaknesses competitors exploit?"

4. "Where do dependencies create unacceptable levels of risk?"

5. "What supply-chain assumption is no longer reliable?"

6. "Where do operational failures undermine leadership confidence?"

7. "Which vendor relationship needs reevaluation?"

8. "What operational issue could create a major setback if ignored?"

Follow-Up Supply-Chain & Operational-Flow Questions (10)

Tone: reflective, clarifying, insight-deepening.

1. "Can you describe a recent supply-chain or workflow disruption?"

2. "What sign indicated the issue was emerging?"

3. "How did the team respond operationally?"

4. "How did people respond emotionally?"

5. "What adjustments were made to manage the disruption?"

6. "What did the disruption reveal about system weaknesses?"

7. "What long-term changes were considered afterward?"

8. "Which dependencies remain fragile or uncertain?"

9. "What opportunities exist to simplify or strengthen your flow?"

10. "What support would help your team handle disruptions more confidently?"

Conclusion

Supply-chain and operational-flow questions uncover the external dependencies and process realities shaping how the organization works day to day. These insights highlight where reliability supports momentum and where external friction slows progress, increases stress, or exposes hidden vulnerabilities.

Strategically, these questions reveal what constraints may delay adoption, implementation, or scaling of new initiatives. Psychologically, they illuminate how operational unpredictability affects morale, urgency, and communication. Understanding these forces gives the advisor a complete picture of the buyer's operational landscape.

As Chapter 8 continues, we will explore industry standards, external triggers, and environmental influences that shape decision-making. Operational flow reveals the practical realities; next, we examine the external forces that shape expectations and urgency.

Reflection Prompt:
Think of a time when supply-chain disruption reshaped an organization's plans. Which question would have revealed that vulnerability sooner?

CHAPTER 8 - SECTION 7 - Industry-Standard and Best-Practice Questions

Introduction

Beyond market trends, economic pressures, and operational realities, every organization is influenced by a set of **industry standards and best practices**—external expectations about how a company in their space "should" operate. These standards can come from peers, analysts, certification bodies, associations, large players in the industry, or dominant customer segments. They influence how organizations evaluate themselves and how they judge whether they're keeping up.

Strategically, industry standards shape priorities, investments, and timing. If peers are adopting new technology, improving workflows, or shifting processes, organizations often feel pressured to follow. Falling behind perceived best practices can create urgency, tension, or defensive decision-making. Understanding which standards the buyer pays attention to reveals what they believe "good" looks like—and whether they feel aligned or behind.

Psychologically, industry standards carry emotional weight. Organizations often compare themselves to competitors or industry leaders, creating feelings of pride, insecurity, momentum, or anxiety. These comparisons shape internal narratives about identity, capability, and direction. These questions help uncover the expectations, pressures, and comparisons influencing decision-making outside the organization.

Interpretation Tip: Listen for statements like "everyone is moving toward…," "the industry expects…," or "we're behind the curve on…" These reveal perceived industry norms. Also note how the buyer describes their competitors—comparison language often hints at aspiration or insecurity.

Coaching Note: Approach this topic with reassurance. Many organizations feel uneasy when discussing gaps in best practices. Your role is to explore, not judge.

Example prompts:

- *"Which industry standards influence how you evaluate success?"*
- *"Where do you feel ahead or behind compared to your peers?"*

Standard Industry-Standard & Best-Practice Questions (8)

Tone: calm, curious, comparison-aware.

1. "Which industry standards most influence your planning?"
2. "Where do you feel aligned with what peers are doing?"

3. "Which best practices are already integrated into your workflow?"

4. "Where do industry expectations help guide your direction?"

5. "Which external benchmarks you pay attention to most?"

6. "Where do customers expect you to follow industry norms?"

7. "Which standards support your long-term goals?"

8. "Where does your team feel confident in meeting industry expectations?"

Intermediate Industry-Standard & Best-Practice Questions (9)

Tone: probing, clarity-seeking, insight-focused.

1. "Where do you feel the organization is slightly behind industry norms?"

2. "Which best practices have been difficult to adopt?"

3. "Where do peers influence your decision-making?"

4. "Which new standards or trends are gaining traction?"

5. "Where do industry benchmarks highlight gaps in performance?"

6. "Which standards require investment or process change?"

7. "Where do expectations shift faster than your team can adapt?"

8. "Which best practices create internal debate or resistance?"

9. "Where does industry direction shape long-term planning?"

Aggressive Industry-Standard & Best-Practice Questions (8)

Tone: direct, truth-exposing, reality-focused.

1. "Where is your organization clearly behind industry standards?"

2. "Which best practice you've delayed that now creates risk?"

3. "Where are competitors setting a bar you're not meeting yet?"

4. "Which industry expectations your team avoids discussing?"

5. "What standard, if ignored, could damage credibility?"

6. "Where does falling behind peers create internal tension?"

7. "Which best-practice gap has been ignored for too long?"

8. "What industry expectation challenges your current capabilities the most?"

Follow-Up Industry-Standard & Best-Practice Questions (10)

Tone: reflective, clarifying, forward-looking.

1. "Can you describe a moment when an industry shift created urgency?"

2. "What triggered your awareness of that shift?"

3. "How did the team respond to the change?"

4. "Which best practices became more important afterward?"

5. "What gaps became visible because of the shift?"

6. "Which improvements were made—and which remain?"

7. "What deeper pattern did this reveal about your industry readiness?"

8. "What would adopting current standards require internally?"

9. "What benefit would closing those gaps create for the organization?"

10. "What future standards do you expect to influence your decisions?"

Conclusion

Industry-standard and best-practice questions reveal the external benchmarks shaping how organizations evaluate their performance and direction. These insights clarify where the buyer feels aligned, where they feel behind, and where peers influence strategic decisions. Understanding industry standards helps the advisor connect discovery to broader expectations, not just internal goals.

Strategically, these questions highlight competitive positioning, market expectations, and emerging trends. Psychologically, they expose feelings of pride, comparison pressure, aspiration, or insecurity—powerful drivers of decision urgency. Industry standards often create invisible pressure that affects planning long before internal teams discuss it openly.

As Chapter 8 continues, we will explore external trigger events, timing pressures, and environmental influences that shape decision movement. Industry standards define the expectations; next, we uncover the events that create momentum.

Reflection Prompt:

Think of a time when peers or competitors influenced an organization's choices. Which industry-standard question would have surfaced that influence earlier?

CHAPTER 8 - SECTION 8 - External-Trigger Questions

Introduction

Beyond market conditions, customer expectations, competition, financial pressures, and industry standards, organizations are often influenced by **external trigger events**—sudden shifts, unexpected disruptions, or new developments that force immediate action. External triggers can include market shocks, technological breakthroughs, competitor announcements, sudden customer churn, global events, or supply-chain failures. Unlike predictable trends, triggers are abrupt and catalytic.

Strategically, external triggers create turning points. They cause organizations to accelerate decisions they were delaying, pause projects they once prioritized, or rethink assumptions overnight. Understanding external triggers allows you to identify the real moments that shape urgency, budget flexibility, and openness to change. These triggers often explain shifts the buyer may not articulate unless asked directly.

Psychologically, external triggers create heightened emotion—stress, excitement, fear, confusion, or renewed determination. People may feel pressured, reactive, or energized depending on how the event influences their role and responsibilities. These questions reveal the emotional interpretation of the trigger, which often matters as much as the trigger itself.

Interpretation Tip: Listen for time-linked statements such as "after that happened," "since last quarter," "right after the announcement," or "once the issue occurred…" These reveal inflection points. Also pay attention to the buyer's tone—external triggers often leave emotional footprints.

Coaching Note: Approach trigger conversations with steady curiosity. These moments can be sensitive or stressful, so your tone should help the buyer reflect without feeling exposed.

Example prompts:

- *"What recent events outside your control have influenced your plans?"*

- *"Where have external shifts changed your timeline or direction?"*

Standard External-Trigger Questions (8)

Tone: calm, time-aware, situational.

1. "What external events have influenced your priorities recently?"

2. "Which shifts caught your attention over the past few months?"

3. "Where have external developments changed your planning?"

4. "Which events created new opportunities for your team?"

5. "Where did external changes help clarify direction?"

6. "Which triggers made you re-evaluate internal processes?"

7. "Where did outside events reinforce your existing strategy?"

8. "Which developments aligned with your long-term goals?"

Intermediate External-Trigger Questions (9)

Tone: probing, insight-driven, pattern-focused.

1. "Which abrupt changes created the most internal conversation?"

2. "Where did external news lead to a shift in expectations?"

3. "Which events revealed new risks or vulnerabilities?"

4. "Where did trigger events create operational challenges?"

5. "Which developments forced adjustments in customer communication?"

6. "Where did triggers impact staffing, resources, or timelines?"

7. "Which events reshaped your budget or investment planning?"

8. "Where did unexpected developments expose gaps in readiness?"

9. "Which patterns in trigger events appear across the past year?"

Aggressive External-Trigger Questions (8)

Tone: direct, sharp, truth-seeking.

1. "Which external event disrupted your plans the most recently?"

2. "What trigger exposed the biggest weakness in your organization?"

3. "Where did leadership struggle to respond to an external shock?"

4. "Which event forced you to change direction abruptly?"

5. "What external shift challenged your assumptions the hardest?"

6. "Which trigger revealed issues you'd avoided addressing?"

7. "Where are you still dealing with the fallout of a recent event?"

8. "What external threat are you least prepared for today?"

Follow-Up External-Trigger Questions (10)

Tone: reflective, clarifying, emotion-aware.

1. "Can you describe the moment you realized the external trigger mattered?"

2. "What early signs hinted the event was about to happen?"

3. "How did your team react emotionally?"

4. "What actions were taken immediately afterward?"

5. "Which processes were tested the hardest during the event?"

6. "What deeper issue did the trigger reveal?"

7. "What changes have been made since then?"

8. "What vulnerabilities remain because of the event?"

9. "What opportunities became visible after the trigger occurred?"

10. "What would help your team respond better to future triggers?"

Conclusion

External-trigger questions uncover the turning points that shape urgency, timing, and strategic shifts. These events often explain why decisions change suddenly, why budgets appear unexpectedly, or why certain projects move to the top of the priority list. Understanding external triggers helps the advisor interpret the emotional and strategic context behind the buyer's current direction.

Strategically, these insights reveal catalysts for action. Psychologically, they illuminate stress points, resilience, and emotional readiness—all essential for guiding meaningful discovery. External triggers bridge the gap between long-term trends and immediate behavior.

As Chapter 8 continues, we will explore environmental influences and timing forces that shape when decisions must—or must not—be made. Trigger events identify what happened; next, we examine how those events affect pressure over time.

Reflection Prompt:

Think of a sudden external event that disrupted your team's plans. Which external-trigger question would have revealed its impact earlier?

CHAPTER 8 - SECTION 9 - Environmental and Contextual-Pressure Questions

Introduction

Organizations don't make decisions in a vacuum—they operate within a complex web of **environmental and contextual pressures**, many of which fall outside traditional categories like competition or regulation. These forces include geographic limitations, cultural context, societal expectations, workforce availability, technological maturity, infrastructure constraints, and even seasonal cycles. These external realities subtly shape how organizations think, act, and prioritize.

Strategically, environmental and contextual pressures influence speed, capacity, and direction. They determine how quickly the organization can innovate, how effectively it can scale, and how resilient it is in the face of change. These pressures often explain variations in performance between similar organizations operating in different environments. They also affect decisions around staffing, expansion, customer focus, and technology adoption.

Psychologically, contextual pressures create ongoing emotional undertones. An understaffed labor market may create anxiety. A geographically dispersed workforce may create disconnection. A region dependent on a single industry may create vulnerability. These contextual elements influence confidence, stability, and willingness to take risks. These questions uncover the environmental backdrop shaping the buyer's mindset.

Interpretation Tip: Listen for factors the buyer describes as "just the way things are here." These reveal environmental realities that can't be easily changed but must be understood. Also note how the buyer speaks about predictability—context often determines what they expect to remain stable or unstable.

Coaching Note: Approach environmental factors as neutral forces, not shortcomings. Many contextual pressures are outside the organization's control, and acknowledging them respectfully helps build trust.

Example prompts:

- *"What environmental factors influence how your team operates?"*

- *"Where do contextual realities shape what's possible?"*

Standard Environmental & Contextual-Pressure Questions (8)

Tone: calm, observational, environment-aware.

1. "Which external conditions influence your team's daily work?"

2. "Where do geographic or regional factors shape your operations?"

3. "Which contextual pressures your industry experiences consistently?"

4. "Where does your environment support strong performance?"

5. "Which seasonal or cyclical factors affect your planning?"

6. "Where do workforce availability trends influence decisions?"

7. "Which environmental conditions remain stable year after year?"

8. "Where does your context give you a natural advantage?"

Intermediate Environmental & Contextual-Pressure Questions (9)

Tone: probing, insight-driven, clarity-seeking.

1. "Where do environmental pressures limit your pace of change?"

2. "Which contextual factors create uncertainty or vulnerability?"

3. "Where does infrastructure or technology maturity influence decisions?"

4. "Which geographic or cultural realities complicate operations?"

5. "Where do environmental pressures affect customer behavior?"

6. "Which contextual shifts could disrupt your plans?"

7. "Where does talent availability shape resource allocation?"

8. "Which environmental factors influence long-term strategy?"

9. "Where do contextual pressures amplify internal challenges?"

Aggressive Environmental & Contextual-Pressure Questions (8)

Tone: direct, realistic, truth-seeking.

1. "Which environmental factor creates the biggest limitation today?"

2. "Where is your context working against your goals?"

3. "Which external reality leadership avoids acknowledging?"

4. "Where does your environment create unavoidable risk?"

5. "Which contextual pressure has the strongest negative impact on performance?"

6. "Where do environmental issues expose deeper operational weaknesses?"

7. "Which external force causes the most frustration internally?"

8. "What contextual condition would require radical adaptation if it worsened?"

Follow-Up Environmental & Contextual-Pressure Questions (10)

Tone: reflective, clarifying, narrative-based.

1. "Can you describe a moment when environmental factors disrupted your plans?"

2. "What early signs signaled the pressure was increasing?"

3. "How did the team respond to the change?"

4. "What internal adjustments became necessary?"

5. "What deeper issue did the environmental pressure expose?"

6. "How has your environment shaped your long-term planning?"

7. "Which contextual conditions remain unpredictable?"

8. "What opportunities have emerged because of your environment?"

9. "What support would help you navigate contextual pressures more effectively?"

10. "What small adaptations could reduce environmental strain?"

Conclusion

Environmental and contextual-pressure questions uncover the forces that surround the organization—elements outside its control but deeply influential in shaping its capabilities and decisions. These pressures reveal constraints, opportunities, and vulnerabilities that make each buyer's situation unique. Understanding these external realities allows the advisor to contextualize discovery in a broader ecosystem rather than viewing decisions in isolation.

Strategically, these insights help reveal why the organization operates the way it does. Psychologically, they uncover the emotional undercurrents shaped by the environment—stability, uncertainty, frustration, or pride. Environmental understanding is essential for advising with empathy and precision.

As Chapter 8 moves to its final section, we will explore the timing forces that influence when decisions must be made, when they can be delayed, and how external and internal pressures create momentum. Environmental pressures define the backdrop; timing forces define movement.

Reflection Prompt:
Think of an organization strongly shaped by its environment or geography. Which contextual-pressure question would have revealed that influence sooner?

CHAPTER 8 - SECTION 10 - Timing-Pressure Questions

Introduction

Timing pressure is one of the most influential—and least discussed—forces affecting organizational decisions. Even when the strategy is clear, the budget is set, and the motivation is strong, **timing** determines when an organization can realistically take action. Timing pressure comes from deadlines, seasonal cycles, internal milestones, fiscal calendars, contract renewals, staffing constraints, customer commitments, or external events that compress the decision window.

Strategically, timing pressure reveals whether the buyer feels urgency, stability, or hesitation. It helps you understand how quickly they need to decide, what events might accelerate movement, and what barriers might slow progress. Timing often determines feasibility more than budget or desire. Without understanding timing pressure, discovery remains incomplete.

Psychologically, timing pressure shapes emotional dynamics—stress, fear of missing a deadline, anxiety around peak seasons, or relief when timelines stabilize. Teams may act reactive under intense timing constraints or overly cautious when timing feels uncertain. These questions reveal how the buyer's timeline influences decision-making behavior, communication, and internal alignment.

Interpretation Tip: Listen for clues like "before the end of the quarter," "after this cycle," "once we get through this period," or "we're waiting on…." These reveal timing anchors and constraints. Also pay attention to inconsistencies; sometimes teams feel "too busy to change," even when change would relieve the pressure.

Coaching Note: Approach timing with practical empathy. Timing constraints are often legitimate—not excuses—and understanding them helps you support the buyer rather than push them.

Example prompts:

- *"What timing factors influence how quickly you can take action?"*

- *"Where do deadlines shape your priorities?"*

Standard Timing-Pressure Questions (8)

Tone: calm, reflective, schedule-aware.

1. "What upcoming deadlines influence your current priorities?"

2. "Where does timing help create clarity for your decisions?"

3. "Which parts of the year feel most predictable for planning?"

4. "Where do cycles or seasons guide your workflow?"

5. "Which timing windows support taking on new initiatives?"

6. "Where does your team feel comfortable adjusting timelines?"

7. "Which internal milestones shape decision-making pace?"

8. "Where does timing align well with your current workload?"

Intermediate Timing-Pressure Questions (9)

Tone: probing, pattern-focused, detail-oriented.

1. "Where does timing pressure create hesitation or caution?"

2. "Which periods of the year limit your capacity for change?"

3. "Where do deadlines compress decision-making?"

4. "Which timing conflicts affect collaboration between teams?"

5. "Where do customer or partner schedules influence your timeline?"

6. "Which timing constraints shape budget release or approval cycles?"

7. "Where does timing pressure impact quality or thoroughness?"

8. "Which workloads become unpredictable throughout the year?"

9. "Where do timing constraints reveal gaps in planning?"

Aggressive Timing-Pressure Questions (8)

Tone: direct, truth-seeking, timeline-revealing.

1. "Which deadline creates the most pressure right now?"

2. "Where does timing prevent you from acting when you should?"

3. "Which timing constraint leadership avoids addressing?"

4. "Where are you running out of time to solve a known issue?"

5. "What timing pressure has already caused delays or setbacks?"

6. "Where do timelines force rushed or reactive decisions?"

7. "Which key window, if missed, creates major risk?"

8. "What timeline assumption may no longer be realistic?"

Follow-Up Timing-Pressure Questions (10)

Tone: reflective, clarifying, forward-looking.

1. "Can you describe a moment when timing pressure shaped a major decision?"

2. "What event or deadline triggered the pressure?"

3. "How did the team respond operationally and emotionally?"

4. "What compromises or adjustments were made?"

5. "What deeper issue did the timing pressure reveal?"

6. "What changes were considered to avoid similar pressure in the future?"

7. "Which timing constraints still affect your planning today?"

8. "What opportunities arise when timing pressure eases?"

9. "What support would help you navigate future timing demands?"

10. "What would an ideal decision timeline look like for your team?"

Conclusion

Timing-pressure questions uncover the temporal forces shaping how organizations make decisions. They reveal urgency, hesitation, capacity, and the windows in which change is feasible. Timing affects resource allocation, emotional readiness, and operational flow more than most internal factors. Without understanding timing, many discovery insights remain disconnected from reality.

Strategically, timing-pressure insights help position conversations around feasibility and urgency. Psychologically, they surface stress patterns, avoidance tendencies, and readiness for action. Timing is often the real reason behind both movement and delay.

With timing addressed, Chapter 8's exploration of external forces is complete. This chapter now provides a full understanding of the environmental, market, financial, competitive, regulatory, and temporal pressures shaping buyer behavior—essential for advanced discovery.

Reflection Prompt:
Think of a decision that was rushed or delayed due to timing constraints. Which timing-pressure question would have revealed that constraint earlier?

Chapter Conclusion

Chapter 8 reveals that external forces shape internal decisions more than most organizations realize. Market conditions, customer expectations, competition, budgets, regulations, and environmental realities form the backdrop of every strategic conversation. These pressures influence timing, urgency, confidence, and resource allocation. Without understanding them, even the most thorough internal discovery remains incomplete.

Strategically, the chapter equips the advisor with a lens for interpreting why decisions accelerate or stall, why priorities rise or fall, and where tension or opportunity originates. Psychologically, it highlights the emotional landscape created by external forces—stress, optimism, uncertainty, or pressure—that drives behavior long before internal discussions begin. These insights help the advisor ask sharper questions and uncover deeper meaning behind surface-level statements.

With Chapters 7 and 8 complete, the reader now has a dual understanding: the internal forces shaping behavior and the external forces shaping context. Together, these perspectives form the foundation for advanced discovery. From here, the book turns to the next major theme, building on internal and external awareness to help advisors navigate decision dynamics with clarity and confidence.

BONUS CHAPTER 1 - Advanced Human Dynamics, Emotion, and Personal-Level Discovery

Chapter Introduction

Most discovery conversations focus on organizational priorities, operational needs, and strategic goals. While these layers matter, they overlook the deepest influence on decision-making: **the individual human being** behind each choice. Bonus Chapter 1 expands the advisor's perspective into the personal, emotional, and psychological space where motivations, fears, aspirations, and internal narratives shape behavior long before formal decision paths activate. This chapter explores discovery at a human depth most sales processes never reach.

Each section is designed to reveal a different dimension of personal experience that influences how people interpret risk, opportunity, and change. Personal motivation shows what drives someone forward. Stress patterns reveal where emotional strain limits clarity or engagement. Change-readiness uncovers the internal resilience or hesitation shaping their willingness to move ahead. Confidence and doubt reveal the emotional states that either strengthen or weaken decision-making.

The middle sections explore how personal priorities and interpersonal dynamics interact with these emotional states. Every individual balances responsibilities they care about, and these priorities influence their support or resistance to new initiatives. At the same time, interpersonal dynamics shape the emotional tone of collaboration. Healthy relationships create energy; strained ones create hesitation. These layers add nuance to discovery, revealing why some stakeholders contribute actively while others retreat into silence.

As the chapter progresses, the advisor gains insight into emotional triggers and information-processing preferences. These elements help explain sudden reactions, communication styles, and how someone absorbs or resists new information. When advisors understand these patterns, they can adapt their approach to make the stakeholder feel supported, respected, and seen—qualities that strengthen trust and promote honest dialogue.

The final sections explore emotional climate and personal vision—two powerful drivers of behavior. Emotional climate shapes how the individual feels day to day, influencing their tone, patience, and engagement. Personal vision reveals the deeper future they are trying to build for themselves. When advisors understand a person's emotional landscape and future aspirations, they gain clarity on why certain decisions feel easy while others feel heavy or risky.

Bonus Chapter 1 is built to help advisors reach a deeper level of discovery—one that integrates empathy, psychological insight, and strategic clarity. These questions help you understand the human realities beneath every organizational conversation. They elevate discovery from transactional Q&A to meaningful dialogue that creates a lasting foundation of trust.

BONUS CHAPTER 1 - SECTION 1 - Personal-Motivation Questions

Introduction

Organizations make decisions, but individuals carry them. Every initiative, priority, hesitation, or objection is influenced by the personal motivations of the people involved. Personal motivation shapes how stakeholders interpret risks, how they respond to uncertainty, and what they privately hope to gain or avoid. Unlike organizational goals—which are often documented and shared—personal motivations are internal and rarely spoken without thoughtful prompting. This section helps the advisor explore what drives each person at a deeper level.

Strategically, understanding personal motivation reveals the forces that shape commitment and resistance. Motivated stakeholders advocate for progress, influence peers, and push through friction. Unmotivated or conflicted stakeholders slow momentum, delay decisions, or redirect attention toward safer alternatives. When you understand an individual's real motivations, you understand how the buying process will behave long before formal decisions appear.

Psychologically, personal motivations reflect values, aspirations, fears, and identity. Some people are motivated by recognition; others by stability or impact. Some seek strategic contribution; others seek relief from stress. When you explore motivation thoughtfully, you learn what makes someone feel proud, secure, respected, or successful. This creates deeper trust and reveals insights they may not share with colleagues.

Interpretation Tip: Listen for subtle emotional signals. Phrases like "it would help me…" or "I've been wanting to…" reveal personal ambition. Comments such as "I'm just trying to keep things stable…" or "I don't want this to fall apart…" reveal personal fear. Personal motivation often hides beneath neutral language.

Coaching Note: Approach motivation with genuine curiosity. Your tone should create a safe, non-judgmental space. People rarely share personal motivations unless they feel respected and understood. When a buyer reveals their personal "why," protect it. Use it to guide alignment—not to manipulate urgency.

Example phrasing:

- *"What matters most to you personally as you work through this?"*

- *"How does this initiative connect to what you want for your own role?"*

Standard Personal-Motivation Questions (8)

Tone: warm, open, rapport-building.

1. "What aspects of your work matter most to you personally?"

2. "Where do you feel the strongest sense of purpose in your role?"

3. "Which goals are you most excited to support this year?"

4. "Where do you feel energized by new opportunities?"

5. "What responsibilities give you the most satisfaction?"

6. "Which parts of this initiative align with your interests?"

7. "Where do you feel confident in the direction things are heading?"

8. "What personal success indicators matter most to you?"

Intermediate Personal-Motivation Questions (9)

Tone: probing, thoughtful, emotionally aware.

1. "Where do you feel the most personal stake in this project?"

2. "Which outcomes matter to you beyond the organizational goals?"

3. "Where does this initiative support your long-term growth?"

4. "Which responsibilities help you feel at your best professionally?"

5. "Where do you hope this project removes frustration or friction for you?"

6. "Which parts of your role you'd like to strengthen moving forward?"

7. "Where do you want more influence or clarity in your work?"

8. "Which personal priorities align with the outcome you're evaluating?"

9. "Where do you crave more stability, recognition, or momentum?"

Aggressive Personal-Motivation Questions (8)

Tone: direct, truth-seeking, respectfully candid.

1. "What do you personally stand to gain if this works?"

2. "What risk would you personally face if this goes wrong?"

3. "Where do you feel under-recognized or under-supported today?"

4. "What part of your role leaves you the most frustrated?"

5. "Where do you feel pressure to deliver results quickly?"

6. "What would make you feel more confident in your own success?"

7. "Where do organizational priorities conflict with your own?"

8. "What outcome do you genuinely want—even if others don't say it out loud?"

Follow-Up Personal-Motivation Questions (10)

Tone: empathetic, reflective, trust-building.

1. "Can you share a moment that made your personal priorities feel clearer?"

2. "What experience shaped what you value in your role today?"

3. "How did that moment influence how you make decisions now?"

4. "Which responsibilities make you feel the most fulfilled?"

5. "What gives you confidence when facing new initiatives?"

6. "What catches your attention when something feels personally important?"

7. "How do you know when something aligns with your values?"

8. "What would help you feel personally supported during this process?"

9. "What would success in this initiative mean for you personally?"

10. "What personal outcome would feel most meaningful to you in the long term?"

Conclusion

Personal-motivation questions bring the advisor closer to the human reality behind every decision. They reveal the hopes, fears, pressures, and ambitions that guide how stakeholders think and behave. When advisors understand these motivations, they gain insight into the emotional and psychological engines driving the buying process.

Strategically, personal motivations influence influence. A motivated stakeholder becomes an advocate. A conflicted stakeholder becomes a decelerator. Personal motivations explain subtle behaviors—why someone slows down, pushes forward, asks deeper questions, or suddenly shifts direction. Understanding these motivations allows you to shape conversations that support individuals rather than pressure them.

Psychologically, personal motivations reveal identity. They show whether someone craves security, recognition, clarity, challenge, or relief. When these motivations are honored, trust deepens. When they are ignored, resistance grows—even when the organizational case is strong. This section helps advisors approach discovery through the lens of humanity rather than hierarchy.

As Bonus Chapter 1 continues, the following sections explore stress patterns, confidence, interpersonal dynamics, emotional triggers, learning styles, and personal vision. Together, they give the advisor a complete map of human behavior—allowing discovery to reach deeper and create genuine alignment.

Reflection Prompt:
Recall a time when a stakeholder supported or resisted a decision for personal reasons rather than organizational ones. Which personal-motivation question would have revealed their "why" sooner?

BONUS CHAPTER 1 - SECTION 2 - Stress-Pattern & Overload Questions

Introduction

Every stakeholder carries stress into the decision process, whether they acknowledge it openly or not. Stress shapes clarity, attention, emotional availability, and willingness to take risks. When someone feels overloaded, they process information differently, respond more cautiously, and may avoid decisions altogether. Understanding stress patterns helps the advisor interpret behaviors that would otherwise seem unpredictable or inconsistent.

Strategically, stress influences decision speed, communication quality, and prioritization. An overloaded stakeholder might delay meetings, skim important details, or default to safe options rather than innovative ones. Stress creates invisible friction that slows progress—not because the stakeholder disagrees with the initiative, but because they lack the bandwidth to engage fully. These questions reveal how workload, pressure, and emotional strain influence the decision environment.

Psychologically, stress is rooted in fear, responsibility, identity, or personal expectations. Some people stress when expectations rise; others stress when clarity fades. Some feel overwhelmed by workload; others by uncertainty or potential conflict. When you explore stress patterns thoughtfully, you uncover emotional dynamics that shape how the stakeholder thinks, reacts, and seeks control.

Interpretation Tip: Listen for expressions like "we're stretched thin," "I've been juggling a lot," "timing is tough," or "we're under pressure right now." These indicate emotional strain. Also observe when someone is overly brief, highly cautious, or slower to respond—behaviors often tied to internal overload.

Coaching Note: Treat stress as a shared human experience, not a weakness. These questions should create relief, not pressure. When stakeholders feel understood, their stress softens, and their openness increases. Your tone should remain steady, warm, and patient.

Example phrasing:

- *"How is the current workload affecting your ability to focus on this initiative?"*

- *"Where do you feel stretched or overloaded right now?"*

Standard Stress-Pattern & Overload Questions (8)

Tone: gentle, patient, supportive.

1. "Which parts of your workload feel the heaviest right now?"

2. "Where do you feel stretched thin across responsibilities?"

3. "What tasks or priorities require the most energy from you?"

4. "Where does your team feel steady and manageable?"

5. "Which responsibilities create the most daily pressure?"

6. "Where do you feel you have enough clarity to stay in control?"

7. "Which moments of your day tend to feel the most demanding?"

8. "Where do you feel supported during busy periods?"

Intermediate Stress-Pattern & Overload Questions (9)

Tone: probing, caring, emotionally perceptive.

1. "Where do competing priorities create pressure for you?"

2. "Which responsibilities you wish you could delegate more effectively?"

3. "Where does stress affect your ability to make decisions confidently?"

4. "Which tasks drain you the most emotionally?"

5. "Where does workload interrupt your ability to think strategically?"

6. "Which expectations feel unclear or overwhelming?"

7. "Where do time constraints limit how deeply you can engage?"

8. "Which responsibilities spike your stress during certain seasons?"

9. "Where do you feel tension building before deadlines or milestones?"

Aggressive Stress-Pattern & Overload Questions (8)

Tone: direct, honest, pressure-aware (still respectful).

1. "What responsibility is overwhelming you the most right now?"

2. "Where are you carrying pressure that others may not see?"

3. "What part of this decision feels hardest to manage emotionally?"

4. "Where is stress hurting your effectiveness or clarity?"

5. "Which priority would you remove if you had the authority?"

6. "Where do you feel dangerously close to burnout?"

7. "What pressure has gone unaddressed for too long?"

8. "Where does stress make you hesitate when you normally wouldn't?"

Follow-Up Stress-Pattern & Overload Questions (10)

Tone: empathetic, reflective, grounding.

1. "Can you describe a moment when you felt overloaded recently?"

2. "What triggered that feeling?"

3. "How did you respond in the moment?"

4. "What helped you regain control or clarity?"

5. "Which patterns do you notice in your stress over time?"

6. "How does stress influence the way you communicate with your team?"

7. "What adjustments help reduce pressure for you?"

8. "What long-term changes would make your workload more manageable?"

9. "What support system would help you maintain clarity during intense periods?"

10. "How do you know when stress is affecting your judgment?"

Conclusion

Stress-pattern questions reveal the emotional and cognitive load stakeholders carry beneath the surface. These pressures often shape decisions more strongly than formal priorities or organizational goals. When the advisor understands how stress influences pace, clarity, and attention, the entire discovery process becomes more human, accurate, and compassionate.

Strategically, stress insights highlight where decision energy is available and where overload may create hidden barriers. Understanding stress patterns helps you avoid misinterpreting delays or caution as resistance—often, they reflect bandwidth limitations rather than lack of interest. This knowledge helps you adjust expectations, pacing, and communication.

Psychologically, stress reveals vulnerability. When stakeholders share how stress affects them, they expose the emotional weight of their role. This creates a deeper relationship built on trust and respect. Reducing stress through clarity, structure, and steady communication becomes part of your value.

As Bonus Chapter 1 continues, you will explore confidence, doubt, personal alignment, interpersonal dynamics, emotional triggers, learning styles, and long-term personal vision. Together, these sections deepen your understanding of human behavior and strengthen your ability to guide meaningful discovery.

Reflection Prompt:
Think of a time when stress—not strategy—shaped a stakeholder's decision. Which stress-pattern question might have surfaced that influence earlier?

BONUS CHAPTER 1 - SECTION 3 - Change-Readiness Questions

Introduction

Change-readiness is one of the most important, yet least explored, dimensions of personal discovery. Even when a solution is logical, beneficial, and aligned with organizational goals, individual stakeholders vary widely in their comfort with change. Some approach new initiatives with curiosity and energy. Others experience hesitation, uncertainty, or fear—even if they believe the initiative is necessary. Understanding change-readiness allows the advisor to interpret emotional tone, anticipate resistance, and support stakeholders more effectively.

Strategically, change-readiness influences momentum. A stakeholder who is ready for change becomes a catalyst, offering insight, feedback, and initiative. A stakeholder who feels unprepared or cautious may create drag—not deliberately, but because the psychological weight of change slows their engagement. When you understand how ready someone feels, you can adjust pacing, communication, and support to match their emotional bandwidth.

Psychologically, change-readiness reflects past experiences, tolerance for ambiguity, personal confidence, and perceptions of stability. People accustomed to frequent change often adapt quickly; those burned by past transitions may proceed carefully. Some fear losing control; others fear losing credibility or security. These questions help uncover how change is *felt*, not just how it is understood intellectually.

Interpretation Tip: Listen for emotional indicators. Statements like "we've had a lot of change already," "I'm not sure the timing is right," or "I like where things are now" reveal readiness levels. Enthusiastic responses signal ease with change; neutral or hesitant language signals caution or fatigue.

Coaching Note: Approach the topic with empathy. Change is emotional. Your tone should validate their feelings while helping them articulate what conditions would make change feel safer, clearer, or more manageable.

Example phrasing:

- *"How comfortable do you feel with this level of change?"*

- *"What helps you adjust smoothly when things shift?"*

Standard Change-Readiness Questions (8)

Tone: supportive, open, gentle.

1. "How comfortable do you generally feel with new initiatives?"

2. "Where do you adapt easily to change in your role?"

3. "What helps you stay grounded during transitions?"

4. "Which types of change feel manageable for you?"

5. "Where have past changes worked well for your team?"

6. "What signs help you trust that a change is positive?"

7. "Where do you feel ready for improvement or adjustment?"

8. "Which aspects of change energize you?"

Intermediate Change-Readiness Questions (9)

Tone: probing, emotionally perceptive, clarifying.

1. "Where does change create uncertainty or caution for you?"

2. "Which past transitions shaped how you respond to change today?"

3. "Where do you feel the need for more information before moving forward?"

4. "Which changes have been the hardest to adjust to?"

5. "Where do you see potential disruption affecting your role?"

6. "Which conditions help you feel more prepared for change?"

7. "Where does your team differ in readiness levels?"

8. "Which parts of this initiative feel most unfamiliar?"

9. "Where do you feel tension between stability and progress?"

Aggressive Change-Readiness Questions (8)

Tone: direct, honest, truth-seeking but respectful.

1. "What part of this change makes you most uneasy?"

2. "Where do you feel unprepared or under-supported for what's ahead?"

3. "What past change left a negative impression that still affects you?"

4. "Where do you fear losing control if this moves forward?"

5. "Which part of your role would be most disrupted by this change?"

6. "What assumption about this change makes you hesitate?"

7. "Where do you see yourself resisting—even quietly?"

8. "What would make this change feel too risky to support?"

Follow-Up Change-Readiness Questions (10)

Tone: reflective, steady, deeply empathetic.

1. "Can you share a moment when a change went better than expected?"

2. "What made that experience successful for you?"

3. "Can you recall a time when change felt overwhelming?"

4. "What caused the stress in that moment?"

5. "How did you regain confidence during that transition?"

6. "What patterns do you notice in how you respond to new things?"

7. "What helps you feel in control during uncertain situations?"

8. "What support would make this upcoming change easier for you?"

9. "What would a healthy pace of change look like for you personally?"

10. "How do you know when you're ready—or not ready—for change?"

Conclusion

Change-readiness questions illuminate the emotional landscape that surrounds any new initiative. They help the advisor understand not just what the stakeholder thinks, but what they *feel*—a vital distinction when navigating decisions that involve uncertainty or disruption. These insights deepen trust and prevent misinterpretation of hesitation as resistance.

Strategically, understanding readiness allows the advisor to match the pace of discovery to the stakeholder's comfort level. Change-readiness often explains the timing, momentum, and engagement patterns that influence the buying journey. When readiness is low, decision-making slows. When readiness is high, progress accelerates naturally.

Psychologically, these questions uncover the emotional roots of change behavior. They reveal fears, fatigue, past wounds, and sources of stability. When these feelings are acknowledged, stakeholders feel safe. When ignored, they become hidden barriers that stall progress. By understanding readiness, the advisor becomes a more thoughtful guide through uncertainty.

As Bonus Chapter 1 continues, the next sections explore confidence and doubt, personal alignment, interpersonal dynamics, and emotional triggers. Together, they create a deeper toolkit for navigating the human side of decision-making with empathy, precision, and insight.

Reflection Prompt:
Think of a moment when someone resisted change for emotional rather than logical reasons. Which change-readiness question would have revealed the truth earlier?

BONUS CHAPTER 1 – SECTION 5 - Personal-Priority Alignment Questions

Introduction

Every stakeholder enters a decision process with their own set of personal priorities—responsibilities they value, goals they want to advance, and pressures they must manage. These priorities shape how they interpret new opportunities and challenges. When an initiative aligns with someone's personal priorities, they engage with clarity and enthusiasm. When it conflicts with those priorities, hesitation emerges, even if the initiative is objectively sound. Understanding personal-priority alignment allows the advisor to connect strategy with the individual's deeper motivations.

Strategically, alignment acts as an accelerant. When a stakeholder sees clear alignment between the initiative and what matters most to them personally, they become an advocate and decision-shaper. Misalignment, however, creates friction. A stakeholder whose working reality conflicts with the initiative's demands may resist, delay, or disengage. These questions help surface whether the initiative strengthens or disrupts the individual's current momentum.

Psychologically, personal priorities reflect identity, values, ambition, and emotional needs. Some stakeholders prioritize stability; others prioritize growth. Some prioritize clarity; others prioritize autonomy. The advisor who understands these priorities gains insight into what will feel encouraging, stressful, or conflicting for the individual. Personal alignment is often the difference between genuine buy-in and silent resistance.

Interpretation Tip: Listen for comments like "I've been trying to focus on…," "My main priority right now is…," or "This could help me solve…" These reveal what the stakeholder values. Pay attention to contradictions between what they say is important and what they spend time on—these often reveal hidden priorities.

Coaching Note: Approach personal priorities with respect. You're not judging them—you're understanding them. The more clarity you gain about what matters to the stakeholder, the more effectively you can help them see how the initiative supports their goals.

Example phrasing:

- *"How does this initiative fit with what matters most to you right now?"*

- *"Which of your priorities does this support—or complicate?"*

Standard Personal-Priority Alignment Questions (8)

Tone: warm, curious, grounding.

1. "What are your main priorities in your role right now?"

2. "Which responsibilities feel most important to you personally?"

3. "Where does this initiative support your current focus?"

4. "Which of your goals does this align with?"

5. "Where do you feel clear about what matters most?"

6. "Which activities give you the strongest sense of progress?"

7. "Where does your daily work reflect your long-term interests?"

8. "Which responsibilities help you feel most fulfilled?"

Intermediate Personal-Priority Alignment Questions (9)

Tone: probing, thoughtful, alignment-seeking.

1. "Where do you see tension between this initiative and your current priorities?"

2. "Which responsibilities would this help simplify or improve?"

3. "Where might this add extra pressure to your workload?"

4. "Which priorities are non-negotiable for you right now?"

5. "Where do you feel pulled in different directions?"

6. "Which aspects of your role are consuming more time than you'd prefer?"

7. "Where would you like to direct more attention?"

8. "Which long-term goals does this support—or distract from?"

9. "Where does this initiative compete with other commitments you carry?"

Aggressive Personal-Priority Alignment Questions (8)

Tone: direct, honest, truth-focused (still respectful).

1. "What personal priority would this initiative disrupt most?"

2. "Where does this conflict with what you're trying to accomplish?"

3. "Which responsibility would this force you to deprioritize?"

4. "Where do you fear losing progress on something that matters to you?"

5. "Which personal goal feels threatened by this initiative?"

6. "Where are you being asked to trade your priorities for the organization's?"

7. "What part of your workload would become harder if this moves forward?"

8. "Where does alignment feel weakest—or absent completely?"

Follow-Up Personal-Priority Alignment Questions (10)

Tone: reflective, supportive, clarity-enhancing.

1. "Can you share a moment recently when your priorities became clearer to you?"

2. "What experience shaped those priorities?"

3. "How do you decide what deserves your attention most?"

4. "What helps you stay true to your priorities during busy periods?"

5. "Which priorities have shifted for you over the past year?"

6. "What does progress in your role look like to you personally?"

7. "What would stronger alignment feel like day to day?"

8. "What change would help reduce conflict between your priorities and new initiatives?"

9. "What support would help you protect your most important priorities?"

10. "How does this initiative fit into your personal direction for the future?"

Conclusion

Personal-priority alignment shapes how stakeholders interpret the demands and benefits of an initiative. When alignment exists, clarity grows and momentum builds. When alignment is missing, friction appears—often subtly at first, then visibly as decisions slow. These questions help advisors understand where the initiative fits into the stakeholder's personal landscape.

Strategically, alignment determines advocacy. People push hardest for the initiatives that support what they value most. They also resist the initiatives that threaten their progress. Understanding this alignment enables the advisor to connect the initiative to each stakeholder's lived experience, not just the organization's goals.

Psychologically, personal priorities reveal identity and purpose. They reflect who the stakeholder wants to be, how they want to work, and what they want to accomplish. When priorities are respected, trust grows. When they're ignored, resistance deepens even if the stakeholder remains polite or cooperative. This section helps advisors navigate these dynamics with clarity and respect.

As Bonus Chapter 1 continues, the next sections explore interpersonal dynamics, emotional triggers, information-processing styles, and personal vision. These layers reveal what shapes the stakeholder's perception, behavior, and emotional engagement in increasingly meaningful ways.

Reflection Prompt:
Think of a stakeholder who supported an initiative because it aligned with their personal goals—even if it wasn't a top organizational priority. Which personal-priority question would have revealed their motivation earlier?

BONUS CHAPTER 1 - SECTION 6 - Discovery When a Prospect Is Emotionally Flooded or Overwhelmed

Introduction

Some of the most challenging discovery conversations happen when the prospect is overwhelmed, emotional, or mentally overloaded. In these moments, they cannot think clearly, evaluate options, or communicate in a stable way. Their nervous system is driving the conversation more than their logic. If you try to push forward, escalate too fast, or interpret their emotional responses as rational responses, the conversation collapses. Your job is not to fix their emotions. Your job is to create enough safety, structure, and calm that clarity becomes possible.

When a prospect is emotionally flooded, their answers become fragmented, inconsistent, or overly dramatic. They may jump between topics, avoid detail, shut down, or over-explain. These reactions are not signs of unwillingness—they are signs of overload. The moment you recognize emotional flooding, you must slow your pace, lower your tone, and remove pressure. Influence is earned through presence, not force.

Your role in these moments is to help the prospect return to a state where thinking is possible. You do this by grounding the conversation. You simplify questions. You reduce the emotional temperature. You give permission for reflection. You avoid escalation until their nervous system stabilizes. This is not about comforting the person. It is about creating conditions where clarity can return. When the emotional temperature lowers, discovery can continue.

The purpose of this section is to show you how to maintain control without adding pressure. You will learn how to recognize emotional flooding early, how to guide the prospect back into clarity, and how to create questions that cut through overwhelm without triggering defensiveness. You will also learn how to interpret the signals that show when the prospect is ready to continue with deeper levels of discovery.

When a prospect is overwhelmed, they are not resisting you—they are resisting the discomfort inside themselves. Your presence is what regulates the moment. Your pacing is what anchors the conversation. Your neutrality is what creates safety. This section gives you the tools to lead through emotional weight without losing momentum, structure, or influence.

Standard Questions (8)

Calm, grounding, simple questions that help stabilize the moment.

1. "Can we slow down for a moment so I can understand this more clearly?"

2. "What part of this feels the heaviest for you right now?"

3. "When you think about everything happening, what stands out the most?"

4. "What's been taking up the most mental space for you today?"

5. "Would it help if we focus on one piece of this at a time?"

6. "What's the part you feel comfortable talking through first?"

7. "Can you walk me through what happened before things felt overwhelming?"

8. "What would feel like a good starting point for us right now?"

Intermediate Questions (9)

These questions go deeper while maintaining emotional safety.

1. "When the pressure builds, what tends to get lost in the noise for you?"

2. "What do you feel you haven't been able to say clearly yet?"

3. "What's the part you've been trying to manage on your own?"

4. "When things become overwhelming, how does that affect your decision-making?"

5. "What's the impact of all this stress on your ability to move forward?"

6. "Which pieces feel urgent, and which pieces feel confusing?"

7. "What expectations—internal or external—are weighing on you the most?"

8. "What tends to happen when this much pressure shows up in your world?"

9. "What would make this conversation feel easier for you right now?"

Aggressive (Direct, Respectful) Questions (8)

These cut through emotional fog and bring the prospect back to grounded truth.

1. "What's the real issue—not the noise—driving this overwhelm?"

2. "What are you afraid will happen if you slow down and look at this honestly?"

3. "What's the part of this situation you've been avoiding the most?"

4. "If nothing changes, what does this emotional cycle continue to cost you?"

5. "At what point does 'overwhelmed' become a reason not to act?"

6. "What decision are you postponing by staying in this emotional space?"

7. "How long have you allowed this level of pressure to control your choices?"

8. "What would happen if you faced the root issue instead of managing symptoms?"

Follow-Up Questions (10)

Reflective, steady, grounding, designed to restore clarity.

1. "When you say it feels overwhelming, what does that mean for you specifically?"

2. "Can you give me an example of when this pressure showed up recently?"

3. "What happened right before you felt things start to escalate?"

4. "What part of your answer feels the most important for us to unpack?"

5. "When you think about the bigger picture, where does this fit in?"

6. "What feels manageable right now, even if the rest doesn't?"

7. "Help me understand how this affects your confidence or clarity."

8. "What's the piece of this that keeps coming back into your mind?"

9. "When you imagine this resolving, what changes first?"

10. "What do you need from me in this moment so we can move forward clearly?"

Conclusion

Emotional flooding is a natural human response. It is not a sign of weakness and not a sign of disinterest. It is a sign that the person is experiencing more pressure than they can process at once. When you slow the conversation, simplify the moment, and reduce the emotional temperature, you help the prospect regain access to their own clarity. This is not persuasion. This is leadership.

When you learn how to navigate overwhelm, you protect the integrity of the conversation. You prevent misinterpretation. You prevent premature decisions. You prevent the prospect from shutting down. This allows the conversation to move forward without force, without tension, and without losing depth.

The goal is not to eliminate emotion. The goal is to anchor the moment so emotion does not control the direction of the call. Once the prospect feels grounded, they can explore consequence, responsibility, and next steps with more honesty. You become the calm center in a chaotic moment—and that is what creates real influence.

Emotional steadiness is one of the highest skills of discovery. When you regulate the moment, you regulate the conversation. When you regulate the conversation, you create clarity. And clarity is what moves people out of overwhelm and into meaningful action.

BONUS CHAPTER 1 - SECTION 7 - Emotional-Trigger Questions

Introduction

Every stakeholder has emotional triggers—specific situations, phrases, past experiences, or pressures that spark strong internal reactions. These reactions may appear as defensiveness, withdrawal, over-explaining, irritation, sudden silence, or accelerated urgency. Emotional triggers influence how people interpret information, how they participate in discussions, and how they respond to risk. Understanding these triggers adds precision and emotional intelligence to discovery.

Strategically, emotional triggers affect decision quality. When emotions spike, clarity drops. People may latch onto minor details, avoid important conversations, or make decisions based on perceived threat rather than actual logic. By uncovering emotional triggers, the advisor can approach sensitive topics with steadiness, anticipate friction, and adjust their communication to prevent escalation.

Psychologically, emotional triggers come from a mixture of past experiences, identity, expectations, and personal vulnerability. A stakeholder who once faced criticism for a failed project may react strongly to uncertainty. Someone who values control may react to ambiguity. Someone who depends on stability may react to rapid change. These questions help reveal the internal sensitivities that shape a person's emotional response to complex decisions.

Interpretation Tip: Pay attention to sudden shifts in tone, energy, pacing, or body language. Emotional triggers often surface quickly: a moment of hesitation, a tightened voice, or a sudden increase in detail. Listen for phrases like "I've had bad experiences with…" or "This makes me nervous because…"—these reveal underlying patterns.

Coaching Note: Handle emotional triggers with care. Your tone should signal safety, patience, and respect. The goal is not to expose emotional vulnerabilities but to understand them well enough to support the stakeholder through moments of tension.

Example phrasing:

- *"What tends to trigger hesitation or stress during tough decisions?"*

- *"Where do certain situations make you react more strongly than others?"*

Standard Emotional-Trigger Questions (8)

Tone: gentle, calm, grounding.

1. "Which situations tend to create emotional strain for you at work?"

2. "Where do you notice stress rising more quickly?"

3. "Which topics require a bit more emotional space for you?"

4. "Where do you prefer extra clarity before feeling comfortable?"

5. "Which interactions feel most sensitive or delicate?"

6. "Where does uncertainty create mild tension for you?"

7. "Which responsibilities carry more emotional weight?"

8. "Where do you appreciate a slower, steadier approach?"

Intermediate Emotional-Trigger Questions (9)

Tone: probing, emotionally aware, thoughtful.

1. "Which past experiences influence how you respond to new decisions?"

2. "Where do high-pressure moments trigger strong reactions?"

3. "Which situations make you feel guarded or cautious?"

4. "Where do certain personalities or communication styles affect your comfort?"

5. "Which unexpected changes tend to unsettle you most?"

6. "Where does fear of being misunderstood influence your reactions?"

7. "Which situations increase your sensitivity to details?"

8. "Where do conflicting opinions trigger emotional tension?"

9. "Which events cause you to shift from calm to alert quickly?"

Aggressive Emotional-Trigger Questions (8)

Tone: direct, respectful, truth-focused.

1. "What situation triggers your strongest emotional reaction?"

2. "Where do you feel defensive before the conversation even starts?"

3. "Which issues make you react more than you'd prefer to?"

4. "Where do you fear being blamed if things go wrong?"

5. "What topic or scenario instantly raises your stress level?"

6. "Where do emotional reactions interfere with your clarity?"

7. "Which part of this initiative triggers the most personal tension?"

8. "What emotion makes decision-making hardest for you?"

Follow-Up Emotional-Trigger Questions (10)

Tone: reflective, steady, emotionally validating.

1. "Can you recall a moment when an emotional reaction surprised you?"

2. "What caused that reaction?"

3. "How did you recognize what was happening internally?"

4. "What helped you regain your emotional balance?"

5. "What patterns do you see in your emotional responses over time?"

6. "How do emotional triggers affect your ability to collaborate?"

7. "What support helps reduce emotional tension for you?"

8. "What boundaries help protect your emotional well-being at work?"

9. "What would help you feel safer during emotionally sensitive conversations?"

10. "How do you want others to approach you when emotions rise?"

Conclusion

Emotional-trigger questions give the advisor deeper insight into the internal reactions that shape behavior. These triggers influence the speed, tone, and quality of decision-making more than most people realize. When stakeholders feel emotionally activated, they see risk more strongly and opportunity less clearly. By understanding these triggers, the advisor can navigate conversations with sensitivity and foresight.

Strategically, emotional triggers reveal potential obstacles to alignment and progress. A single trigger can slow collaboration, shift priorities, or derail momentum. When these triggers are understood, they become manageable rather than disruptive. The advisor can adjust communication style, pacing, or clarity to match the stakeholder's emotional landscape.

Psychologically, this section reveals the hidden experiences shaping who the stakeholder is today. It highlights their vulnerabilities, strengths, and emotional patterns. When these are acknowledged respectfully, trust deepens. Stakeholders feel seen, not judged. This creates a more resilient foundation for deeper discovery and more complex decisions.

As Bonus Chapter 1 continues, the next sections explore information-processing styles, personal vision, and future orientation. These layers complete the portrait of how individuals interpret, respond to, and internalize the decision journey.

Reflection Prompt:
Think of a moment when a stakeholder reacted strongly to a seemingly small issue. Which emotional-trigger question here would have revealed the deeper cause earlier?

BONUS CHAPTER 1 - SECTION 8 - Learning-Style & Information-Processing Questions

Introduction

Every stakeholder absorbs information differently. Some need detail; others need high-level clarity. Some prefer visuals; others prefer discussion. Some make sense of decisions by exploring possibilities; others need step-by-step certainty. These differences in learning style and information processing shape how stakeholders interpret the initiative, how quickly they engage, and how confidently they participate in decision-making. Understanding these differences helps the advisor communicate in a way that supports clarity rather than confusion.

Strategically, learning styles influence how smoothly the decision process unfolds. A stakeholder who receives information in their preferred style processes uncertainty more comfortably and participates with greater clarity. A stakeholder who receives information in a mismatched style may appear disengaged, skeptical, or resistant—not because they disagree, but because they don't yet understand. These dynamics often explain why certain meetings feel productive while others feel strained.

Psychologically, information-processing preferences reflect cognition, personality, past experiences, and emotional safety. People who value structure need predictability; those who value exploration need openness. Some stakeholders avoid details because details overwhelm them; others avoid high-level explanations because they crave precision. When advisors adapt to these preferences, they help stakeholders feel competent, centered, and respected.

Interpretation Tip: Listen for subtle cues such as "Can you show me?", "Walk me through this," "I need to see the big picture," or "Let's slow down." These statements reveal how the stakeholder takes in information. Also watch pacing—fast processors jump in quickly; reflective thinkers need time to absorb before engaging.

Coaching Note: Avoid assuming that one style is better than another. Cognitive diversity strengthens decision-making. Your role is to match your communication to each stakeholder's processing style so they feel understood, not rushed.

Example phrasing:

- *"What helps information make the most sense to you?"*

- *"How do you prefer to learn about new processes or ideas?"*

Standard Learning-Style & Information-Processing Questions (8)

Tone: curious, supportive, respectful.

1. "How do you prefer to receive new information?"

2. "What helps you learn most effectively during complex discussions?"

3. "Where do visuals help you understand ideas more clearly?"

4. "Which explanations make new concepts easier for you to grasp?"

5. "Where does high-level information feel comfortable?"

6. "Which types of details help you feel grounded?"

7. "Where do structured steps support your understanding?"

8. "What kind of communication helps you stay focused?"

Intermediate Learning-Style & Information-Processing Questions (9)

Tone: probing, insightful, pattern-seeking.

1. "Where do you need more detail to feel confident?"

2. "Which topics require a slower pace for you to process fully?"

3. "Where does too much information create overload?"

4. "Which formats—verbal, written, visual—help you most?"

5. "Where do you need the big picture before diving into specifics?"

6. "Which information gaps make decisions harder for you?"

7. "Where does timing affect how well you absorb new ideas?"

8. "Which types of explanations help you avoid confusion?"

9. "Where do you need repetition or reinforcement for clarity?"

Aggressive Learning-Style & Information-Processing Questions (8)

Tone: direct, honest, clarity-focused (still respectful).

1. "What type of information consistently confuses or frustrates you?"

2. "Where do you feel rushed when trying to process new details?"

3. "Which explanations feel overwhelming or unclear?"

4. "Where do you avoid engaging because the information feels mismatched?"

5. "Which communication styles shut you down emotionally?"

6. "What format makes it hardest for you to make sense of the initiative?"

7. "Where does lack of structure make you feel uncertain?"

8. "What part of this process is hardest for you to understand quickly?"

Follow-Up Learning-Style & Information-Processing Questions (10)

Tone: reflective, thoughtful, grounding.

1. "Can you share a moment when someone explained something in a way that clicked for you?"

2. "What made that approach work so well?"

3. "Can you recall a moment when communication created confusion?"

4. "What do you think caused the disconnect?"

5. "How do you typically make sense of complex information?"

6. "What helps you feel more centered when learning something new?"

7. "What patterns do you notice in your understanding process?"

8. "What would make this initiative easier for you to process?"

9. "What type of support helps you gain clarity fastest?"

10. "How can we tailor communication to match your learning preferences?"

Conclusion

Learning-style questions uncover the cognitive and emotional preferences that shape how stakeholders understand information. These preferences influence their engagement, confidence, and ability to assess risk or opportunity. When advisors honor these differences, they create an environment where stakeholders feel capable, respected, and prepared.

Strategically, understanding learning styles allows the advisor to tailor communication to support clarity across the entire decision group. Some stakeholders need synthesis; others need detail. Some need discussion; others need examples. When communication matches cognition, momentum builds naturally.

Psychologically, these insights reveal deeper patterns in how people make sense of their roles and responsibilities. They highlight the mental frameworks that bring comfort, reduce stress, and create confidence. They also uncover sources of confusion that might otherwise appear as resistance or disengagement.

As Bonus Chapter 1 continues, the next sections explore personal-vision questions and long-term emotional meaning. These insights complete the human-centered lens that complements the organizational and strategic exploration of earlier chapters.

Reflection Prompt:
Think of a stakeholder who seemed resistant until the information was presented differently. Which learning-style question here would have revealed their preference earlier?

BONUS CHAPTER 1 - SECTION 9 - Emotional-Climate Awareness Questions

*(Note: This is **not** the same as organizational climate from earlier chapters. This section focuses on **an individual's personal emotional climate**—the internal emotional environment that shapes how they show up day to day.)*

Introduction

Every individual carries a personal emotional climate—a blend of mood, stress load, outlook, energy level, and internal dialogue that shapes their engagement throughout the day. While external circumstances influence this climate, much of it forms from within: personal habits, expectations, emotional resilience, self-talk, and past experiences. When advisors understand a stakeholder's emotional climate, they gain insight into how that person processes feedback, interprets challenges, and makes decisions under pressure.

Strategically, emotional climate affects the stability and consistency of the decision process. A stakeholder with a calm internal climate listens more openly, communicates with clarity, and navigates complexity with steadiness. A stakeholder experiencing emotional turbulence may appear indecisive, defensive, or impatient—not from lack of interest but from internal strain. Emotional climate often explains the "why" behind unpredictable or inconsistent behavior.

Psychologically, emotional climate reflects how someone moves through the world. It reveals their sensitivity to pressure, their emotional bandwidth, and their internal readiness for change. Some individuals carry optimism and resilience even through difficulty; others carry tension or exhaustion without realizing how deeply it influences their responses. This section helps the advisor explore these internal patterns thoughtfully and respectfully.

Interpretation Tip: Pay attention to pacing, tone of voice, and subtle shifts in mood. Rapid changes can signal emotional fluctuation. Consistent calm, consistent tension, or consistent caution often point to long-standing emotional patterns.

Coaching Note: Approach emotional climate with care. The goal is not to diagnose, judge, or analyze. The goal is to understand how the person's internal state influences their external behavior—and to support them accordingly.

Example phrasing:

- *"How would you describe the emotional environment you're carrying into your work lately?"*

- *"Where do you feel emotionally steady—and where do things feel unsettled?"*

Standard Emotional-Climate Awareness Questions (8)

Tone: soft, warm, steady.

1. "How has your general mood been as you move through recent work?"

2. "Where do you feel emotionally steady and grounded?"

3. "What parts of your day feel emotionally clear and manageable?"

4. "Where do you feel the most internal calm?"

5. "Which responsibilities bring you a sense of ease or balance?"

6. "Where does emotional steadiness support your decisions?"

7. "Which interactions leave you feeling more centered?"

8. "Where do you feel emotionally open and comfortable?"

Intermediate Emotional-Climate Awareness Questions (9)

Tone: thoughtful, perceptive, gently probing.

1. "Where do emotional ups and downs influence your clarity?"

2. "Which responsibilities create emotional heaviness for you?"

3. "Where do you feel emotionally drained by your workload?"

4. "Which situations cause your mood to shift quickly?"

5. "Where do emotional patterns affect your willingness to engage?"

6. "Which tasks make you feel emotionally overloaded?"

7. "Where does emotional turbulence make decisions harder?"

8. "Which moments leave lingering emotional tension?"

9. "Where do you need emotional space before making important decisions?"

Aggressive Emotional-Climate Awareness Questions (8)

Tone: direct, honest, emotionally precise.

1. "What emotion is dominating your work experience right now?"

2. "Where do you feel emotionally unstable or unsettled?"

3. "Which recurring emotion slows your decision-making?"

4. "Where are you emotionally exhausted?"

5. "What internal pressure has been building without release?"

6. "Where does emotional fatigue undermine your confidence?"

7. "Which emotional state interrupts your ability to collaborate?"

8. "What part of your emotional climate feels unsustainable?"

Follow-Up Emotional-Climate Awareness Questions (10)

Tone: reflective, validating, emotionally grounding.

1. "Can you recall a recent moment when your emotional climate felt positive and strong?"

2. "What contributed to that emotional balance?"

3. "Can you recall a moment when your emotional climate felt unsettled?"

4. "What triggered that shift?"

5. "How did you regain emotional steadiness?"

6. "What patterns do you notice in your emotional fluctuations?"

7. "What practices help you maintain emotional clarity?"

8. "What would support a healthier emotional climate in your work?"

9. "What emotional boundaries help protect your energy?"

10. "How do you want to feel as you navigate this decision process?"

Conclusion

Emotional-climate questions help the advisor understand the internal emotional environment each stakeholder brings into their work. These internal states shape pacing, clarity, tone, and decision behavior. When emotional climate is stable, the individual engages with confidence and thoughtfulness. When emotional climate fluctuates or destabilizes, their responses become harder to predict.

Strategically, emotional climate explains much of the decision momentum—both forward movement and hesitation. These insights help the advisor determine when to slow down, when to simplify communication, and when to offer reassurance. Understanding emotional climate also prevents misinterpretation of behavior that might otherwise appear as lack of commitment.

Psychologically, emotional climate reflects the stakeholder's inner world—how they process pressure, carry stress, and regain balance. When advisors make space for these internal experiences, they deepen trust and create emotional safety. This leads to more honest conversations, clearer insight, and a more supportive decision environment.

As Bonus Chapter 1 approaches its final section, the next exploration focuses on **Personal Vision & Future Orientation**, completing the emotional and psychological map that helps advisors engage with the whole person behind every decision.

Reflection Prompt:
Think of a stakeholder whose behavior changed depending on their internal state. Which emotional-climate question would have surfaced that shift earlier?

BONUS CHAPTER 1 - SECTION 10 - Personal-Vision & Future-Trajectory Questions

Introduction

Every stakeholder carries a personal vision for their future—a mixture of hopes, ambitions, and imagined possibilities that shape how they interpret decisions today. Personal vision influences motivation, risk tolerance, and the willingness to commit to change. When advisors understand the future a stakeholder is trying to build for themselves, they gain powerful insight into the emotional logic behind their choices.

Strategically, personal vision affects long-term decision alignment. A stakeholder who sees an initiative as a step toward their desired future will advocate strongly, even when the process becomes difficult. A stakeholder who sees the initiative as a threat to their trajectory may resist quietly or disengage. These questions surface whether the decision supports, disrupts, or is irrelevant to the individual's personal path.

Psychologically, personal vision reflects identity, aspiration, and emotional purpose. Some want to grow. Some want stability. Some want recognition. Some want to simplify their work. These visions guide how people interpret change, challenge, and opportunity. When advisors connect an initiative to a person's future vision, they create meaning that strengthens commitment.

Interpretation Tip: Listen for long-term language: "I want to," "I imagine myself," "Where I'm heading," "Eventually I'd like to…" These statements reveal the internal future the stakeholder is building. Also pay attention to hesitation—silence around the future often signals uncertainty or emotional fatigue.

Coaching Note: Approach personal vision without intrusiveness. You're helping the stakeholder articulate a future they care about—not challenging it. Your tone should be respectful, inspired, and patient.

Example phrasing:

- *"Where do you see your role evolving over the next few years?"*

- *"How does this initiative connect to the future you want for yourself?"*

Standard Personal-Vision & Future-Trajectory Questions (8)

Tone: warm, encouraging, forward-looking.

1. "Where do you see your role evolving in the coming years?"

2. "Which parts of your future feel most exciting to you?"

3. "Where do you hope to grow or expand your skills?"

4. "Which responsibilities support your long-term goals?"

5. "Where do you feel momentum in your development?"

6. "Which opportunities align with your future direction?"

7. "Where do you want more influence or impact over time?"

8. "What does a fulfilling next chapter look like for you?"

Intermediate Personal-Vision & Future-Trajectory Questions (9)

Tone: thoughtful, probing, horizon-focused.

1. "Where do you feel uncertainty about your long-term path?"

2. "Which future goals feel most important to you now?"

3. "Where does your current role support your aspirations?"

4. "Which responsibilities hold you back from future growth?"

5. "Where do you want more stability or clarity moving forward?"

6. "Which skills do you want to sharpen for your future trajectory?"

7. "Where do you imagine yourself taking on new challenges?"

8. "Which long-term priorities influence how you evaluate decisions today?"

9. "Where does this initiative align—or conflict—with your future vision?"

Aggressive Personal-Vision & Future-Trajectory Questions (8)

Tone: bold, honest, purpose-seeking (still respectful).

1. "What future do you genuinely want—but rarely say out loud?"

2. "Where do you feel your current path is too limited?"

3. "Which personal ambition feels blocked right now?"

4. "Where do you fear stagnation if nothing changes?"

5. "Which part of your role no longer fits the future you want?"

6. "What future path would you pursue if pressure wasn't a factor?"

7. "Where do you worry that this decision will shape your future negatively?"

8. "What long-term desire is driving your feelings about this initiative?"

Follow-Up Personal-Vision & Future-Trajectory Questions (10)

Tone: reflective, clarifying, gently revealing.

1. "Can you share a moment when your future vision became clearer to you?"

2. "What influenced that moment of clarity?"

3. "How has your personal vision changed over the years?"

4. "Which experiences shaped your long-term aspirations?"

5. "What helps you feel connected to your future direction?"

6. "What signals tell you you're moving toward the right future?"

7. "What adjustments would help align your work with your vision?"

8. "What would a healthier or more inspiring future look like for you?"

9. "What support would help you move toward your long-term goals?"

10. "How does this initiative fit into the life you want to build?"

Conclusion

Personal-vision questions reveal the deeper hopes, ambitions, and emotional trajectories that guide how stakeholders interpret decisions. When an initiative aligns with these visions, commitment grows naturally. When it conflicts, even subtly, resistance spreads quietly beneath the surface. This section helps advisors understand not just what the stakeholder wants to do now, but who they want to become in the future.

Strategically, personal vision is a powerful predictor of advocacy. People fight for what they believe moves them closer to the future they desire. They hesitate when decisions feel misaligned with their purpose. Understanding this alignment enables the advisor to position the initiative as part of a meaningful future story rather than just another organizational task.

Psychologically, personal vision reflects identity. It reveals what brings meaning, pride, growth, or security. When advisors connect with personal vision authentically, they strengthen trust and create conversations that reach beyond mechanics into purpose. This deepens the relationship and improves the quality of the decision journey.

With this section complete, **Bonus Chapter 1 is fully finished**. You now have a complete 10-section chapter exploring the human elements—emotions, priorities, internal patterns, and personal aspirations—that influence every decision. This chapter elevates the book into a more complete psychological and strategic framework.

Reflection Prompt:
Think of a stakeholder whose long-term aspirations shaped how they responded to a decision. Which personal-vision question would have revealed their ambitions earlier?

BONUS CHAPTER 1 — Chapter Conclusion

Bonus Chapter 1 uncovers the personal and emotional forces shaping how individuals participate in decision-making. These forces are often invisible on the surface but powerful in their influence. Motivation, stress, change-readiness, confidence, personal priorities, emotional patterns, and future aspirations all combine to create a complex internal environment. Understanding these layers helps the advisor interpret behavior accurately instead of making assumptions.

Strategically, the insights from this chapter reveal why decisions accelerate, stall, or shift unexpectedly. When advisors understand interpersonal dynamics, emotional triggers, and information-processing preferences, they can adapt communication and pacing to support clarity. When they understand personal vision and emotional climate, they can connect initiatives to meaning rather than mechanics. These perspectives turn confusion into clarity and friction into alignment.

Psychologically, this chapter gives advisors the tools to humanize discovery. People feel safer when their inner experience is understood and respected. They share more openly, engage more deeply, and collaborate more authentically. This emotional connection strengthens decision-making and creates a more honest, trustworthy relationship between advisor and stakeholder.

As you move into Bonus Chapter 2, the focus shifts from internal human experience to **future-state thinking, innovation readiness, opportunity acceleration, and strategic foresight**. Together, these two bonus chapters complete the book's exploration of discovery—from internal emotion to external evolution—giving advisors the most comprehensive framework for understanding human and organizational decision behavior.

BONUS CHAPTER 2 - Introduction

Future-State, Innovation, and Strategic Foresight Discovery

Bonus Chapter 2 expands discovery into a new dimension: the future. While earlier chapters explored present needs, emotional drivers, internal dynamics, and current obstacles, this chapter shifts the lens forward. It focuses on how stakeholders imagine, anticipate, and prepare for what comes next. The future is rarely discussed directly, yet it shapes almost every decision people make. By exploring the future openly, advisors help stakeholders reveal deeper aspirations, hidden concerns, and strategic tensions that influence their choices long before implementation begins.

Each section in this chapter uncovers a different facet of future thinking. Some sections explore vision—what stakeholders *want* to create. Others focus on uncertainty—what they fear or what they must prepare for. Still others examine capability, readiness, alignment, barriers, and imagination. Together, these elements create a complete map of how individuals and organizations think about tomorrow, not just today.

Strategically, future-oriented discovery helps advisors identify whether an initiative is built on strong foundations or fragile assumptions. It reveals whether the organization is prepared for disruption, open to innovation, or limited by outdated systems. It exposes whether decision-makers are driven by ambition, caution, or the pressure to "keep up." These insights guide advisors toward recommendations that will hold up under both current and future conditions.

Psychologically, the future brings both excitement and pressure. Some stakeholders speak about the future with energy and optimism. Others speak about it with worry, fatigue, or guarded neutrality. This difference matters. The emotional tone of future thinking influences risk tolerance, commitment, and decision speed. Understanding these tones allows advisors to navigate conversations with empathy and precision, giving stakeholders the space to explore their hopes and fears without judgment.

The chapter also includes imaginative and boundary-free questions that help stakeholders step outside limitations. Many organizations limit their thinking without realizing it. By removing constraints—temporarily—these questions unlock possibility. Imagination reveals truths that rational conversations keep hidden: dreams, hidden motivations, and unrealized potential. Even when the ideas seem unrealistic, the underlying desires are deeply practical and highly actionable.

When taken together, the sections in this chapter create an advanced, future-focused discovery toolkit. Advisors gain the ability to interpret behavior, anticipate resistance, strengthen alignment, and position their solutions with greater strategic clarity.

BONUS CHAPTER 2 - SECTION 1 - Future-State Vision Questions

Introduction

Every organization operates inside a picture of the future—some clear, some vague, some inspiring, and some reactive. That picture shapes how decisions are made today. Whether leaders talk about their future openly or keep it tucked away in strategy decks, future-state vision influences investment, risk tolerance, innovation appetite, and priority-setting. This section explores how stakeholders imagine the next chapter of their organization, department, team, or role—and how that vision affects decision momentum.

Strategically, future-state vision acts as a compass. When the future is clear, decisions align naturally. When the future is blurry, decisions drift, stall, or compete for attention. A defined future gives direction; an undefined future creates hesitation. These questions help reveal whether stakeholders are making decisions based on a strategic destination or simply reacting to short-term pressures.

Psychologically, future-state thinking reflects hope, ambition, fear, and identity. Some leaders imagine progress; others imagine protection. Some picture growth; others picture stability. These visions guide emotional energy—what excites them, what scares them, and what feels worth the effort. Understanding this allows the advisor to connect the initiative to something meaningful rather than mechanical.

Interpretation Tip: Listen for the level of detail in the stakeholder's description. Vague visions often indicate uncertainty, internal misalignment, or fear of overcommitting. Clear visions suggest strong goals, personal investment, or confident leadership. The tone they use to describe the future—optimistic, cautious, neutral—reveals emotional direction.

Coaching Note: Approach future conversations with curiosity rather than challenge. People share more openly when they don't feel evaluated. Your role is to understand how they imagine tomorrow so you can understand today's decisions with greater insight.

Example phrasing:

- *"If everything goes well, what do you want this organization to look like in a few years?"*

- *"What future are you trying to move toward—not just the next task, but the bigger picture?"*

Standard Future-State Vision Questions (8)

Tone: open, imaginative, grounded.

1. "What do you hope your organization looks like in a few years?"

2. "Where do you see the team growing or evolving?"

3. "What future improvements feel most important to you?"

4. "Where do you want to see greater stability or consistency?"

5. "Which long-term opportunities excite you the most?"

6. "Where do you imagine your processes working more smoothly?"

7. "Which future goals feel the most achievable from where you stand now?"

8. "What does a strong future-state look like for your team?"

Intermediate Future-State Vision Questions (9)

Tone: probing, structured, forward-thinking.

1. "Where does your current direction align with your future vision?"

2. "Which gaps stand between where you are and where you want to be?"

3. "Where do you need new capabilities to reach your future goals?"

4. "Which long-term risks shape your desired direction?"

5. "Where do you feel unsure about the future trajectory?"

6. "Which decisions today carry the biggest long-term impact?"

7. "Where do you see the greatest opportunity for future growth?"

8. "Which internal processes need to evolve for your future-state to work?"

9. "Where do potential future changes influence how you plan today?"

Aggressive Future-State Vision Questions (8)

Tone: direct, bold, deeply truth-seeking.

1. "What future are you avoiding talking about because it feels risky?"

2. "Where does your current path make your desired future unrealistic?"

3. "Which long-term assumption may no longer be true?"

4. "What future outcome do you fear the most?"

5. "Which ambition feels too big to admit openly?"

6. "Where will your current limitations eventually become roadblocks?"

7. "What future direction would force uncomfortable change?"

8. "What long-term vision is quietly driving your decisions—even if no one says it out loud?"

Follow-Up Future-State Vision Questions (10)

Tone: reflective, thoughtful, meaning-seeking.

1. "Can you share a moment when your future vision became clearer to you?"

2. "What experiences shaped how you see the future today?"

3. "How has your long-term direction evolved over time?"

4. "What helps you stay focused on the future when short-term pressure builds?"

5. "What signs tell you you're moving toward your desired future?"

6. "What early progress would make you feel more confident in your future-state?"

7. "What part of your future vision feels the most personal or meaningful?"

8. "What could make your desired future easier to reach?"

9. "What obstacles feel the most significant as you look ahead?"

10. "How do you want this initiative to influence your long-term direction?"

Conclusion

Future-state vision questions reveal the long-term perspective that shapes how stakeholders evaluate today's decisions. These visions influence the direction, pace, and emotional tone of the decision process. When the future feels clear, stakeholders act with confidence. When the future feels uncertain, hesitation appears even in simple conversations. Understanding a stakeholder's long-term view provides vital context for interpreting their motivations and concerns.

Strategically, this section highlights where alignment exists—or where it doesn't. When organizational decisions match the future-state vision, momentum builds naturally. When decisions conflict with that vision, friction grows quietly in the background. These questions enable the advisor to position solutions within the larger story the stakeholder is trying to create for their organization.

Psychologically, future-state visions anchor identity and meaning. They reveal what leaders hope to build, protect, or transform. When advisors connect initiatives to these deeper aspirations, they help stakeholders feel understood and supported. This strengthens trust, enriches discovery, and clarifies the path forward.

As Bonus Chapter 2 continues, the next sections explore innovation resistance, long-term outcomes, scenario planning, and barriers to breakthrough performance. Together, they form a comprehensive framework for understanding how the future shapes today's decisions.

Reflection Prompt:
Think of a stakeholder who pursued a difficult initiative because it aligned with their long-term vision. Which future-state question would have revealed their deeper purpose earlier?

BONUS CHAPTER 2 - SECTION 2 - Innovation-Resistance Questions

Introduction

Organizations often talk about innovation as if everyone welcomes it, but real innovation introduces uncertainty, disruption, learning curves, and emotional risk. Even when change is beneficial, people resist it for reasons that feel personal, practical, or protective. Innovation resistance is rarely about the idea itself—it's about the impact the idea might have on control, stability, identity, and workload. This section helps advisors uncover the subtle and overt forms of resistance that shape how stakeholders respond to new approaches.

Strategically, innovation resistance influences the adoption of new systems, processes, and initiatives. A team that resists innovation slows implementation, questions decisions repeatedly, or clings to old methods. A team that embraces innovation engages with curiosity and adapts quickly. Understanding where resistance lives—and why—helps the advisor navigate the emotional and operational challenges innovation brings.

Psychologically, resistance often stems from fear: fear of losing competence, fear of visibility, fear of increased expectations, or fear of repeating past failures. Some people resist innovation because they value predictability; others resist because change threatens their perceived stability or status. These questions illuminate these psychological forces so the advisor can address them with empathy and strategy.

Interpretation Tip: Listen for defensive language, hesitant pacing, or overemphasis on "how we've always done it." Subtle comments like "That sounds complicated," "We tried something like that," or "Our team just isn't built for that" often signal deeper resistance patterns. Pay attention to who resists and who supports—both reveal internal influence.

Coaching Note: Treat resistance as information, not opposition. People resist because they care about something—clarity, competence, stability, or control. When you understand the source of resistance, you can guide the conversation in a way that feels safe rather than confrontational.

Example phrasing:

- *"What makes innovation feel exciting—or challenging—for your team?"*

- *"Where do new ideas tend to meet hesitation?"*

Standard Innovation-Resistance Questions (8)

Tone: open, calm, judgment-free.

1. "Where do new ideas feel easy for your team to explore?"

2. "Which types of changes your team usually adapts to well?"

3. "Where does innovation fit naturally into your workflow?"

4. "Which recent improvements felt smooth or positive?"

5. "Where do small adjustments feel manageable for your group?"

6. "Which team members tend to welcome new approaches?"

7. "Where have new solutions helped reduce stress or simplify work?"

8. "What past innovations worked well for your team?"

Intermediate Innovation-Resistance Questions (9)

Tone: probing, neutral, insight-seeking.

1. "Where do new ideas tend to meet hesitation?"

2. "Which types of innovation create confusion or discomfort?"

3. "Where have past changes created stress for your team?"

4. "Which concerns do people voice when new approaches are introduced?"

5. "Where does the team struggle to let go of old processes?"

6. "Which responsibilities make people wary of trying something unfamiliar?"

7. "Where does innovation create the biggest learning curve?"

8. "Which internal habits slow the adoption of new methods?"

9. "Where is innovation embraced in theory but resisted in practice?"

Aggressive Innovation-Resistance Questions (8)

Tone: direct, honest, clarity-demanding.

1. "What part of innovation feels like a threat to your team?"

2. "Where does your group resist change even when the benefits are clear?"

3. "Which past failure still influences resistance today?"

4. "Where do people avoid innovation to protect their comfort zone?"

5. "Which roles feel most vulnerable when new ideas arrive?"

6. "What internal belief creates the strongest resistance to innovation?"

7. "Where does fear of looking unprepared slow down progress?"

8. "What innovation would your team reject immediately—and why?"

Follow-Up Innovation-Resistance Questions (10)

Tone: reflective, steady, psychologically supportive.

1. "Can you recall a time when innovation felt overwhelming for the team?"

2. "What caused the tension in that moment?"

3. "How did people react emotionally or behaviorally?"

4. "What helped reduce resistance over time?"

5. "What did that experience teach you about how the team handles change?"

6. "Which parts of innovation feel personally challenging for you?"

7. "What support makes new ideas easier to accept?"

8. "What conditions help resistance soften naturally?"

9. "Where would small wins help strengthen openness to innovation?"

10. "How can we introduce new ideas in a way that feels safe and manageable?"

Conclusion

Innovation-resistance questions uncover the emotional and structural forces that make new ideas difficult to adopt. These forces often operate quietly beneath the surface, shaping tone, engagement, and pace. When advisors understand where resistance originates, they can guide innovation more thoughtfully and avoid misinterpreting hesitation as rejection.

Strategically, these insights reveal barriers to progress. Innovation may be necessary, but adoption depends on readiness, clarity, and emotional safety. When resistance is addressed respectfully, organizations move more smoothly into improvement. When resistance is ignored, even strong initiatives struggle to gain traction.

Psychologically, innovation resistance reflects vulnerability and self-protection. These questions help stakeholders express concerns they might otherwise keep hidden—fears of losing control, of appearing incompetent, or of repeating past challenges. When these emotions are understood, innovation becomes less threatening and more collaborative.

As Bonus Chapter 2 continues, the next section explores long-term value and outcome questions—helping stakeholders articulate the results they hope innovation will produce. Together, these sections deepen future-state clarity and align decisions with meaningful direction.

Reflection Prompt:
Think of a past initiative where resistance slowed progress. Which innovation-resistance question here would have revealed the source sooner?

BONUS CHAPTER 2 - SECTION 3 - Long-Term Outcome & Value Questions

Introduction

Every meaningful decision carries both immediate benefits and long-term consequences. While short-term outcomes are easy to measure—cost, effort, timing—the long-term value of an initiative determines whether the organization grows, stabilizes, or struggles. Long-term outcomes shape sustainability, capability-building, competitive positioning, and future resilience. This section helps uncover how stakeholders think about impact beyond the present moment.

Strategically, long-term thinking separates reactive organizations from forward-moving ones. Some teams evaluate decisions based on what solves today's problems; others evaluate based on how today's decisions will shape the next several years. Understanding which lens a stakeholder uses helps the advisor anticipate how they will interpret risk, opportunity, and timing. Long-term value often determines whether a stakeholder commits with confidence or hesitates out of caution.

Psychologically, long-term thinking reflects mindset, identity, and emotional investment. Some individuals naturally think in multi-year arcs; others think in short bursts due to pressure, workload, or environment. Long-term perspectives often reveal someone's sense of responsibility, vision, fear of regret, or hope for better outcomes. When advisors understand this perspective, they can frame decisions in a way that resonates with the stakeholder's deeper priorities.

Interpretation Tip: Listen for language that signals time orientation. Phrases like "next quarter," "this year," or "immediate results" indicate short-term focus. Phrases like "down the road," "over time," or "in the future" reveal long-term thinking. Notice whether their desired outcomes center on relief, protection, improvement, or transformation.

Coaching Note: Encourage long-term reflection without dismissing short-term realities. Many stakeholders want long-term value but feel trapped by immediate pressures. Your role is to help them balance both lenses with clarity and confidence.

Example phrasing:

- *"When you look beyond today, what outcomes matter most to you long-term?"*

- *"What value do you hope this delivers years from now?"*

Standard Long-Term Outcome & Value Questions (8)

Tone: steady, thoughtful, future-aware.

1. "What long-term outcomes matter most for your team's success?"

2. "Where do you see value growing over time?"

3. "Which improvements would make the biggest difference long-term?"

4. "Where do you hope to see sustained progress?"

5. "Which outcomes would still matter years from now?"

6. "Where do you want long-term stability or consistency?"

7. "Which results feel worth investing in over time?"

8. "Where do you imagine long-term benefits outweighing short-term effort?"

Intermediate Long-Term Outcome & Value Questions (9)

Tone: probing, clarifying, horizon-focused.

1. "Where do short-term needs conflict with long-term value?"

2. "Which decisions today will have the strongest impact years from now?"

3. "Where do you see gaps between current performance and desired outcomes?"

4. "Which long-term risks concern you the most?"

5. "Where do you hope this initiative strengthens your future readiness?"

6. "Which areas require long-term investment rather than quick fixes?"

7. "Where do long-term goals guide your decision-making?"

8. "Which outcomes help the organization stay competitive over time?"

9. "Where does long-term value matter more than immediate results?"

Aggressive Long-Term Outcome & Value Questions (8)

Tone: direct, bold, truth-seeking.

1. "What long-term risk are you ignoring because the short-term need feels urgent?"

2. "Where will current decisions create future problems if left unaddressed?"

3. "Which long-term goal has been postponed too many times?"

4. "Where do short-term pressures blind the organization to future impact?"

5. "Which future outcome are you most afraid of missing?"

6. "Where do you fear regret if the long-term value isn't pursued now?"

7. "What will become harder—and more expensive—if delayed further?"

8. "Which long-term opportunity requires bold action, not caution?"

Follow-Up Long-Term Outcome & Value Questions (10)

Tone: reflective, grounding, meaning-focused.

1. "Can you describe a time when long-term thinking paid off for your team?"

2. "What made that decision valuable over time?"

3. "Can you recall a moment when short-term thinking created future challenges?"

4. "What did you learn from that experience?"

5. "What helps you stay committed to long-term goals under pressure?"

6. "How do you measure progress toward long-term outcomes?"

7. "What future benefits feel most meaningful to you personally?"

8. "What obstacles make long-term planning difficult?"

9. "What support would help you balance short-term needs with long-term value?"

10. "How do you hope this initiative shapes your future direction?"

Conclusion

Long-term outcome questions illuminate the deeper arc of organizational and personal decision-making. They help the advisor see beyond immediate tasks to understand the future impact stakeholders care about most. These insights reveal whether the organization is driven by short-term relief or long-term resilience, and how that orientation influences timing, investment, and advocacy.

Strategically, long-term thinking determines which initiatives endure. When stakeholders see clear long-term value, they are more likely to persist through challenges, gather support, and take ownership of the outcome. When the long-term impact is unclear, hesitation grows and short-term pressures dominate. Understanding these dynamics helps advisors guide conversations with foresight.

Psychologically, long-term outcome thinking reveals hope, fear, ambition, and responsibility. It shows what the stakeholder wants to protect, build, or transform over time. When advisors connect an initiative to these deeper aspirations, they elevate the conversation from planned to meaningful. This strengthens trust and creates shared purpose.

As Bonus Chapter 2 continues, the next section explores scenario planning—how stakeholders imagine potential futures, prepare for uncertainty, and navigate complexity. These perspectives deepen the advisor's understanding of how the organization approaches both risk and opportunity over time.

Reflection Prompt:
Think of a decision that created long-term impact—positive or negative. Which long-term value question would have surfaced the key insight earlier?

BONUS CHAPTER 2 - SECTION 4 - Scenario-Planning Questions

Introduction

Scenario planning helps organizations anticipate future conditions rather than react to them. It invites stakeholders to consider multiple possible outcomes—best case, worst case, and everything in between. While leaders often think about the future in broad terms, they rarely articulate detailed scenarios unless prompted. This section explores how stakeholders imagine potential futures and how those imagined futures influence the decisions they make today.

Strategically, scenario planning reveals whether the organization is preparing for uncertainty or hoping circumstances will remain stable. Some teams think proactively, sketching out various paths and preparing for disruption. Others make decisions as though the future will mirror the present. Understanding how a stakeholder thinks about alternative outcomes helps the advisor forecast decision behavior, risk tolerance, and prioritization.

Psychologically, scenario thinking exposes how individuals emotionally relate to uncertainty. Some embrace unknowns with curiosity. Others feel anxious or threatened by unpredictable conditions. These emotional reactions shape their decision-making, their openness to innovation, and their willingness to commit to long-term strategies. Scenario-planning questions allow you to identify these underlying attitudes toward uncertainty.

Interpretation Tip: Listen for how stakeholders talk about extremes. If they dismiss worst-case scenarios entirely, they may be avoiding discomfort. If they dwell excessively on negative outcomes, they may struggle with fear-based planning. Balanced scenario thinking reveals a mature and intentional approach to uncertainty.

Coaching Note: Approach these conversations with a tone that encourages exploration rather than prediction. Scenario planning is not about accuracy—it is about readiness. Encourage stakeholders to think broadly without feeling pressured to forecast the perfect outcome.

Example phrasing:

- *"What possible futures are you preparing for as you consider this decision?"*

- *"How do different scenarios influence the choices you're evaluating?"*

Standard Scenario-Planning Questions (8)

Tone: open, curious, exploratory.

1. "Which future scenarios do you consider when planning ahead?"

2. "Where do you see potential opportunities in different outcomes?"

3. "Which possibilities feel most realistic from your perspective?"

4. "Where do you want to be prepared no matter what happens?"

5. "Which external factors could shape your future direction?"

6. "Where does your team already consider multiple potential paths?"

7. "Which scenarios would you like to understand more clearly?"

8. "Where do you feel confident in how your team handles change?"

Intermediate Scenario-Planning Questions (9)

Tone: probing, analytical, perspective-expanding.

1. "Where could unexpected changes create new opportunities?"

2. "Which scenarios worry you the most, and why?"

3. "Where do you feel uncertain about how the future might unfold?"

4. "Which internal vulnerabilities could be exposed under certain conditions?"

5. "Where would your strategy shift if a major disruption occurred?"

6. "Which assumptions need to be re-evaluated across scenarios?"

7. "Where do best-case and worst-case outcomes diverge most sharply?"

8. "Which scenarios would strain your team's current capabilities?"

9. "Where does preparing for multiple futures feel difficult or unclear?"

Aggressive Scenario-Planning Questions (8)

Tone: bold, forward-projecting, truth-seeking.

1. "What scenario are you avoiding because it feels uncomfortable?"

2. "Where could your current strategy collapse under pressure?"

3. "Which assumption, if proven wrong, would create major risk?"

4. "Where are you underprepared for a sudden market shift?"

5. "Which scenario represents your organization's greatest vulnerability?"

6. "What future event would force immediate change?"

7. "Which potential outcome challenges your current confidence the most?"

8. "What scenario requires a level of readiness you don't currently have?"

Follow-Up Scenario-Planning Questions (10)

Tone: reflective, steady, grounding.

1. "Can you share a past moment when a scenario you anticipated came true?"

2. "What helped you navigate that situation effectively?"

3. "Can you recall a moment when an unexpected event caught you unprepared?"

4. "What did that experience teach you about planning ahead?"

5. "What signals help you recognize when a scenario is shifting?"

6. "How do you balance hope and caution when thinking about the future?"

7. "What would help your team prepare more confidently for uncertainty?"

8. "Which scenario deserves deeper planning attention now?"

9. "What early steps could strengthen readiness across outcomes?"

10. "How do you want to respond when the unexpected happens?"

Conclusion

Scenario-planning questions reveal how stakeholders think about uncertainty, complexity, and possible futures. These insights help advisors understand whether the organization is preparing thoughtfully for change or reacting to the moment without considering potential outcomes. When scenario thinking is strong, organizations act intentionally. When it is weak, decisions are driven by immediate pressure rather than long-term resilience.

Strategically, scenario insights help advisors tailor recommendations for durability. Understanding best-case, worst-case, and most-likely paths allows advisors to position solutions that remain valuable across changing conditions. It also helps expose hidden risks that may affect implementation, adoption, or long-term results.

Psychologically, scenario thinking uncovers emotional readiness. Stakeholders who fear uncertainty may seek excessive detail or delay decisions. Those who embrace uncertainty may move too quickly without stress-testing their assumptions. By understanding these tendencies, advisors can help teams find a balanced approach to future planning.

As Bonus Chapter 2 continues, the next sections explore breakthrough barriers and opportunity acceleration—two areas closely tied to how organizations respond to the possibilities revealed by scenario thinking.

Reflection Prompt:
Think of a time when a team was either well-prepared or completely unprepared for an unexpected shift. Which scenario-planning question here would have revealed that readiness earlier?

BONUS CHAPTER 2 - SECTION 5 - Breakthrough-Barrier Questions

Introduction

Every organization reaches a point where progress slows, not because the team lacks intelligence or effort, but because unseen barriers limit forward movement. These barriers often form gradually—old habits, outdated processes, limited capacity, unchallenged assumptions, fear of conflict, or structural constraints. Breakthrough-barrier questions help uncover what is preventing the team from reaching the next level of performance, innovation, or clarity.

Strategically, breakthrough insight reveals where the organization's growth is constrained. While leaders may talk about "improving efficiency" or "doing more with less," the real breakthrough often requires confronting deeper issues: misaligned priorities, overloaded teams, cultural resistance, or the absence of clear ownership. When these barriers are surfaced, the advisor gains precision about what must change before meaningful progress can occur.

Psychologically, breakthrough barriers reflect emotional comfort zones and long-standing protective behaviors. People often resist acknowledging barriers because doing so exposes vulnerability or disrupts familiar rhythms. Some hesitate to challenge established norms; others avoid difficult conversations or fear the weight of new expectations. These questions help reveal the psychological architecture behind those constraints.

Interpretation Tip: Listen for statements like "that's just how we do it," "we've tried before," "leadership isn't ready," or "timing never feels right." These phrases often point to underlying blockers. Breakthrough moments rarely come from a single problem—they come from understanding a pattern.

Coaching Note: Approach this section with balance. Your tone must be courageous but empathetic. Breakthrough conversations often feel exposing, and stakeholders must feel safe to speak honestly about challenges without feeling judged.

Example phrasing:

- *"What is the biggest barrier preventing your team from reaching the next level?"*

- *"Where do you feel stuck, even though you know progress is possible?"*

Standard Breakthrough-Barrier Questions (8)

Tone: curious, supportive, improvement-oriented.

1. "Where do you feel progress slows down most often?"

2. "Which tasks or processes seem to hit the same walls repeatedly?"

3. "Where does the team get stuck even when the goal is clear?"

4. "Which responsibilities feel heavier than they should?"

5. "Where do you see opportunities that haven't been fully unlocked yet?"

6. "Which routines or habits feel outdated now?"

7. "Where do you feel the team is close to a breakthrough?"

8. "Which small changes could remove everyday friction?"

Intermediate Breakthrough-Barrier Questions (9)

Tone: probing, insightful, pattern-seeking.

1. "Where do invisible barriers limit your team's performance?"

2. "Which decisions take longer than they should—and why?"

3. "Where does uncertainty or misalignment slow momentum?"

4. "Which processes feel overcomplicated or unclear?"

5. "Where do skill gaps create bottlenecks?"

6. "Which assumptions no longer fit your current reality?"

7. "Where do internal silos restrict collaboration or speed?"

8. "Which obstacles require leadership attention to overcome?"

9. "Where do you see the same problems resurfacing over time?"

Aggressive Breakthrough-Barrier Questions (8)

Tone: bold, direct, breakthrough-focused (still respectful).

1. "What is the biggest barrier you've been avoiding addressing?"

2. "Where do leadership decisions create unnecessary limitations?"

3. "Which internal habit is holding the organization back the most?"

4. "Where do you know change is needed but no one wants to initiate it?"

5. "What is the hidden friction that people talk about privately but not publicly?"

6. "Where does your current structure make progress almost impossible?"

7. "Which behavior or mindset must change before any breakthrough happens?"

8. "What uncomfortable truth would accelerate progress if it were spoken openly?"

Follow-Up Breakthrough-Barrier Questions (10)

Tone: reflective, clarifying, courage-building.

1. "Can you describe a moment when a barrier became impossible to ignore?"

2. "What made that barrier stand out to you?"

3. "How did the team respond in that moment?"

4. "What deeper issue did that barrier reveal?"

5. "What past attempts have been made to overcome it?"

6. "What prevented those attempts from succeeding?"

7. "What small step could begin shifting that barrier today?"

8. "What support would make overcoming the barrier feel achievable?"

9. "What would progress look like once the barrier is removed?"

10. "How would the organization transform if this breakthrough occurred?"

Conclusion

Breakthrough-barrier questions uncover the structural and psychological limits preventing progress. These barriers often shape decisions quietly, restricting momentum even when the team is motivated, intelligent, and aligned. When advisors understand these constraints, they can help stakeholders shift from surface-level adjustments to meaningful change.

Strategically, breakthrough insights reveal where hidden inefficiencies, cultural resistance, or leadership dynamics impact progress. These revelations enable advisors to focus on what truly matters—the levers that drive transformation rather than the symptoms that disguise deeper issues. Breakthrough barriers are often the key to unlocking long-term value.

Psychologically, this section helps uncover the emotional comfort zones and fears that prevent teams from challenging the status quo. When stakeholders feel safe acknowledging these limits, they shift from defensive patterns to problem-solving mindsets. This emotional pivot often marks the beginning of renewal, innovation, or strategic realignment.

As Bonus Chapter 2 continues, the next section explores opportunity acceleration—how organizations can move faster on initiatives that matter most once breakthrough barriers are understood and addressed.

Reflection Prompt:
Think of a time when a single hidden barrier held back significant progress. Which breakthrough-barrier question here would have uncovered it sooner?

BONUS CHAPTER 2 - SECTION 6 - Opportunity-Acceleration Questions

Introduction

Most organizations have opportunities sitting right in front of them—moments where progress could happen faster, results could come sooner, or momentum could be captured more decisively. But opportunity rarely accelerates itself. Teams get absorbed in routines, distracted by urgent tasks, or slowed by incomplete information. Opportunity-acceleration questions help identify where the organization could move more quickly and confidently toward meaningful gains.

Strategically, understanding opportunity acceleration reveals where high-value initiatives are stuck behind slow processes, unclear ownership, or caution. Some opportunities only emerge for a short window; others require bold action to capture their full value. These questions help the advisor identify which opportunities deserve speed, which require alignment, and which need structural support.

Psychologically, acceleration requires belief and emotional readiness. Stakeholders may hesitate because they fear moving too quickly, disrupting stability, or overcommitting. Others feel energized by speed and want to capitalize before conditions shift. Opportunity-acceleration questions uncover the emotional drivers behind pacing—excitement, anxiety, confidence, or uncertainty.

Interpretation Tip: Listen for phrases like "we should have done this sooner," "we keep circling back," "timing is important," or "we're losing ground here." These statements signal areas where acceleration may be possible—or necessary. Opportunity windows often close quietly, not dramatically.

Coaching Note: Encourage honest reflection without implying pressure. Opportunity acceleration is not about rushing—it's about identifying where momentum can be harnessed instead of wasted. Your tone should inspire clarity, not urgency for urgency's sake.

Example phrasing:

- *"Which opportunities would benefit most from earlier action?"*

- *"Where could progress move faster if conditions were clearer?"*

Standard Opportunity-Acceleration Questions (8)

Tone: optimistic, curious, encouraging.

1. "Which opportunities feel most promising right now?"

2. "Where do you see momentum already building?"

3. "Which initiatives could progress with a little more focus?"

4. "Where does your team show readiness for faster action?"

5. "Which opportunities align well with current strengths?"

6. "Where do you see a clear path to early wins?"

7. "Which projects feel close to moving forward?"

8. "Where does increased clarity make acceleration easier?"

Intermediate Opportunity-Acceleration Questions (9)

Tone: probing, strategic, momentum-focused.

1. "Where do slow processes reduce the value of emerging opportunities?"

2. "Which opportunities are time-sensitive or window-based?"

3. "Where do you feel the organization is moving too cautiously?"

4. "Which decisions, if made sooner, would create stronger results?"

5. "Where does unclear ownership slow progress?"

6. "Which opportunities depend on quick alignment across teams?"

7. "Where does hesitation reduce competitive advantage?"

8. "Which opportunities are too important to delay?"

9. "Where do you see early traction that could be amplified?"

Aggressive Opportunity-Acceleration Questions (8)

Tone: bold, challenging, urgency-revealing (without pressure).

1. "What opportunity is slipping through your fingers right now?"

2. "Where is unnecessary caution holding you back?"

3. "Which high-value initiative deserves immediate focus?"

4. "Where are you losing momentum by waiting?"

5. "Which unmet opportunity could change your trajectory if accelerated?"

6. "What process slows you down more than you're willing to admit?"

7. "Which opportunity requires a decisive move—soon?"

8. "Where does delay create the greatest strategic risk?"

Follow-Up Opportunity-Acceleration Questions (10)

Tone: reflective, clarifying, forward-moving.

1. "Can you describe a time when acting quickly created a strong outcome?"

2. "What conditions made fast action possible?"

3. "Can you recall a moment when hesitation cost you an opportunity?"

4. "What did that experience teach you about timing?"

5. "What signals tell you an opportunity is worth accelerating?"

6. "What support increases your comfort with faster progress?"

7. "What internal steps could make movement smoother?"

8. "What would early success look like for this opportunity?"

9. "What would prevent unnecessary delays in this case?"

10. "How do you want to manage pace as you move forward?"

Conclusion

Opportunity-acceleration questions reveal where momentum is available but underutilized. These insights help advisors identify which initiatives deserve earlier attention, clearer decisions, or strengthened ownership. When opportunities move too slowly, value erodes. When they accelerate appropriately, organizations gain efficiency, competitive advantage, and emotional energy.

Strategically, understanding acceleration points helps advisors guide the organization toward proactive, not reactive, decision behavior. It highlights where speed can amplify value rather than create unnecessary pressure. These insights also reveal the difference between initiatives that require caution and those that benefit from forward momentum.

Psychologically, opportunity acceleration exposes emotional readiness. Stakeholders who feel confident seek progress. Those who feel uncertain hesitate. Understanding this emotional layer helps advisors support stakeholders in ways that reduce fear and build alignment. Acceleration becomes a shared choice—not a forced pace.

As Bonus Chapter 2 continues, the following sections explore capability building, future-threat awareness, strategic alignment, and transformation readiness—rounding out a complete view of how organizations prepare for and navigate the future.

Reflection Prompt:
Think of a missed opportunity that could have changed an organization's trajectory. Which acceleration question here would have revealed its urgency sooner?

BONUS CHAPTER 2 - SECTION 7 - Capability-Building Questions

Introduction

Every long-term strategy depends on capabilities—the skills, systems, habits, and capacities that allow an organization to execute effectively. While goals set the direction, capabilities determine whether those goals are reachable. Many organizations underestimate the gap between what they want to achieve and what they are currently equipped to deliver. Capability-building questions help uncover these gaps so that advisors can guide stakeholders toward realistic, sustainable progress.

Strategically, capability insights reveal where potential is limited by current constraints. A team may have a strong vision for the future but lack the expertise, structure, or operational muscle to reach it. These gaps can lead to stalled initiatives, overworked teams, or underperforming outcomes. Capability-building questions identify where strengthening systems, training, teamwork, or leadership development will accelerate success.

Psychologically, capability gaps often create emotional tension. People may feel overwhelmed, insecure, or protective when their team's limitations become visible. Others may feel energized by conversations about growth and improvement. Understanding both the functional and emotional components of capability-building allows advisors to support the organization with respect and precision.

Interpretation Tip: Listen for uncertainty around skills, bandwidth, or infrastructure. Phrases like "we're stretched thin," "we don't have the right tools," or "we need more confidence in this area" reveal underlying capability concerns. Also pay attention to who expresses confidence versus who expresses caution—this often indicates internal misalignment.

Coaching Note: Approach capability gaps with an empowering tone. The goal is not to expose weakness but to illuminate opportunity. Capability-building becomes exciting when stakeholders feel hopeful and supported rather than evaluated.

Example phrasing:

- *"What capabilities will you need to achieve your long-term goals?"*

- *"Where does your team need support or development to move forward confidently?"*

Standard Capability-Building Questions (8)

Tone: supportive, clear, grounded.

1. "Which strengths does your team rely on most today?"

2. "Where do you already have strong capability foundations?"

3. "Which skills support your long-term goals?"

4. "Where does your current expertise align well with future needs?"

5. "Which capabilities help your team perform consistently?"

6. "Where does your team feel confident in its abilities?"

7. "Which systems or processes already work well for you?"

8. "Where do you see capability growth beginning naturally?"

Intermediate Capability-Building Questions (9)

Tone: probing, constructive, insight-seeking.

1. "Where do capability gaps limit your progress?"

2. "Which responsibilities require skills you're still developing?"

3. "Where does bandwidth limit execution speed or quality?"

4. "Which capabilities will become more critical in the next few years?"

5. "Where do outdated processes slow your team down?"

6. "Which tools or systems are no longer keeping up with demand?"

7. "Where do you need stronger cross-team coordination?"

8. "Which capability gaps create the most risk for your strategy?"

9. "Where does your team feel uncertain about future requirements?"

Aggressive Capability-Building Questions (8)

Tone: direct, honest, challenge-oriented (but respectful).

1. "What capability gap is holding your organization back the most?"

2. "Where are you relying on workarounds instead of building competence?"

3. "Which skills are missing but rarely discussed openly?"

4. "Where would failure occur if capabilities aren't strengthened soon?"

5. "What process or system is no longer acceptable for your future goals?"

6. "Where does your team lack the confidence needed to scale?"

7. "What capability shortfall creates the greatest long-term vulnerability?"

8. "Which part of your strategy is unrealistic without capability development?"

Follow-Up Capability-Building Questions (10)

Tone: reflective, encouraging, clarifying.

1. "Can you recall a time when improved capabilities changed your results?"

2. "What made that shift possible?"

3. "Can you share a moment when capability gaps created unexpected challenges?"

4. "What did that experience teach you?"

5. "What early steps could strengthen your team's confidence today?"

6. "What type of support or training would create the greatest impact?"

7. "Which small habits would improve capability over time?"

8. "What would capability success look like one year from now?"

9. "What internal alignment is needed to support capability growth?"

10. "How do you want your team to feel as their capabilities expand?"

Conclusion

Capability-building questions illuminate the foundation upon which long-term progress depends. They help advisors understand whether the organization has the skills, systems, and structure required to pursue its vision with confidence. Without these insights, initiatives risk becoming overambitious, under-resourced, or misaligned with reality.

Strategically, capability awareness highlights where investments in people, tools, or processes are necessary to achieve sustainable momentum. These insights allow advisors to support organizations in building competence rather than relying on short-term effort or hope. Capability-building becomes an intentional path rather than a reactive scramble.

Psychologically, these questions help stakeholders acknowledge both their strengths and their limitations with clarity and confidence. When capability gaps are addressed with support rather than criticism, teams feel empowered to grow. This creates an environment where improvement feels attainable rather than overwhelming.

As Bonus Chapter 2 continues, the next sections explore future-threat awareness, strategic alignment, and transformation readiness—rounding out an advanced framework for future-oriented discovery.

Reflection Prompt:
Think of a time when capability gaps limited the success of a project. Which capability-building question here would have surfaced the issue earlier?

BONUS CHAPTER 2 - SECTION 8 - Future-Threat Awareness Questions

Introduction

Every organization faces threats that could disrupt stability, slow progress, or challenge long-term goals. Some threats are external—market shifts, technology changes, regulatory updates, or competitor moves. Others are internal—talent gaps, outdated processes, cultural resistance, misalignment, or overreliance on fragile systems. Future-threat awareness questions help uncover how stakeholders perceive these risks, how they mentally prepare for them, and how they respond when warning signs appear.

Strategically, understanding threat awareness reveals whether leaders are proactive or reactive in safeguarding their future. Some organizations anticipate disruption and plan ahead; others recognize threats only when they become unavoidable. These differences shape both the timing and quality of decisions. When threat awareness is strong, organizations move with foresight. When it is weak, they drift into vulnerability.

Psychologically, threat perception is tied to fear, confidence, past experiences, and emotional tolerance for uncertainty. Some stakeholders see threats as catalysts for improvement; others experience them as stress triggers that lead to avoidance or defensiveness. These emotional responses influence how openly threats are discussed—and whether they turn into proactive planning or quiet anxiety.

Interpretation Tip: Listen for the level of specificity in how stakeholders describe threats. Vague answers often signal avoidance or lack of awareness. Clear, concrete concerns reveal thoughtful vigilance. Also pay attention to tone—fear-based descriptions differ from strategic ones.

Coaching Note: Approach threat conversations with steadiness. The goal is not to amplify fear, but to illuminate realities that can be planned for. Use a calm, grounded tone to help stakeholders feel supported rather than exposed.

Example phrasing:

- *"What future threats do you want to prepare for before they become urgent?"*

- *"Where do you see potential risks that deserve more attention?"*

Standard Future-Threat Awareness Questions (8)

Tone: steady, clear, calmly observant.

1. "Which long-term risks are on your radar right now?"

2. "Where do you see potential challenges emerging over time?"

3. "Which external changes could affect your future direction?"

4. "Where do you want more protection or stability?"

5. "Which internal vulnerabilities deserve periodic attention?"

6. "Where do shifting trends influence your planning?"

7. "Which areas require ongoing vigilance?"

8. "Where does future uncertainty shape your decisions today?"

Intermediate Future-Threat Awareness Questions (9)

Tone: probing, analytical, horizon-scanning.

1. "Where do you feel exposed if conditions change suddenly?"

2. "Which threats would have the greatest long-term impact?"

3. "Where do slow-developing risks go unnoticed until too late?"

4. "Which internal limitations increase vulnerability?"

5. "Where do dependencies create hidden threat pathways?"

6. "Which competitive moves could disrupt your plans?"

7. "Where might regulatory or industry shifts introduce new risks?"

8. "Which threats would require immediate action if triggered?"

9. "Where does lack of visibility make risk assessment difficult?"

Aggressive Future-Threat Awareness Questions (8)

Tone: direct, bold, protective, truth-seeking.

1. "What threat are you most afraid will catch you unprepared?"

2. "Where could a single failure create cascading consequences?"

3. "Which risk is being underplayed or ignored internally?"

4. "Where would a major disruption expose your biggest weakness?"

5. "Which threat feels urgent, even if no one speaks about it openly?"

6. "Where do you see danger that others underestimate?"

7. "What future event could critically damage momentum?"

8. "Which vulnerability could jeopardize your long-term strategy?"

Follow-Up Future-Threat Awareness Questions (10)

Tone: reflective, clarifying, courage-building.

1. "Can you recall a time when a threat emerged faster than expected?"

2. "How did your organization respond in that moment?"

3. "What did you learn from that experience?"

4. "Can you describe a threat you recognized early and prepared for well?"

5. "What contributed to that preparedness?"

6. "What early signals help you identify emerging threats?"

7. "What internal support would strengthen your readiness?"

8. "What would a balanced threat-preparation plan look like for you?"

9. "What could help reduce fear while increasing vigilance?"

10. "How do you want your organization to respond when new threats appear?"

Conclusion

Future-threat awareness questions illuminate how stakeholders perceive, anticipate, and emotionally interpret risk. These insights help advisors understand where organizations are vulnerable, where they are prepared, and where denial or avoidance may be creating silent exposure. Without this understanding, even well-designed strategies can fail under pressure.

Strategically, threat awareness helps organizations prepare for uncertainty with intentionality rather than panic. It highlights areas that require monitoring, strengthening, or restructuring. By surfacing these concerns early, advisors help teams build resilience and agility, ensuring the future does not catch them off guard.

Psychologically, threat conversations reveal how individuals experience uncertainty—whether they respond with courage, caution, avoidance, or strategic thinking. These emotional patterns influence the pace and quality of decisions. Addressing threats with calm curiosity helps stakeholders feel supported while maintaining clarity.

As Bonus Chapter 2 continues, the next sections explore strategic alignment and transformation readiness—two areas that determine how well organizations integrate insights into action.

Reflection Prompt:
Think of a time when a threat was recognized too late. Which future-threat awareness question here would have surfaced it earlier?

BONUS CHAPTER 2 - SECTION 9 - Strategic-Alignment Questions

Introduction

Strategic alignment is the backbone of effective decision-making. Even the most valuable initiative fails when it does not fit the organization's direction, priorities, or resource realities. Alignment determines whether a decision moves forward smoothly, encounters friction, or stalls entirely. This section explores the degree to which stakeholders see the initiative as supporting, enhancing, or complicating their strategic goals.

Strategically, alignment affects everything from speed of approval to quality of execution. When an initiative fits naturally into the organization's priorities, support builds quickly and collaboration forms easily. When alignment is weak, conversations become circular, priorities compete, or the initiative becomes overshadowed by louder, more urgent needs. These questions help advisors understand how the initiative fits into the broader strategic landscape.

Psychologically, alignment reflects personal belief, internal logic, and emotional investment. If someone feels the initiative strengthens their vision, they become a champion. If they feel it distracts from their mission, they become hesitant—even if they do not say so explicitly. Alignment is both intellectual and emotional, and uncovering it requires careful listening and thoughtful exploration.

Interpretation Tip: Pay attention to language like "this fits," "this conflicts," "this competes," or "this strengthens." Also listen for hesitation when discussing other priorities—lack of clarity about alignment often reveals deeper uncertainty or contradictory expectations between departments.

Coaching Note: Approach alignment with neutrality. Your role is not to force alignment, but to uncover how the stakeholder sees the bigger picture. Your tone should invite honesty and clarity without judgment.

Example phrasing:

- *"How well does this initiative support your current strategic direction?"*

- *"Where does this fit—or conflict—with what matters most right now?"*

Standard Strategic-Alignment Questions (8)

Tone: clear, calm, perspective-building.

1. "Where does this initiative support your broader goals?"

2. "Which priorities does it reinforce for your team?"

3. "Where do you see natural alignment with your current direction?"

4. "Which existing strategies does this complement?"

5. "Where does the initiative feel like a logical next step?"

6. "Which areas of progress does this help accelerate?"

7. "Where does it strengthen efforts already underway?"

8. "Which goals become easier to reach with this in place?"

Intermediate Strategic-Alignment Questions (9)

Tone: probing, thoughtful, integrative.

1. "Where does this initiative compete with other priorities?"

2. "Which goals does it support more strongly than others?"

3. "Where is alignment present but not yet clear to the full team?"

4. "Which strategic objectives require this initiative to move forward?"

5. "Where do conflicting priorities influence your evaluation?"

6. "Which teams need to be aligned for this to succeed?"

7. "Where might alignment shift over time as needs evolve?"

8. "Which constraints limit alignment right now?"

9. "Where would strategic clarity strengthen decision-making?"

Aggressive Strategic-Alignment Questions (8)

Tone: bold, honest, clarity-demanding (still respectful).

1. "What part of this initiative does *not* align with your strategy?"

2. "Which priority must give way if this moves forward?"

3. "Where does leadership say one thing is a priority but act differently?"

4. "Which strategic goal is being ignored or overshadowed?"

5. "What contradiction exists between your goals and this initiative?"

6. "Where does misalignment create hidden risk?"

7. "What assumption about alignment may be misleading the team?"

8. "Where does this initiative force a choice between two strategic paths?"

Follow-Up Strategic-Alignment Questions (10)

Tone: reflective, clarifying, alignment-strengthening.

1. "Can you recall a moment when strong alignment made a past initiative successful?"

2. "What created that alignment?"

3. "Can you share a time when misalignment led to missed outcomes?"

4. "What lessons came from that experience?"

5. "What helps you determine alignment early in a decision?"

6. "What would stronger alignment look like for this initiative?"

7. "What conversations are needed to build shared understanding?"

8. "What signals tell you an initiative fits the strategy well?"

9. "What would reduce misalignment across teams?"

10. "How do you want alignment to shape next steps?"

Conclusion

Strategic-alignment questions reveal how well an initiative fits into the organization's priorities, constraints, and long-term direction. Alignment determines whether decisions feel natural or forced, whether momentum builds or stalls. Without alignment, even the best ideas struggle. With alignment, progress becomes inevitable.

Strategically, alignment insight helps advisors position their solutions accurately—not by overselling, but by connecting to the priorities that matter most. It helps stakeholders see how the initiative affects their goals and resource planning. Misalignment becomes visible early, preventing wasted effort or unrealistic expectations.

Psychologically, alignment reflects belief and emotional investment. People want to feel that their decisions contribute to a meaningful direction. When alignment is clear, confidence grows. When it's unclear, hesitation deepens. These questions help uncover both the intellectual logic and the emotional truth behind the stakeholder's position.

As Bonus Chapter 2 approaches its last section, the next focus is transformation readiness—the ultimate test of whether the organization is prepared to evolve, adapt, and pursue meaningful change.

Reflection Prompt:
Think of a time when an initiative succeeded because the strategy was clear and aligned. Which strategic-alignment question here would have confirmed that certainty sooner?

BONUS CHAPTER 2 - SECTION 10 - Transformation-Readiness Questions

Introduction

Transformation requires more than desire. It requires readiness—emotional, operational, cultural, and strategic. Many organizations express interest in change, but not all are prepared for the demands that transformation creates. Readiness involves capacity, clarity, leadership alignment, resilience, and the willingness to adopt new behaviors. This section explores how prepared stakeholders truly feel for meaningful transformation and what conditions must exist for change to take root.

Strategically, transformation readiness determines the likelihood of long-term success. When readiness is high, organizations adapt quickly, respond well to disruption, and sustain progress even when challenges arise. When readiness is low, even well-designed initiatives falter. Decisions slow, resistance grows, and teams revert to old habits. Readiness questions help advisors understand whether the foundation is strong enough for the change being considered.

Psychologically, readiness includes emotional thresholds: tolerance for uncertainty, resilience under pressure, and willingness to leave behind familiar routines. Some stakeholders embrace transformation with optimism; others feel anxious, skeptical, or protective of the status quo. Understanding these emotional patterns helps advisors support stakeholders with empathy and realism.

Interpretation Tip: Listen for emotional commitments such as "we're ready," "we're stretched," "this is a big step," or "we need more preparation." These statements often reveal the true internal landscape. Readiness has gradients—not binaries—and your questions help map where the organization stands across that spectrum.

Coaching Note: Approach readiness with honesty and care. Transformation is demanding, and people need space to express concerns without fear of judgment. Your tone should communicate that readiness is not a pass-or-fail test—it is an opportunity for clarity and preparation.

Example phrasing:

- *"How prepared do you feel for the level of change this initiative may require?"*

- *"Where do you feel ready—and where do you feel uncertain?"*

Standard Transformation-Readiness Questions (8)

Tone: warm, steady, exploratory.

1. "Where do you feel ready for meaningful change?"

2. "Which parts of this initiative feel manageable for your team?"

3. "Where does the organization already show adaptability?"

4. "Which upcoming changes align with your current strengths?"

5. "Where do you see early signs of transformation beginning?"

6. "Which responsibilities support readiness for new approaches?"

7. "Where do you feel confident in your team's ability to evolve?"

8. "Which past successes show that change is possible?"

Intermediate Transformation-Readiness Questions (9)

Tone: probing, perspective-building, clarifying.

1. "Where does your team need more preparation for upcoming changes?"

2. "Which capabilities must strengthen before transformation begins?"

3. "Where do current routines resist new expectations?"

4. "Which parts of your culture help—or hinder—change?"

5. "Where does communication need to improve for readiness to grow?"

6. "Which groups feel most uncertain about what's coming?"

7. "Where might bandwidth limitations affect transformation efforts?"

8. "Which leadership behaviors will influence readiness the most?"

9. "Where do readiness and hesitation coexist within the team?"

Aggressive Transformation-Readiness Questions (8)

Tone: direct, truth-seeking, respectful.

1. "What part of this transformation are you least prepared for?"

2. "Where will resistance appear first—and why?"

3. "Which part of your culture is not ready for this level of change?"

4. "Where would transformation collapse without stronger leadership commitment?"

5. "What expectation feels unrealistic with your current capacity?"

6. "Where do you personally feel unprepared to support the change?"

7. "Which hidden fear could derail transformation if not addressed?"

8. "What part of this effort demands a readiness you don't yet have?"

Follow-Up Transformation-Readiness Questions (10)

Tone: reflective, supportive, realistic.

1. "Can you recall a time when your organization handled major change well?"

2. "What made that experience successful?"

3. "Can you describe a transformation that struggled or failed in the past?"

4. "What lessons came from that experience?"

5. "What would increased readiness look like for you personally?"

6. "What support would help your team feel more prepared?"

7. "What steps could reduce uncertainty before moving forward?"

8. "What early wins would create confidence in the change process?"

9. "What boundaries or structure would protect your team during transition?"

10. "How do you want the transformation to feel as it unfolds?"

Conclusion

Transformation-readiness questions reveal whether the organization is emotionally, operationally, and culturally prepared for meaningful change. Without readiness, even well-designed plans struggle. With readiness, organizations evolve with confidence and resilience. These questions uncover the real conditions that determine whether transformation is possible or premature.

Strategically, readiness insight helps advisors avoid pushing change too quickly or too slowly. It highlights where preparation is needed—capabilities, communication, culture, leadership, or mindset. When advisors understand these factors, they can help stakeholders create strong foundations that support sustainable transformation.

Psychologically, readiness reflects emotional courage and vulnerability. People must feel supported, capable, and aligned before taking bold steps into the unknown. By encouraging honest conversations about readiness, advisors strengthen trust and lay the groundwork for smoother transitions.

Reflection Prompt:
Think of a major change that succeeded or failed due to readiness. Which transformation-readiness question would have clarified preparedness earlier?

BONUS CHAPTER 2 - SECTION 11 - Constraint-Free Imagination & Vision Expansion Questions

Introduction

Most decision-making discussions stay within the boundaries of what feels possible, practical, and safe. But breakthrough insights often emerge when people are invited to imagine without limits—even briefly. Constraint-free imagination removes the pressure of budget, approval, timing, and responsibility. When the mind is allowed to explore openly, deeper hopes surface, hidden frustrations become visible, and unspoken desires rise into clarity. This section gives stakeholders the space to articulate what they truly want before reality narrows the path.

Strategically, imagination opens doors that limitations keep closed. When stakeholders think freely, they reveal the outcomes that matter most to them. These insights help advisors understand the deeper motivation behind decisions—not just what the stakeholder wants to solve, but what they want to *create*. Imagination also uncovers the opportunities people consider impossible, too risky, or too ambitious under normal conditions. These "ideal-state" ideas often illuminate the direction strategy should truly move toward.

Psychologically, constraint-free thinking reduces emotional pressure. People feel safer exploring unrealistic or exaggerated ideas because they aren't committing to them—they're experimenting. This safety removes self-censorship and exposes authentic preferences, frustrations, and values. It also helps reveal fears disguised as limitations since imagination exposes what someone might pursue if fear, risk, or judgment disappeared.

Interpretation Tip: Listen for themes that repeat in their imaginative answers. Even unrealistic ideas reveal realistic desires: simplicity, recognition, control, relief, innovation, or stability. When stakeholders imagine freely, they often express their deepest needs with surprising honesty.

Coaching Note: Treat imaginative statements as clues, not commitments. Your role is to help the stakeholder reconnect those imaginative insights to practical next steps—not to dismiss them as "unrealistic." Imagination is often the cleanest path to truth.

STANDARD IMAGINATION & VISION EXPANSION QUESTIONS (16)

Tone: open, curious, possibility-focused.

1. "If you could wave a magic wand and fix one part of your operation, what would change first?"

2. "In a perfect world, how would this process work from start to finish?"

3. "If nothing held you back, what would you want this team to accomplish?"

4. "What would the ideal version of your role look like?"

5. "If every tool worked exactly as you wished, how would your day feel different?"

6. "What would your dream version of this initiative deliver?"

7. "If resources weren't a factor, what would you build or improve right now?"

8. "What outcome would make your life noticeably easier?"

9. "If you could simplify one recurring challenge, which would you choose?"

10. "What would a friction-free year look like for your team?"

11. "If you could enhance one capability instantly, which would you choose?"

12. "What would success look like if everything clicked perfectly?"

13. "If you could shape the future without limitations, what direction would you choose?"

14. "What ideal support system would help you perform at your best?"

15. "If you could automate any task or responsibility, what would go first?"

16. "What would an ideal partnership with outside providers look like for you?"

INTERMEDIATE IMAGINATION & VISION EXPANSION QUESTIONS (18)

Tone: probing, thoughtful, creative but grounded.

1. "If you could redesign this department from scratch, what would be different?"

2. "Where would you invest first if you were granted unrestricted funding?"

3. "If internal politics didn't exist, what decision would you make immediately?"

4. "What future would you pursue if you had complete authority?"

5. "If you could reset one long-standing process, which would you restart?"

6. "What do you wish your team could stop doing entirely?"

7. "If you could speed up one initiative dramatically, which would you choose?"

8. "What do you secretly wish your organization could do—but never admits?"

9. "If time were not a constraint, what project would you pursue first?"

10. "What would your ideal cross-team collaboration look like?"

11. "If you could solve one systemic issue permanently, which one matters most?"

12. "What would your future state look like if you could remove all obstacles?"

13. "If your team could gain one super-skill overnight, which skill would it be?"

14. "What do you wish leadership understood without you needing to explain it?"

15. "If you could eliminate one recurring point of stress, what would disappear?"

16. "What innovation would you adopt instantly if risk wasn't part of the equation?"

17. "If you could duplicate a part of your team's success, which part would you replicate everywhere?"

18. "What bold idea would you pursue if no one could say no?"

AGGRESSIVE IMAGINATION & VISION EXPANSION QUESTIONS (16)

Tone: direct, bold, truth-extracting, still respectful.

1. "What would you change tomorrow if no one could push back?"

2. "What dream outcome feels too big to admit during normal discussions?"

3. "What radical improvement would you pursue if you didn't have to defend it?"

4. "Which limitation frustrates you most—but you pretend to accept it?"

5. "If you could remove one decision-maker from the process entirely, who would it be?"

6. "What painful process would you erase forever if given the chance?"

7. "What would your organization look like if fear played zero role in decisions?"

8. "Which success are you capable of achieving but haven't pursued out of caution?"

9. "If you could break one rule without consequences, which rule would you eliminate?"

10. "What do you want to implement that everyone else is too afraid to try?"

11. "If you could replace one major system immediately, which one would disappear?"

12. "What initiative would you launch if you weren't worried about failure?"

13. "What would you pursue if you didn't have to negotiate with other departments?"

14. "Which constraint feels like the biggest lie your organization has accepted?"

15. "If you could rebuild your strategy with total freedom, what would be non-negotiable?"

16. "What bold shift would transform your work if you didn't limit yourself?"

Conclusion

Imagination-based discovery reveals the truth that structured, rational conversation often hides. When stakeholders imagine without inhibition, they expose what they value most, what burdens them, and what they deeply want but rarely voice. These insights are powerful because they reflect desires free from fear, politics, or practicality.

Strategically, these questions uncover direction, intention, and aspiration. Even the most unrealistic answers carry usable insight: clarity about outcomes, clarity about frustrations, and clarity about motivation. Advisors who understand these imaginative truths gain a clearer picture of what stakeholders will champion, resist, or prioritize as decisions unfold.

Psychologically, constraint-free thinking bypasses internal filters—perfectionism, self-doubt, organizational constraints, fear of judgment. In this state, stakeholders express the raw ideas that fuel passion and creativity. When these ideas surface, advisors gain access to a deeper emotional landscape, making it easier to build alignment and trust.

This section completes the second bonus chapter's exploration of the future—not just the future that feels possible, but the future that feels desirable. Here, imagination becomes the doorway to truth.

BONUS CHAPTER 2 - Conclusion

Bonus Chapter 2 brings the future into sharp focus. Throughout these sections, stakeholders explored not only where they stand today but where they believe they are heading—and where they fear they may end up if conditions shift. This long-range perspective helps advisors guide decision-making with more accuracy, empathy, and strategic intelligence. Understanding the future context gives every insight deeper meaning.

Strategically, the chapter exposes the forces that shape long-term success: readiness, capability, alignment, innovation, resilience, and imagination. Advisors who understand these forces can help organizations prepare intentionally rather than reactively. They can position their solutions as bridges to the future rather than patches for the present. This strengthens advocacy, clarifies direction, and elevates decision quality.

Psychologically, the chapter reveals the emotional truths that influence how stakeholders approach tomorrow—hope, fear, pride, uncertainty, excitement, and ambition. By navigating these emotions with calm clarity, advisors build trust and create space for honest exploration. When the future feels understood, it becomes less intimidating and more actionable.

As you move into the next chapter, the focus shifts again—from foresight to unbounded imagination. Chapter 11 builds on everything gathered here, inviting stakeholders to think beyond practical constraints and explore the fullest expression of what they want. It becomes the creative complement to the strategic depth of this chapter, completing the most comprehensive future-oriented discovery framework in the book.

BONUS CHAPTER 3 - Introduction

Hidden Drivers, Ethical Pressures & Deep-Structure Discovery

Chapter 13 brings the book into its deepest psychological territory. While earlier chapters explored visible behaviors, stated goals, clear barriers, and recognizable emotional patterns, this chapter focuses on the forces people rarely name but consistently feel. These hidden drivers—ethical tension, identity, invisible cost, momentum patterns, emotional memory, ownership confusion, trust, emotional logic, unspoken ambition, and organizational energy—shape decisions far more strongly than formal strategy ever can. When advisors understand these silent influences, they gain the ability to interpret behavior with nuance and accuracy.

Most decision processes are influenced by far more than budgets, deadlines, and business goals. People navigate internal pressure, personal standards, reputation concerns, emotional triggers, and the expectations of others. Yet these influences often go unspoken, because they feel too complex, too personal, or too politically risky to address directly. This chapter creates a structured, thoughtful way to explore those forces respectfully. It gives advisors a way to uncover what people truly carry beneath the surface.

Strategically, the insights from this chapter reveal the true conditions surrounding a decision. For example: ethical pressure explains quiet hesitation; professional identity explains strong preferences; invisible costs explain fatigue; momentum patterns explain unexplained delays; emotional memory explains fear; unclear ownership explains inconsistency; low trust explains guarded conversation; emotional logic explains misalignment; ambition explains motivation; and energy explains readiness. Each section exposes a different layer of reality—together forming a complete picture of why decisions unfold as they do.

Psychologically, these questions introduce a rare level of emotional safety and validation. Stakeholders often feel relieved when someone finally asks about the pressures they have been carrying silently. When people feel understood without judgment, their communication becomes clearer, more honest, and more grounded. This emotional clarity improves decision-making far more than pushing for logic or speed.

Another purpose of this chapter is to give the reader a deeper sense of confidence when handling complex, sensitive, or high-stakes conversations. Many professionals sense these hidden forces but lack the language to explore them respectfully. The questions in this chapter serve as doorways—gentle enough to invite openness, yet precise enough to reveal meaningful truth. When used skillfully, they help stakeholders articulate the emotional reality behind their choices.

This chapter is also designed to make the advisor more emotionally intelligent. By learning to notice the patterns beneath the surface—tone shifts, hesitations, contradictions, and unspoken tension—advisors gain the ability to support stakeholders in ways that feel safe, strategic, and deeply human. The goal is not to fix people's emotional challenges but to understand how those challenges influence the decision in front of them.

By the time the reader finishes this chapter, they will have the tools to uncover the forces that most people never articulate. These insights elevate discovery from a set of questions into a genuine understanding of the human experience of decision-making.

BONUS CHAPTER 3 - Section 1 - Ethical Pressure & Integrity Tension Questions

Ethical pressure is one of the most quietly influential forces in any decision-making process. People want to act with integrity, yet they often face expectations, constraints, and subtle influences that make the right path feel complicated. Ethical tension doesn't always come from dramatic wrongdoing. More often, it shows up in small compromises, unspoken obligations, or internal conflict about how choices affect people, fairness, or long-term trust. This section helps uncover those pressures so advisors can understand the deeper emotional and moral landscape behind decisions.

Strategically, ethical pressure often shapes timing, alignment, communication, and the level of support a stakeholder is willing to give. When someone feels morally conflicted, they slow down, hesitate, become overly cautious, or over-justify their actions. When they feel ethically aligned, they move with confidence and conviction. Understanding ethical tension allows advisors to see the "hidden brakes" influencing progress—brakes that rarely appear in surface-level discussions.

Psychologically, integrity tension creates emotional weight. People feel responsible for protecting their team, honoring commitments, and acting according to their personal values. When these values conflict with organizational expectations, internal stress grows. Stakeholders may feel torn between loyalty and honesty, between speed and fairness, or between personal ethics and political realities. Ethical pressure also affects how comfortable someone feels advocating for a decision publicly.

Interpretation Tip: Listen closely to statements like "I don't want to step on toes," "this feels sensitive," "there are politics here," or "I'm trying to do the right thing." These phrases signal that ethical pressure is present, even if the speaker avoids naming it. Ethical tension is rarely stated directly—it's revealed through hesitation, tone, and the way people explain their choices.

Coaching Note: Approach ethical questions with calm neutrality. These conversations must feel safe. Ethical concerns are deeply personal, and stakeholders may fear judgment or exposure. Your tone should invite honesty, deepen clarity, and help them explore their values without feeling cornered. Your role is not to solve their ethical conflict but to understand how it shapes their decisions.

Example phrasing:

- *"Where do your values influence how you think about this decision?"*

- *"What part of this feels sensitive or morally complicated?"*

Standard Ethical Pressure & Integrity Questions (8)

Tone: respectful, calm, inviting honesty.

1. "Where do you want to make sure this decision aligns with your values?"

2. "Which parts of this process feel ethically important to you?"

3. "Where do you want to protect fairness for your team or customers?"

4. "Which expectations feel clear and comfortable for you?"

5. "Where do you want to maintain transparency?"

6. "Which responsibilities feel especially important for doing this the right way?"

7. "Where do you want to avoid misunderstandings or mixed signals?"

8. "Which outcomes matter to you for reasons beyond the business impact?"

Intermediate Ethical Pressure & Integrity Questions (9)

Tone: probing, thoughtful, morally aware.

1. "Where do you feel subtle pressure that influences the decision?"

2. "Which parts of this process feel ethically gray or unclear?"

3. "Where do expectations conflict with what feels right to you?"

4. "Which decisions affect people in ways you're thinking carefully about?"

5. "Where might transparency need to be strengthened?"

6. "Which choices have reputational impacts that matter to you?"

7. "Where do political dynamics complicate the ethical picture?"

8. "Which values guide you most when things feel uncertain?"

9. "Where could ethical tension affect momentum or comfort?"

Aggressive Ethical Pressure & Integrity Questions (8)

Tone: direct, courageous, truth-seeking (still safe and respectful).

1. "What ethical concern are you carrying that you haven't said out loud yet?"

2. "Where are you being asked to do something that feels off to you?"

3. "Which expectation feels unfair—even if you tolerate it?"

4. "Where are you protecting people from consequences they should actually face?"

5. "What political pressure is shaping this decision more than it should?"

6. "Where does the 'right thing' conflict with the 'easy thing'?"

7. "What part of this decision makes you uncomfortable ethically?"

8. "Where would your integrity feel compromised if this went the wrong way?"

Follow-Up Ethical Pressure & Integrity Questions (10)

Tone: reflective, grounding, encouraging honesty.

1. "Can you recall a moment when ethical tension shaped a past decision?"

2. "What made that moment stand out to you?"

3. "How did others respond when ethics became part of the conversation?"

4. "What did that experience teach you about doing the right thing under pressure?"

5. "What signs tell you that an ethical concern is starting to grow?"

6. "What helps you stay anchored to your values when decisions become difficult?"

7. "What would support look like if you had to navigate an ethical dilemma again?"

8. "How do you want people to feel about your role in this decision?"

9. "What outcome would make you feel proud of how you handled this?"

10. "How do you want your values to show up in the next steps?"

Conclusion

Ethical pressure and integrity tension reveal some of the deepest drivers behind decision-making. These forces operate quietly, often beneath the surface of formal goals, data, or organizational responsibilities. When advisors understand these pressures, they gain insight into why certain decisions accelerate, stall, or shift direction unexpectedly. Ethical concerns are rarely rooted in logic—they are rooted in personal belief, responsibility, and care for others.

Strategically, this section helps uncover hidden constraints that numbers, timelines, and priorities cannot explain. Ethical tensions influence communication, stakeholder alignment, advocacy, and risk tolerance. When these tensions are understood and respected, advisors can support stakeholders in ways that honor both their integrity and their strategic goals. Without this understanding, advisors risk misinterpreting hesitation as resistance instead of moral caution.

Psychologically, ethical conversations create space for authenticity. Stakeholders who feel safe voicing their concerns often make clearer, more grounded decisions. They feel more confident in their choices because those choices align with their personal values. This alignment reduces regret, increases commitment, and strengthens trust between the advisor and the stakeholder.

As Chapter 13 continues, the next sections explore other hidden drivers that shape decisions—identity, invisible costs, emotional logic, trust, and ambition. Together, these sections reveal the deeper human truths that guide organizational behavior, completing the most advanced layer of discovery in the book.

BONUS CHAPTER 3 - Section 2 - Professional Identity & Role-Driven Decision Questions

Every decision-maker carries a professional identity—a personal sense of who they are, who they want to be, and how they believe they should show up in their role. This identity acts as a quiet compass, shaping choices long before data or recommendations enter the conversation. Professional identity influences risk tolerance, communication style, priorities, pace, and even emotional responses to pressure or change. This section explores how identity drives decisions in ways stakeholders rarely articulate openly.

Strategically, identity alignment determines whether someone champions a decision or withdraws from it. If a decision supports how a stakeholder sees themselves—such as being a protector, innovator, stabilizer, problem-solver, or builder—they naturally lean in. If the decision threatens that identity, even unintentionally, friction surfaces. Advisors who understand a stakeholder's professional identity gain insight into motivations that no spreadsheet or org chart can reveal.

Psychologically, identity ties deeply to self-worth, pride, reputational concerns, and emotional safety. People make decisions not only for the organization, but for the story they want to tell about themselves. They want to feel competent, respected, valued, and aligned with their personal standards. When a decision threatens those internal narratives—like exposing a gap, creating risk, or shifting responsibility—individuals may hesitate, resist, or seek reassurance.

Interpretation Tip: Listen for identity-defining language such as "I'm the kind of person who…," "My job is to protect…," "I always make sure…," or "I see myself as…." These statements hint at internal narratives that shape their choices. Identity-driven decisions are rarely about the task—they are about the meaning behind the task.

Coaching Note: Approach identity with respect and curiosity. Professional identity can be a point of pride or vulnerability. Invite exploration without telling people who they are or how they should feel. Your tone should help them articulate their internal expectations clearly, without pressure or judgment.

Example phrasing:

- *"How does this decision connect to the role you see yourself playing in the organization?"*

- *"Where does your professional identity guide your choices here?"*

Standard Professional Identity Questions (8)

Tone: warm, curious, supportive.

1. "How do you describe your role when you're at your best?"

2. "What part of your work feels most aligned with who you are?"

3. "Where do you feel most confident in your responsibilities?"

4. "Which decisions feel natural for you to lead?"

5. "Where do you want to make the greatest impact?"

6. "Which strengths define you professionally?"

7. "Where do you feel your role brings out your best qualities?"

8. "Which responsibilities feel most connected to your values?"

Intermediate Professional Identity Questions (9)

Tone: thoughtful, probing, identity-aware.

1. "Where does your role shape how you evaluate this decision?"

2. "Which expectations influence how you show up as a leader?"

3. "Where do you feel the weight of responsibility most strongly?"

4. "Which tasks challenge your sense of identity?"

5. "Where do you feel stretched beyond how you naturally operate?"

6. "Which parts of your identity guide your risk tolerance?"

7. "Where do you feel your contributions are misunderstood or undervalued?"

8. "Which expectations conflict with how you see yourself professionally?"

9. "Where does this decision support—or disrupt—the role you want to play?"

Aggressive Professional Identity Questions (8)

Tone: direct, courageous, identity-revealing.

1. "What part of this decision threatens your sense of professional identity?"

2. "Where do you feel pressure to be someone you're not?"

3. "Which expectation feels unfair given the role you actually play?"

4. "Where do you carry responsibility that others don't recognize?"

5. "What part of this decision challenges your confidence the most?"

6. "Where are you expected to lead without being given authority?"

7. "Which part of your identity are you trying to protect in this process?"

8. "Where do you feel unseen for the role you truly play in this organization?"

Follow-Up Professional Identity Questions (10)

Tone: reflective, empathetic, grounding.

1. "Can you recall a moment when you felt fully aligned with your role?"

2. "What made that moment meaningful for you?"

3. "Can you think of a time when identity tension affected a decision?"

4. "What did that experience teach you about yourself?"

5. "What helps you feel grounded in who you are when pressure rises?"

6. "How do you want others to perceive your leadership or contribution?"

7. "What part of your identity do you want to strengthen moving forward?"

8. "What boundaries help you maintain integrity within your role?"

9. "What kind of support helps you show up as your best self?"

10. "How do you want your professional identity to influence this decision?"

Conclusion

Professional identity is one of the most powerful—yet least discussed—drivers of decision-making. When advisors understand how individuals see themselves, they gain a deeper view into motivation, resistance, ambition, and fear. Identity influences how stakeholders communicate, what they prioritize, and what they avoid. Ignoring identity means missing the emotional core of decision behavior.

Strategically, identity insights help advisors tailor conversations to match the stakeholder's internal compass. When recommendations resonate with identity, decisions become easier, more confident, and more energized. When identity feels threatened, even strong business cases encounter friction. Knowing this difference allows advisors to position solutions in ways that reinforce, rather than challenge, the stakeholder's sense of self.

Psychologically, identity-based discovery builds trust. It gives stakeholders space to articulate who they are, what they value, and how they want to contribute. This creates a deeper connection and a more honest dialogue. People make clearer decisions when they feel understood—not only for their role, but for their identity within it.

As Chapter 13 continues, the next section explores invisible costs—the burdens organizations feel but rarely name. These hidden pressures shape momentum just as strongly as identity and ethics, and uncovering them strengthens your understanding of the deeper forces at play.

BONUS CHAPTER 3 - Section 3 - Invisible Cost & Hidden Burden Questions

Every organization carries costs that do not appear on financial statements—costs that drain energy, slow progress, and quietly shape decisions. These invisible costs include emotional exhaustion, frustration, lost time, damaged trust, unclear communication, reputation risk, and the silent weight of chronic inefficiency. Because these burdens are not easily quantified, stakeholders rarely discuss them openly. Yet these hidden pressures influence decisions as strongly as budgets or deadlines. This section helps bring those costs into the light.

Strategically, invisible costs often determine whether an initiative feels necessary, overdue, or avoidable. When hidden burdens rise, leaders become more receptive to change—even if surface-level metrics look stable. When burdens are unacknowledged, resistance grows because the true strain is not recognized. Advisors who uncover invisible costs gain a clearer understanding of why progress feels easy or difficult, even when the "official" reasoning seems unrelated.

Psychologically, hidden burdens shape emotional bandwidth. People tolerate inefficiency for a while, but eventually these quiet pressures become distracting or demotivating. Some stakeholders absorb stress silently out of loyalty or habit. Others carry emotional weight because they feel responsible for fixing what isn't theirs to solve. Understanding these internal burdens helps advisors interpret tone, hesitation, clarity, and urgency more accurately.

Interpretation Tip: Listen for soft statements like "it's fine," "we make it work," "it's not a big deal," or "we manage." These phrases often mask deeper costs people are used to tolerating. Invisible burdens become normalized over time, and stakeholders may need supportive questioning to articulate them clearly.

Coaching Note: Approach invisible costs with empathy and patience. These burdens often involve frustration, disappointment, or emotional fatigue. Your tone should help stakeholders feel safe admitting what they've been carrying—sometimes for years. You're not just uncovering obstacles; you're validating the human experience behind them.

Example phrasing:

- *"Where does this current approach cost more energy than it appears on the surface?"*

- *"What hidden burdens affect your team that don't show up in reports?"*

Standard Invisible Cost & Hidden Burden Questions (8)

Tone: calm, empathetic, uncovering.

1. "Where does extra effort go unnoticed in your daily work?"

2. "Which tasks take more energy than people realize?"

3. "Where do you see small inefficiencies adding up over time?"

4. "Which responsibilities feel heavier than they appear on paper?"

5. "Where does communication require more work than it should?"

6. "Which processes create subtle frustration for your team?"

7. "Where are people silently carrying additional workload?"

8. "Which issues drain time even though they look minor from the outside?"

Intermediate Invisible Cost & Hidden Burden Questions (9)

Tone: probing, clarifying, weight-revealing.

1. "Where do invisible costs impact performance or morale?"

2. "Which recurring issues create emotional strain or fatigue?"

3. "Where does the team feel overextended even when metrics seem stable?"

4. "Which inefficiencies have become 'normal' but still drain energy?"

5. "Where do internal expectations create quiet pressure?"

6. "Which tasks are performed only because no one has challenged their necessity?"

7. "Where are people absorbing stress that leadership doesn't see?"

8. "Which responsibilities are taking more than they give back?"

9. "Where are hidden burdens shaping decisions behind the scenes?"

Aggressive Invisible Cost & Hidden Burden Questions (8)

Tone: bold, truth-seeking, pressure-releasing.

1. "What hidden cost is wearing your team down the most?"

2. "Which burden has been tolerated for far too long?"

3. "Where are people quietly burning out?"

4. "Which problem is draining energy but rarely discussed openly?"

5. "Where does the real cost differ sharply from the reported cost?"

6. "What inefficiency do people complain about privately but ignore publicly?"

7. "Which invisible burden would disappear if people felt empowered to address it?"

8. "Where are you sacrificing more than the organization realizes?"

Follow-Up Invisible Cost & Hidden Burden Questions (10)

Tone: reflective, supportive, air-clearing.

1. "Can you recall a time when an invisible burden finally became visible?"

2. "What changed once it was acknowledged?"

3. "Can you describe a hidden cost that went unaddressed for too long?"

4. "What did that experience teach you?"

5. "What signs help you recognize when invisible burdens are rising?"

6. "What type of support helps reduce hidden strain?"

7. "What small changes would relieve pressure for your team?"

8. "What would progress look like if these invisible costs decreased?"

9. "What would help make hidden burdens easier to discuss internally?"

10. "How do you want your team to feel when dealing with these challenges?"

Conclusion

Invisible costs are among the most powerful forces shaping organizational behavior. They drain energy quietly, distort decision-making, and influence emotional readiness long before a formal decision is made. Advisors who surface these hidden burdens gain access to a layer of truth that stakeholders rarely express without thoughtful prompting. When invisible costs become visible, clarity improves and progress accelerates.

Strategically, understanding hidden burdens helps advisors pinpoint the true causes behind slowdowns, resistance, or burnout. These costs often explain why teams appear functional on the surface yet struggle to maintain momentum. By identifying invisible strain, advisors can position their solutions as relief—not just improvement. This reframes the initiative as a source of energy rather than another demand.

Psychologically, acknowledging hidden burdens gives stakeholders validation. It grants permission to express frustration they have been carrying silently. This emotional release often builds trust, reduces defensiveness, and makes individuals more open to change. When people feel seen, they feel lighter—and lighter teams make clearer decisions.

As Chapter 13 continues, the next section explores momentum and stagnation patterns—the rhythms that determine how organizations move when facing opportunity or challenge. Together, these sections reveal forces that operate beneath the surface but drive outcomes more strongly than formal processes ever could.

BONUS CHAPTER 3 - Section 4 -Momentum & Stagnation Pattern Questions

Introduction

Every organization has a rhythm—a natural way it speeds up, slows down, circles back, or gets stuck. These patterns show up in how teams adopt new ideas, manage conflict, execute priorities, and respond to uncertainty. Some teams move quickly when clarity appears but stall when alignment lags. Others surge forward during urgency but lose energy once pressure fades. These patterns often operate beneath awareness, yet they shape nearly every important decision.

Strategically, momentum patterns reveal how the organization behaves under real conditions—not ideal ones. Advisors who understand these rhythms can predict decision speed, anticipate stalls, and identify when momentum is rising or slipping. Stagnation patterns, on the other hand, point to where the organization routinely hesitates: approvals, communication gaps, leadership alignment, unclear ownership, or fear of disruption. These insights help advisors plan interactions and recommendations with much greater precision.

Psychologically, momentum ties to emotions—excitement, confidence, relief, frustration, doubt, and fatigue. Stagnation often reflects fear of being wrong, fear of conflict, or the comfort of routine. People move faster when they feel safe, supported, and aligned. They stall when uncertainty feels heavy, when responsibilities are unclear, or when emotional energy is low. Understanding these emotional currents helps advisors interpret pauses and progress more accurately.

Interpretation Tip: Pay attention to the words stakeholders use to describe pace: "we're circling again," "we lost steam," "we're finally moving," or "we got stuck." These phrases reveal more than status—they reveal patterns. Momentum and stagnation rarely happen randomly. They repeat until identified.

Coaching Note: Approach momentum discussions without judgment. These patterns are normal and often rooted in survival instincts. Your goal is to help the stakeholder notice the pattern—not feel blamed for it. When they see their own rhythm, they gain the ability to shift it intentionally.

Example phrasing:

- *"Where does your team naturally move quickly?"*

- *"Where does momentum stall, even when the goal is clear?"*

Standard Momentum & Stagnation Questions (8)

Tone: observational, curious, neutral.

1. "Where does your team usually build momentum easily?"

2. "Which types of projects tend to move forward without friction?"

3. "Where do decisions flow smoothly from idea to action?"

4. "Which responsibilities consistently get done on time?"

5. "Where do you notice progress happening without much effort?"

6. "Which processes feel steady and predictable?"

7. "Where does early clarity lead to quick movement?"

8. "Which situations bring out your team's best pace?"

Intermediate Momentum & Stagnation Questions (9)

Tone: probing, pattern-seeking, honest.

1. "Where does momentum slow down, even when priorities are clear?"

2. "Which steps in your process create repeated stalls?"

3. "Where do approval cycles disrupt progress?"

4. "Which tasks get delayed most often—and why?"

5. "Where does misalignment consistently reduce speed?"

6. "Which moments make the team hesitate before acting?"

7. "Where does momentum depend too heavily on a single person?"

8. "Which patterns of stagnation have become predictable?"

9. "Where does the organization confuse motion with progress?"

Aggressive Momentum & Stagnation Questions (8)

Tone: direct, courageous, clarity-demanding.

1. "What pattern of stagnation has everyone accepted but no one addressed?"

2. "Where does your team lose momentum for reasons no one names?"

3. "Which decision gets stuck in endless loops?"

4. "Where does fear—not strategy—cause slowdown?"

5. "Which internal behavior repeatedly drains momentum?"

6. "Where would momentum skyrocket if one blocker disappeared?"

7. "Which part of your process is so slow it feels unacceptable?"

8. "Where does progress collapse the moment pressure fades?"

Follow-Up Momentum & Stagnation Questions (10)

Tone: reflective, validating, insight-deepening.

1. "Can you recall a time when your team built strong momentum quickly?"

2. "What conditions helped that happen?"

3. "Can you think of a moment when stagnation became obvious?"

4. "What triggered that stall?"

5. "What patterns have been consistent across past initiatives?"

6. "What emotional cues signal that momentum is rising or falling?"

7. "What support helps your team move through hesitation?"

8. "What early actions help prevent stagnation before it starts?"

9. "What would it look like if your team shifted its momentum pattern intentionally?"

10. "How do you want momentum to feel during upcoming decisions?"

Conclusion

Momentum and stagnation patterns reveal how an organization actually behaves—not how it claims to behave. These rhythms determine project speed, decision clarity, and the overall experience of working inside the organization. Advisors who understand these patterns can anticipate movement, read emotional signals more accurately, and support stakeholders in shifting their approach when needed.

Strategically, these insights expose the true pacing mechanisms inside the organization. Some slowdowns are structural; others are emotional. Some momentum is driven by clear priorities; other momentum evaporates when uncertainty appears. Knowing these distinctions allows advisors to tailor their guidance to the team's natural rhythm instead of fighting against it.

Psychologically, momentum ties heavily to emotional readiness and confidence. When teams feel aligned, supported, and energized, momentum builds. When teams feel stretched, uncertain, or unprotected, stagnation rises. Helping stakeholders name these rhythms creates self-awareness that often leads to healthier decisions and smoother execution.

As Chapter 13 continues, the next section explores decision regret and emotional memory—the powerful forces that shape how people respond to new choices based on past experiences. This deepens the understanding of how history influences behavior in the present.

BONUS CHAPTER 3 - Section 5 - Decision Regret, Lessons & Emotional Memory Questions

Introduction

Every decision-maker carries a history of past choices—some that worked well and others that left emotional marks. These past experiences create "decision memory," a lens through which stakeholders view new opportunities. Decisions that ended badly often create caution, fear, or skepticism. Decisions that went well create confidence, speed, and openness. This section explores how past decisions, emotional memory, and unspoken regret shape current behavior more than people realize.

Strategically, decision history affects pacing, advocacy, and risk tolerance. Stakeholders who have been burned in the past often hesitate even when conditions are favorable. Those who have experienced success may push forward more aggressively than circumstances justify. Advisors who understand the emotional residue from past decisions gain the ability to interpret behavior with nuance rather than judgment. They can also anticipate where a stakeholder may need reassurance, clarity, or a different type of support.

Psychologically, regret plays a powerful role. It can create overcorrection, indecision, or persistent doubt. Some stakeholders carry quiet embarrassment about decisions that failed. Others hold onto pride from decisions that went well. These emotional anchors shape their identity, confidence, and internal narratives. Emotional memory is not about the facts—it's about how past outcomes made them feel. Understanding this emotional history is essential for uncovering deeper motivations and fears.

Interpretation Tip: Listen for coded language like "we tried that once," "we don't want to repeat mistakes," "last time was painful," or "we learned a few lessons." These statements are often small windows into much bigger emotional experiences. Stakeholders rarely reveal decision regrets directly—they hint at them indirectly.

Coaching Note: Approach decision history with compassion. Past failures often represent moments of vulnerability. Your tone should acknowledge the emotional reality without dwelling on blame. The goal is not to revisit the past, but to understand how the past shapes the present.

Example phrasing:

- *"Which past decisions still influence how you think about this situation today?"*

- *"What experiences taught you something important about how you approach new initiatives?"*

Standard Decision Regret & Emotional Memory Questions (8)

Tone: gentle, reflective, open.

1. "Which past decisions taught your team something meaningful?"

2. "Where have previous choices shaped your approach today?"

3. "What past experiences influence how you evaluate opportunities?"

4. "Where did a previous decision work out better than expected?"

5. "Which lessons from past projects guide you now?"

6. "Where have past wins built confidence in your team?"

7. "What positive experience do you hope to repeat?"

8. "Which past outcomes continue to shape expectations?"

Intermediate Decision Regret & Emotional Memory Questions (9)

Tone: probing, curious, insight-driven.

1. "Where did a past decision create frustration or disappointment?"

2. "Which missteps taught you something important about your process?"

3. "Where do you see caution today because of something that happened before?"

4. "Which past choices would you approach differently now?"

5. "Where did expectations fail to match reality in a previous initiative?"

6. "Which emotional experiences—positive or negative—still influence your approach?"

7. "Where did communication break down in past decisions?"

8. "Which decisions created lasting impact, good or bad?"

9. "Where do you feel pressure not to repeat a previous mistake?"

Aggressive Decision Regret & Emotional Memory Questions (8)

Tone: direct, honest, emotionally revealing (still respectful).

1. "Which past decision still creates regret for you today?"

2. "Where did a previous choice damage trust or confidence?"

3. "Which decision felt like a failure—even if others moved on?"

4. "Where did you feel responsible for an outcome that didn't go well?"

5. "What experience still shapes your caution more than it should?"

6. "Which painful moment changed the way you approach risk?"

7. "Where did you feel misunderstood or unsupported during a major decision?"

8. "Which past regret silently influences your behavior now?"

Follow-Up Decision Regret & Emotional Memory Questions (10)

Tone: grounding, healing, clarifying.

1. "Can you describe the moment you realized that decision was going off track?"

2. "What emotions were present in that situation?"

3. "How did the team respond to the fallout?"

4. "What did that experience teach you about communication or clarity?"

5. "How do you evaluate risk differently now because of that moment?"

6. "What helped you recover confidence after a difficult decision?"

7. "Which strengths emerged from the experience, even if it was painful?"

8. "What reassurance helps you move forward when the past feels heavy?"

9. "What steps prevent old patterns from repeating today?"

10. "How do you want your past experiences to shape the next decision—in a positive way?"

Conclusion

Decision regret and emotional memory shape far more than most leaders acknowledge. These experiences influence how stakeholders interpret risk, approach collaboration, and respond to opportunities. Advisors who understand these emotional histories create space for clarity, healing, and more grounded decision-making. Without recognizing decision memory, it's easy to misinterpret hesitation as resistance rather than caution shaped by experience.

Strategically, uncovering past experiences allows advisors to design conversations that address emotional truths. They can help stakeholders avoid repeating harmful patterns and reinforce positive ones. When advisors understand what worked and what hurt, they gain insight into how to position new initiatives in ways that feel safe, meaningful, and aligned with the stakeholder's history.

Psychologically, acknowledging past regret creates emotional release. Many decision-makers carry burdens silently because they fear appearing weak or responsible. When advisors make space for honest reflection, stakeholders often reconnect with confidence, clarity, and hope. This fosters courage and momentum for future decisions.

As Bonus Chapter 3 continues, the next section explores ownership and accountability—the forces that determine who feels responsible, who steps forward, and who steps back when decisions matter most. Together, these sections reveal deep emotional architecture that shapes real-world outcomes.

BONUS CHAPTER 3 - SECTION 6 - Ownership, Accountability & Responsibility Clarity Questions

Introduction

Ownership is the backbone of execution. No matter how strong a strategy appears, no initiative survives without clear responsibility. Yet in many organizations, ownership is murky. People assume someone else is handling a task, wait for direction, or avoid taking charge because the lines of accountability feel risky or unclear. This section helps reveal who truly feels responsible, who is uncertain, and where accountability breaks down behind the scenes.

Strategically, ownership clarity determines progress speed, decision quality, and follow-through. When responsibility is well-defined, teams move with confidence and purpose. When responsibility is scattered or unspoken, even small tasks become complicated. Advisors who understand real ownership—not the theoretical version on the org chart—gain insight into where decisions may stall, who controls momentum, and where alignment must be strengthened.

Psychologically, ownership carries emotional weight. Some stakeholders step forward naturally because responsibility empowers them. Others hesitate because ownership exposes them to judgment, pressure, or the potential for failure. Still others take on too much because they fear letting people down or believe no one else will do it "right." Understanding these emotional dynamics helps advisors interpret behavior more accurately and respond with empathy.

Interpretation Tip: Listen for statements like "that's not really my area," "I help where I can," "we all own it," or "leadership decides that." These phrases often reveal diffusion, avoidance, or confusion about responsibility. Ownership is rarely as clear as organizations claim. Genuine ownership reveals itself through consistency, voice, and commitment—not job titles.

Coaching Note: Approach ownership conversations with neutrality, not accusation. The goal is not to assign blame but to understand structure, comfort, and expectations. Your tone should help stakeholders explore their role honestly without fear of being judged or pressured.

Example phrasing:

- *"Who feels most responsible for moving this forward?"*

- *"Where does ownership feel clear—and where does it feel uncertain?"*

Standard Ownership & Accountability Questions (8)

Tone: clarifying, steady, neutral.

1. "Where is ownership already clear for this initiative?"

2. "Which responsibilities are well-defined today?"

3. "Where do you feel confident in your role in this process?"

4. "Who typically takes charge when decisions need to be made?"

5. "Where do teams collaborate well without confusion?"

6. "Which tasks naturally fall into place?"

7. "Where does accountability feel strongest within your group?"

8. "Which responsibilities match your strengths and expectations?"

Intermediate Ownership & Accountability Questions (9)

Tone: probing, honest, structure-revealing.

1. "Where does ownership become unclear during execution?"

2. "Which responsibilities feel shared but not truly assigned?"

3. "Where do tasks fall through the cracks?"

4. "Which decisions lack a clear owner today?"

5. "Where does communication break down around who is responsible?"

6. "Which steps depend on people who are already overloaded?"

7. "Where is accountability uneven across teams or leaders?"

8. "Which responsibilities feel unfairly distributed?"

9. "Where would clarity reduce confusion or hesitation?"

Aggressive Ownership & Accountability Questions (8)

Tone: direct, truth-seeking, disruption-friendly.

1. "Who claims ownership publicly but avoids it privately?"

2. "Where is responsibility intentionally avoided?"

3. "Which critical task has no real owner—even though everyone assumes it does?"

4. "Where does leadership expect accountability without providing authority?"

5. "What responsibility are you being asked to own without proper support?"

6. "Who steps back when pressure rises, leaving others to carry the load?"

7. "Which part of this initiative fails because accountability is fragmented?"

8. "Where does confusion around ownership create the highest risk?"

Follow-Up Ownership & Accountability Questions (10)

Tone: reflective, stabilizing, reinforcing clarity.

1. "Can you recall a time when ownership was perfectly clear and things moved smoothly?"

2. "What made that situation work so well?"

3. "Can you think of a time when lack of ownership caused frustration?"

4. "What was the emotional impact of that moment?"

5. "How do you recognize when ownership is starting to drift?"

6. "What helps you feel confident in taking responsibility?"

7. "What support strengthens your ability to own a decision?"

8. "What boundaries help prevent responsibility overload?"

9. "How can ownership be shared without creating confusion?"

10. "What would clarity around roles change for the team moving forward?"

Conclusion

Ownership is one of the most underestimated forces behind execution. Without clear responsibility, even the best strategies lose momentum. Stakeholders may hesitate, duplicate effort, or wait for direction they assume someone else will provide. Advisors who uncover true ownership gain a more accurate and honest view of how decisions will unfold in real conditions—not ideal ones.

Strategically, ownership insights reveal where alignment, process, or leadership clarity needs strengthening. When advisors understand who truly governs movement within the organization, they can position solutions in a way that aligns with power dynamics, workload, confidence levels, and resource realities. This leads to smoother adoption, faster progress, and less friction.

Psychologically, ownership touches core human themes—pride, fear, accountability, validation, pressure, and self-protection. Some stakeholders embrace responsibility; others avoid it for reasons tied to identity, past experiences, or emotional safety. Acknowledging these factors helps advisors support people in ways that honor both competency and well-being.

As Chapter 13 continues, the next section explores trust and psychological safety—forces that determine whether stakeholders speak honestly, raise concerns early, and collaborate openly. Together, these deep-structure drivers reveal the emotional architecture behind organizational behavior.

BONUS CHAPTER 3 - Section 7 - Trust & Psychological Safety Questions

Trust is the foundation that determines how openly people communicate, how quickly they move, and how honestly they share concerns. When trust is strong, conversations flow freely, challenges surface early, and decisions feel collaborative. When trust is weak, people hold back. They hide doubts, soften criticism, filter truth, and avoid difficult topics. Psychological safety—the sense that speaking up won't lead to embarrassment, conflict, or punishment—shapes the quality of every conversation inside an organization.

Strategically, trust affects alignment, speed, and decision quality. A team that lacks psychological safety will not raise risks early, even when those risks jeopardize the initiative. They avoid conflict to maintain harmony, which ironically leads to bigger issues later. In contrast, high-trust environments share information quickly and transparently, leading to stronger decisions and smoother execution. Advisors who understand trust dynamics can anticipate where communication blocks or hidden resistance may appear.

Psychologically, trust reflects emotional vulnerability. People decide whether to share openly based on past experiences, team culture, and perceived judgment from others. Some individuals speak freely because they feel safe. Others hesitate because past conversations taught them that honesty carries consequences. These emotional memories shape the entire decision process—often without stakeholders realizing it.

Interpretation Tip: Listen for phrases like "I don't want to step on toes," "this stays between us," "we have to be careful," or "I can't say that in a bigger meeting." These statements reveal trust levels more accurately than formal descriptions of "culture" ever will. Psychological safety shows up in tone, hesitation, and what people *don't* say.

Coaching Note: Create a space where honesty feels welcome. Trust-related conversations must feel supportive, not exposing. Your tone should communicate confidentiality, curiosity, and respect. When people sense psychological safety with you, they will share truths they don't share internally.

Example phrasing:

- *"Where do people feel safe speaking openly—and where do they hold back?"*

- *"How much trust exists within the group making this decision?"*

Standard Trust & Psychological Safety Questions (8)

Tone: warm, safe, inviting open expression.

1. "Where does your team communicate openly and comfortably?"

2. "Which relationships support honest conversations?"

3. "Where do you see strong levels of trust inside the group?"

4. "Which team members feel safe raising difficult topics?"

5. "Where does transparency come naturally?"

6. "Which discussions feel productive and respectful?"

7. "Where do you sense emotional security within the team?"

8. "Which environments encourage thoughtful dialogue?"

Intermediate Trust & Psychological Safety Questions (9)

Tone: probing, calm, insight-seeking.

1. "Where does the team hold back from being fully honest?"

2. "Which discussions feel tense or guarded?"

3. "Where does fear of judgment influence communication?"

4. "Which roles or personalities affect psychological safety the most?"

5. "Where do people hesitate before raising concerns?"

6. "Which past experiences shaped current trust levels?"

7. "Where does conflict avoidance limit progress?"

8. "Which decisions require higher trust than currently exists?"

9. "Where does the team rely on informal conversations to stay aligned?"

Aggressive Trust & Psychological Safety Questions (8)

Tone: direct, courage-inducing, truth-seeking (still safe).

1. "Where do people pretend to agree because they don't feel safe disagreeing?"

2. "Which individual makes honesty difficult for others?"

3. "Where does your team hide problems until they become urgent?"

4. "What truth is never spoken in group settings but discussed privately?"

5. "Where does fear—not respect—shape how people communicate?"

6. "Which leadership behaviors erode psychological safety?"

7. "Where do people change their tone depending on who is in the room?"

8. "What topic would dramatically improve things if it could be discussed openly?"

Follow-Up Trust & Psychological Safety Questions (10)

Tone: reflective, grounding, relationship-focused.

1. "Can you recall a moment when honesty led to a positive outcome?"

2. "What made that conversation feel safe?"

3. "Can you think of a time when lack of trust caused unnecessary stress?"

4. "What was the emotional impact of that moment?"

5. "How does the team respond when someone raises a difficult concern?"

6. "What helps people feel heard and respected?"

7. "What builds trust most effectively within this group?"

8. "What erodes trust quickly?"

9. "What would psychological safety look like during future decisions?"

10. "How do you want communication to feel moving forward?"

Conclusion

Trust and psychological safety determine the emotional climate of decision-making. Without them, even highly skilled teams struggle. People withhold information, soften truth, or stay silent to avoid conflict. Advisors who understand these dynamics can identify hidden barriers earlier and help create a space where honest conversations become possible. Trust is not an accessory—it is a structural component of effective decision-making.

Strategically, trust affects speed, alignment, and execution quality. Teams with low trust move cautiously and unpredictably. Teams with high trust move confidently and collaboratively.

Understanding trust levels allows advisors to navigate interactions with precision, knowing when to push, when to support, and when to slow down to rebuild safety.

Psychologically, trust reflects emotional security. People contribute more openly when they feel respected, protected, and valued. By creating a safe conversational environment, advisors give stakeholders permission to express concerns they have never voiced. This honesty leads to better decisions, deeper alignment, and stronger outcomes.

As Chapter 13 continues, the next section explores Emotional Logic—the inner reasoning patterns that guide decisions before logic is even applied. Understanding how feelings shape choices strengthens your ability to interpret motivations and anticipate behavior.

BONUS CHAPTER 3 - Section 8 - Emotional Logic & Feeling-Based Decision Questions

Introduction

Every decision contains two layers: the logical explanation and the emotional truth underneath it. People use logic to justify choices, but they use emotion to *make* them. Emotional logic is the internal reasoning people use to interpret risk, meaning, and direction. It shapes how decisions feel, not just how they appear on paper. This section uncovers the emotional drivers that influence confidence, hesitation, urgency, and the overall comfort someone has with a given path.

Strategically, emotional logic reveals why traditional business justifications—such as ROI, efficiency, or deadlines—do not always move people. Advisors often assume that a clear business case should create alignment, but stakeholders respond based on how a decision feels: safe or risky, aligned or uncomfortable, exciting or overwhelming. Understanding emotional logic helps advisors position decisions in ways that resonate with the stakeholder's personal sense of security, identity, and values.

Psychologically, emotional logic forms from past experiences, self-perception, organizational culture, and internal narratives. Some stakeholders prioritize harmony because conflict feels threatening. Others favor speed because stagnation feels intolerable. Some avoid risk because past failure carries emotional weight. Others embrace bold action because it aligns with how they see themselves. These emotional patterns shape every decision they make—even if they cannot fully articulate them.

Interpretation Tip: Listen for emotional clues hidden inside logical statements. Phrases like "this just feels risky," "I'm not sure about this," "something seems off," or "that feels right" reveal emotional logic at work. Emotions often appear subtly—in the tone, the pace of speech, or the moments where someone pauses before answering.

Coaching Note: Approach emotional reasoning with respect. Emotions are not weaknesses— they are signals. Your goal is not to "correct" emotional logic, but to understand it. When people feel seen emotionally, they become more open, honest, and confident in their choices.

Example phrasing:

- *"How does this decision feel to you—not just logically, but personally?"*

- *"Where do emotions influence how you interpret this situation?"*

Standard Emotional Logic Questions (8)

Tone: warm, calm, personally reflective.

1. "How does this decision feel to you right now?"

2. "Where do you feel confident about the path ahead?"

3. "Which aspects feel comfortable and clear?"

4. "Where does this decision feel aligned with what you value?"

5. "Which outcomes feel emotionally meaningful to you?"

6. "Where do you feel steady about your next steps?"

7. "What part of this feels reassuring?"

8. "Where does this choice feel like a natural fit?"

Intermediate Emotional Logic Questions (9)

Tone: probing, compassionate, insight-focused.

1. "Where do emotions influence your comfort with this decision?"

2. "Which parts feel uncertain or uneasy?"

3. "Where does past experience affect how you interpret this choice?"

4. "Which risks feel heavier emotionally than they look on paper?"

5. "Where do you feel pulled in two emotional directions at once?"

6. "Which expectations create emotional pressure for you?"

7. "Where does the decision feel big, even if the task is small?"

8. "Which outcomes would bring emotional relief if achieved?"

9. "Where do emotions slow down your decision-making?"

Aggressive Emotional Logic Questions (8)

Tone: direct, courageous, emotionally revealing.

1. "What emotional fear sits underneath your hesitation?"

2. "Where does this decision feel risky in a way you haven't said out loud?"

3. "Which past emotion is clouding your view of the present situation?"

4. "What feeling would you prefer to avoid as this decision unfolds?"

5. "Where do you feel protective of yourself or your team?"

6. "Which emotion makes this decision harder than it appears?"

7. "What emotional truth have you been softening in the conversation?"

8. "Where does this choice challenge how you want to feel at work?"

Follow-Up Emotional Logic Questions (10)

Tone: validating, grounding, helping people deepen emotional awareness.

1. "Can you recall a moment when following your emotional logic led to a good decision?"

2. "What made that moment feel right?"

3. "Can you describe a time when ignoring your emotional signals caused problems?"

4. "What did that teach you about listening to your intuition?"

5. "What emotions show up most often during high-stakes decisions?"

6. "How do you distinguish between helpful intuition and protective fear?"

7. "What emotional support helps you move forward when decisions feel heavy?"

8. "Which emotional cues tell you a decision is aligned with your values?"

9. "Which cues tell you something is off?"

10. "How do you want to feel as you move into the next phase of this decision?"

Conclusion

Emotional logic is one of the most important—and most overlooked—drivers of decision-making. Advisors often focus on data, processes, and outcomes, but decisions live in the emotional space between fear and confidence, uncertainty and clarity, safety and vulnerability. Understanding emotional logic allows advisors to interpret behavior accurately and respond with empathy and precision.

Strategically, these insights help advisors shape conversations that truly resonate. When they understand emotional drivers, they can position solutions in ways that feel safe, motivating, and aligned with the stakeholder's deeper values. Emotional clarity leads to stronger alignment, better pacing, and more sustainable decisions.

Psychologically, exploring emotional logic builds trust. Stakeholders feel validated and understood when their emotional reactions are acknowledged rather than dismissed. This opens the door to deeper truth-telling, more honest collaboration, and decisions made with confidence rather than pressure.

As Chapter 13 continues, the next section will explore Quiet Ambition & Unspoken Desire—the inner motivations people rarely share, yet rely on when deciding what truly matters to them.

BONUS CHAPTER 3 - Section 9 - Quiet Ambition & Unspoken Desire Questions

Introduction

Every stakeholder carries ambitions they rarely voice. Some aspirations feel too personal, too bold, or too politically sensitive to share openly. Others are held quietly because the stakeholder fears judgment, pushback, or unwanted attention. Quiet ambitions drive decisions subtly—they influence risk tolerance, preference, urgency, and the level of emotional investment a stakeholder feels. This section helps uncover the hidden desires that shape decision-making beneath the surface.

Strategically, unspoken desires can accelerate alignment or create invisible resistance. When a solution supports a stakeholder's personal ambition—such as gaining influence, building expertise, stabilizing their team, or elevating their reputation—they move faster and more decisively. When a solution threatens those ambitions or fails to support them, hesitation surfaces. Advisors who understand these hidden motivations gain access to a powerful predictor of stakeholder behavior.

Psychologically, ambition is tied to identity, self-worth, and personal meaning. Many people downplay their ambition because they fear appearing selfish or overly driven. Others hide their desires because past environments punished ambition. Some simply struggle to articulate what they want most. Quiet ambition often expresses itself through subtle cues: increased engagement, emotional energy, unusual hesitation, or deeper questioning.

Interpretation Tip: Listen for hints like "I've always wanted…," "Someday I hope…," "I don't usually talk about this, but…," or "If I'm honest…" These moments signal that a deeper ambition is present. Unspoken desire often appears in small disclosures rather than bold statements.

Coaching Note: Approach ambition with encouragement, not pressure. Many stakeholders guard their aspirations closely. Your tone should communicate that ambition is normal, valuable, and relevant—not something to hide. The goal is never to extract ambition, but to create a safe path for them to express it.

Example phrasing:

- *"What personal goal would feel meaningful for you as this decision unfolds?"*

- *"Where does this opportunity connect with something you want on a deeper level?"*

Standard Quiet Ambition Questions (8)

Tone: warm, curious, personal.

1. "What part of this opportunity feels personally meaningful to you?"

2. "Where do you want to grow professionally through this process?"

3. "Which outcomes align with what you hope to build for yourself?"

4. "Where does this decision connect with long-term goals you value?"

5. "Which responsibilities help you feel most fulfilled in your role?"

6. "Where do you want to make a lasting impact?"

7. "What strengths are you hoping to use more often?"

8. "Which contributions matter most to you personally?"

Intermediate Quiet Ambition Questions (9)

Tone: probing, supportive, insight-oriented.

1. "Which personal aspirations shape how you see this decision?"

2. "Where do you feel a pull toward greater responsibility or visibility?"

3. "What professional milestone does this opportunity help you move toward?"

4. "Which ambitions feel important but rarely get discussed?"

5. "Where do you wish you had more influence or ownership?"

6. "Which achievements would bring personal satisfaction beyond business results?"

7. "Where do you want your work to leave a stronger mark?"

8. "What role do personal goals play in how you evaluate risk?"

9. "Where do your hopes and the organization's goals naturally align?"

Aggressive Quiet Ambition Questions (8)

Tone: direct, courageous, truth-revealing (but respectful).

1. "What ambition do you rarely admit—even to yourself?"

2. "Where do you want increased authority but hesitate to say it?"

3. "Which goal feels too big or too personal to express openly at work?"

4. "Where do you want recognition that you aren't currently receiving?"

5. "What outcome would elevate your reputation in a meaningful way?"

6. "Where would success in this decision advance your personal path?"

7. "Which ambition scares you because you want it so deeply?"

8. "What desire influences your decisions, even if you never voice it?"

Follow-Up Quiet Ambition Questions (10)

Tone: reflective, safe, insight-deepening.

1. "Can you recall a moment when achieving a personal goal felt deeply rewarding?"

2. "What emotions were present in that moment?"

3. "What did that experience teach you about what you value?"

4. "How do you usually recognize when an ambition is guiding your choices?"

5. "What type of support helps you feel confident pursuing personal goals?"

6. "What fears surface when you think about expressing your ambitions openly?"

7. "Which parts of your ambition feel energizing?"

8. "Which parts feel vulnerable?"

9. "What would progress look like if you honored these ambitions more intentionally?"

10. "How do you want your personal goals to influence your next steps?"

Conclusion

Quiet ambition is one of the most powerful, yet hidden, drivers of decision behavior. It shapes how stakeholders interpret opportunities and risks, how quickly they move, and how emotionally invested they become. Advisors who uncover these deeper motivations gain access to a level of insight that transforms the quality of collaboration and communication.

Strategically, understanding ambition allows advisors to position solutions in ways that align with personal meaning. When recommendations match a stakeholder's unspoken desires, alignment strengthens and decisions accelerate. When ambition is ignored or misunderstood, friction appears, even if business logic seems clear.

Psychologically, ambition reflects identity, pride, confidence, and hope. By giving stakeholders permission to express their aspirations, advisors create space for honesty and empowerment. This strengthens trust and allows people to envision decisions not just as tasks, but as meaningful steps in their professional journey.

As Chapter 13 continues, the final section explores Organizational Energy & Capacity—the emotional "fuel levels" that determine how prepared a team is to take on new challenges. Together, these insights complete the deep-structure layer of your discovery ecosystem.

BONUS CHAPTER 3 - Section 10 - Organizational Energy & Capacity Questions

Introduction

Every organization operates with an emotional energy level—an internal "fuel tank" that influences how people think, respond, and take action. This organizational energy shifts based on workload, morale, clarity, conflict, recent wins, hidden stress, leadership dynamics, and internal culture. When energy is high, teams take initiative, collaborate smoothly, and embrace new opportunities. When energy is low, even simple tasks feel heavy. This section explores how emotional capacity shapes decision-making in ways that are rarely measured but strongly felt.

Strategically, organizational energy is directly tied to momentum, adoption, and execution. Advisors may present strong recommendations, backed by data and logic, only to discover that the team is too drained to move. Other times, teams push forward enthusiastically because the emotional climate supports action. Understanding the energy level behind a decision helps advisors anticipate speed, readiness, and how much support the team will need.

Psychologically, energy reflects emotional experience—stress, hope, frustration, pride, confusion, optimism. People can only sustain so much change before fatigue sets in. When energy is depleted, teams become reactive rather than proactive. They avoid innovation, resist responsibility, and retreat into familiar routines. When energy is strong, they lean into learning, take healthy risks, and collaborate with enthusiasm.

Interpretation Tip: Notice when stakeholders laugh lightly about being "spread thin," or when they say "we're doing our best," "we're trying to keep up," or "it's been a long season." These statements reveal emotional and energetic strain. Energy is often felt in tone first, long before anyone admits it directly.

Coaching Note: Approach energy questions with empathy. Emotional capacity is not a weakness—it is a signal that the team needs alignment, recovery, or support. Your tone should give stakeholders permission to be honest without fear of appearing resistant or uncommitted. Energy-focused discovery often brings relief because it acknowledges what people have been quietly carrying.

Example phrasing:

- *"Where does the team feel energized right now?"*

- *"Where does the workload feel heavier than the organization admits?"*

Standard Organizational Energy Questions (8)

Tone: calm, observational, supportive.

1. "Where does your team feel energized at the moment?"

2. "Which responsibilities feel manageable and steady?"

3. "Where is the group working with good rhythm and confidence?"

4. "Which projects bring the team a sense of momentum?"

5. "Where does communication feel smooth and reliable?"

6. "Which areas feel emotionally stable right now?"

7. "Where do people seem engaged and interested?"

8. "Which tasks feel easy for the team to handle?"

Intermediate Organizational Energy Questions (9)

Tone: probing, grounded, honest.

1. "Where does the team feel stretched or fatigued?"

2. "Which tasks require more energy than expected?"

3. "Where does workload create emotional strain?"

4. "Which projects feel heavier than their size suggests?"

5. "Where does the team struggle to sustain momentum?"

6. "Which responsibilities drain energy more than they contribute?"

7. "Where does uncertainty reduce capacity to take on more?"

8. "Which moments reveal the team's current limits?"

9. "Where does emotional fatigue influence decision-making?"

Aggressive Organizational Energy Questions (8)

Tone: direct, bold, tension-revealing (but empathetic).

1. "Where is the team running on emotional fumes?"

2. "Which project should pause because the team doesn't have the capacity?"

3. "Where is burnout present but unspoken?"

4. "Which responsibilities are overwhelming the team the most?"

5. "Where is lack of energy sabotaging progress?"

6. "Who is carrying too much simply because no one else stepped in?"

7. "Which initiative would collapse without a few people overworking?"

8. "Where has the team quietly accepted an unsustainable workload?"

Follow-Up Organizational Energy Questions (10)

Tone: reflective, restorative, emotionally grounding.

1. "Can you recall a time when the team felt energized and connected?"

2. "What helped create that energy?"

3. "What past situations drained the team more than expected?"

4. "What warning signs appeared before energy dropped?"

5. "What helps the team recover emotional bandwidth?"

6. "Which leaders or behaviors restore energy rather than drain it?"

7. "What small changes would lighten emotional load right now?"

8. "What would momentum feel like if the team rested or realigned?"

9. "How can energy levels be protected during upcoming decisions?"

10. "What does a healthy, energized team look like to you?"

Conclusion

Organizational energy is one of the most accurate predictors of whether decisions will gain traction. Advisors who ignore emotional capacity may overestimate readiness and misunderstand hesitation as resistance. But when advisors understand energy levels, they see the truth behind pacing, adoption, and execution. Energy is not a soft concept—it is a core operational reality.

Strategically, energy insights help advisors match their recommendations to the team's emotional bandwidth. They can introduce new ideas at the right moment, adjust pacing, or provide additional support when capacity is low. This increases adoption and reduces friction. When energy is high, advisors can help stakeholders channel that momentum into decisions that matter most.

Psychologically, acknowledging energy honors the human side of work. Teams are made of people with limits, emotions, and needs—not machines. When stakeholders feel seen, they become more open, more honest, and more engaged. Energy-focused discovery builds trust by validating the emotional reality of organizational life.

With this section, Chapter 13 reaches its full depth. You have now explored the most powerful hidden drivers behind decision-making: ethics, identity, invisible cost, momentum, emotional memory, ownership, trust, emotional logic, ambition, and energy. Together, these layers reveal the complete emotional architecture that shapes organizational behavior.

BONUS CHAPTER 3 — Conclusion

Bonus Chapter 3 completes the deepest layer of discovery by revealing the emotional, ethical, and psychological architecture behind human decision-making. Throughout these sections, the questions guided stakeholders gently toward truth—truth about what pressures them, motivates them, scares them, inspires them, and shapes their choices. When advisors understand these hidden forces, they gain a far clearer understanding of why decisions accelerate, stall, or shift unexpectedly.

Strategically, these insights strengthen every part of the discovery process. Ethical pressure explains caution. Identity explains personal investment. Invisible costs explain fatigue. Momentum patterns explain pacing. Emotional memory explains sensitivity. Ownership reveals risk. Trust explains communication gaps. Emotional logic reveals reasoning. Ambition exposes direction. And organizational energy reveals readiness. Together, these layers provide the most complete context for decision behavior.

Psychologically, this chapter deepens empathy and expands emotional awareness. It helps advisors see stakeholders not as roles or titles but as people navigating complex internal landscapes. When advisors honor these inner realities, they build deeper trust, stronger alignment, and more meaningful collaboration. Decisions become less about persuasion and more about clarity.

The work of this chapter prepares the reader for the final chapter of the book—the formal unveiling of the Discovery Operating System. With a full understanding of the visible and hidden forces shaping decisions, the reader is now ready to learn the structure that underlies every question in this book and ties the entire discovery experience together with clarity and purpose.

Why Discovery Breaks (The Real Problem)

Discovery does not break down because salespeople or consultants ask poor questions. In fact, many professionals ask thoughtful, well-structured, and logically sound questions—yet still receive vague answers, partial truths, or polite deflection. The real failure point in discovery is not the quality of the question, but the **reaction the question triggers**. Questions often create perceived threat, and when threat appears, resistance follows.

Resistance is not a sign of unwillingness or bad intent. It is a protective response. People resist questions when they sense potential exposure, loss of control, judgment, obligation, or future commitment. A simple question can feel consequential if the answer implies responsibility, reveals uncertainty, challenges prior decisions, or narrows future options. As the importance of the decision increases, so does the emotional weight attached to each answer—and with it, the likelihood of resistance.

This is why discovery must be reframed. The objective is not to extract information as efficiently as possible. The objective is to create **permission** for honest information to emerge. Permission is earned when the other person feels safe, unpressured, and respected in how their answers will be used. Effective discovery is not about getting answers quickly; it is about creating the conditions where real answers are possible.

The Psychology of Resistance in Discovery

Every discovery question initiates a silent internal process long before an answer is given. While the words of the question may sound neutral, the listener is immediately evaluating what the question *means*, not just what it asks. This evaluation happens subconsciously and often within seconds, shaping whether the response will be open, guarded, or evasive.

The first evaluation is **intent**. The listener is asking, *"Why are you asking this?"* If the purpose of the question is unclear, the mind fills in the gap—often assuming judgment, manipulation, or pressure. When intent feels ambiguous or self-serving, resistance forms as a protective measure. Clear intent lowers threat; unclear intent amplifies it.

The second evaluation is **risk**. Here the listener asks, *"What happens if I answer honestly?"* Honest answers can carry consequences: exposure of weakness, internal conflict, budget constraints, authority gaps, or past mistakes. If the perceived downside of honesty outweighs the benefit, the answer will be filtered, softened, or redirected. Resistance is not about deception—it is about minimizing perceived risk.

The third evaluation is **control**. This is the question most professionals underestimate: *"What does this obligate me to next?"* People resist discovery when they sense that an answer will narrow options, force a decision, or accelerate a process they are not ready to enter. When questions feel like stepping stones toward loss of autonomy, resistance increases—even if the question itself seems reasonable.

Resistance intensifies under specific conditions. Authority imbalances heighten caution, especially when someone feels evaluated by an expert, consultant, or executive. Identity threats trigger self-protection when questions imply incompetence or poor judgment. And when discovery feels like interrogation rather than collaboration, the conversation shifts from exploration to defense. Understanding these psychological dynamics is essential, because discovery succeeds not by overcoming resistance—but by preventing it from forming in the first place.

Identity Protection (Why Smart Buyers Withhold)

One of the most overlooked causes of resistance in discovery is identity protection. Most discovery frameworks assume that resistance is about tactics, trust, or timing, but they fail to account for something far more personal: people instinctively protect their sense of competence, judgment, and credibility. This is especially true with experienced buyers, executives, and decision-makers who have built their careers on being capable and decisive.

People do not withhold information because they are dishonest. They withhold information because certain answers threaten how they see themselves or how they believe others see them. Questions that imply poor judgment, missed signals, or failed decisions activate self-protection. When identity feels at risk, accuracy gives way to preservation. The buyer's priority shifts from clarity to dignity.

This is why discovery resistance often shows up in predictable ways. Buyers defend underperforming vendors because admitting failure feels like admitting error. They over-rationalize weak results to preserve internal consistency. They avoid specifics that might expose gaps in oversight. They minimize problems to maintain authority and confidence in front of others. These behaviors are not obstacles to discovery—they are signals that identity feels unsafe.

The governing rule of effective discovery is simple and absolute: **never make someone choose between honesty and dignity**. When a question threatens personal credibility, the answer will protect identity, not truth. Skilled salespeople and consultants design discovery conversations that allow buyers to remain competent while being candid. When dignity is preserved, honesty follows.

Power, Status, and Role Dynamics

Discovery resistance is not uniform; it changes based on who is answering the question and where they sit within the organization. The same question can feel collaborative to one person and threatening to another. Power, status, and role shape how questions are interpreted, and failing to account for these dynamics is one of the fastest ways to trigger resistance—especially in complex or multi-stakeholder conversations.

Executives tend to resist questions that feel like audits or evaluations. They are accustomed to being the decision authority, not the subject of diagnosis. When questions imply oversight, second-guessing, or scorekeeping, answers become strategic rather than transparent. Mid-level leaders often resist questions that expose internal misalignment, political tension, or execution gaps. Their resistance is less about ego and more about self-preservation within the organization. Junior stakeholders, on the other hand, resist questions that force them to speak "upward" or comment on decisions made above their authority. The risk for them is not being wrong—it is being seen as disloyal, uninformed, or out of bounds.

Power-aware discovery requires a deliberate shift in posture. Questions must be asked **with authority**, not **at authority**. This means positioning yourself as a peer in problem-solving rather than an examiner collecting data. Effective discovery frames questions as shared exploration—*"Let's look at this together"*—instead of diagnosis. Language that sounds analytical or evaluative too early increases defensiveness, even when the intent is helpful.

When power dynamics are respected, discovery feels collaborative instead of invasive. Buyers are more willing to share context, nuance, and uncertainty when questions honor their role rather than challenge it. Skilled communicators do not flatten hierarchy or ignore status; they navigate it carefully, allowing each stakeholder to participate without risking position or credibility.

Structural Causes of Resistance (Fix These First)

Before improving the quality of discovery questions, it is essential to remove the structural conditions that create resistance in the first place. Many discovery breakdowns occur not because the question is wrong, but because the environment surrounding the question makes it feel unsafe. When structure is flawed, even well-intentioned questions are interpreted as interrogative or self-serving.

Poor framing is one of the most common errors. Questions asked without context force the listener to guess at intent, and when intent is unclear, the mind defaults to caution. A question that appears neutral to the asker can feel evaluative or transactional to the listener if its purpose has not been established. Context reduces suspicion. Without it, resistance rises.

Bad sequencing is another major source of friction. Questions about "why," budget, authority, or decision-making asked too early often feel premature and invasive. These questions signal consequence before safety exists. When buyers sense that the conversation is moving toward commitment before trust is established, they respond by withholding or deflecting. Timing errors compound this problem. Diagnostic questions posed before psychological safety is in place shift the conversation from exploration to defense.

Tone and pace complete the structure. Speed creates pressure, even when none is intended. Rapid-fire questions feel like interrogation, not collaboration. Precision without warmth creates emotional distance, making the interaction feel clinical rather than human. Effective discovery slows the conversation down, balances clarity with empathy, and allows space for thoughtful answers. Fixing these structural issues first ensures that resistance does not appear before the real discovery even begins.

Pre-Framing: Lowering Resistance Before Questions

Pre-framing is the point at which discovery either succeeds or fails. Long before a question is asked, the listener is already assessing intent, risk, and consequence. Pre-framing addresses those concerns *before* they turn into resistance. When done well, it makes even difficult questions feel reasonable, purposeful, and safe.

Effective pre-framing begins with intent transparency. When people understand why a question exists, they no longer need to defend against hidden agendas. Explaining the purpose of a question signals respect and collaboration rather than extraction. Permission-based language further reduces pressure by making it clear that participation is voluntary, not forced. When people know they are not being cornered, their answers become more candid.

Outcome alignment strengthens pre-framing by positioning the question as serving the listener's interests, not just the asker's objectives. When buyers see how a question helps create clarity, avoid mistakes, or protect outcomes they care about, resistance softens. Normalizing uncertainty completes the process. By signaling that not having a perfect answer is acceptable, the question becomes an invitation to think rather than a test to pass.

The governing principle is simple: people answer hard questions when they understand *why* the question exists and feel safe saying, "I'm not sure." Pre-framing creates that safety. Without it, even well-crafted questions trigger defense. With it, discovery becomes a cooperative process of exploration instead of a guarded exchange of information.

Question Design That Invites Real Answers

Discovery questions should feel collaborative, not extractive. When a question feels like it is pulling information out of someone, resistance follows. When it feels like a shared attempt to understand a situation, people participate willingly. The difference is not subtle, and it has nothing to do with being softer or less precise. It has everything to do with how the question positions the relationship between the two parties.

High-trust question design often begins indirectly. Indirect entry questions allow the conversation to approach sensitive topics gradually rather than confronting them head-on. Externalized questions shift the focus away from the individual and onto patterns, situations, or environments, reducing personal exposure. Range-based questions give people safe boundaries to answer within, making it easier to be honest without feeling boxed into a single admission. Assumptive neutrality removes judgment from the question entirely, signaling that no particular answer is expected or preferred.

When these elements are present, the emotional experience of discovery changes. The question feels like an invitation rather than a challenge. It communicates partnership instead of evaluation. The listener experiences the conversation as *"Let's look at this together,"* rather than *"Explain yourself."* That shift in posture is what allows real answers to surface—answers that are accurate, nuanced, and usable—without triggering defensiveness or withdrawal.

Emotional Awareness Without Escalation

Unacknowledged emotion creates resistance. When tension, hesitation, or frustration is present but ignored, it does not disappear—it goes underground. Buyers become guarded, answers become mechanical, and discovery loses depth. At the same time, poorly handled emotion creates shutdown. Over-labeling, mislabeling, or drawing too much attention to emotion can make people feel exposed or analyzed, which stops the conversation entirely.

Effective discovery requires emotional awareness without escalation. This means noticing emotional signals without magnifying them. A slight pause, a change in tone, or a vague answer often carries more meaning than the words themselves. Skilled communicators acknowledge tension lightly, without spotlighting it or forcing it into the open. They reflect what is sensed in a way that invites clarification, not defense.

Validation plays a critical role here, but it must be precise. Validating experience does not mean agreeing with conclusions or endorsing decisions. It simply acknowledges that the person's perspective makes sense given their situation. This distinction keeps discovery grounded and professional. When emotion is handled with restraint and respect, discovery remains human rather than clinical—and trust deepens instead of eroding.

Buyer Narratives & Self-Deception

Not all resistance in discovery is defensive. In many cases, it is unconscious. Buyers often operate within narratives that help them make sense of past decisions, current results, and future plans. These narratives are not intentionally misleading; they are simplifying stories that preserve consistency and reduce internal tension. When discovery questions challenge these stories too directly, resistance emerges—not because the buyer is hiding something, but because the narrative feels necessary to maintain coherence.

Buyers tend to protect the version of events that allows them to avoid hard tradeoffs. A story that explains underperformance without requiring change feels safer than one that exposes difficult choices or missed opportunities. Over time, these narratives become familiar and unquestioned.

Discovery questions that collide with them can feel disorienting or threatening, even when asked respectfully.

Effective discovery does not attempt to dismantle these narratives abruptly. Instead, it gently surfaces contradictions, blind spots, and gaps by widening the lens. This approach allows the buyer to notice inconsistencies on their own, rather than having them pointed out. When done skillfully, discovery invites reflection instead of embarrassment, and curiosity instead of defensiveness. The goal is not to correct the buyer's story, but to expand it enough that new understanding can emerge naturally.

Internal Politics & Invisible Stakeholders

In many discovery conversations, resistance does not belong to the person answering the questions. It belongs to someone who is not in the room. Internal politics, unspoken hierarchies, and competing priorities often shape what can be said openly and what must be carefully managed. When these dynamics are ignored, discovery produces incomplete or misleading information—not because the buyer is uncooperative, but because they are navigating forces beyond the conversation.

There are consistent signals that invisible stakeholders are influencing the dialogue. Authority becomes vague. Decisions are attributed to "we" without clarity on who that includes. Timelines stretch without explanation. Language becomes cautious, conditional, or overly measured. These patterns indicate that answers are being filtered through internal considerations such as approval risk, political exposure, or fear of misalignment.

Effective discovery must surface these dynamics without creating tension or conflict. This requires asking in ways that feel safe rather than accusatory. Alignment is explored collaboratively, not challenged. Veto power is identified indirectly, without forcing the buyer to name obstacles they may feel uncomfortable exposing. When handled correctly, discovery brings internal realities into view without putting the buyer in a compromised position. The goal is not to provoke internal conflict, but to understand it well enough to navigate it responsibly.

Managing Resistance in Real Time

Resistance rarely announces itself directly. It shows up subtly, woven into the way answers are delivered rather than what is said. Deflection, humor, intellectualizing, topic changes, or questioning the question itself are all signs that the conversation has crossed into perceived risk. These behaviors are not disruptions to discovery—they are feedback. They indicate that something in the moment feels unsafe, premature, or consequential.

The most common mistake professionals make when resistance appears is trying to overpower it. Pushing harder, justifying the question defensively, or rephrasing the same question more aggressively only increases threat. These responses signal that the asker is more invested in getting an answer than maintaining trust. Once that signal is sent, the quality of information drops sharply, even if the conversation continues.

What works instead is subtle course correction. Light acknowledgment lets the other person feel seen without being put on the spot. Slowing the pace reduces pressure and gives space for reflection. Re-anchoring intent reminds the buyer why the question exists and how it serves the conversation, not just the outcome. Offering optionality restores a sense of control, which immediately lowers resistance. When handled this way, resistance often dissolves on its own— and the conversation naturally returns to depth without confrontation.

Re-Entry Strategies After Deflection

When a discovery answer is partial, vague, or avoided, the instinct for many professionals is to press immediately for clarity. This often backfires. Deflection is a signal that the topic carries perceived risk, not that the conversation should stop. Effective discovery treats deflection as a timing issue, not a failure.

A soft reset allows the conversation to continue without tension. By letting the moment pass and shifting briefly to adjacent context, pressure dissipates. Expanding the frame before returning to the topic gives the buyer a broader perspective, which often makes the original question feel less personal or consequential. Contrast can also be introduced by exploring extremes or alternatives, making the true answer easier to reveal without direct exposure.

Referencing patterns or third parties further reduces personal risk. When buyers can speak about trends, common situations, or anonymized examples, they often disclose more than they would in direct self-reference. Once safety is re-established, returning to the original topic feels natural rather than forced. The objective is not to corner the buyer, but to reach understanding through patience and structure. The goal of re-entry is always **completion without confrontation**.

Reading the Answer (Not Just Hearing It)

Discovery does not end when an answer is given. It continues in how that answer is interpreted. Effective discovery requires **answer calibration**—the ability to recognize not just what was said, but how and why it was said that way. Many discovery failures occur because answers are accepted at face value when they are actually filtered, protective, or incomplete.

Polite answers aim to keep the conversation smooth without revealing much. Strategic answers are designed to manage perception, timing, or leverage. Protective answers shield identity, authority, or internal dynamics. Incomplete answers may sound cooperative but leave out key context or constraints. None of these are inherently negative; they are natural responses to perceived risk. The mistake is treating them all as final.

Once an answer is calibrated, the next move becomes clear. Some situations call for gentle probing to add clarity. Others benefit from reframing the question to reduce exposure. At times, the wisest choice is to park the issue temporarily and return later, when more trust or context exists. Skilled discovery is not about exhausting every topic immediately—it is about knowing when to advance, when to pause, and when to let the conversation mature. Reading the answer correctly preserves trust while steadily increasing accuracy.

Silence as a Trust Tool

Silence reduces resistance when it is used with intention. In discovery, silence is not an absence of skill; it is often the clearest signal of confidence and respect. When a question is followed by immediate clarification, reassurance, or additional commentary, pressure increases and thinking space disappears. Silence, by contrast, gives the other person room to process without being rushed toward an answer.

Silence signals patience. It communicates that there is no penalty for reflection and no expectation of immediacy. This alone lowers perceived risk. When people are not hurried, they are more likely to move past surface responses and speak with greater honesty. Silence also removes pressure by shifting control back to the person answering. They no longer feel managed by the pace of the conversation.

Most professionals talk too soon. They rescue the buyer from discomfort, interrupt emerging insight, or fill the space out of habit. In doing so, they inadvertently prevent clarity from forming. When silence is held calmly and without judgment, it often invites the buyer to complete their own thought more fully. Used this way, silence becomes a powerful trust tool—one that deepens discovery without a single additional word.

Repairing Trust When a Question Misses

Even elite communicators misstep. Discovery conversations are dynamic, and no amount of preparation eliminates the possibility that a question lands poorly. What separates skilled professionals from average ones is not the absence of mistakes, but the ability to recognize and repair them quickly without undermining credibility.

Effective recovery begins with retraction that is calm and proportional. Over-apologizing draws unnecessary attention to the misstep and can make the moment feel larger than it is. Instead, a brief acknowledgment followed by clarification of intent reassures the other person that no harm was intended. Resetting tone is equally important. Slowing down, softening delivery, and removing urgency signals that the conversation remains collaborative rather than corrective.

Re-establishing collaboration completes the repair. When the buyer feels that the conversation is once again a shared exploration rather than an evaluation, trust stabilizes. Mistakes do not erode trust on their own; they are expected in real conversations. Trust is lost when misalignment is ignored or pushed through. Addressed early and cleanly, a missed question often strengthens credibility rather than weakens it.

Ethical Discovery (The Non-Negotiable Core)

This framework is not manipulation. Its purpose is not to extract information through pressure, tactics, or psychological leverage. Ethical discovery is grounded in respect for autonomy, dignity, and informed choice. When discovery crosses into coercion, the information gained may be usable in the short term—but trust is permanently damaged.

Ethical discovery sets clear boundaries. There is no cornering, no trapping, and no forced disclosure. Questions are invitations, not demands. A buyer's right to pause, reflect, or decline is honored without penalty. Respect for "not ready" answers preserves psychological safety and ensures that when disclosure does happen, it is voluntary and reliable.

The core belief that guides this work is simple: **discovery is collaboration under uncertainty, not interrogation under pressure**. Both parties are navigating incomplete information and shared risk. When discovery is conducted ethically, it builds clarity, alignment, and trust—regardless of whether a deal moves forward. This standard protects relationships, reputations, and outcomes long after the conversation ends.

Preparing for High-Stakes Discovery

High-stakes discovery requires a different level of preparation. Executive-level conversations and complex deals involve greater visibility, higher consequences, and more internal exposure. In these environments, resistance is not a flaw—it is a rational response to risk. Successful discovery at this level is built deliberately, not improvised.

Micro-agreements create momentum without commitment. Small, mutual confirmations about purpose, scope, or direction establish alignment before deeper questions are introduced. Progressive disclosure allows information to unfold in layers, rather than demanding full transparency all at once. Each step builds confidence that the conversation is safe and worthwhile. Safety stacking reinforces this by consistently demonstrating respect, patience, and neutrality over time, rather than relying on a single moment of rapport.

Consistency in tone and intent ties everything together. Executives pay close attention to whether words and behavior align across the conversation. When tone remains steady and intent remains clear, even difficult questions feel natural rather than invasive. In this way, high-stakes discovery becomes a logical progression instead of a confrontation. Hard questions do not feel forced—they feel inevitable, because the groundwork has already been laid.

Application Path (Next Build Steps)

This framework is designed to be modular, adaptable, and practical. Each section can stand on its own, yet together they form a complete architecture for discovery in sales, consulting, and high-stakes conversations. Because the focus is on reducing resistance rather than memorizing scripts, the material translates across industries, deal sizes, and roles without losing effectiveness.

From here, the framework can be expanded into full written chapters that explore each concept in greater depth, supported by examples and scenarios. It can be converted into sales discovery training that helps professionals diagnose resistance in real time and respond with precision. For consultants, it can serve as a diagnostic model that improves engagement quality, alignment, and trust before recommendations are ever made.

The framework also lends itself to a practical playbook for difficult conversations and a structured language library that provides ready-to-use phrasing to lower resistance without manipulation. Each path preserves the same core principle: discovery works best when it is intentional, ethical, and collaborative. How it is applied depends on the audience—but the foundation remains the same.

Safety-Setting Statements *(Lower nervous system activation before depth)*

Safety-setting statements establish the emotional conditions required for honest discovery. Before a prospect can think clearly, reflect openly, or explore sensitive topics, their nervous system must register that the conversation is not a test, an evaluation, or a trap. These statements quietly reduce perceived risk by signaling patience, neutrality, and respect. When safety is present, resistance decreases and clarity becomes possible.

15 Safety-Setting Statements & Questions

1. "There's no right or wrong answer here."

2. "This isn't about evaluating you—it's about understanding the situation clearly."

3. "You don't need to have this fully figured out yet."

4. "We're just trying to get clarity, not arrive at conclusions."

5. "There's no pressure to answer this perfectly."

6. "This is simply a thinking conversation, not a decision conversation."

7. "If something feels unclear, that's completely fine."

8. "We're exploring, not judging."

9. "You can answer this at whatever level feels comfortable."

10. "Nothing you say here commits you to anything."

11. "This is about understanding the landscape, not assigning fault."

12. "It's okay if your thoughts are still forming."

13. "We're not looking for certainty—just accuracy."

14. "This conversation is meant to be useful, not stressful."

15. "If an answer changes as we talk, that's normal."

Safety-setting statements are the foundation of ethical and effective discovery. They calm the nervous system, lower defenses, and remove the fear of consequence that causes guarded answers. When prospects feel safe, they think more clearly, speak more honestly, and remain engaged even as the conversation deepens. These statements do not weaken discovery—they strengthen it by making depth possible. Without safety, discovery stays shallow. With safety, truth emerges naturally.

Permission & Autonomy Statements *(Restore control to reduce resistance)*

Permission and autonomy statements restore a sense of control at moments when discovery could feel intrusive or consequential. Resistance often emerges not because a question is unreasonable, but because the prospect feels they are losing agency. These statements lower defensiveness by making it clear that participation is voluntary, pacing is flexible, and the conversation is collaborative rather than compulsory.

15 Permission & Autonomy Statements & Questions

1. "Can I ask something that may help us see this more clearly?"

2. "If this isn't useful to explore right now, we can set it aside."

3. "We don't have to go into detail unless it feels helpful."

4. "You're free to pass on this if it doesn't feel relevant."

5. "We can come back to this later if now isn't the right moment."

6. "Only share what you're comfortable sharing."

7. "This is optional—feel free to answer at a high level."

8. "If you'd rather not explore this today, that's completely fine."

9. "We can slow this down or pause here if you'd like."

10. "There's no expectation to resolve this right now."

11. "Let me know if this question feels premature."

12. "You can stop me anytime if this isn't landing well."

13. "This is meant to support clarity, not create pressure."

14. "We can approach this from a different angle if that's easier."

15. "I want this to be useful for you—guide me on where to focus."

Permission and autonomy statements prevent resistance by returning control to the buyer at precisely the moments where pressure might otherwise build. When people feel they can opt out, slow down, or redirect, they become more willing to engage honestly. These statements do not weaken discovery; they strengthen it by ensuring participation is voluntary and informed. Autonomy creates safety, and safety allows deeper, more accurate discovery to occur.

Dignity-Preserving Statements *(Protect identity while inviting honesty)*

Dignity-preserving statements protect the prospect's sense of competence while creating space for truth. When discovery touches past decisions, missed opportunities, or underperformance, people instinctively guard their identity. These statements prevent shame, defensiveness, and self-justification by separating the *person* from the *outcome*. When dignity is preserved, honesty becomes possible without self-embarrassment.

15 Dignity-Preserving Statements & Questions

1. "Most capable people run into this at some point."

2. "This is more common than people realize."

3. "Nothing about this suggests poor judgment."

4. "Given what you were dealing with at the time, that makes sense."

5. "Hindsight always makes these situations look cleaner than they felt."

6. "This isn't about mistakes—it's about understanding the context."

7. "A lot of smart decisions don't show their limits until later."

8. "Anyone in your position would have faced similar constraints."

9. "This says more about the environment than your ability."

10. "It sounds like you were working with the information you had."

11. "There's no failure here—just learning."

12. "This doesn't reflect a lack of effort or attention."

13. "Plenty of strong leaders describe this exact pattern."

14. "This wasn't obvious at the time, even to experienced people."

15. "Understanding this now doesn't invalidate what you did then."

Dignity-preserving statements neutralize one of the strongest forces behind discovery resistance: identity threat. When people feel their competence or credibility is at risk, they protect themselves with rationalization or avoidance. These statements remove that threat by honoring context, effort, and intention—without excusing outcomes. By allowing prospects to remain competent while being candid, dignity-preserving language unlocks deeper truth and more accurate discovery. Honesty follows naturally when dignity is not on the line.

Normalization Statements *(Reduce isolation and shame)*

Normalization statements reduce resistance by helping prospects understand that their challenges are neither unique nor personal failures. When people believe they are alone in a struggle, they protect themselves through minimization, humor, or deflection. Normalization removes that isolation by placing the issue in a broader context, allowing the prospect to engage without feeling exposed or singled out.

15 Normalization Statements & Questions

1. "I hear this a lot in situations like yours."

2. "This tends to show up when things get complex."

3. "Most teams don't notice this until it becomes visible."

4. "You're not the only one navigating this."

5. "This is a very common pattern at this stage."

6. "I've seen this emerge in otherwise well-run organizations."

7. "This usually appears before people realize it's happening."

8. "A lot of capable groups experience this quietly."

9. "This is something many people adapt to without realizing it."

10. "It often looks manageable until you step back and examine it."

11. "Most people don't connect these dots right away."

12. "This is more widespread than it gets credit for."

13. "Many teams assume this is 'just how things are.'"

14. "This isn't unusual given the pressure you're under."

15. "What you're describing fits a familiar pattern."

Normalization statements replace self-protection with openness by removing the emotional weight of isolation. When prospects realize that their situation is shared by others, shame dissolves and curiosity returns. These statements do not minimize the issue—they make it safer to explore. By placing challenges within a broader pattern, normalization lowers defensiveness and invites more honest reflection, allowing discovery to move from avoidance to clarity.

Intent-Clarifying Statements *(Prevent misinterpretation of questions)*

Intent-clarifying statements remove one of the most common sources of resistance in discovery: uncertainty about motive. When buyers don't understand *why* a question is being asked, they often assume pressure, judgment, or acceleration toward a decision. Clarifying intent up front prevents misinterpretation and allows sensitive topics to be explored without triggering defensiveness.

15 Intent-Clarifying Statements & Questions

1. "The reason I'm asking is so we don't make assumptions."

2. "This helps me understand the full picture—not to push a decision."

3. "I ask this so we don't overlook something important later."

4. "This isn't about moving faster—it's about being accurate."

5. "I want to be careful not to fill in gaps incorrectly."

6. "This question is about context, not commitment."

7. "I'm asking so we can avoid unintended consequences."

8. "This gives us clarity before we talk about options."

9. "I want to make sure I'm not misreading the situation."

10. "This helps me tailor the conversation appropriately."

11. "I'm asking now so we don't have to revisit it under pressure later."

12. "This isn't about qualification—it's about understanding."

13. "I want to respect your constraints, not challenge them."

14. "This question prevents us from chasing the wrong solution."

15. "I'd rather ask now than assume and be wrong."

Intent-clarifying statements reduce resistance by removing ambiguity around motive. When buyers understand that a question exists to create accuracy—not pressure—they are far more willing to answer honestly. These statements preserve trust while allowing necessary discovery around money, authority, risk, and consequences. Clear intent turns sensitive questions into collaborative checkpoints rather than perceived traps, keeping discovery grounded and ethical.

Emotional Containment Statements *(Acknowledge emotion without amplifying it)*

Emotional containment statements allow emotion to be recognized without allowing it to take over the conversation. In discovery, emotion often surfaces alongside complexity, pressure, or consequence. Ignoring it creates resistance, but over-engaging it turns discovery into therapy. These statements strike the balance by acknowledging what's present while keeping the conversation focused, grounded, and productive.

15 Emotional Containment Statements & Questions

1. "I can hear there's some weight to this."

2. "That sounds like it's been frustrating."

3. "It makes sense that this would feel heavy."

4. "We don't need to unpack all of that—just enough to understand."

5. "There's clearly some history here."

6. "I can tell this hasn't been simple."

7. "That reaction makes sense given what you've been dealing with."

8. "We don't have to stay here long—just enough for clarity."

9. "There's emotion attached to this, and that's understandable."

10. "I'm not trying to dig into this—just acknowledge it."

11. "We can keep this practical while still recognizing the impact."

12. "This sounds like it's carried some pressure."

13. "I hear the tension without needing to analyze it."

14. "We don't need to relive it—just understand it."

15. "Acknowledging this helps us move forward cleanly."

Emotional containment statements preserve trust by acknowledging emotional reality without escalating it. They signal awareness, respect, and restraint—three qualities that keep discovery professional and human at the same time. When emotion is neither ignored nor over-examined, resistance decreases and clarity improves. These statements help maintain momentum while honoring what's present, allowing discovery to continue without derailment.

Re-Entry Softeners *(Return to avoided topics safely)*

Re-entry softeners make it possible to return to important topics that were previously avoided without creating confrontation or pressure. In discovery, partial or redirected answers are often a sign of timing, not refusal. These statements allow the conversation to re-approach sensitive areas after trust, context, or clarity has increased, keeping discovery constructive rather than adversarial.

15 Re-Entry Softeners & Questions

1. "Can we circle back to something you mentioned earlier?"

2. "I want to revisit this gently, if that's okay."

3. "Earlier you touched on something that feels important."

4. "Now that we have more context, this may be easier to explore."

5. "Something you said earlier stood out to me."

6. "With what we know now, this might look a little different."

7. "I didn't want to interrupt earlier, but I'd like to return to this."

8. "This feels like a good moment to come back to that point."

9. "We can stay high-level, but I want to make sure we don't miss this."

10. "You mentioned this briefly before—can we expand on it a bit?"

11. "I'd like to reconnect this to what you shared earlier."

12. "This may land differently now than it did earlier."

13. "I want to make sure I understood what you meant before."

14. "Let's revisit this with the perspective we've built."

15. "If it still feels relevant, I'd like to return to this."

Re-entry softeners allow discovery to reach completion without force. By lowering the emotional cost of returning to sensitive topics, they transform deflection into opportunity. These statements respect timing, restore choice, and preserve collaboration. When used skillfully, re-entry softeners deepen discovery while maintaining trust, ensuring that important information surfaces naturally rather than under pressure.

Ethical Boundary Statements *(Explicitly reject manipulation)*

Ethical boundary statements make integrity visible. When buyers carry skepticism from past sales pressure or negative consulting experiences, they listen less to questions and more to intent. These statements establish clear boundaries around influence, pace, and outcome, signaling that discovery is being conducted in good faith. When integrity is explicit, trust accelerates.

15 Ethical Boundary Statements & Questions

1. "My goal isn't to push you anywhere."

2. "This conversation should be useful whether we work together or not."

3. "Clarity matters more than closing."

4. "If this doesn't make sense to pursue, that's okay."

5. "I'm not here to convince you—just to understand."

6. "You don't owe me a decision."

7. "I'd rather slow this down than rush it incorrectly."

8. "This isn't about selling you something—it's about getting clarity."

9. "If the answer ends up being 'not now,' that's a valid outcome."

10. "There's no upside for either of us in forcing this."

11. "My responsibility is accuracy, not persuasion."

12. "I don't want you agreeing just to be polite."

13. "This only works if it genuinely makes sense for you."

14. "We can stop here if this isn't adding value."

15. "I'm comfortable with whatever conclusion you reach."

Ethical boundary statements reduce resistance by removing fear of manipulation. They make it clear that discovery is not a funnel toward a predetermined outcome, but a process of honest evaluation. When buyers know they won't be pressured, they engage more openly and provide more accurate information. These statements separate trusted advisors from transactional sellers, reinforcing credibility and long-term trust regardless of the final decision.

Closure-Stabilizing Statements *(End difficult moments without emotional residue)*

Closure-stabilizing statements help regulate the end of emotionally weighted or high-consequence moments in discovery. Even productive conversations can leave emotional residue if they end abruptly or without acknowledgment. These statements provide psychological closure, allowing the buyer to feel respected, grounded, and unpressured as the conversation transitions forward.

15 Closure-Stabilizing Statements & Questions

1. "I appreciate you being open about that."

2. "That was helpful context—thank you."

3. "We can pause here and pick this up later."

4. "Nothing needs to be decided today."

5. "I know that wasn't easy to talk about."

6. "That gave me a much clearer picture."

7. "Let's let that settle for a moment."

8. "We've covered what we needed for now."

9. "There's no need to push this any further today."

10. "We can revisit this when it feels right."

11. "I respect you sharing that."

12. "That was enough depth for now."

13. "We can take a breath and move on."

14. "Thank you for trusting me with that."

15. "We're in a good place to pause."

Closure-stabilizing statements prevent emotional carryover by ending discovery moments with calm and respect. They signal that nothing further is required in the moment and that the conversation can continue later without penalty. By providing clean closure, these statements preserve trust, reduce lingering stress, and leave the buyer feeling regulated and valued—setting the stage for thoughtful next steps rather than reactive decisions.

THE DISCOVERY SPEED CHECKLIST

The Cost of Speed in Discovery

Speed is the biggest enemy of understanding. When you move too fast in a discovery call, you lose the thread of the conversation, skip emotional cues, and drift away from the structure that creates clarity. Most advisors don't realize they're accelerating. The shift happens quietly. A moment of internal pressure. A desire to sound prepared. A rush to get to the "important" part of the call. But prospects feel this shift instantly. They become guarded, vague, or disconnected. The conversation loses depth.

This checklist exists because the signs of rushing are subtle. They show up in tone, pacing, assumptions, and the way you interpret the prospect's answers. Once speed enters the conversation, discovery becomes fragile. You lose control without realizing it. Your questions become less effective. The prospect's answers become thinner. Progress slows even as you move faster.

To remain in command, you must constantly regulate your pace. Slowing down is not weakness—it is discipline. It keeps the conversation grounded, centered, and emotionally safe. It allows the prospect to reflect instead of react. It helps you follow the structure instead of chasing the moment. The checklist on the next pages is your tool for staying steady. It tells you when you've drifted, how to regain control, and how to return to a pace that supports true insight.

Use this guide as a recalibration tool before every call, during challenging moments, and after each conversation to evaluate your discipline. When you learn to control the tempo, you learn to control the room. And when you control the room, discovery becomes cleaner, deeper, and far more effective.

How to Tell If You're Going Too Fast in the Call — And How to Fix It Instantly

Most sales reps and consultants don't realize they're moving too quickly until the call is already slipping away. Speed creates pressure. Pressure creates resistance. Resistance kills discovery. This checklist gives you real-time indicators that you've left the calm, grounded rhythm needed for elite-level discovery.

Use this before the call, during the call, and immediately after to calibrate your pace.

SECTION 1 — SIGNS YOU ARE GOING TOO FAST (INTERNAL)

These signals come from *you*. When you notice them, slow down immediately.

Internal Pressure Signs

- ☐ You feel a sudden urge to "get to the point."

- [ ] You're thinking about the close instead of the next question.
- [ ] Your breathing is shallow or your voice tightens.
- [ ] You feel rushed even when the prospect isn't rushing you.
- [ ] You're trying to sound smart instead of curious.
- [ ] You feel uncomfortable with silence and fill space quickly.
- [ ] You're afraid the prospect may lose interest if you slow down.

Internal Thinking Errors

- [ ] You assume you know the real problem too early.
- [ ] You jump to solutions in your mind before the prospect finishes.
- [ ] You catch yourself predicting answers instead of listening.
- [ ] You're mentally skipping steps in the order of operations.
- [ ] You're trying to "steer" the conversation instead of discovering truth.

SECTION 2 — SIGNS YOU ARE GOING TOO FAST (EXTERNAL)

These signals come from the *prospect*. They reveal that your pace has surpassed their emotional comfort level.

Prospect Behavior Signals

- [ ] Their answers get shorter.
- [ ] They begin giving vague, surface-level responses.
- [ ] They start explaining instead of reflecting.
- [ ] They repeat themselves as if you missed something.
- [ ] They say things like "It's complicated," but don't elaborate.
- [ ] They become overly polite — a sign of emotional retreat.
- [ ] They talk quickly or defensively.

Prospect Energy Signals

- [ ] They seem mentally scattered or overwhelmed.
- [ ] Their tone rises or becomes pressured.
- [ ] Their pace accelerates to match yours.
- [ ] They stop correcting details — a sign they've disengaged.
- [ ] They "gloss over" important information to keep up.

SECTION 3 — SIGNS THE CONVERSATION STRUCTURE IS BREAKING

If any of these occur, it means the sequence has been disrupted.

☐ You are asking consequence questions before establishing clarity.

☐ You are moving to authority or budget too early.

☐ You are challenging before emotional safety is established.

☐ You are following up inconsistently or skipping follow-ups entirely.

☐ You are accepting vague answers at face value.

☐ You're moving to the next topic before the current one is resolved.

☐ You are escalating without permission.

☐ You feel like you're "dragging" the prospect instead of guiding them.

SECTION 4 — THE RESET PROTOCOL: HOW TO FIX SPEED IN REAL TIME

If you check even **one** of the boxes above, follow this reset protocol.

Step 1 — Pause

☐ Stop talking.
☐ Take one silent breath.
☐ Let the moment settle.

Step 2 — Slow the Rhythm

Use any of these grounding statements:

- "Let's slow down for a moment so I can understand this clearly."
- "I want to go back to something important you said."
- "Before we move forward, I want to make sure we're not skipping anything."
- "Can we stay here for a moment?"

These statements gently retake control without pressure.

Step 3 — Ask a Clarifying Question

Examples:

- "When you said ___, what did that mean for you specifically?"
- "Can you walk me through that piece again?"
- "What's the part I might be missing?"

Clarifying questions instantly slow the pace and deepen the conversation.

Step 4 — Reset Emotional Temperature

Use a calm tone, lower your volume, lengthen your pauses.

Your voice regulates their nervous system.

Step 5 — Re-Enter the Correct Order of Operations

Move back to whatever stage you skipped:

- Establish → Diagnose → Consequence → Conflict → Criteria → Authority → Budget → Timeline → Commitment

Speed disappears when sequence is followed.

SECTION 5 — SPEED-PROOF YOUR NEXT CALL (PRE-CALL CHECKLIST)

Review this checklist for 30 seconds before your call:

- ☐ My goal is clarity, not speed.
- ☐ I will not assume the problem.
- ☐ I will listen longer than I speak.
- ☐ I will let silence work for me.
- ☐ I will not rush consequence.
- ☐ I will not escalate without permission.
- ☐ I will follow up until clarity appears.
- ☐ I will move in sequence, not in reaction.
- ☐ I will stay emotionally neutral.
- ☐ I will recap the answers at the end of the discovery process
- ☐ I will slow down every time the prospect speeds up.

This primes your mindset and protects the structure of the call.

SECTION 6 — THE 10-SECOND SELF-CHECK (DURING THE CALL)

If at any point you feel the call slipping, ask yourself:

- ☐ "Who is driving the pace right now?"
- ☐ "Am I responding or reacting?"
- ☐ "Did I skip a step because *I* felt rushed?"
- ☐ "Am I following the prospect or guiding them?"
- ☐ "Is this answer clear enough for me to move forward?"

If the answer to any of these feels uncertain, slow down immediately.

SECTION 7 — A FINAL REMINDER

Speed is almost always a sign of internal pressure, not external necessity.
When you slow the conversation, you increase clarity.
When you increase clarity, you create movement.
When you create movement, you never need to push.

Speed is the enemy of insight.
Slowness is the foundation of authority.

This checklist exists to help you stay in control of yourself first — because the person who controls themselves controls the conversation.

Mastery Lives in the Moments You Slow Down

The difference between an average advisor and an elite one is not talent. It's pacing. The best advisors know how to move slowly enough for truth to emerge. They don't rush. They don't react. They don't let internal pressure dictate their rhythm. They create space—space for thought, space for honesty, and space for clarity. That space is where influence lives.

This checklist is not simply a tool. It is a guardrail. It protects you from speeding past the cues that matter most. It keeps you aware of your tendencies and reinforces the discipline needed to lead high-quality conversations. Every time you use it, you sharpen your awareness. You strengthen your presence. You become more intentional with the way you guide discussions.

The more you practice slowing down, the more predictable your outcomes become. You start seeing patterns earlier. You recognize emotional shifts instantly. You hear what others miss. And you no longer get pulled into the prospect's urgency or anxiety. You become the steady point in the conversation—the person who anchors the moment and brings the prospect back into clarity.

Mastery in discovery is not about knowing more. It's about noticing more. And you can only notice more when you slow down enough to see the truth. This checklist is your reminder that clarity always beats speed, presence always beats pressure, and discipline always beats intensity.

Use it often. Use it intentionally. Use it until slowing down becomes your natural way of leading every conversation you enter.

Book Conclusion — The Discovery Conversation That Changes Everything In Sales And Consulting

Discovery is not a step in the sales process. It is the process. It is the psychological engine that determines whether the prospect reaches real clarity, whether you uncover the full truth, and whether the relationship turns into something meaningful, valuable, and transformative. When done well, discovery becomes a strategic advantage that few advisors ever master — not because they lack talent, but because they never learned how to see beneath the surface.

This book was created to change that.

Across every chapter, you have learned that discovery is not about memorizing questions. It is about understanding intention. It is about sequencing conversations with purpose. It is about recognizing emotional distance before it becomes a barrier. It is about seeing implications, contradictions, tension, risks, and consequences long before the prospect has language for them. It is about helping people think more clearly than they have in months, or sometimes years.

You now have a complete system — not a script, not a template, not a list of prompts — but a full diagnostic architecture that lets you navigate complexity with confidence. You can establish safety, reveal truth, uncover aftermath, map misalignment, explore internal conflict, surface decision criteria, identify political influencers, understand risk, test readiness, and follow the natural arc of a conversation without force, pressure, or insecurity. You have the tools to remain calm when the prospect becomes uncertain. You have the frameworks to guide someone through their own thinking without disrupting their dignity. You have the ability to turn scattered frustration into structured clarity.

This book gives you leverage, but not the kind used to push people. The leverage that matters is the leverage of **insight** — the kind that awakens a prospect to their own reality so deeply that returning to the old pattern becomes impossible. When someone finally sees the consequences of staying the same, the conversation shifts. Urgency becomes internal. Momentum becomes natural. Decisions become mature. And the relationship becomes grounded in mutual respect instead of transactional pressure.

Mastering discovery transforms you.
You stop chasing prospects.
You start guiding them.
You stop trying to be impressive.
You start becoming essential.
You stop fearing difficult conversations.
You start seeking the truth that sits inside them.

With repetition, you will begin to hear the unstated meaning behind a phrase… notice the hesitation behind an answer… sense the contradiction behind a confident tone… and guide the person toward insight with precision and ease. What once felt complicated will feel obvious. What once felt stressful will feel natural. What once felt unpredictable will become structured, predictable, and fully within your control.

But most importantly, discovery will elevate the way you serve people.
You will help them understand their world more clearly.
You will help them see what they've been tolerating.
You will help them reconnect to their goals.
You will help them see patterns they've outgrown.
You will help them protect their future from the cost of avoiding the truth.

This book is the beginning of that transformation, not the end of it.

Return to these sections often.
Review the questions.
Study your own conversations.
Observe your emotional patterns.
Pay attention to the hidden moments.
Refine your timing, tone, and neutrality.
Practice the sequence until it becomes instinct.

If you do, discovery will stop being something you perform.
It will become part of who you are — a way of thinking, a way of listening, a way of leading, and a way of seeing people with depth and clarity.

And when you reach that point, you will discover something profound:

Discovery is the conversation that changes everything — for the prospect, for the opportunity, and for

The Training That Permanently Changes How Your Team Communicates, Sells, and Makes Decisions

How To Work With Scott:

If you're reading this, something inside your organization or process isn't working the way it should. Deals are taking longer than they need to. Conversations feel vague and or confusing. Prospects aren't giving straight answers. Leaders are repeating the same guidance over and over without seeing a real shift in behavior. Your team may be busy, but they're not moving revenue or clarity forward at the pace you expect. And if you've been in business long enough, you already know the truth: communication problems *always* become performance problems.

That is exactly what Scott specializes in diagnosing and fixing.

When Scott steps into your organization, the guessing stops. Your team will discover how to uncover what is really happening inside a conversation—whether it's with a customer, a prospect, or a member of your own leadership team. Instead of chasing surface-level explanations or getting thrown off by resistance, they develop the ability to stay grounded, ask the right questions, and guide the discussion toward clarity and commitment. This is not motivational speaking. Nothing about this is temporary. Scott rewires the way people think, respond, and communicate so that the changes show up in every meeting, every call, and every deal.

Companies hire Scott in because the cost of unclear communication has finally become too high to ignore. They're tired of salespeople who sound confident but never get to the truth. They're tired of leaders who can't extract what's actually happening inside their teams. They're tired of watching conversations drift, deals stall, and culture weaken because nobody is equipped to create structure or emotional steadiness in the middle of uncertainty. And more than anything, they're tired of being dependent on the "naturally talented few" while everyone else struggles.

Once Scott trains your team, that dynamic disappears. People begin to understand problems at their root instead of at the surface. Conversations go deeper, faster. Resistance loses its power. Prospects open up. Leaders start getting straight answers instead of vague updates. The culture shifts because clarity becomes normal. Accountability becomes easier. Decision-making becomes cleaner. Sales cycles move faster, not because of pressure, but because of understanding.

Every engagement is built for real-world application. It doesn't matter whether Scott is training your sales team, developing your leaders, or building a communication framework for your entire organization—your people will walk out knowing how to control conversations, navigate emotion, and create the kind of clarity that drives performance upward.

To explore bringing Scott into your organization, here's what you need to know. Scott does not offer free consulting on a discovery call. The conversation you schedule is a fit call and see if you are a good fit. You will discuss the problem you're trying to solve, the outcomes you need, the training or event you're considering, and the investment required. If there is alignment, you will move forward. If there isn't, Scott will tell you directly and respectfully.

If you are committed to improving your team's performance, culture, and communication, this is your next step. If you are looking for a brainstorming session or free advice, it isn't.

Schedule your call by dialing this number **808-364-9906**.

The results you want will not come from working harder. They come from teaching your organization how to think and communicate at a higher level. That is what Scott does better than anyone.

Call now: **808-364-9906**.